EMPIRE OF DIAMONDS

EMPIRE of DIAMONDS

Victorian Gems in Imperial Settings

Adrienne Munich

University of Virginia Press
© 2020 by the Rector and Visitors of the University of Virginia
All rights reserved
Printed in the United States of America on acid-free paper

First published 2020

ISBN 978-0-8139-4400-5 (hardcover)
ISBN 978-0-8139-4401-2 (ebook)

1 3 5 7 9 8 6 4 2

Library of Congress Cataloging-in-Publication Data
is available for this title.

Cover art: Diamond texture (Aeya/iStock) and calligraphic vintage elements (Extezy/iStock)

For Maxwell Justus Munich

Contents

Acknowledgments ... ix

Introduction: Diamond Stories, Diamond Settings ... 1

I. India: Gems from the Gods ... 21

1. Conversions of the Last Maharajah of the Punjab and His Koh-i-noor Diamond ... 31
2. The Moonstone's Sacred Masculinity ... 46
3. Imitation India in Robert Louis Stevenson and Arthur Conan Doyle ... 56
4. Kim as Jewel and Crown ... 71

II. England: Diamond Metropole ... 83

5. Diamond Games for a Dead Man ... 91
6. *Ivanhoe*'s Racialized Legacy to English Diamond Novels ... 114

III. South Africa: The Karoo Setting ... 143

7. True Stories on the Diamond Fields ... 151
8. The Scramble and the Scramblers ... 159
9. Domestic Romance Adventures on the Diamond Fields ... 171
10. Disavowed, Dispossessed Boers in Charlotte Mansfield and Olive Schreiner ... 193

Epilogue: America—A Diamond Is for Everyone ... 207

Notes	219
Bibliography	249
Index	265

Illustration gallery follows page 130

Acknowledgments

Virtually all inquirers about my research responded with a diamond story of their own, about family intrigue, smuggled diamonds that saved lives, love mixed with greed and ostentation, diamond desires, diamond dealing, wonder and awe, blood diamonds, and, particularly in New York, relatives in the diamond business. I first acknowledge these tellers of tales. Though their tone indicated they were sharing secrets, their plots resemble those interpreted in this book. Tellers confirm the compelling nature of diamond stories.

I have mined many institutions, becoming more conscious of diamond miners' risks. I honor those ordinary diggers, some named in this book, their accounts having landed in safer, climate-controlled repositories. Some of those writings are preserved in Special Collections of Sterling Library at Yale University. The Africana Research Library in Kimberley, South Africa, conveys a visceral sense of what the Diamond Fields must have been like; the librarian's residence was razed when diamonds were found in its flower beds. Blessedly, the 1887 library building stands, its rich offering intact. The beautiful National Library of South Africa in Cape Town, South Africa, contains astonishing documents about the Diamond Fields. The New York Public Library yields great riches, among them the Lionel Pincus and Princess Firyal Map Division and the Dorot Jewish Division. The elegant Science, Industry, and Business Library (of recent memory) harbored indispensable material and an anonymous librarian who volunteered diamond lore. The J. Walter Thompson Diamond Information Center Collection at the John W. Hartman Center for Sales, Advertising, and Marketing History, David M. Rubenstein Rare Book and Manuscript Library, Duke University, furnished unique images and advertising memos. I thank them for a fellowship to work in the collection, with special thanks to Josh Rowley, Reference Archivist. The Library Company of Philadelphia, James Green, Librarian, not only granted a fellowship but also sent me information long after I had used their local services in a setting so lovable that one librarian had his ashes interred in a wall. I've been welcomed at university libraries at Rice, Kansas, Yale, and of course my own institution, Stony Brook, with its richly supplied books and hospitable staff at the Matoo Center for India Studies, S. N. Sridar, Director. I read hard copies of nineteenth-century periodicals in the Newberry Library in Chicago. The Library and Photography Archives of the Royal Collection at Windsor Castle lent me a desk in its stony home.

In the many years that I've taken to assemble materials and to write fragments of the larger story that forms *Empire of Diamonds,* friends, students, and colleagues responded. Audiences at Rice University, the University of Kansas, the Gardiner Seminar at Yale University, the CUNY Victorian Seminar, the North Atlantic Victorian Studies Association, British Women Writers, and the Parkes Collection for Jewish Studies, Southampton University, have pointed out errors of my ways and have introduced me to scholars throughout the world. My fortune in colleagues has been extraordinary. Nancy Tomes told me about the Hartman Center for Advertising at Duke University with their collection from the J. Walter Thompson advertising firm, introduced me to the librarian, and offered a room and advice in her Durham home. Andrew Nicolson took time out from his researches at the University of Chicago Library to read and explain Bengali, Hindi, and Sanskrit in Tagore's virtuoso lapidary. I wrote my first diamond article about the blockbuster film *Titanic* with Maura Spiegel, a perfect collaborator, who has also responded to drafts of this book. Peter Manning at Stony Brook lent me his father's better diamond merchants' tie for talks. Kim Cox and Anthony Teets, first doctoral students and then colleagues, have been a part of this book almost forever. Melissa Bradshaw not only read parts of this book but also allowed me to set aside writing about diamonds to co-edit two books about Amy Lowell. My Stony Brook colleagues Ann Kaplan, Celia Marshik, Drew Newman, Ayesha Ramachandran, Ben Robinson, Mike Rubenstein, and Susan Scheckel made me grateful for university communities. Stony Brook IT staff members Jomy Muttathil and Ralph Molaro keep my devices and my storage systems up to date with energy and extreme patience. Writing group Tanya Agathacleos, Carolyn Berman, Deborah Lutz, Caroline Reitz, and Talia Schaffer read versions of subsequently published diamond articles; Drake Stutesman reminded me to write in prose; Herb Sussman, Carole Silver, Norman Levy, Karen Chase, Tricia Lootens, Paula Krebs, Paul Armstrong, Rachel Brownstein, Rachel Jacoff, Richard Kaye, Diana Diamond, Anne Humpherys, Nancy Henry, Patricia Spacks, Tim Alborn, Martha Vicinus (who suggested how to lasso my files into shape by following diamond wherever it led), Bob Patten (the most exacting reader ever: Hopkins and Marilyn are for him), Betsy Gitter, Bunny Kolodner, and Hilary Beattie helped animate the otherwise solitary writing experience. Fate placed Larry and Edith Malkin as my neighbors. Edith recounted her memories of her diamond merchant father in Belgium and Larry, author and journalist, encouraged me to write less like an academic. Their friend John de St. Jorre offered his perspectives as a seasoned writer. Priti Joshi, Pryia Atwal, Norman Levy, Susan Gubar, and Karen Starr are among those who encouraged my writing about ethnic groups, though I remain concerned about offending. John Maynard reminded me every week for decades of humanistic and scholarly values. Among those astute readers of drafts, none has been more constant than my treasured Stony Brook colleague Mike Tondre. My two sons gave me contrary advice, useful at contrary moments: Matthew counseled persistence, and Edwin reminded me of other pleasurable options. Listening to Edwin afforded memorable times, and heeding Matthew—who also responded to drafts—enabled me to finish. My husband, Dick, provides me with the best kind of rock. Max brought his magical perspective, and his spirit infuses my days.

Portions of this book in different forms appeared in essay collections published by University of North Carolina Press, Palgrave/Macmillan, Ila Palma, and Rutgers University Press.

Finally, I thank University of Virginia Press Editor Eric Brandt, who guided me with confidence, grace, and generosity. Amid conflicting advice, he reinforced my own intentions. Readers he supplied offered careful, rigorous perspectives, reminding me of the ideals of academic discourse. The editors at Virginia form a wondrous team.

I am responsible for errors and opinions, though the latter have been honed by those mentioned and those I've forgotten, to whom I apologize. All have provided reminders that a community exists who care about stories and listen to them and to each other.

EMPIRE OF DIAMONDS

INTRODUCTION

Diamond Stories, Diamond Settings

> Believing, with Max Weber, that man is an animal suspended in webs of significance he himself has spun, I take culture to be those webs, and the analysis of it to be therefore not an experimental science in search of law but an interpretive one in search of meaning.
> —Clifford Geertz, *The Interpretation of Cultures*

This book concerns fictional and factual stories about diamonds, focusing on the Victorian period, when Britain controlled the world's diamonds. Demonstrating that the diamond empire still holds sway, a newspaper advertisement headed "Every Object Has a Story," which appeared near Valentine's Day in 2017, affirms a connection between stories and diamonds whose apparently inessential entwinement can be traced to a nineteenth-century formation that this book calls a diamond empire (figure 1). As if it were a message to this author, the advertisement continues: "worth finding, worth telling." Illustrating the claim that story inheres in valued objects, an illustration features a large, heart-shaped diamond that even in black and white radiates its facets from the page, joining stories to affairs of the heart, "worth" having multiple meanings. A story about a big diamond, it suggests, not only is about love but is also a story of exceptional material value, thus worth more than other stories. Readers learn that the 31.25-carat diamond sold for \$3,947,000.[1] Announcing extraordinary prices and sizes conforms to diamond stories explored in this book. Diamond prices, so the advertisement indicates, and this book will confirm, contribute to the erotic

EVERY OBJECT HAS A STORY

worth finding, worth telling

 INVITING CONSIGNMENTS, FEBRUARY 14
for our May auction of Fine Jewelry.
415 Madison Avenue #1418, New York.
Heart-shaped diamond wt. 31.25 cts.,
sold for $3,947,000
Contact: 617.874.4305, newyork@skinnerinc.com

Figure 1. "Every object has a story." That the storytelling object is a diamond confirms stories about diamonds as having special interest. That the diamond is heart-shaped links its cost to matters of the heart and gifts men bestow on women. The advertisement appeared in the *New York Times* right before Valentine's Day 2017. (Image courtesy of Skinner, Inc., www.skinner.com)

and cultural power that underlies the stories that formed a diamond empire during the age of Queen Victoria, an empire whose realm extends to our own moment.

Qualities unique to diamond allow it to constitute an empire, one worthy of stories. Diamond's imaginative potential rests on its unique structural properties. It is pure crystallized carbon, its molecules arranged in such a way to distinguish it from other minerals containing the same element, such as graphite and coal. Unlike those materials, too, diamond is transparent. Moreover, its cellular construction produces the hardest mineral on earth. Instrumentally, its hardness means that only a diamond can facet diamonds. Diamond gems would not exist as we know them without diamond dust as a faceting polish. Their inimitable hardness earns respect, even awe, crucial to their symbol-making powers.

Hardness alone would not earn diamond its status as an empire-forming gem. Diamonds are called "blazers" for a reason. They can seem on fire. Diamond has the power to addict the eye, a fatal attraction attributed to its unique reflective and refractive qualities, a combination highest of all gemstones. A diamond on a body in certain lights gleams like nothing else, and thus captures and arrests attention. Humans take pleasure in glitter: a physiological trigger draws people to the gem. Those of us susceptible to its allure cannot help ourselves: we are hooked. As late as the thirteenth century in Belgium, diamond sparkle became enhanced by increasingly precise means of faceting, satisfying European taste for shine over size.[2]

Diamonds often phosphoresce, apparently gleaming of their own volition. In his Indian lapidary, *Mani-mālā, or A Treatise on Gems* (1879), Raja Sir Sourindro Mohun Tagore identified phosphorescence as a basic quality of diamond: "It is phosphorescent on being exposed to sunshine and remains so until it is removed or even when covered with cloth or leather or paper."[3] In an influential nineteenth-century English lapidary, Charles William King also incorrectly attributes phosphorescence as unique and generic to all diamonds: "The Diamond is highly electric, attracting light objects when heated by friction; and alone amongst gems has the peculiarity of becoming phosphorescent in the dark, after long exposure to the sun's rays."[4] Though, in fact, all diamonds do not phosphoresce, that gleam adds to diamond lore, the collection of folk knowledge and fact that elevates diamond to its position of supremacy.[5] Suggesting animate life within the object, diamond glow adds to its imperial meanings.

Efforts at counterfeit, called "paste"—not merely imitation as in rhinestone and cubic zirconia in later times—began very early, perhaps before the

Romans. Hand-cut glass was backed with foil, or inferior stones received such enhancements. Glass imitations have a higher refraction, so they glitter more but do not reflect with the same intensity. Early efforts to synthesize diamond came to nothing or little until the twentieth century. Now, diamonds can be manufactured to become indistinguishable from the real thing.[6] Under controlled circumstances, a blowtorch can produce a diamond.[7] A recent story about transformation, transmutation, and true alchemy tells of a dead man becoming a diamond. Alice Gregory in the *New Yorker* wrote of the conceptual artist Jill Magid, who had permission to disinter the cremated ashes of Mexican architect Luis Ramiro Barragán Morfin to take a small portion for refining into a 2.02-carat diamond.[8] The lugubrious twist in Magid's diamond story is the exhumation of the architect's ashes, not their refinement into a diamond. Since the beginning of the twenty-first century, businesses offer refinement to any and all paying for a diamond made from human or animal ashes.

Although manufactured diamonds cannot be distinguished from mined ones, diamonds discussed in this book erupted from the center of the earth after having violently penetrated earth's thin crust eons earlier. In the sensational language of former mining editor Matthew Hart, "A billion years ago a barrage of meteorites pounded the infant Earth. The bombardment lasted some 400 million years. . . . In this model, the diamond on someone's finger might contain at its center a dot of a jewel whose antiquity goes back 10 billion years."[9] Diamond origins, like diamond prices, inspire large figures: "The ages of diamonds themselves span hundreds of millions of anniversaries."[10] Huge numbers increase human awe, boggling the mind by vindicating the eye's entrancement.

Diamonds' great value depends on a myth that they are rare. On the contrary, sufficient quantities are found here on earth. In addition, they populate outer space. A different book might have been entitled *Universe of Diamonds*. A librarian at the Science, Industry, and Business branch of the New York Public Library recounted a story about a recently discovered diamond planet, 55 Cancri e.[11] "There are diamond meteor showers out there," he added. As soon as the diamond planet was identified, *Forbes magazine* began calculating its worth as $26.9 nonillion—nonillion being thirty zeros in the United States, fifty-four zeros in the United Kingdom. The sparkle emanating from a planet in our Milky Way galaxy, invisible to the naked eye, was given a dollar amount that can never be realized but rather was aimed to astound. Were prospectors able to exploit 55 Cancri e, diamonds' dollar value would plummet. This book recognizes awe about diamond supply and diamond worth like that inspired by galactic diamonds. Diamond-rich itself, Planet Earth turns in a diamond-bestrewn atmosphere.

The diamond empire also draws on a misconception that diamond is indestructible. According to some reports attracting readers with amazing factoids, all diamonds ever mined, ever made into jewels or drilling tips, exist in the world today. This is not the case. Diamonds can be broken or chipped, scratched or cloven. More decisively, they can be vaporized, though perhaps those stones exist in the mists of time. The French scientist Antoine Lavoisier demonstrated as early as 1772 that diamond could burn entirely, like charcoal, to produce gas.[12] In very high heat, 1405 degrees Fahrenheit, they oxidize, forming carbon dioxide that can displace air and asphyxiate a person. Their lethal disappearing act has been omitted from diamond lore.[13] Diamond power is stronger than reality, inducing symbolic structures authorizing it.

The source of any diamond cannot be reliably mapped. One cannot confidently know where it was mined. Moreover, recut diamonds lose identifying marks, making a stone vulnerable to disguise. That quality has a dark side. Once a diamond is recut, not even an expert could certify whether it was cut down from a stolen gem. Shape-shifting diamonds are created for thieves and plots. Criminals contribute to the diamond empire's population.

Because carbon is plentiful, mineralogists do not give diamonds a "place of eminence," while lapidaries rank them among gems as the most precious.[14] Once diamond moves from rough mineral to fabricated gem, it enters webs of signification, webs that intersect and produce myriad meanings dependent on the places where their meanings emerge. In line with Clifford Geertz's concept of culture as a system of signs where everyone is "suspended in webs of significance" spun by humans in response to complex realities, this book embarks on a search for located and particular meanings, mostly found in stories, short and long, true and fictional, attributed to a made object with unique vitality.[15] For a diamond to mean a thing or many things, it needs interpretative fashioning, a faceting with frequently blinding diamond lights glistening before the eyes. It calls out for imperial movements propelled by cultural interpretation to give diamonds that swing, or, in some circles, that bling.

When might one begin becoming aware of a diamond empire? Would it be as late as 1876 when Queen Victoria officially became Empress of India, that diamond-worshipping subcontinent? An essential setting because of the centrality of gems in the Hindu worldview, India brings centuries of gemological lore from religious texts, the Vedas and Puranas, into the diamond empire. Nevertheless, the Royal Titles Act confirmed a British diamond empire but did not initiate it. Significant Victorian writings about Indian diamonds as building blocks of an empire of diamonds described in this book precede the newly proclaimed empress by decades.

Periodization involves choices that depend on emphasis, on a sense of rhythms in history, and above all, on values that can imbue an event with historic weight. The year 1850 marks such a key moment when Britain's diamond empire crystallizes into awareness. At that mid-century year, a solemn ceremony placed in Queen Victoria's outstretched hands the Koh-i-noor Diamond, tribute from the annexation of the Punjab, a huge territory in northern India ruled precariously by the Sikhs in the similarly precarious person of ten-year-old Maharajah Duleep Singh.[16] The governor-general of India interpreted the ritualized conferring of the legendary Asian diamond as a symbol of conquest. It was more: it confirmed an empire of diamonds within Britain's political influence. To fix on a moment when the most contested gem in the Eastern world passed to the Queen of England promotes an organization of meaning this book recognizes as an empire beginning in the Victorian era but also establishing significations continuing beyond that period. The transfer of the Koh-i-noor, for the first time to a country in the Western hemisphere, enfolds Britain in imperial diamondiferous splendor.

From the point of view of a diamond empire, such international events as Victoria's Diamond Jubilee (1897) marking Victoria's sixty-year anniversary on the throne verifies a diamond empire within Victoria's realm. A diamond empire found its first embodiment in a queen who might herself have seemed indestructible, with nine attempts on her life, surviving nine live childbirths, and outliving three of those children. Nevertheless, the diamond empire's imperial reach extended past 1897. More enduring than Victoria, the diamond empire did not die in 1901 with the Queen but has lived on in recognizable forms up to our moment and may well live beyond it.

This book centers on the period called "Victorian" to lay out and interpret symbolic structures that define the diamond empire. Although the empire persists in different forms after the Queen's death, the two empires, political and imaginative, share symbolic elements and. for a while, sites on the world map. There is a reason for that. Victoria's realm, eventually labeled the British Empire, included all the diamond-producing locations in the world: India, South Africa, and Australia. For a while, boundaries of the diamond empire in the cultural imagination and its place within the British Empire are congruent. Without mentioning that congruity, or perhaps not being conscious of it, print literature in English provided many and varied accounts of the stone itself, increasing in this period and endowing it with rare fervor. Diamonds appear in Victorian writings—magazine articles, short fiction, long novels, and very long poems. The diamond empire is not synonymous with the British Empire, but its influences and beliefs permeate its imperial reaches.

Maps delineate three imperial settings that organize this book. Location of stories, all written in English for English-speaking readers, are differently shaped according to the prominent places on the pink map that also form a diamond empire. Australia takes a marginal role in the empire, although Down Under receives little more than respect for enlarging a diamond empire within British borders. Australian prospectors for gold found brownish stones, rarely of gem quality. Those pebbles, most under five carats, seemed to promise more. Tagore's gemological compendium mentioned earlier identifies Australia as a recently found diamond possibility: "Australia was generally known to be the land of gold, but now it bids fair to be the land of Diamonds too. . . . In 1851, Mr. E. H. Hargraves, and the Rev'd. W. B. Clarke, referred to . . . a number of gems including what they called rather vaguely, 'a small one of the Diamond kind,' which was found in Reedy Creek, near Bathurst."[17] Producing neither celebrity diamonds nor best-selling stories, Australian pale brown diamonds did not notably fire a diamond imagination, though they did enlarge a sense of connection between the British and diamond realms. Australia became a major red- and pink-diamond-producing area after the period considered in this book.

Brazil entered the empire not for production but for trade. From about 1725 to the early 1870s, Brazil was the main diamond source after Indian supplies became depleted. The Portuguese government claimed the stones as crown property and circumscribed a district under its control, subject to special laws and regulations preventing admission of unlicensed diamond-seekers, while the military prevented dishonesty among the workers.[18] Those miners were imported African slaves sent to Minas Gerais, its central municipality renamed Diamantina. Hence, although most Brazilian diamonds landed in London, many to be sent to Antwerp or Amsterdam to be polished, the South American setting itself did not generate English plots; the diamonds arrived in the London market, traded by London-based firms. For symbolic purposes, diamonds from Brazil to London become assimilated as English diamonds without the Brazilian setting producing English stories.

An exception to the anonymity of Brazilian diamonds in Victorian literature is Wilkie Collins's *The Evil Genius: A Domestic Story* (1886). A bag of Brazilian diamonds disappears from a hapless ship bound for London markets, deliberately run aground and looted. Without describing the diamonds themselves, Collins reports only their £5,000 value. After their initial pilfering, they briefly reappear but then disappear entirely after about seventy pages. Although the novelist might have built on his diamond knowledge, gleaned as authority for his romance novel *The Moonstone* (1868), Collins's later work merits only passing mention to confirm that the diamond empire limits its literary sway to settings delineating Queen Victoria's realm; that sun neither rose nor set on Brazil.

Then in 1867, a discovery of vast diamond fields in what is now South Africa decisively consolidated the diamond empire within the British realm. The expanding diamond fields produced too many stones for traditional upper-class consumers of them—mainly royalty, nobility, and gentry—and this decade marked a culmination of diamond novels and diamond stories. There is an apparent dynamic between print culture and fiscal needs. Did novels and articles promote demand for increasingly plentiful diamonds at a time when commercial publicity did not feature them? That avalanche of flamboyant diamond advertisements waits for America, as described in the epilogue. Before that and without a direct marketing plan, print culture about diamonds promoted a commercial agenda. As a corollary suggestion for understanding the proliferation of diamond stories, the gem invaded general consciousness after 1850—diamonds glittering in the cultural skies. As the most famous, imperially contested diamond in history, the Koh-i-noor sparked that attention, inspiring articles, legends, photographs, literary works, and a place of honor in the Great Exhibition of 1851. The South African diamond discovery then intensified diamond discourses, diamond networks, and diamond desires.

What could one glean from the correlation between the British Empire's controlling the world's diamonds and the proliferation of print material about them? Once seized on as a topic or motif, what did print literature make of them? These are questions underlying *Empire of Diamonds*—an exploration of various significations given to diamonds in writings leading up to and through a time of "diamond mania."[19] It is a book about varied but specific ways writers in English constructed a diamond empire, literary gems both large and small. Diamond takes on different significations in different kinds of works, depending on their setting. In that sense, the diamond empire resembles other empires in that its parts do not constitute a rational whole but are yoked together by conquest. As with the Roman Empire, the cultures, peoples, languages, and ethnologies brought under its mantle differ greatly. Affirming the centrality of imagination for understanding a culture's methods of changing history by organizing its meanings, the three parts of this book discuss three settings that form an empire in their common marshalling of diamond power. At the same time, each setting evaluates and interprets the stone in different ways, demonstrating that diamond functions as a common imperial symbol for superior power while also conforming to local realities. This book also mirrors that imperial consciousness, respecting cultural differences among its parts. India, England, and South Africa exist within the empire, but their social systems do not mirror each other.

Imperial Webs and Networks

Empire in my title refers to sway over a disparate, disconnected realm that differs socially and culturally in its parts, a place that can be mapped in fragments on a world map and in personal experience. Students of empire recognize that the concept of empire itself depends on metaphor to be comprehended by different imperial subjects in different locations. Robert MacDonald argues for "the metaphorical construction of empire," citing Althusser's use of "ideology" and signifying practices of discourse.[20] Kathryn Tidrick also emphasizes empire as a state of mind: "I assume that what was distinctively English about the enterprise was not people's motives for going there but what they believed themselves to be doing when they got there."[21] Tidrick's "there" gestures outward to those settings people went to, bringing with them their consciousness and constructions of empire.[22] Empires encompass different kinds of people, called "races" by Victorian ethnologists. Heterogeneous peoples appear in settings that are neither home nor away and where encounters with objects take on uncanny meanings. My use of empire, too, recognizes that beliefs construct the diamond empire, ensconcing legends in fiction, reportage, and historical accounts.

In addition to English imperial consciousness, Tidrick also recognizes that empire in the nineteenth century is primarily an evangelical, middle-class enterprise, a contention that is borne out in most texts under examination here. Missionaries contributed to imperial energies while religious adherents bought diamonds from these imperial areas. Diamonds glittering on middle-class women's necks, ears, and fingers convey a class conviction concerning its destined authority over more benighted inhabitants of annexed territories. Lest those diamond-buying men and diamond-wearing women slip into overweening pride and pleasure, their evangelical consciousness adds moral valences projected onto an object of great veneration or of forbidden desire, bringing it down to humble earth. Following Max Weber's formulation that unites Protestant ethics and capitalist energy, Evangelicals can love diamonds, but they should not fully enjoy them.[23] Readers absorb a moral message about sins of covetousness, lust, and pride embedded in diamond stories.

In the following pages, texts and images disclose differences in diamond meanings according to localized beliefs and concerns. Cultural interpretation in the mode of what Clifford Geertz calls "thick description" illuminates a culture's diverse practices, representations, and communicative exchanges. This method resembles the literary practice of close reading insofar as attention to textual nuance and texture uncovers that plenitude or thickness in levels of literary meanings.[24] Attention to text and social context demonstrates the thick construction of diverse parts of the diamond empire. Moreover, settings in this book assign diamonds to different social ranks: the three parts trace a trajectory from Indian diamonds identified with Asian princes in part 1; with English royalty, aristocratic families, and gentry in part 2; and with all seekers in South Africa where class and rank give way to wealth and the pursuit of money in part 3. Finally, in the epilogue, diamonds move to an America where diamonds are sought by all while bearing values and trappings of their British origins.

Not only does the mineral itself require manufacture to constitute its empire, but the diamond empire itself requires fabrication to be recognized as an entity. "Webs of significance," Geertz's phrase, connect imperial meanings within an entity conceived and organized as an empire that contains both common characteristics and radical differences. A web—or in a later critical vocabulary, a network—of meanings connects them. *Network,* a term notably used by Bruno Latour, signifies connections between persons and things or objects in a culture. His anthropological sociology proposes a problem-solving model that can be applied to thinking about diamonds. In *We Have Never Been Modern,* Latour refers to "delicate webs" in alluding to Ariadne, the Cretan princess whose thread to guide Theseus through a labyrinth modeled multiple ways of solving the same puzzle. Arachne the spider would be Geertz's weaver, whereas Ariadne is Latour's. I am guided both by Geertz's cultural poetics in uncovering symbolic significances of diamond and by Latour's object-oriented account, where irreducibly physical properties lead to diamond's prominence. Latour's reliance on incommensurate dimensions that nonetheless are linked by a thread is also instructive in conceiving the concept of empire: "None of these is commensurable, yet there they are, caught up in the same story."[25] Latour refers to Ariadne's thread in order to make sense of disparate but connected stories: "To shuttle back and forth, we rely on the notion of translation, or network. Suppler than the notion of system, more historical than the notion of structure, more empirical than the notion of complexity, the idea of network is the Ariadne's thread of these interwoven stories. . . . The delicate networks traced by Ariadne's little hand remain more invisible than spiderwebs."[26] Settings in this book are incommensurable in that they cannot be mapped seamlessly onto one another, but they cohere, attached by a diamond thread, to constitute an empire. This book bears out the force of Geertz's attention to symbolic meanings while also sharing in the general spirit of Latour's focus on the actual agency of objects whose properties offer humans various simultaneous paths to decode its uses.

Diamond, with its physical properties (Latour) and symbolic power (Geertz), radiates meanings in an imperial web to capture its disparate elements. A diamond network is based on a common agreement that the gem exerts unique force. Economically, diamond desire depends on their being just out of one's fiscal comfort zone, a reason for manipulation of supplies.[27] We might not pay so much attention to diamonds were they local, cheap, and plentiful. Or, if we did notice them, they might not be conceived as having powers to form an empire. Psychologically they would not add to a person's self-importance; socially they would not add stature. Mined in far-off places and transported across seas, they acquire an often-suspicious lineage from their provenance. Unlike coal, diamonds are not indigenous to the British Isles. Arriving on English shores as foreign luxuries, they are reverenced with religious and heretical fervor. Such worship involves eliding those responsible for their production and place in imperial trade.

Despite common belief about the supreme preciousness of diamond, their partnership with humans varies according to location. Consequently, this book uses "settings" in two ways. The setting for a gem varies depending upon placement—on a gendered body, on a shrine, in a chest, in the heavens. Set in a crown, a throne, or a god's forehead, a diamond proclaims supernatural power. Set as jewels for adornment, diamonds signify economic prowess and financial success. In that social realm, diamond meanings are driven by the increasingly dominant engine of fashion. Fashion's characteristically constant change echoes enormous and dizzying cultural alterations in all areas of Victorian social life.

Setting also denotes a place. Meanings form in those settings that denote the "there" in the British Empire. Diamond provides a symbol seeming to steady, even still, great shifts in notions of domestic and foreign, home and abroad. In the context of great imperial circulation of goods and people, diamond's adamantine structure seems to take in and fix what is dislocated. Diamond becomes a symbol for permanence, seeming to counter both personal and political instabilities, including social problems within marriage as an institution and political disturbances such as what were regarded as little wars in India and Africa, including great land grabs in India and Africa. Their facets constitute a hard and glittering object whose very structure speaks of constancy. The two meanings of setting converge and clash in writings examined here, and those conflicts reveal cultural work performed by awe-inspiring diamonds.

Victorian diamonds sparkle within colonial encounters, the "imperial settings" of the title. Each setting in this book places diamonds in foreign contexts, ones that engender meanings. Diamonds are associated with strange peoples, most often with Jews. Centuries of Jewish traders were central to distribution in all settings, even in India, where Indian Jews reputedly descended from the Lost Tribes. English writers adopt Indian lore about diamond power recorded by Indian gemologists. English stories about Indian diamonds discussed in this book are influenced by religious beliefs expressed in the Vedas and Puranas, which lapidaries, used as textbooks for knowledge about the powers of gemstones, expanded and varied, constituting rich gemological lore. Beliefs that diamond delivers punishments from the gods of Eastern and Western religious creeds carries over into English writings about Indian diamonds.

In England and South Africa, nineteenth-century Jewish traders, pawnbrokers, and bankers cannot be separated from the jewels they traded, owned, or stole. Inhabiting the center of London's diamond market, Jewish networks form part of diamond economics and diamond meanings.[28] Once the diamond empire is extended to South Africa, black natives are linked with Jews to shock adventurers out of their complacency yet to reassert their Anglo-Saxon superiority. The mind-changing encounter of peoples on the Diamond Fields forms part of their meanings, particularly in cultural maneuvers to wipe racialized fingerprints from diamond gems. Diamonds like to pass as pure white.[29]

Symbolic Scintillations: Diamond as Fetish

Diamond's fetish quality provides a common thread connecting different meanings assigned to diamonds in the settings of this book. Insisting on interchange among peoples as an essential component of the meaning of fetish, anthropologist William Pietz locates the etymology of fetish as a word, *fetiço*, meaning "made thing," used in exchanges between Portuguese traders and West Coast Africans: "The fetish, then, not only originated from, but remains specific to, the problematic of the social value of material objects as revealed in situations formed by the encounter of radically heterogenous social systems."[30] That problematic also inheres in a diamond empire, which creates and sustains diamond fetish power in all its settings. Fetishes are vivified by specific exchanges among unequal peoples. In a series of influential articles, Pietz grapples with the "problem" of the fetish during the sixteenth- and seventeenth-century age of exploration. His concern bears upon the later era of this book's inquiry: "There emerged a new problematic concerning the capacity of the material object to embody—simultaneously and sequentially—religious, commercial, aesthetic, and sexual values."[31] Like the earlier era of Pietz's attention, the nineteenth century saw commercial and cultural exchanges within an increasingly technologically produced consumer, commodified economy. The colonial encounter described in his anthropological analysis of fetish also applies to symbolic diamond meanings within the diamond empire delineated in this book. Set in that imperial web, diamonds assume sentimental, fiscal, and sacred properties, all jostling for primary attention.[32] In all their settings, diamonds are fetishized with meanings shaped by their location.

Although Pietz cautions readers to respect the term's "sinister pedigree" owing to its origins in unequal, racialized power relations, many theories have found the concept of fetish indispensable.[33] In anthropological, psychoanalytic, and Marxist uses, fetish functions as a religious superstition for the first, a symptom for the second, and a blindness about an object's fabrication for the third.[34] In all areas the object becomes mystified, infused with living spirit. Applied to diamond, "fetish" denotes how traces of the supernatural inhere in a fabricated piece of rock. Both Marx and Freud appropriated the anthropological term. In Marx, the commodity appears as if by a miracle, independent of laborers required for its production. Such a reception elides the system of production and exploitation; in Freud, an impotent man gains sexual power by means of a common object he endows with enabling potency.[35] Marx refers to the commodity as a "social hieroglyphic" that people try to decipher.[36] In his allusion to the nineteenth-century mistaken view that Egyptian hieroglyphics was not a phonetic but a picture language, Marx points to a nineteenth-century tendency toward concrete thought. Victorians animated stuff not only as souvenirs but with spirit, if not soul. As fetish, diamond functions like a materialized guardian angel and promises unending love, immortality, or, at the least, invincibility. In a contradictory belief, diamond also curses its possessor. As fetish, its hardness confirms masculinity. For instance, Asian potentates valued huge, named diamonds, the stone's frequently blood-ridden history confirming a victor's superior virility. A masculine spirit, based on chemical properties, animated the coveted gem.

Fetish as a concept has been applied to nineteenth-century social structures. Recognizing common ground among anthropological, Marxist, and

Freudian uses of the term and placing these uses in debate, the cultural critic Jon Stratton refers to developing social practices of Western peoples in which psychological forces join with capitalist imperatives to increase consumption. In that developing consumer culture, which becomes increasingly visible in the mid-nineteenth century, spectacularized female bodies carry excessive symbolic meanings that contain the fetish sense of awe, as if a spirit inhabited them. In such cases, the body's importance resides in its display as an aestheticized fetish, an item of connoisseurship. In English texts explored in this book, a woman takes part in a trophy system that nonetheless maintains diamond power as a male prerogative. As a fetish, a trophy woman displays the male's importance.

Once fetishized as a proof of men's prowess, a female body becomes alienated from itself, worshipped in isolated body parts. Stratton articulates the process that he calls "cultural fetishism" during the development of nineteenth-century consumer culture, when "the male eroticisation and spectacularisation of the female body" was taking place "at the same time that the male body is conscientiously hidden from view."[37] The female body displaying diamonds stands for consumer culture and for the striving men who supply the gems. Thus, in nineteenth-century consumer culture, masculine values are central to a fetish exchange in which the social contract deeds diamond-bearing to women as a sign of male power. The jewels variously represent a declaration of national invincibility, family prowess, and racial superiority at a moment when England is knowing itself as the British Empire and such confidence is both challenged and reasserted. Social systems wobble, causing diamonds that represent them to distract from those uncertainties by means of their eye-popping dazzle and a belief that shine might emanate from a supernatural force.

In contrast to cultural fetishism as a gendered exchange, the fetish charge of Indian diamonds directly applies to men. In displaying their own beauty and wealth, Indian princes cover themselves in large gems to affirm their masculine, divine right to rule.

Relying on diamond fetish power but stripping that faith of some of its mystification, a South African symbolic economy typically calculates diamond worth in hard figures. The newly mined stones become commercial objects with fluctuating monetary values, yet whose mystification as manufactured rarity needs preservation to maintain immense profitability. A diamond digger who scores many stones might enhance his masculine status on the personal level. Transferred to business and multiplied greatly, the diamond industry affirms the virile superiority of a place controlling diamond markets—a diamond business empire, politically ensconced, that becomes tyrannical, closing off competition. A successful enterprise of this kind relies upon diamond's fetish quality. Eventually, at the end of the era encompassed in this book, diamond prices seem naturally ordained rather than controlled by a syndicate with secretive forces securing the gems' allure. For Victorian political economies, financial considerations subtend spiritual symbolism. Diamond prices may be calculated with cold efficiency, but diamonds often glitter in the celestial sphere, elevated by faith in their earthly value.

Immortal Symbol, Eternal Sign

In a stunning example of enveloping diamond in divine light removed from sordid economics, the Jesuit poet Gerard Manley Hopkins in "That Nature is a Heraclitean Fire and of the comfort of the Resurrection" (1888) elevates a diamond to its highest symbolic pinnacle. Emotional forces that dread impermanence obscure a fetish quality that gives authority to the "immortal diamond" at the end of the poem. Those believers in a holy covenant glorify Christian immortality in the face of constant change on earth: "Million-fuelèd, nature's bonfire burns on." The poet ordinarily fills his poems with homage to the created world, even when he feels utterly alienated from it, even when its storms and mountains wrack him. An exception is his shining diamond that in the poem opposes "the residuary worm." Above and apart from nature's bonfire, diamond resists all flames. "Immortal diamond," that ecstatic, culminating phrase ending his extended sonnet, arrives at an eschatological climax to a meditation on constant decay within the created world.[38] Glossing Heraclitus's philosophy about fire as the fundamental element fueling change and flux in the world, Hopkins represents Nature in a rush of tumultuous images, from clouds to man, "this Jack, joke, potsherd" whose body and whose best mind burns to ash. Unlike creation's annihilating fires, diamond in the poem defies Nature's fate. Diamond transforms Heraclitean fire into eternal light and life for those Christians believing in the Incarnation and the Resurrection. "In a flash," mortal coil can become "immortal diamond," the phrase repeated twice in a litany of faith. This is holy alchemy.

The poet emerged from writing his "terrible sonnets," in which tormented religious doubts find no relief: "Comforter, where, where is your comforting?" he cries out in "No worst, there is none" (poem 65), with only divine silence to increase his suffering.[39] By contrast, "comfort" in the title of "That Nature is a Heraclitean Fire" turns earthly death to immortal diamond for believers, safe out of nature's remorseless flames. As in powerful metaphors, a core of fact lends credence to its climatic ending. Nevertheless, in the heat and pressure required to form diamond from carbonized bodies, as in the case of Luis Ramiro Barragán, diamonds exist within time and are thus subject to time's revenges.

As symbol of immortality, Hopkins's diamond is a wondrous fabrication. Diamonds, as noted above, are subject to vaporization. But Hopkins's phrase "immortal diamond" reinforces a cultural truth about diamond indestructibility. Because of increasing knowledge of diamond formation after the African diamond discovery, Hopkins might have known that they are produced by great heat, and hence his invocation of Heraclitean fire recalls diamonds to those who know their origins in earth's fiery core, though they too are vulnerable to a kind of Heraclitean vaporization. Rather, the poet elevates diamond production in great heat to spiritual miracle. Facing death (Hopkins died the next year), the poet finds solace in transformation to immortal diamond. That diamond beyond time would not be visualized as a dull, rough one. To have its exalted position, its force, and its power, readers see it shining as a beautifully faceted thing, a gemstone beyond price, beyond death.

Extending a diamond empire with religious overtones to the present moment, such a promise as Hopkins's achieves an earthly, contradictory glorification in British artist Damien Hirst's 2007 *For the Love of God* (see plate 1). The work consists of an eighteenth-century human skull with human teeth, encased in platinum and encrusted with 8,601 "flawless" diamonds. Apparently, the title of the work refers to an exclamation by the artist's mother about the shape her son's future works might take. A pious phrase incorporated into common parlance retains its religious context. It is a homey reference and a son's extravagant response hardened into lugubrious art. The diamond skull attracts and chides, telling of human decay and yet affirming the paradox of immortal death. The skull underlying its encrustation ("pavé" in the jewelry world) supports its meaning: this was once a real but unnamed person, whose bones were likely unconsecrated and on the commodity market and whose life is largely undocumented.[40] Those unembellished, whitish teeth are enamel, the most mineralized and therefore the hardest part of the human body, not carbon as in bones but inorganic calcium phosphate.

Does the work offer comfort along with dread? Is this what the love of God has come to in a materialistic age? Is this fetishized skull an object of special devotion?[41] As a memento mori, *For the Love of God* displays little humility about human clay—no poor potsherd here, no Jack, perhaps a little joke about flamboyant, extravagant defiance of inevitable death. Part of its shock value resides in its being an actual person's head, its bones still there under its platinum shield. As what remains after death in bone and teeth, the work reminds the viewer of those universally humble human origins of the man we might as well call Jack. With an additional gleam from the largest diamond, pear-shaped, pink, and 52.40 carats, the elaborately crafted jewel in its forehead recalls diamonds embedded in a Hindu god's forehead. A practice in India, the diamond in a deity's forehead has been taken up in the Western imagination to lend sacred allure to big diamonds. This visual iteration resonates as a contradictory judgment about Western idolatry. As a fellow human, the diamond skull smiles at the viewer. Or maybe it opens its jaws to bite. The Hopkins poem offers diamond comfort beyond our mortal coil, whereas the Hirst work offers awesome diamond dread, embedded in what remains on earth. Regarding this book, the diamond skull confidently presented as art offers a comment on and example of ways a diamond empire can rule.

Bearing in mind the disparate areas in empires, the three parts of this book attend to three imperial settings: India, England, and South Africa. In each setting a different literary genre dominates, partly influenced by how writings conjure those locations and the values given to diamonds there. The late Victorian works discussed in part 1 on Indian-denominated diamonds are romances, where they evoke a jeweled setting, referred to possessively and familiarly as "the jewel in her crown." Indian diamonds carry over a religious aura into English writings, originating in ancient beliefs. They glitter with danger, temptation, and sin, warnings found in both Hindu and Christian concepts of a diamond's power. To denote diamonds as Indian, authors such as Wilkie Collins in *The Moonstone,* Robert Louis Stevenson in "The Rajah's Diamond," Sir Arthur Conan Doyle in "The Sign of Four" and "Adventures of the Blue Carbuncle," and Rudyard Kipling in *Kim* evoke an exotic place where diamonds not only are encrusted on swords but also shine in the Indian air. Royal men cover themselves in the gems. They kill for them. Subtended by religious belief, diamond heat is often infernal.

Part 2 turns from the Indian setting to newly forming English political and social identity, with diamond as its multifaceted symbol. Lord Tennyson's allegorical narrative poem *Idylls of the King* recasts a medieval source to recount a promising but doomed imperial endeavor that reflects Victorian concerns about changing power structures in which male power is diffused. That failed political effort is juxtaposed with Dickens's business account in *Little Dorrit* of chicanery made possible by forms of governmental authority based, like new business enterprises, on an alienated, corporatized model. In both poem and novel, diamonds are signs of misplaced authority. Added to issues of national identity formation, the second chapter of part 2 addresses the question of race as part of Englishness, a problem that grows entangled with stories about diamonds, initiated in the fabricated history of Sir Walter Scott's *Ivanhoe* and taken up by its Victorian descendants in Anthony Trollope's *The Eustace Diamonds,* George Eliot's *Daniel Deronda,* and Amy Levy's *Reuben Sachs,* all realist novels. Greed and ostentation, reverence and politics, anti-Semitism and nationalism weave their sinister and seductive ways into the diamond novels discussed there. Diamonds considered as English embed in their symbolism concerns about a country's becoming an empire, shifts in family and gender values, and worries about the racial purity within that political entity—immigrants challenging a bounded self-identity, conceived as racially pure, racially white—whose members are born within the British Isles.[42] Because diamonds shine like nothing else, the symbol serves to distract from immense social change by seeming changeless.

South Africa, the setting of part 3, confirms the reach of a diamond empire under British control. Surely the most cataclysmic global event for the developing diamond empire was the unique discovery of diamonds in rivers and then a kind of soil called kimberlite in what became known as South Africa. In a continent labeled dark with uncharted territories and natives' incomprehensible lifestyles, languages, and beliefs, all regarded as savage, Occidental upstarts counterfeited blue blood with white diamonds. Unlike in earlier diamond mining, now prospectors from anywhere could stake a claim to find diamonds while others could freely observe the process—to photograph or write about it. Trading often occurred in the open. And anyone able to pay the price could own diamonds—in fact, were encouraged to do so. South African writing presents a diamond culture more complete than available in other settings, from digging them up to making them precious and their finders either rich or destitute. Stories in this setting do not ignore conditions of producing the sparkle in the gem. Generic blending characterizes writings about South African diamonds—to the point that fiction moves into history, manufacturing what are considered facts. Often memoirs read like novels, novels read like history, and fictions sometimes contain sections akin to technical manuals. Forgotten diamond novels, along with those of well-known writers H. Rider Haggard and Olive Schreiner, register their stories alongside memoirs, journalism, and letters to warm readers with the African sun of the diamond discovery that changed the imperial map.

Empire of Diamonds ends with an epilogue tracing the emigration of the diamond empire to America, where its meanings, democratized, are largely consolidated and imported from imperial meanings. Advertising and publicity campaigns affirmed that the British lost the war but reigned in America's diamond empire. Empire of diamonds is a fraught, chaotic, and often compelling realm, revealing its imaginative force in an object that exceeds ordinary desires. Because diamonds scintillate and thereby can addict, a message disclosed by interpreting myriad relationships between the diamonds and humans as explored in *Empire of Diamonds* may likely go unheeded: be wary. Rather than being "a girl's best friend," as Marilyn Monroe memorably sings in an updated film version of gold digger Lorelei Lee, as created in Anita Loos's *Gentlemen Prefer Blondes* (1925), diamonds in this book are often associated with death, whether a promise as in Hopkins or a warning as in Hirst, or as an occasion for crime or marriage in the texts dazzlingly recorded by Victorian writers of fictions and facts.

I
India

Gems from the Gods

> The best of the inorganic world being gemstones, it is no wonder that the sages have rightly appreciated the quality of divine fire in the production of gemstones.
>
> —Murthy on Rig Veda

The jewel in her crown is not only an imperial metaphor. That boast about India as the acme of the British Empire is grounded in the diamond heart of Indian beliefs. Long before India was a twinkle in the British imperial eye, it knew itself in jeweled terms. Moreover, diamonds came from India. Before the eighteenth century, along with Borneo, it was the world's only known diamond source. Moreover, Indians themselves regarded gems as the keystone to their signifying system, an essential part of their worldview. In pre-Hindu sacred writings—Vedas and Puranas—all aspects of life could be known and understood by studying the properties of gemstones. According to S. R. N. Murthy, who translated five gemological studies from Sanskrit, "Gemmology [*sic*] was considered to be one of the well-known 64 arts to be learnt by every individual in ancient India."[1] Beliefs expressed in Hindu hymns reveal the centrality of jewels to Indian culture and illuminate their sustaining aura in the imperial imagination. The Indian world was charged with the glory of gems, traces of which underwrite the British elevation of India. Indian diamonds hover over the empire of imperial imagination as a well-wrought crown.

Diamonds carried individual Indian identities centuries, even millennia, before blue-dyed Britons became civilized Anglo-Saxons. Diamond mining in India started at the "dawn of history"[2] along with diamond lore that places diamonds from the gods in Krishna's hands.[3] As sacred objects, many are secreted in temple treasuries only viewable by the gods. The Rig Veda, the oldest collection of Sanskrit Vedic hymns (1200–900 BC), specifies myriad ways that gems were woven into the very fabric of Hindu culture. Sacred writings assume continuities among all experience so that economic value, religious practice, medical lore, political power, aesthetic allure, and erotic pleasures join in a holistic guide about how to live with gems, how gems live with people, and how gems signify sacred relationships between people and deities.

Profusions of Indian gems attracted adventurers and mythmakers to the subcontinent. Marco Polo's account of his voyages along the Silk Road stimulated hunters for wealth to venture eastward in search of gems.[4] Kublai Khan traveled with Marco Polo; thus, the explorer's spirit hovers over Samuel Taylor Coleridge's "Kubla Khan," where the ruler's "stately pleasure dome" may well have been imagined as gem-encrusted. Sanskrit gemological lore was also carried into Europe to a huge audience by texts such as *The Thousand and One Nights*, a collection of medieval tales, considered of Arabic and Persian origins, where luxurious rooms drip with precious gems. The tales incorporated accounts of Sinbad the sailor's voyages to a diamond-besprinkled valley. In European translations (the first in English in the early eighteenth century) Sinbad's adventures associated almost inaccessible gems with the mysterious East. The significance to the Western imagination of this one compilation of tales cannot be overstated.

Following Marco Polo, merchant travelers took to the seas. One such seventeenth-century seeker, Jean-Baptiste Tavernier (1605–1689), became sufficiently enchanted that he robed himself in a turbaned Eastern costume, opening doors to princely treasuries and enabling him to obtain storied gems to sell to such diamond-addicted luminaries as the Sun King, Louis XIV. Tavernier's *Travels in India* (1676) described encounters with Indian princes and their treasuries, further whetting Western appetites. In the late eighteenth and nineteenth centuries, ancient gemological lore that spelled out symbolic and sacred meanings became of greater interest in the West when the East–West diamond trade increased. Attending to Indian gemological writings, nineteenth-century English lapidaries responded to a demand for diamond knowledge that could retain the diamond mystification useful for the imagination and the market.

Lore about diamonds also appears in Indian lapidaries that specified powers and functions depending upon assessments of color, shape, and purity. Hindus seeking their fortune told or a cure for an ailment are advised to wear diamonds according to the gem's caste, gender, and medicinal properties. One such precept provides a gloss on England's crown jewel as an epithet for the essence of empire: "The fronts of regal palaces should burn with pure diamonds." According to Tagore in *Mani-Mālā*, such an architectural feature promises protection from "every kind of evil," providing that the diamonds are "Brahmin diamonds of the clearest water and thus efficacious for all people."[5] Such extravagant advice challenges Western ways of sorting out the world, assigning social classes to gems and recommending extravagant display. In visualizing a diamond-fronted palace, readers in the West both confront an exotic worldview and confirm Occidental fantasies about Indian jeweled environments. Furthermore, an assessment of good, male, Brahmin diamonds as "pure," signals a gendered and moral register. Whatever else, the diamond palace distinctly locates its provenance in an Indian, primarily Hindu, imaginary. This palace façade sutra occurs in a unique work by Tagore, a renowned scholar, musician, philanthropist, and member of the prominent Tagore family who compiled a remarkable lapidary. Tagore, also mentioned in the introduction, strung together Indian wisdom about gems, imagined as beads to a necklace, with the knots between the beads taken from British commentary and he compiled and translated it all into Hindi, Bengali, Sanskrit, and English. Inspired by gem lore lovingly transmitted to him as a young boy— "I can see myself sitting on the lap of my gentle mother, while she amused me by trying to impress on my mind the names of different kinds of precious stones"—Tagore disseminated such instilled wisdom at a time when gems were increasingly absorbed into Western beliefs and treasuries.[6] Tagore's work arrived at a prime Victorian moment for interest in diamonds.

Tagore underscores India's legacy to British fascination with diamonds as deriving from the veneration of gems deemed "precious" in early Sanskrit texts and gemological works. The earliest of these, possibly in the third or first century BC, a Sanskrit text, Kautilya's *Arthasatstra,* includes what is considered the first reference to diamond. It appears in a consideration of governance and economics. Diamond was recognized for its brilliance and for its economic worth, with hoarding and trading a part of its cultural legacy.[7] In the Rig Veda a hard mineral, perhaps a diamond, was worshipped as originating in divine fire.[8] A hymn invoking Universal Fire places diamond for a phase of its life deep in the earth, where it acquires its powers. This account anticipated scientific descriptions of diamond origins, unknown until the nineteenth century, while affirming the gem's sacred attribution. Vedic diamonds mineralize divinity.

While diamond was revered, it was not always benevolent; its influence often included violence and malice. Associated in the Rig Veda with Indra, the thunder and war god, the stone that is probably what is now known as diamond forms part of the god's supreme weaponry.⁹ Before they were ornamental signs of wealth, before they enhanced palaces, thrones, and royalty, diamonds formed part of the gods' killing machines. Accessories to war, they are covered in blood and, as a sign of power, they dazzle to mesmerize and to terrorize. As efficacious for palace façades, so Indian princes implanted their bodily façades with diamonds as proofs of their power. To cover the rajah's body in gems was to astonish viewers with his sacred invulnerability (figure 2).

Rulers owned the purest and largest Indian diamonds, usually designated as male diamonds. They belonged to kings because, according to one myth of origin, they sprang from invincible Bala, king of the Danavas. In some versions of this myth of origins, Bala, or Vala, is a demon and therefore immortal.

Figure 2. Yadavindra Singh, Maharajah of Patalia, 1941. To cover the prince's façade with diamonds ensures invincibility and asserts power. (Cartier/Nadler; Vendome Press)

Though evil and indestructible, Bala boasted a pure lineage so that when he agreed to the gods' request and sacrificed himself to them, his bones became the seeds of gems that retained the demonic body's extraordinary power and purity.[10] Everywhere the unique seeds of Bala's immolation dropped, whether in water or earth, diamonds grew.[11]

The Bala myth recorded by the fifth-century lapidary *Radnadīpikā* (*Examination of Precious Stones*), by Buddha Bhatta, establishes one strand of symbolic meanings of diamonds not only in India but in cultures that inherit those meanings.[12] The Indian diamond, according to this account, comes into being at the threshold between the gods and mortals; it carries within it a seed of divinity. Transformed into diamonds, Bala is converted into a possession of the gods. From an anthropological perspective about objects that contain within them an eternal spirit, the *Radnadīpikā* formulates a fetish pedigree for diamonds. Because the stones are animated by the king's demonic spirit, they are power fetishes, desired and feared. As talismans or charms they also carry the blessing of power, seeming to sanctify and authorize those kings who possess them. Suffused with the malign spirit of Bala, first property of the gods and then of royalty, diamonds may cause horrendous consequences to those possessing them. *Radnadīpikā's* Bala offers a dark myth of origin for diamonds, an aspect often overlooked in face of the gem's ability to dazzle. Diamond worship embraces the devotee in the terrible grip of its sacred nature.

As the palace sutra reveals, diamonds are categorized by gender, caste, economics, health, and moral justice. Masculine, feminine, and neuter genders are recognized by shape, color, and inclusions, considered flaws. Masculine diamonds are the best, most revered, and useful in chemical and medical operations. A feminine diamond brings grace and fertility, whereas a neuter diamond destroys energy and brings weakness and disappointment. Male rulers owned the largest, purest, whitest circular diamonds among regalia signifying their power: "That diamond which has eight facets, six angles, brilliant, emits spectral light, of the waters of clouds and appears to float on water is called male diamond."[13] The best male diamonds possess universal medicinal powers, whereas female diamonds only help women. Hermaphrodite diamonds could be useful for impotence. "That diamond which is flat, rounded or elongated is female; and the one which is rounded and dark coloured angled as also slightly heavy is called the hermaphrodite."[14] To wear the wrong-gendered diamond brings misfortune, whereas the right diamond begets desired outcomes. For instance, according to Varahamihira's *Brhatsamhita* 16, "Ladies desiring male children should not wear any and all kinds of diamond; they should wear only such diamonds which resemble a square pattern or triangle or a grain or vagina."[15] Diamonds also impart desired effects when incorporated in prayers: "Women can always escape the curse of sterility by adorning a goddess decked with diamonds."[16] Flawed diamonds cause pregnant women to miscarry.

Like humans, diamonds are organized in a delineated class system. Four castes of diamonds—Brahmin, Vaisya, Kshatriyas, and Súdras—bestow upon the owner specific benefits. A Brahmin diamond, the most valuable, pure white, confers blessings from the gods. Vaisya produces fame, wisdom, and skill in the fine arts, whereas Kshatriyas generate success, power, and victory over enemies. The best diamonds of the Súdras induce benevolence in the owner and make him healthy and wealthy. Tagore points out the rigid caste system, echoing social organization: "As the promiscuous intercourse of one caste with another gives rise to mixed castes among mankind, so it is with diamonds, the mixed classes of which are fraught with great troubles to man."[17] Diamonds exhibiting impurities and flaws betray their mixed-caste origins and need to be avoided because they are the source of serious consequences, ranging from loss of family dignity to death.

Global economics influence diamond meanings by disseminating some Indian beliefs in the course of commercial exchanges. Indian diamonds had been known in the Mediterranean world, but regular exports had begun because of the intensification of trade between India and Europe in the sixteenth century.[18] Indians sold leftovers from the stones' sacred and royal uses, penetrating Western markets by traders affiliated with the East India Company. From the moment diamond becomes a commodity, it enters the underground market as well. Diamond mining has always included the risk of the miners finding ingenious methods of secreting stones. Tavernier reported that Indian miners often swallowed valuable diamonds; a merchant reported to him that one of his workmen concealed a diamond in the corner of his eye.[19] Developing Victorian literary genres of fiction discussed in this part—sensation, detective, and mystery among others—found diamond lore ready-made for plots.

In fact, Indian diamonds often arrive in Western lands with stories of their own. Large Indian diamonds are endowed with names, pedigrees, and personalities. Their life stories extend centuries longer than human biographies. Celebrities, named diamonds achieved the status of superheroes or gods. Attributes given to those diamonds when they were part of the Indian worldview carry over to British culture, assimilating into Western meanings and values while carrying traces of their Indian origins.

This brief overview of Indian gemology's vast influence draws attention to the resonance of diamonds specified as Indian in English fiction. The jewel of Britain's empire wrote itself into national literature. Embellished and changing as they assimilate to a time and place, Hindu beliefs in diamond power become colored by Protestant values, some puritanical guilt mingling with materialistic awe and amorous desire. Indian diamonds rarely appear in Victorian stories as purely benevolent or as merely beautiful. Further, as we will see, Indian diamonds arrive with contemporary consciousness of British imperial transgressions, notably the Sepoy Rebellion, also called the Indian Mutiny of 1857. As Gautam Basu Thakur asserts, "Every single narrative about the Rebellion contains discussions of imperial concerns with material objects."[20] Bala's demonic vigor as well as the Christian devil's animates Victorian Indian diamond stories.

Deeply influential on Western beliefs about the gems, the moral force implicit in Hindu gemological writing can be discerned in the power given to Indian diamonds in English writings. But their moral force may also be converted to a Protestant register by the various authors who write versions of romances with an Indian diamond heart. As a material object, famous Indian diamonds are absorbed into royal and aristocratic treasuries, their notorious message usually ignored. As a metaphor, the jewel in her crown incorporates knowledge, mystification, spirituality, and unimaginable wealth that places India as the special favorite, the glittery charm that quickened and thereby affirmed the British imperial imagination.

1

Conversions of the Last Maharajah of the Punjab and His Koh-i-noor Diamond

The year 1850 initiated a diamond empire within the imperial reaches of Britain when Queen Victoria received the Koh-i-noor diamond from British annexation of the Punjab. Known and heralded before its arrival on English shores, the diamond continued to cause a sensation. It suffered indignities as well as honors. This chapter intertwines the legend and fate of the celebrity diamond with that of its last Indian owner, Maharajah Duleep Singh, and mingles their influence on both fictional and factual Victorian stories.

Carrying a venerable legend, the Koh-i-noor enjoyed a fame that depended as much upon biography as it did upon beauty. With what the *Chambers' Edinburgh Journal* considered "Oriental extravagance," Nadir Shah in 1739 named an already-famous large stone "Koh-i-noor" in Persian, translated as "Mountain of Light."[1] Both the name and its Indian attribution are relatively recent. To call the large, fabled diamond "Indian" may seem to erase its origins before the subcontinent was known by that name. Much later, when its move from the Punjab to England might recommend a name change to veil its extraordinarily bloody history and to assimilate to a new regime, its Persian name persisted.

Its name preserved its legend. Often the locution "it is said" indicates that a legend informs history. "It is said" carries traces of an oral tale handed down, the current teller recounting the story without verifying it. Though the Koh-i-noor fascinates beyond mere economic price, its speculative worth earned it a value not in currency but in nourishment as "two and a half days' food for the whole world."[2] Intended to spin the mind, the legendary calculation splendidly ignored considerations of both fluctuating currency rates and the varying appetites of the whole world's peoples. Defying rationality, the diamond achieved such valuation despite ample evidence that it was neither the most lustrous nor the largest of storied gemstones.[3] Legendary features also contribute to the portrayal of the real Indian prince who owned it, in part because the diamond's luster shaped his life. In telling about the Koh-i-noor's fate joined with that of the last Asian prince who possessed it, "it is said" marks that kind of legendary construction where fact is trumped by the insistence of myth. Legend endows the Koh-i-noor with agency as a personage, a few Victorian chapters of which intersect with the fate of Duleep Singh, last maharajah of the Punjab. Unlike the prince's story, barely noted in Western histories of the Raj (except for British Sikhs, who honored him at the centenary of his birth), the Koh-i-noor legend has attracted huge audiences that pay a hefty tariff to place themselves on a conveyor belt to glide past this diamond. It is the last display of the Jewel House in the Tower of London, where as a treasure of the Crown, it proclaims its Britishness.

The journey to its current position lasted millennia, if its legend is taken as gospel. The Koh-i-noor's notoriety rests upon its first being a gift from a god, then its plunder by belligerent men with princely East Asian lineages, and finally its alteration to regal British identity. In following the stages of the diamond's transformations, the concept of conversion usefully organizes a relatively recent chapter in the adventures of the Koh-i-noor—becoming British.[4] Conversion connects the diamond's sacred legend with the biography of Duleep Singh, also a convert.[5] In the context of the Raj, "conversion" describes a radical but imperfect transformation of the two immigrants. Already pacified by two Anglo-Sikh wars and within a few years of each other, the diamond and the prince entered England as strangers in the land owing to an invitation they could not refuse.

So triumphantly were the two heralded that rituals, ceremonies, and hospitality endowed them with a role that muted their potential danger to the idea of an Englishness based on Victorian racial taxonomies. Their welcome also mutes the considerable price they paid in being so celebrated. The very terms of their arrival in England maintained boundaries that preserved marks of their difference, so that they remained imperial trophies. While signaling their Asian origins in their names, their conversion makes of them not merely Christian and British but permanently Oriental. Maharajah and diamond undergo aesthetic, cultural, and religious conversions that are inextricable from imperial identity politics.

The maharajah's radical conversion from Punjab ruler to British subject is revealed by comparing portraits of the prince. When Duleep Singh was seven, his position was rendered in the context of his advisors in a Mughal-style miniature watercolor, *Durbar of Maharaja Dalip Singh* (c. 1845), probably by Hasan-al-din of the Sikh School in Lahore (see plate 2). Two years a maharajah, the boy presides in this painting over equally resplendent councilors.[6] In contrast to Western perspectival conventions, the painting renders surface rather than depth, its distinguished subjects absorbed into rhythmic patterns: the terrace where the durbar (court or formal meeting) takes place, the architectural framing, and the elaborate borders.[7] Duleep Singh, seated in the center on a cushion, focuses the design, a green halo marking his supremacy. The nobles' dress differs slightly, and their heads provide rhythmic variations on a theme. The plumed *jigha* crowning their turbans surpass each other in glory. Turban ornaments—the *jigha* and the *sairpaich* (clustered ornaments of jewels in precious metal settings)—are symbols of royalty as introduced in India by the Mughals.[8] The watercolor tells Western eyes differences in ways of seeing and in depicting authority. The princely boy is enclosed and among others. Furthermore, the watercolor depicts an idealized council meeting where the boy prince seems the center of authority. In fact, his mother, Jind Kaur, acted as regent and brought her son along to durbars as part of his education.[9]

Western paintings depict different but idealized versions of Duleep Singh's role as an Eastern prince. In contrast and as a visual record of the prince's radical conversion, two paintings depict the youth in trappings of his origins. *Portrait of Duleep Singh* (1852) by George Duncan Beechey (see plate 3) and *Portrait of Maharaja Duleep Singh* (1854) by Franz Xavier Winterhalter (see plate 5), oil on canvas portraits, convey an ideology embedded in aesthetics. The artists converted a bejeweled Duleep Singh into a visual language not of his own culture, endowing his images with European values. While taking the prince out of his Punjabi context, the paintings charm the viewer with an expectation that includes the trace of the diamond he inherited. In embodying that imperial metaphor in their different ways, the paintings portray the young maharajah as a jewel in his own right but in Queen Victoria's crown.

The first portrait uses oil paint, canvas, and portrait conventions to rework the Indian subject to a European way of depicting sovereignty.[10] George Duncan Beechey left for India when his English commissions dried up, becoming court painter of Indian potentates and Raj officials. Duleep Singh commissioned his portrait at the request of Lord Dalhousie, governor-general of the vast Punjab that the prince had surrendered.[11] Conventions of Western portraiture present an intimate close-up of a fourteen-year-old exotically clad royal. Ravishing textures—glowing yards of draped silks, limpid dark almond eyes—tell viewers he is not English. Jewels dominate his likeness and exemplify the otherness of his masculinity in contrast to a Western prince's regal attire.[12]

Compared to the lively boy with leg extended and hand petting his dog in the Lahore watercolor miniature, Beechey's composition encourages Western fantasies about opulently clad Asian princes posed to resemble Western sovereigns. A fantasy itself, Duleep Singh's 1852 portrait was painted after he had been ceremoniously removed from his realm with British rituals of treaties and agreements. As Maharajah of Nowhere, he was royally housed in a luxurious compound at Fatehgarh with the title and trappings of a prince, including an allowance, yet without territory, freedom of movement, or access to his treasury of jewels, or *toshkhana*. An emblem of the British acquisition of the Punjab, he is offered to British officials not as a ruler but as booty.

Lord Dalhousie placed Duleep Singh under the guardianship of Dr. and Mrs. John Spencer Login, devout Christians who acted both in the place of parents and as protectors of Crown property. Their contradictory roles carry through in Duleep Singh's life. In another sign of false authority, the portrait masks his captivity by endowing the maharajah with meticulously depicted jewels that might denote his own splendid wealth and power. Those very jewels actually are his by permission, chosen by his guardian who inventoried and guarded the Lahore treasury, including jewels.[13] With that self-satisfied but unconscious irony characteristic of paternalistic authority, Login gave some of Duleep Singh's own jewels to him as birthday presents, as he reported in an 1849 letter to his sister: "I had the pleasure of presenting to the Maharajah on the morning of his birthday, a *lakh* of rupees worth of his own jewels from the toshkhana which I had been empowered by Government to select and present to him. . . . When I congratulated him on his appearance, he innocently remarked that on his last birthday he had worn the Koh-i-noor on his arm!"[14] Login expresses his pleasure in possessing the young prince as a ward of Empire in giving back his former possessions as gifts that now signify benevolent dictatorship. And Duleep Singh's remark about his wearing the Koh-i-noor, whatever its affect—longing, pride, anger, all lost in quotation—recalls the missing jewel. The wonder of it shows in Login's exclamation point. The young prince will always be lit by the reflected rays of the diamond he gave up. His comment indicates that he knew it. Eighteen forty-nine is the year that Duleep Singh surrendered the Koh-i-noor.

According to gemological wisdom, Duleep Singh's Indian jewels would have proclaimed his power. His jeweled turban signifies his status and religion. In Sikhism, the turban is an essential article of faith, adopted by all adherents, who never cut their hair. Appropriated from a sign of status to a religious garment, the unadorned Sikh turban affirms the equality of all male adherents. However, in the portrait, as in the miniature (where servants wear plain turbans), precious jewels distinguish this youth from the democracy of his faith. Pearls and emeralds in the *sairpaich* add another layer to his authority, while the *jigha* transforms the plume depicted in the miniature as a feather-shaped jewel composed of diamonds, emeralds, and pendant pearls. According to Bernard S. Cohn, "Kings in the medieval Hindu tradition were the controllers of the earth and its products, and in cosmographic terms jewels were the essence of the earth, its most pure and concentrated substance. Thus, the cloth turban with its associated jewels brought together all the powers of the earth."[15] Sikh rulers adopted this symbolic system.[16]

From a Western perspective, large emerald and pearl hoop earrings indicate the prince's slide from Indian prince to Raj trophy. His earrings resemble those in the Indian watercolor, but their meaning has shifted from masculine and powerful to exotic and effeminate, reflecting centuries of the English effeminizing of India.[17] Duleep Singh's adorned head seems an artifact, a curiosity in a British display, picked up in an Indian bazaar. In context, his portrait for the governor-general is a souvenir of British power, conceived as a gift.

The rest of the maharajah's jewelry reinforces the double message conveyed by his turban. Sumptuous necklaces of huge pearls, large rubies and spinels, with a great spherical emerald and diamond drop, might seem sufficient adornment. Yet those splendid ornaments on his torso highlight a portrait jewel. Placed in the center of the painting, an ivory miniature of Queen Victoria emphasizes this deposed maharajah's affiliation with the British Empire. Because of its location and subject, the jewel could hold its own even were it not encircled by large oval diamonds. Queen Victoria's image colonizes the center of her captive's portrait, assigning it a significance that differs from the jewel's provenance. In 1838 it was given to Duleep Singh's officially acknowledged father, Maharajah Ranjit Singh, by Lord Auckland when he visited the Punjab not long before Ranjit Singh's death.[18] Annexation of the Punjab a decade later alters the meaning of the gift. The portrait jewel that initially formed part of a diplomatic, reciprocal gift exchange between rulers now signifies that the wearer could be regarded as an honored possession.[19] In the Beechey portrait, the Maharajah's and the Queen's three-quarter profiles mirror each other. The portrait jewel marks a cordial yet subservient affiliation, a sign of amity at the same time as it signifies almost a familial, hierarchical relation.[20] Such jeweled portraits combine "opulence with intimacy" and signify, in Diana Scarisbrick's happy phrase, "dynastic pride and private affection."[21] The portrait jewel appears almost like an identity tag when worn by this prince in the context of his absorption into Queen Victoria and Prince Albert's domestic life.

The portrait jewel so centrally placed offers conflicting meanings to the royal family's embrace of this deposed yet privileged prince. On the one hand, a predominant interpretation would see poignancy in the jewel as a brave disguise of the prince's demotion. The location of the Queen Victoria portrait jewel would then celebrate Duleep Singh—elegant, handsome, and young—as a newborn child of the empire. Representing a sovereign-child relationship that had faded between the monarch and her British subjects but was revivified in the colonial relation, he would exemplify what came to be known as the "Peter Pan" theory regarding Asians.[22] Like Lost Boys, they never grow up. His very youth seems to confirm ethnographic precepts that the Indian lived in an earlier stage of civilization than the more advanced British. On the other hand, a question of the status of the portrait jewel on the breast of a deposed prince dramatizes the role of royalty that conflicts with official positions that have prevailed over time. According to Priya Atwal's recent challenge to views about nation, the portrait jewel would be considered as a sign of a more equal status to the Queen as a royal personage. In Victoria's approving eyes, the portrait jewel testifies to Duleep Singh's status as a royal, with privileges above those of other titled aristocrats of her court. That opinion and accompanying affection were at odds with officials where the portrait jewel places its wearer in a dependent relationship, the owner being at the mercy of views where the idea of blood predominated over royal ranks that disregarded national boundaries.[23] Like a precious toy, his setting was already precarious but increasingly so when he inevitably became too grown up and too British. An official view that respected bloodlines above status, seated in part in the India Office, voiced aggressively by Dalhousie, ultimately prevailed. Duleep Singh stood on a liminal threshold, becoming a problematic gentleman, unequal but accustomed to privileges accorded to him by his affectionate queen's acceptance of royalty over the category of race.

Given Login's wonder at Duleep Singh's "innocent" memory of wearing his own diamond as a birthday ornament and the separation of the prince from the legendary stone, the missing diamond leaves its trace on the prince's image in the Beechey painting. Arm bracelets, called "bazubands," one of the Koh-i-noor's Punjabi settings, encircle Duleep Singh's arms. It is said that

Ranjit Singh, called the "Lion of the Punjab" for his ruthless military prowess despite being blind in his left eye, so loved looking at the Koh-i-noor that he placed it on the right side of his horse's bridle to see its sparkle as he rode.[24] Given Indian lore about the gem's power, he no doubt displayed it to broadcast his prowess. Ranjit Singh also wore on his right arm a bazuband of three diamonds, the Koh-i-noor in the center (see plate 4). According to Indian diamond lore, a diamond destroys all enemies when worn on the arm.[25]

Undisputed in power, the Koh-i-noor boasts a legend beyond time. Skeptics may question whether the Punjabi diamond is that same very large, shining stone that, in 1000 BC or maybe 3000 BC, Krishna received as a gift to mankind from Surya, the sun god. Millennia later and now much smaller, a remarkable irregularly shaped gem of between 286 and 186 carats enters history when it is said to carry a curse that will be rained down on the head of the various sultans, shahs, maharajahs, Mughals, Indians, Persians, Afghanis, Turks, Sikhs, Hindus, Muslims who poke out eyes by the hundreds, chop off countless heads, rob, pillage, vandalize, deceive, and destroy to obtain it.[26] In exchange, they or their families will die or live miserably.

The end of the Koh-i-noor's Asian history in 1850 marked a new chapter for its legend. The great diamond, whose history had been notoriously bloody and whose origins are mythical, changed nationalities once again as an item of exchange in the transfer of the Punjab to the British. Characterizing the diamond's legend as the captured legacy of kings, Dalhousie recognized the value of the Koh-i-noor "as a historical symbol of conquest in India."[27] The diamond had already traveled to England where it officially became a royal possession, after a series of comical events, squabbling over what was the appropriate entity to convey the jewel to Queen Victoria—the East India Company or the governor-general—and its emissary misplacing it, when the Queen received the jewel at the 1850 ceremony at Buckingham Palace. The fragment of Indian lore arrived just in time to star in Henry Cole and Prince Albert's 1851 Great Exhibition of the Works of Industry of All Nations, where, in a gilded cage, it was the object of awe and disappointment.

Whereas the transfer of the Koh-i-noor to Queen Victoria's very hand marks a first step in the gem's gender and national conversion, it takes another giant step in its political conversion with its appearance as display in the Great Exhibition.[28] Its placement, not in the Indian Pavilion in the company of other Indian precious stones, but in the British section where it could be admired both as a dazzling proof of British power and an object to be evaluated and assessed by the eyes of the *hoi polloi*, marks a change in the stone's meaning. The Koh-i-noor now was stripped of its setting, though it was exhibited with two flanking diamonds, as if in the bazuband. It was encased in a disproportionately large gilded cage surmounted by a large English crown. Its metaphoric gender conversion at the Great Exhibition was anticipated in the transfer from powerful male Asian rulers to the Queen and future Empress of India.

The Koh-i-noor had become an epitome of Empire. Humiliated by its confinement, though captured as a treasure, it became absorbed in a common light. William Paxton's genius in making a "Crystal Palace" served to transform the rainbow magic of a diamond into what looked like a dull lump of glass, as if the diamond had ceded its reflective powers along with its Asian identity. Isobel Armstrong analyzes the stone's metamorphosis from impressive gem to lusterless mineral under the leveling sunlight of the all-glass structure.[29] The demotion of the Koh-i-noor from a stone of Nadir Shah's inspired naming to an inferior simulacrum of the great hall that housed it marked its symbolic status from a sequestered rarity to a logo for Empire. Having a greyish cast to begin with, it is no wonder that the humor magazine *Punch* rechristened the caged jewel "Mountain of Darkness."[30]

In its varied Asian incarnations, one as an eye of a peacock in Shah Jehan's Peacock Throne, the earlier version of the diamond might have been viewed by a few hundreds. In the Crystal Palace, it showed itself to any and everyone who gathered in hordes to gape at it, as the *Illustrated Exhibitor* pointed to its mass audience on July 12, 1851: "That stone is now in Hyde Park, and may be seen by any working man in the country for a shilling."[31] In light of newly forming economies, the diamond was poised on the threshold of being regarded as a commodity whose price was subject to a calculation in which gawking common workers played a part.[32] In the Beechey portrait a year after the opening of the Crystal Palace, Duleep Singh in his orchestrated jewels appears analogous to his former diamond. Like the diamond in its gilded cage, he sits on a gilded upholstered throne-like chair, in contrast to the elaborate platform thrones of East Asia where the ruler kneels on a cushion.

A year after the Beechey painting, Duleep Singh converted to Christianity. Apparently according to his own convictions and without proselytizing from guardians or teachers, he became a Protestant. When he was removed from Lahore, no Sikh counselors accompanied him, nor did he carry with him the sacred text of the Sikh religion, the Gurū Granth Sāhib Ji. His mother, with whom he had an affectionate and mentoring relationship, was banished from his company. His new religious conviction needs to be considered in that context. Without anyone practicing his religion and with the affectionate Logins, who consciously determined to set a Christian example without overtly preaching the Gospel, the maharajah embraced their Protestant faith. We cannot know the emotional and social process involved.[33] Gauri Viswanathan explores the complexities of conversion, pointing out that religion is a "category of identification," not a "transhistorical, transcultural essence."[34] The prince's religious conversion clearly takes part in what she calls its "constituting activity in the world."[35] His desire to convert apparently arrived out of the blue to Login when he received a letter from the young prince: "You will be surprised to learn of my determination to embrace the Christian religion. I have long doubted the truth of the one I was brought up in, and convinced of the truth of the religion of the Bible, which I have made Bhajun Lal [his Brahmin tutor] read a portion of it to me."[36] That Duleep Singh's conversion would have political consequences was recognized immediately; Lord Dalhousie commented to a friend about Duleep Singh's wish to convert: "Politically, we would desire nothing better, for it destroys his influence forever."[37]

Dalhousie instructed Login on the timetable for the prince's conversion: "If Duleep Singh is to go to England, let him be quietly baptized before he goes and by his own name of Duleep Singh."[38] British officials cautiously maintained that his religious conviction was stirred by the maharajah's freely acquired revelation of Christian truth. Yet the "little maharajah," or "little prince" as Dalhousie and others often called him, was enveloped in a Christian atmosphere, biblical phrases echoing in his head, Christian love manifested by the Logins' example.[39] Dalhousie recognized imperial triumph: "This is the first Indian prince . . . that has adopted the faith of the stranger. . . . God prosper and multiply it!"[40] In that context, Dalhousie's insistence that the prince keep his Sikh name draws attention to his use as a political logo: Duleep Singh converted but retained a dual identity, a mixture, not a solution, of Sikh and British. That the maharajah retained his title and name but relinquished the religion signified by "Singh" (borne by all male Sikhs) brought him within the fold, confirming British religious supremacy, whereas his costumes, jewels, and his name enfold him in what would be regarded as an Oriental identity.[41]

When Duleep Singh converted, he presented his shorn sable locks—a lustrous, magnificent, and typically Victorian gift—to Lady Login, an offering suitable for British creative and commemorative uses. In entering a new community, Duleep Singh places his formerly Sikh hair into a British woman's hands, performing an intimate conversion ritual. Although a lock of his hair, unconventionally given to Lady Login, has recently almost miraculously surfaced, what happened to the conversion hair has, at least for now, been lost to history.[42]

In a mirroring ritual, Dalhousie counseled Login to wait until Duleep

Singh left the Punjab to "put the Bible in his hands."[43] On the day before Duleep Singh left for England, he received an elaborate leather-bound, inscribed Protestant Bible from Dalhousie who claimed never to have doubted the justice of "dethroning the boy." Given that his vast lands as well as his *toshkhana* had been seized, the governor-general's inscription might seem rather too pointed, for it promised "an inheritance richer by far than all earthly Kingdoms."[44] The King James Bible, in patriotic terms referred to as "the secret of Her greatness," testifies to the prince's formation as a British subject, while his appearance and name indicates his value as a Punjabi subaltern. The youth became a justificatory legend of that Protestant secret of British rule. After his religious conversion, the prince followed his Koh-i-noor to London.

Victoria and Albert welcomed Duleep Singh fondly as a royal prince.[45] Two of the young princes posed in Indian garb to be photographed. Victoria sketched Duleep Singh, and he posed for cartes de visite in Sikh garments. In line with her respect for international royal status, Queen Victoria deemed his rank as equal to a prince of the realm, with its accompanying privileges, and vigorously defended that decision in memoranda answering governmental objections. That dual identity is dramatically encoded in the commissioned painting *Portrait of Maharaja Duleep Singh,* by Franz Xavier Winterhalter, favored artist of Queen Victoria and Prince Albert (see plate 5).

Winterhalter posed the nearly sixteen-year-old prince as both a Sikh warrior, and thus hypermasculine, and as a silken, bejeweled exotic, a feminized Indian. Intricately draped and patterned cloth enwraps him yet reveals his bent knee. His feet in a balletic position provide front and profile views of his Indian slippers, gold and embroidered, with curved toe echoing the shape of the *jigha*'s jeweled plume. In addition to turban jewels, the maharajah wears his emerald and pearl hoop earrings, pearl necklace, and portrait jewel. Queen Victoria fondly noted in her journal that Duleep Singh generally wore the portrait jewel in her presence. An additional significant jeweled element—the sword—presents another dimension to the representation of the Punjab, its militaristic edge both evoked and contained. The British admired the Sikhs for their fierce martial talents, but the pictured curved jeweled sword has been tamed of its warlike function to become absorbed in a performance of Asian soldiery. Its shape echoes its human subject's curves, and the grip with its jeweled design of rubies and sapphires suggests its Oriental origins.

Not only is the prominently placed sword a sign of martial prowess and Oriental masculinity, but it also alludes to Duleep Singh's rejected religion. Influenced by the Mughal weapon, a *talwar,* and used by Central Asian peoples, it carries a religious meaning to the Sikhs. English travelers in an earlier century described Sikh sacred dining rituals in which the sword served to sanctify the Sikhs' difference from other non-Sikh diners. The Sikh would unsheathe his sword, pass it over the food as he prayed, and then would freely eat. In some Sikh prayers, the sword is a metaphor for God.[46] Although the Sikh sword, the *kirpan,* usually a smaller dagger, derives from the *talwar,* Duleep Singh's sword recalls the sanctified nature of the Sikh weapon, always sheathed unless in a dire situation. In any case, it is unlikely that the royal family would have regarded the sword with alarm. Immediately after the British defeated the Sikhs, the East India Company recruited them into their army where they fought with the British against their enemies: "the remnants of the Mughals and their despised Hindu neighbors of the Ganges Valley."[47] Duleep Singh's sword thus represents a friendly, yet foreign, militarism tinged with a discarded religion.

In contrast to the Beechey portrait, Winterhalter's Duleep Singh performs his Sikh origin, wearing not his clothes but a costume, as if fitted out for a fancy-dress ball, such as those the royal couple was fond of hosting during the 1840s and 1850s. The balls enacted a political and national agenda by conveying messages through dressing up.[48] In the portrait, Maharajah Duleep Singh functions as a representative of the Raj, localized in the painting by a filmy depiction of Lahore in the background.[49] For this performative purpose, Winterhalter's Indian prince does not present himself as a Christian, although under the fringed turban his barbered hair style is English gentlemanly. Posing as a Sikh carries a reminder of the diamond he surrendered.

The Koh-i-noor in fact left its anecdotal trace on Winterhalter's painting. The topic of the diamond arose during a sitting when Queen Victoria asked Lady Login if her ward regretted giving up the Koh-i-noor. Victoria's question itself indicates that she associated the maharajah with his alienated diamond. Learning that Duleep Singh would like to see the diamond, Victoria sent to the Tower for it and placed the jewel in his hands. According to her journal, the prince gazed at the stone for a long time before re-placing the Koh-i-noor in Victoria's hands, saying, "It is to me Ma'am the greatest pleasure thus to have the opportunity as a loyal subject, of myself tendering to my sovereign the Koh-i-noor."[50] This pronouncement, along with the hand-to-hand exchange, echoes the original ceremony and also resembles Duleep Singh's presentation of his hair to Lady Login as a sacramental sign of his religious conversion. It is even more closely a parallel to his hair cutting, for the diamond had already submitted to a cutting with ritual implications.

The prince might have taken a while to recognize the Koh-i-noor he was handed because it was much smaller and in a different aesthetic form. When it was bestowed on Victoria, the Koh-i-noor had already undergone reshaping, probably many times, if the legend is to be believed. It is said that originally when Krishna received it from the deity, it was enormous. From Sultan Alâ-ed-Deen over centuries to Babur, founder of the Mughal Empire, "it is said that the stone then weighed seven hundred and ninety-three carats. Tavernier described it a century later as weighing two hundred and eighty carats, having been thus reduced by an unskilled stone-cutter."[51] When Ranjit Singh "acquired the Kohinoor, it had already been cut in the Indian fashion" and had possibly lost another hundred carats in weight.[52] Whether a piece of Babur's great stone is the one now in the Tower of London can be considered a matter of faith in relics.

The years preceding its arrival on British soil, its appearance, importance, and personhood were fodder for journalists. *Chambers' Edinburgh Journal,* which described its size still in its bazuband as 279 carats, "diminished by cutting and polishing and . . . not being shaped as a brilliant," characterized it as having a legend larger than its actual appearance: "The Koh-i-noor, like many other great personages of history, is not indebted much too external form. It is not cut so as to sparkle like a brilliant, but returns the beholder's gaze with a cold, steady glare, fit to make a nervous man wink."[53] Soon after the British report, an American journalist, Caroline Brown, observed its translation to a dimly lit country, along with its gender, religious, and aesthetic conversions. She suggests that the great gem had become both diminished and trivialized:

> It was now transferred from the land of waving palms and burning skies, of gorgeous birds and savage jungle-dwellers, of enervating heat and sudden floods, to a region whose colors by comparison were dull and cold, whose skies were obscured by mist, whose landscape was one of gently cultured beauty. It became the bauble of a Christian Queen.
>
> When the Queen first saw the Kohinoor, it was shallow, dull-gray with a large flat top imperfectly smoothed, around which were cut numberless tiny facets, irregular in size. These facets surmounted a plain smooth oblong, with three distinct, visible flaws. The stone emitted a dull light, which tended to confirm its evil reputation.[54]

Once again, the Koh-i-noor's bad rap shadowed it.

Being somewhat off in color, with inclusions and an asymmetrical shape, the diamond disappointed its new British owners. It had gone through life with a reputation for matchless color and for awe-inspiring size. Indian faceting practices valued preservation of size rather than symmetry or maximum brilliance. Yet even hundreds of carats smaller, the diamond underwent yet another cutting, another national adjustment.⁵⁵ Prince Albert decided that it needed refashioning.

The very year that Beechey depicted Duleep Singh in India and a year before the prince cut his Sikh hair, the Koh-i-noor underwent surgery with ceremony, pomp, and media attention. A renowned diamond cutter was imported from Amsterdam for the operation, and a figure no less legendary than the Duke of Wellington took part in the ritual, as did Prince Albert. Whereas technology determined the instruments, the process resembled an elaborate initiation ceremony: "Mr. Voorsanger of the great Coster firm of Amsterdam was brought over to do the work. A steam engine of 4 hp was set up in the Crown jewellers' workshops. Prince Albert set the stone in the dop, or holder, and the Duke of Wellington started up the wheel. For thirty-eight days of twelve hours the patient Voorsanger bent over the wheel. The Koh-i-Noor lost 81 carats in weight . . . but gained very little in brilliance. . . . After all its associations with death, torture and depositions, the Koh-i-Noor, the ancient stone of the great Mogul Emperors, shines with a peaceful radiance among the brilliant splendor of the Regalia in the Tower of London."⁵⁶

The writer of the above passage, officer of the Order of the British Empire, describes the Westernized diamond as if malign elements attributed to the Koh-i-noor had been tamed by its Western cutting. Perhaps warrior-hero Wellington, who assumed an honorary, even priestly, role in the surgery, contributed to its pacification. While acknowledging the original's dull surface and admitting the European cuts diminished without improving its brilliance, the writer preserves the diamond's legendary allure. It is less, but it is more. Like the conversion ceremony of its last Indian possessor, the Koh-i-noor was converted, a sign of which is its cutting, to an apparent passivity; like Duleep Singh's conversion appeared to Lord Dalhousie, its malign influence might have been exorcised forever. Like Duleep Singh's conversion, the newly shaped diamond retained its exotic aura by keeping its Persian name.

Not only does possession of the Koh-i-noor signify the power of the possessor, but it is said that the diamond itself *contains* the power, as would a fetish. Radical cutting according to Western protocols in itself marks its conversion from an Indian to a European stone, yet with its curse seemingly intact. Can we believe that the diamond retained its demonic force when the duke died in September 1852, a few months after his presiding over the cutting? Or that the prince consort's role in its conversion eventually led to his own untimely demise at age forty-two? Beliefs about the Koh-i-noor illustrate a problematic of conversions, never absolute and retaining a spirit of a former identity, this one dreadful.

The Koh-i-noor's bestowal to Victoria underscores its gender conversion. Because so many of its Central Asian male potentates who temporarily held on to the diamond came to bloody endings or their lives were dogged with misfortune, it is said that the Koh-i-noor cursed the men who possessed it. Given the suspicion that cutting may have left a residue of the diamond's destructive energy, no English male sovereign has worn it. Regarding it as a woman's adornment, Queen Victoria had it set successively in a brooch, a tiara, and a circlet. The path to final conversion occurred upon Queen Victoria's death. Reduced and Europeanized, the Koh-i-noor was embedded in the primary symbol of Christianity. At the center of a Maltese cross, in the center of a British crown, worn on the forehead of Queen Alexandra, wife of Queen Victoria's son, Edward VII, an anointed sovereign, the Koh-i-noor was converted into a sign not only of power but of the secret of British Protestant greatness (see plate 6). No longer merely a royal bauble and adornment to enhance a queenly bosom or neck, as a crown jewel of the British Empire, the Koh-i-noor achieved British imperial sanctity. Like the Mughals, the British claimed that their authority was confirmed by a relationship to divinity. In its diminished state, this Indian diamond is finally, literally, a jewel in her crown. The Koh-i-noor is made a British, Protestant, and female royal. Queen Alexandra seemed to inherit male Indian style as well as the Indian diamond. Her coronation photograph shows her sitting on a throne-like chair—like Duleep Singh in the Beechey portrait—and festooned with diamonds, pearls, and gems from crown to beyond her waist and around her wrists. Queen Alexandra's bejeweled array emulates an Indian male potentate, and in this guise, she represents the gender conversion undergone by the diamond jewel in her crown.

The legendary diamond transmutes politics into a physical form that parallels the biography of the benighted mascot of the English Royal House of Hanover. Both disguise with jeweled exhibitionism the pacification leading to their conversions. Ranked as a prince, Duleep Singh had adopted signs of British masculinity, wearing tweeds and shooting on his Yorkshire estate. In some photographs, he looks no different from English aristocracy and royalty, including the Prince of Wales, who joined his shooting parties. His name gives him away, but no longer carries the same aura as his diamond. Later in his life, angry, disillusioned, no longer treasured, and erratically seeking an identity, the prince converted back to Sikhism. Despite this formal conversion, he received a Christian burial in England, the service held in the church he endowed. European jewels are generally not interred, but the Koh-i-noor, now identified with royal women, participated in a funeral, that of Queen

Elizabeth, consort of George VI and mother of Elizabeth II. In 2002 her coffin bore the royal diamond embedded in her own refashioned crown.

The human Duleep Singh, regarded as much an object as the fabled stone, occupies only a few chapters—the Victorian ones—of the legend of the Koh-i-noor. Both were celebrated as trophies of imperial triumph. Diamond identity endorses the maharajah's entry into British history colored with romance rather than merely as a poignant footnote in the history of the British acquisition of the Punjab. Duleep Singh's gleaming legend ends with his youth. In his lapidary, C. W. King describes him as no more a prince but merely a "private gentleman about town."[57] In oil paints, though, he remains timeless and beautiful, a bearer of jewels, importing India as a place of sparkling exoticism to cast a domesticated luster on Queen Victoria's court and beyond. He wanders amid the fringes of fictions about Indian diamonds discussed in following chapters. And his diamond? To this day, four Asian countries claim it. Though a Solomonic solution might be to cut the diamond again, this time in four pieces, and return it to its claimants—India, Afghanistan, Iran, and Pakistan—the Koh-i-noor will likely remain British, Christian, royal, and female, converted, that is, while preserving Indian potency in its name.

2

The Moonstone's Sacred Masculinity

> What jeweled Ornaments should be worn to ward off evil Astral Influences? When the Sun is evil, the ruby; when the Moon, the diamond.
> —*Mani-Mālā*

With his attention on the Second Anglo-Sikh War and the Kohi-noor Diamond as booty, Wilkie Collins set his 1868 sensation novel, *The Moonstone: A Romance,* during those war years, 1848–49, just months before the diamond journeyed to the Queen's court and at the very moment that the sequestered Duleep Singh was contemplating his conversion to Protestantism. The novelist had followed Duleep Singh's fate, locating his own marvelous tale near the castle that the maharajah leased before purchasing his own estate. Yet Collins's "Preface" situates the political origin of his romance of intrigue, greed, and true love at an earlier moment marking the British sovereignty over the subcontinent with the 1799 defeat of Tipu Sultan at the Siege of Seringapatam.[1] Bernard S. Cohn's analysis of that event explains the centrality of Collins's opening setting and the metaphor of India as a crowning imperial achievement: "The capture of Seringapatam in 1799 and the final defeat of Tipu Sultan begin the direct involvement of the [East India] Company's government in a systematic effort to explore and document India's past. . . . This victory, combined with Lord Lake's entry in Delhi in 1803, ended whatever doubts there were that the British were now the conquerors of India. . . . The death of Tipu, the arch villain in the emergent British hagiography of India, provided the necessary counterpoint to construction of the British as valorous, virtuous, and above all, triumphant conquerors."[2] Cohn's formulation clarifies the context of Collins's challenge to British imperial pride in his use of a diamond as a multivalent symbol of imperial might. Casting a shadow on British virtue, James Mill's 1858 recounting of the event in his *The History of British India* notes that soldiers stripped Tipu's sumptuously clothed body of its jewels: "He had an amulet on his arm; but his ornaments, if he wore any, were gone."[3] The "ornaments" carry emblematic significations that bear on the powerful diamond in *The Moonstone*. In his choice of religious settings, Collins plots domestic and religious reverberations of such desecration.

An English army officer's violent theft of a fictional, immense Indian diamond, the Moonstone, from Tipu's body initiates the plot. Captain Herncastle slaughters three Brahmin guards, inheritors of centuries of shadowing the stone to reclaim it for their faith. The English military looting replicates the Muslim plunder of the Moonstone. Tipu Sultan, a devout Muslim ruling a majority of Hindus, merged its sacred and militaristic meanings, embedding the contested jewel in his sword.[4] Lauren Goodlad argues for regarding Tipu as a reflection of Maharajah Ranjit Singh, the Sikh ruler who possessed the Koh-i-noor shortly before the initial action of the plot.[5] In line with religious significations of Indian diamonds, argued throughout this part about India, however, the significant religious difference between Sikh Ranjit Singh and Muslim Tipu Sultan renders whatever similarities between the maharajah and the sultan secondary in the meanings attributed to the diamond. In always capitalizing "Diamond," the novel gives it prominence as a character, one whose religious conversions have been forced upon it. Collins's romance adds a British Protestant chapter to the Moonstone's long history where a wrong committed to it, this time by the British, requires restitution. The novel traces the Diamond's bloody path back to its setting as a holy Hindu relic, referred to in the novel as a "sacred gem."[6] By its temporary residence in an English manor house, the author domesticates the Diamond's aura, bringing imperialism home.[7] The gemstone confirms its vitality by its phosphorescence, glowing in the dark, as if inhabited by a moon god. Thus, *The Moonstone* chronicles the Diamond's entry into Protestant England as a hostage, then its return to its sanctified iconicity in a gem-encrusted religion Collins refers to as idolatrous. The novel romances the stone.[8]

Slaying Tipu Sultan and looting his Mysore treasure may confirm temporal British power, but that victory is trumped by the Moonstone's sacred dominion.[9] Gabriel Betteredge, steward of the Victorian country manor that stands as a microcosm of Protestant England, perceives the Diamond as animated with a malign spirit: "Here was our quiet English house suddenly invaded by a devilish Indian Diamond" (46).[10] Without irony about Captain Herncastle's role in the "invasion," Gabriel delivers—as his Christian archangelic name implies—a religiously inflected message. The religious motif signals a source from Indian hymns, which also export their gender and class attributions to Collins's Indian diamond. In referring to the devilish Moonstone's demonic presence, Gabriel's attitude recalls Indian lore about the demon Bala's sacrifice and resembles the sutras in an English register about curses because of a diamond's improper use. Collins adds to the curse (and to the prominence in his novel of the flawed Koh-i-noor as model) by referring to the "complexity" of the stone's valuation: "There was a defect, in the shape of a flaw, at the very heart of the stone" (50). The author used King's condemnation of cutting the Koh-i-noor that destroyed its historical and mineralogical significance and his lapidary opinion that the brilliant cut reduced the stone to a "mere lady's bauble, of but second water, for it has a greyish tinge."[11] That flaw and its off-color serve as an emblem of the novel's politics of imperial ambivalence.

If the Moonstone's restoration to its Hindu sacred function seems a kind of justice, Collins's "Preface" also appears to legitimate European nationality to both Indian gems. It traces the origins of his fictive diamond to two actual Indian diamonds while regarding them as European: "With reference to the story of the Diamond, . . . it is founded . . . on the stories of two of the royal diamonds of Europe. The magnificent stone, which adorns the top of the Russian Imperial Sceptre, was once the eye of an Indian idol [figure 3]. The famous Koh-i-Noor is also supposed to have been one of the sacred gems of India; and . . . to have been the subject of a prediction, which prophesied certain misfortune to the persons who should divert it from its ancient uses" (3–4).[12] Possession apparently deeds the stones to Europe.[13] Yet the author's noting Indian beliefs leaves open an ethical question about ownership of sacred objects. As with the Koh-i-noor, the Hindu belief in the gemstone's power remains as a fact in its history, adding to its allure as a sign of British triumph, while preserving its inalienable and disturbing religious otherness.

Those generic features of the novel that have placed it primarily as a narrative of detection in an imperial context have not given sufficient attention to the Moonstone's religious meanings.[14] The author adopts the passive locution typical of retelling legends to relieve the teller of its reliability: "supposed to have been."[15] The Russian gem was "once the eye of an Indian idol." Collins protects himself from portraying an object of Hindu veneration as anything other than idolatry. The author has it both ways without apparent irony: his fictional diamonds are sacred stones but to idol worshippers. He does not

Figure 3. Diagram of the Orloff, showing its eyeball shape. (J. Walter Thompson Diamond Information Center Collection, Box 27, John W. Hartman Center for Sales, Advertising, and Marketing History, David M. Rubenstein Rare Book and Manuscript Library, Duke University)

acknowledge their fetishized status in Europe. Both of Collins's diamonds are converted to anointed Western royal power in the Orloff's imperial scepter and the Koh-i-noor in a royal treasury, later part of royal regalia. Collins outlines the symbolic system through the rituals of conversion that his models had undergone in the decade preceding publication of *The Moonstone* and the politics involved in their fictional resolution. The actual gems on which Collins's Diamond is based survive as idols of Western monarchical devotion, both now embedded in religiously anointed symbols of European sovereignty.

The first teller of Collins's multi-narrated tale is an unnamed officer in the attack on Tipu Sultan; the juxtaposition of the storming of Seringapatam with the sordid Herncastle family quarrel connects domestic and foreign conflicts. The linkage indicates that the novel will be an imperial family romance. The speaker, whose first lines are addressed "to my relatives in England," is a cousin of an addict, sot, and murderer. The bad soldier, John Herncastle, brother of Lady Verinder, wills the gem to his niece Rachel, most likely to allow its curse to wreak his vengeance on the family. In Collins's genealogy, the stone was dedicated to Vishnu the Preserver, thus retaining its militaristic male identity throughout its Asian history, from the Hindus to "the conquering Mohammedans" and finally to the plundering British military and the murderer of the Indian guards. The stone's violent past is also deeded to this English microcosm in the Verinder estate located close to the first of Duleep Singh's English properties.

When the Koh-i-noor became British and the Orloff became Russian, the storied gems changed genders, one through Catherine the Great's ownership and the other through Victoria's. With its bestowal on Rachel, the fictional stone changes both gender and class. Victoria's public identification with ordinary queens of her realm appears here as a legacy from John Ruskin's "Of Queen's Gardens," where good women are exhorted to emulate queens and to rule pacifically over their households. The Moonstone conveys a trace of both sacredness and royalty when it is given to a young woman who possesses a "sovereign will" (323). It is used as a bauble by a girl who wants to be good but, like Victoria, is possessed of a temper and a mind of her own. In wearing the Moonstone, Rachel emulates Queen Victoria's treatment of the Koh-i-noor by wearing it as "a brooch in the bosom of her white dress" (77). Thus, the transfer of the Moonstone to a British girl mimes the ceremony of Queen Victoria receiving the Koh-i-noor. In a symbolic gesture of the social movement from royal power, Rachel receives the Moonstone on her eighteenth birthday, on her reaching her majority, the same age as Victoria when she ascended to the throne.

Confirming Collins's witty comparison of queen to Queen, Gabriel Betteredge likens his own speech upon servants giving Rachel's birthday gifts to Victoria's annual speech to Parliament: "I follow the plan adopted by the Queen in opening Parliament—namely the plan of saying much the same thing regularly every year. . . . My speech (like the Queen's) is looked for as eagerly as if nothing of the kind had ever been heard before" (70–71). Though Collins mocks Gabriel's hyperbolic comparison, analogies between Victoria and her subjects preserved the monarchy as a potent icon. Readers can link Rachel's diamond birthday gift and Victoria's reception of her Koh-i-noor as a ritualistic imperial ceremony. To reinforce his allusion to Victoria, Collins calls the birthday girl "queen of the day" (76).

The Moonstone's phosphorescence suggests it harbors a living spirit. To prevent the stone from awakening her with its "moony light," Rachel places the stone at bedtime in an Indian cabinet, signifying both her private ownership and its Indian origins, much as Victoria at first treated her Indian diamond as private treasure and Indian souvenir. Rachel's fragile setting for her temporary brooch signals the Diamond's wandering ways, in gender, class, and national origin.[16] For the duration of the novel—nearly to its very last pages—the Moonstone changes class from Sir John Herncastle's spoil of war, to an imperious aristocratic girl's Indian bauble, to the loot of a son of a banker who is also a common thief. The Moonstone moves, in other words, down the British class hierarchy to where its iconic meanings threaten to be absorbed into the capitalist economy "having the Diamond cut into separate stones . . . to make it a marketable commodity" (459).

A class system places Godfrey Ablewhite lower than his cousin Rachel because her aunt, his mother, married a prosperous nobody. The union of Godfrey's parents denoted his mother's descent in class: "There was terrible work in the family when the Honourable Caroline insisted on marrying plain Mr. Ablewhite, the banker at Frizinghall. . . . He had presumed to raise himself from a low station in the world—and that was against him" (266). Proud yet aware of his humble origins: "I had no ancestors" (265), defensively rages Mr. Ablewhite père, wrongly assuming that Rachel has broken her engagement to his handsome son because of her Herncastle blood. Despite disavowal of such snobbery, the honest, solid lawyer Bruff's credulity about blue blood survives his awareness of its excesses: "The Herncastle blood has its drawbacks, I admit. But there *is* something in good breeding after all!" (268). There apparently *is* something potentially dangerous in a misalliance as well, resembling the warnings in Hindu writings against wearing the wrong class of diamond. Godfrey dies ignominiously disguised as an ordinary sailor with a big black beard, his brown face a complexion no blue blood would inherit. His criminal activities as a forger and embezzler give common legal labels separating individual misdeeds from their analogues in imperialist crimes.

Miss Clack, an impoverished relative and the second narrator, needs to be considered in her religious enthusiasm, despite Collins's satirical portrayal. She is a legitimate branch of the Protestant Verinder family, regarding the Diamond as devilish, but secretly coveting wealth, inheritance, and Godfrey Ablewhite, exploiter of such pious spinsters. As claimed in the introduction, empire is authorized as centrally an evangelical project, Miss Clack being one of its unthinking adherents. Mouthing Calvinistic-inflected maxims, she swells English imperial missionary ranks. In its Protestant phase, ownership of the Diamond belongs for a time to the religion that Collins mocks in this character who is seemingly irrelevant to politics but essential to them.

The Moonstone becomes domesticated yet without becoming docile. What had been revered in the Brahmin culture and prized in the Muslim hierarchy has taken on Western values, potentially commodified, not by Rachel who receives it as a gift, but by Godfrey Ablewhite who steals it for the money. Godfrey's name has been noticed for the obvious hypocrisy of his philanthropic religious leadership. Apparently, Collins originally conceived of Ablewhite as a man of the cloth but changed, perhaps at Dickens's request.[17] Had Collins maintained Godfrey as the Reverend Ablewhite, he would have directly connected a Protestant minister to the Moonstone's religious adventures. As it is, the churchly Ablewhite intends to desecrate the Moonstone in not only a Brahmin but an evangelical context. Whereas the Muslim Tipu Sultan's desacralized stone retained its rank and militancy, the Protestant Godfrey Ablewhite degrades it even further by valuing it as a marketable means of sustainable immorality. Charming churchly spinsters, he keeps a costly mistress by embezzling funds as trustee of a minor, needing the Diamond to cover for his misappropriation. He represents the novel's anti-Everyman, a caricature of Victorian religious hypocrisy, moral turpitude, and class hybridity.

Yet Collins, who read King's lapidary and adopted diamond lore as well as diamond facts, recounts the Diamond's downward mobility while retaining what King noted as its wicked power. As John Reed pointed out, Collins dates Murthwaite's letter locating the Moonstone's return on the very year that Queen Victoria received the Koh-i-noor.[18] The feminized recut Koh-i-noor also preserved its destructive force, visited on the vast imperial theater in King's version of the legend: "The Brahmin sage who studies the Book of Fate is probably not dispossessed of his hereditary superstition touching the malign powers of this stone when he thinks upon the so speedily following Russian war, that completely annihilated the prestige of the British army, the legacy of Wellington's successes, and upon the events of the Sepoy mutiny, three years later, that caused the very existence of England as a nation to hang for months upon the magnanimous forbearance of one man: an ugly truth, however much we may affect to ignore it."[19] Distancing himself from the Brahmin sage with his apparently rational perspective on the Diamond as fetish, King's historical allusions to British defeats nevertheless grant credibility to the Koh-i-noor's curse as an ugly truth of its power, as if it were a bone shard from demonic Bala. With a similarly semi-credulous tone about the doom of Wellington and Prince Albert in the description in chapter 1 of the European cutting of the Koh-i-noor, King could not entirely discount the efficacy of its curse. Reading King provides Collins a logic for imbuing his Moonstone with beliefs also enshrined in Hindu hymns about the alignment of diamond with divine meanings. The Moonstone eventually shines again within fiercely warlike, masculine Hindu beliefs dedicated to the moon.

The romance of the Moonstone tells that a gem suffering from Western humiliations of religion, class, and gender can be restored to holy Hindu stature. It can be de-converted first from the terrible Mughals and their "Mohammedan" beliefs and then from civilized Protestants with their family crimes and hypocrisies to return to its ferocious Hindu sacred status. Collins maps the Moonstone's reabsorption into its original culture far from where it was ripped from Tipu Sultan's sword and the murdered Brahmins. Narrative balance might argue for the Moonstone's return to Seringapatam, a South Indian city filled with Hindu shrines and objects of pilgrimage dating to the ninth century and a setting that might render poetic justice regarding the British crime against the Moonstone. A genealogical table found in "Essays in Indian Antiquities," published in 1858 by James Prinsep and Edward Thomas, reveals that the Rajas of Mysore, who took Seringapatam in 1610, were of the Lunar Dynasty of Rajputs.[20] These displaced Rajas were then conquered by Tipu Sultan, leaving their moony but cursed legacy as a sign of their defeat.

In beginning with the British murderous theft at Seringapatam and ending with its return to Kattiawar, Collins initiates an arc rather than a circle of lunar peoples. He apparently was guided in his brilliant resolution by J. W. S. Wyllie, a promising young civil servant who spent two years in Kattiawar and wrote a well-regarded study of that region. Collins wrote to him for a recommendation of a setting free of both Muslim and colonial influence.[21] For his diamond's final triumph, Wyllie provided the novelist with an even purer Hindu lunar site than Seringapatam. Kattiawar, the final setting, rids the Diamond of Muslim and colonial associations. The ending ritual serves as purification rite; the setting frees the Diamond of pollution.

Collins places the sacred shrine with the embedded Moonstone in the north, in the "wild regions of Kattiawar (and how wild they are, you will understand, when I tell you that even the husbandmen plough the land, armed to the teeth), fanatically devoted to the old Hindoo religion — to the ancient worship of Bramah and Vishnu" (469). Becoming Hindu once again, the yellow diamond returns to its ancient and fiercely masculine site. As it reverses the religious trajectory of the diamond, so the novel reverses its gender identity, placing it in a location so dangerously masculine that industrious "husbandmen" need to arm themselves as they plant their crops. Further, taken as a metaphor, the laboring farmer ploughing the land enforces the Moonstone's return to aggressive sexuality as well as to masculine gender, while its return to a city sacred to the moon preserves its divine status. To clarify the meaning of the Moonstone's return, British anthropological hierarchies were more favorably inclined to what Raj administrators classified as the "martial" as opposed to the "non-martial" ethnic groups. Like Sikhs, the Rajputs belonged to the martial category. In Collins's scheme, they cannot be comprehended in the context of Christian dogma. They cannot be converted actually or conceptually. Collins's final setting remains wild, inaccessible, and unconquered. The sacred gem returns to passionate devotees, inconceivable to evangelicals embarking on conversion missions. Miss Clack's narration thus serves to highlight an absolute irreconcilability between her worldview and that of the Kattiawar Rajputs, her gender also throwing difference in setting between self-denying evangelicals and militaristic Rajputs into even starker relief.

That Collins sought a location in northern India and conveyed its religious practices demonstrates that he characterized his diamond not merely as a generalized "Indian" diamond. Specifically a Hindu Rajput diamond, the Moonstone is restored to a territory dedicated to the veneration of major Hindu deities, ruled by devotees of the moon. Murthwaite's letter delivers a donnish lecture about sacred spots, much of which conveys information Collins learned from Wyllie: "Two of the most famous shrines of Hindoo pilgrimage are contained within the boundaries of Kattiawar. One of them is Dwarka, the birthplace of the god Krishna. The other is the sacred city of Somnauth." (469).[22] Collins has significantly reset his diamond so that it is not merely a fictionalized version of his two Indian diamond models but is religiously Hindu. The "few Mahometan families . . . are afraid to taste meat of any kind" (469) for fear of being killed for eating sacred cow meat. The Moonstone returns to the Dwarka temple that was built on the site of Krishna's palace. To add to the complex significance of Collins's carefully mapping the symbolic journey of his diamond, Somnauth, "the sacred city," contains one of the most important Shiva temples and, though sacked many times, yet remains a place of pilgrimages, such as the one Murthwaite witnesses. Somnauth means "protector of the moon god," for it is said that it is the place where the moon was freed of a curse.[23]

In his published work, Wyllie describes the lunar significance of the "far-famed Temple of Somnásth": "the porticoes and pyramid-like domes, the courts and columned aisles that surrounded them, and the numerous subordinate shrines which, as satellites, heightened the splendor of this chosen dwelling of the Lord of the Moon" (325). In that Somnath temple, Wyllie describes a "diamond-eyed image of Krishna tended by a small colony of monks" (342). Collins resets the restored Moonstone, knowing about that most appropriate setting for his moony diamond in the Somnath temple. To intensify the restoration, "the moonlight of the East, pouring in unclouded glory over all" (471) blesses the Moonstone and its adherents. In addition, the Rajput Hindus of this territory are part of the ethnic group Chandravanshi, House of the Moon, or lunar people who are descended, it is said, from Krishna. More clearly than in Seringapatam, the Lunar People of Rajput rule Kattiawar, where the Moonstone affirms a spirit, Rajput Hindu in affiliation, aggressively masculine in gender, and lunar in clan origins. Finally, the symbolic status and sacred meaning of the Moonstone's name is clarified, its "moony light" that Rachel fears divinely correct.

Readers view the final placement of the sacred stone mediated by Murthwaite, whose sun-darkened skin and costume of a "Hindoo-Boodhist from a distant province" (470) grant him entry to the shrine.[24] Murthwaite's disguise throws a murky parallel light on the darkened Godfrey Abelwhite's failed effort. More directly relevant to passing as an Other, Murthwaite compares to Ezra Jennings as a liminal figure who draws upon Indian understanding, considered foreign, idolatrous, and far from an acceptable Protestant outlook. The ending needs Murthwaite as the solution to the stealing of the stone needs Ezra Jennings, medical assistant to the appropriately named doctor, Mr. Candy, who had drugged Blake, inadvertently allowing Ablewhite to take the Diamond. Jennings, a half-caste whose dark/light hair discloses symbolic racial typing, is essential to solving the mystery. Jennings also bears a genealogical trace to medicinal information in the Vedas. Not certified as a Western doctor, he possesses knowledge that includes Eastern practices and a hallucinatory drug, made from poppies imported from India.

Collins suggests imperial envy in his evocation of a place tantalizingly beyond English imaginative powers. Lacking the narrative possibility of a view unmediated by the West, Collins fabricates a pseudo-Indian in Murthwaite, an Orientalist who can pass in the novel as a native and translate to the reader a foreign religion without being its adherent. Something is lost in translation, but that loss underscores Collins's narrative difficulties in depicting a cultural chasm that makes the Other unknowable.[25] Here, too, Collins inquired of Wyllie whether the disguised Orientalist scholar would be credible. In that sense, Murthwaite is a figure for the author. How otherwise to disclose sanctity impenetrable to Western eyes?[26] At the end, the Diamond gathers its imperial meanings, views about empire that are implicit in its violent, irresistible aura. The Diamond, as Collins finally sets it, does not belong to Britain. In locating the Diamond's return to a place closed off to invaders, the final view of the Moonstone as recounted by a disguised Westerner brings romance to English-speaking readers in mediating for them that rapturous triumph of the repatriated, reconverted gem and the aggressive moon people who reverence it.

3

Imitation India in Robert Louis Stevenson and Arthur Conan Doyle

*I*ndia. The very word conjures diamonds to such an extent that Robert Louis Stevenson and Arthur Conan Doyle do not need to know much about either India or diamonds to link the two. In their stories about diamonds, geography replaces gemology. These two authors remap India on to other settings and rely on the fame of Indian-named diamonds to embody the power of evil. Gems in their tales transmit a strong moral warning, redolent of Protestant distrust of luxury. It is as if Bala, the demon whose bones turned into diamonds as recounted in the fifth-century lapidary *Radnadīpikā,* had become a Calvinist. Those who resolve the diamond dilemma in stories by both authors resist diamond allure and deliver sermons on their corrupting influence. Wafting an Indian aura, the diamond tales of Stevenson and Doyle sprinkle diamond dust, endowing their stories with sparkling greed so to measure morality in gems.

"That Accursed Stone": "The Rajah's Diamond"

Robert Louis Stevenson's *New Arabian Nights* (1878; 1882) emerged from nineteenth-century Orientalist attention to the compilation of tales also known as *The Thousand and One Nights' Entertainment.* With many English versions published for every level of reader, the stories counted as common knowledge among readers of all classes and locations in the British Isles.[1] Except for one story, "The Rajah's Diamond," there is no Arabia in Stevenson's *New Arabian Nights.* Evidently to satisfy Western readers' expectations,

Stevenson offered an elaborately structured story about a diamond from the East. In the original Arabian tales, opulence offers wonder without condemnation of luxury. For instance, in a narrative from *The Arabian Nights,* a sultan enters a hall furnished with "the richest stuffs of India." Waterfalls from the mouths of massive gold lions magically transform into diamonds and pearls as the fountain streams arc through the air.[2] The gem-bestrewn atmosphere informs English writers' Indian evocations. As in tales from *The Arabian Nights,* Stevenson describes swift transformations of characters' fortunes from high to modest to low or from lowly to exalted. He also swiftly changes settings in "The Rajah's Diamond" from London to Paris, finally scattering three naïve characters who serendipitously encounter the diamonds to various colonies as a kind of expiation for their handling the stone. However, unlike in his Arabian model, jewels in Stevenson's story are sinful. A diamond can elevate a man's social class but with moral cost. Enchantment by diamonds disguises their wickedness.

Stevenson adapted the *Arabian Nights* narrative style to tell European stories. His nested tales with provisional endings herald the subsequent tale—similar to one method in *The Arabian Nights* of embedding one story in another. "The Rajah's Diamond" consists of four tales with overlapping characters, while each tale also introduces new characters whose moral measure is tallied by degrees of resistance to a rajah's huge diamond, the object that dominates the four tales. Stevenson admits his Occidental appropriation by alluding to an "Arabian Author" as its source.[3] Each story ends with the English narrator confirming the Arabian author's account and recounting characters' eventual fates. The English narrator or editor thus usurps the Arabian teller's authority, demonstrating in each story how a hapless and handsome male character's temporary alliance with the diamond escapes suffering under its malign power. In alluding to the Arabian stories, Stevenson's sophisticated method takes on a comically ironic tone, a contemporary send-up of the magical atmosphere of *The Arabian Nights,* but then adding an even more solemn moralizing to the ending. In line with the fates of characters in *The Arabian Nights,* people are catapulted from one class to another and change locations with amazing rapidity, as if by a genie or magic carpet. By depriving characters of their wealth, they are ultimately taken off the hook. The great diamond is not.

In the first tale, "Story of the Bandbox," young, handsome, and emptyheaded Harry Hartley, whose elite education affords him entrée as secretary and errand boy to Major Vandeleur's London household, is the first of three unworldly, good-looking young men who escape a diamond spell only by emigrating. Straight from school, he enters an establishment harboring a fabulous collection of diamonds acquired by the gold-digging wife; Harry's main function is to lose the diamond contents of a bandbox that Lady Vandeleur tries to smuggle before she abandons her unpleasant old husband. The most notable diamond in the Vandeleur collection was a gift to the old man from a Rajah of Kashgar.

The renowned diamond bears an unlikely provenance. Kashgar, an ancient Chinese city on the Silk Road, was an object in the Great Game, an intrigue between Russia and Britain for hegemony in Asia. The Rajah of the title lords it over Kashgar, but history records no Kashgar rajahs. By 1865 the Muslim Yakub Bey or Beg ruled the city, signing a treaty in 1874 with Russia and Great Britain as part of the Great Game, a central motif in Rudyard Kipling's *Kim*.[4] Its deceptive pedigree notwithstanding, the diamond provides a link among the stories, as if the tales were parts of a legend such as that of the Koh-i-noor. In Stevenson's story, the Rajah of Kashgar bestows "the sixth diamond of the world" on an English officer who performs treasonous favors for him. Evoking the Koh-i-noor's translation, Mountain of Light, the Rajah's Diamond goes by the name of "the Eye of Light, as the Orientals poetically termed it—the Pride of Kashgar."[5] Cut from similar British cloth as John Herncastle in *The Moonstone,* Major-General Sir Thomas Vandeleur, CB, "a man of sixty, loud-spoken, and domineering" (114), serves the rajah against his own country, committing heinous crimes, the enormity of which are only revealed at the end.

As in *The Moonstone* and tales discussed in this chapter, the diamond made him do it. Evidently the major was respected until he visited the rajah's treasures and monomaniacally desires to possess the diamond: "Honor, reputation, friendship, the love of country, he was ready to sacrifice all for this lump of sparkling crystal" (167). Though the major's enumerated crimes might seem exaggerated, his transgressions join in horror those in legends about real Indian diamond legends: "He falsified frontiers, he connived at murders, he unjustly condemned and executed a brother officer . . . ; lastly, at a great danger to his native land, he betrayed a body of his fellow-soldiers and suffered them to be defeated and massacred by thousands" (167). Like other diamonds with a shady past, the brilliance, beauty, and value of the sixth in the world belie its contaminated spirit. Animated by a Hindu fetish that punishes its misuse, the rajah's diamond leads everyone who eyes it on a path to hell.

As in magical tales from the *Arabian Nights,* the diamond "transforms" the returning General Vandeleur "from an obscure and unpopular soldier into one of the lions of society" (89).[6] The great stone also draws to it "one of three or four best dressed women in England, not only a gem of the finest water in her own person, but she showed herself to the world in a very costly setting" (90). Mirroring the gem—"one gem had attracted another" (90)—her status is measured on a consumer register, altering the diamond from a military trophy to a trophy wife's fashion statement.

In the second tale, "Story of the Young Man in Holy Orders," Stevenson turns from crimes of a military officer to those of a strikingly handsome yet studious clergyman, who is instantly corrupted by his accidental finding of the smuggled diamond. Cloistered with his religious books, he knows nothing of the world until his encounter with the Eye of Light: "There lay before him . . . a diamond of prodigious magnitude of the finest water. It was of the bigness of a duck's egg; beautifully shaped, and without a flaw; and as the sun shone upon it, it gave forth a lustre like that of electricity, and seemed to burn in his hand with a thousand internal fires" (116). Phosphorescence emanates from Christian hellfire fueled by Indian diamond lore. Reverend Rolles regards the diamond in a limited biblical context: "He knew . . . that he who possessed it was set free for ever from the primal curse" (151). The reverend might avoid the primal curse—sweating from his labors—but he breaks three commandments: coveting, stealing, and bearing false witness.

Upon uncovering the Eye of Light buried in a garden, Rolles hides it, lies to the police, and seeks financial rather than moral redemption. Wanting to unload his loot, Rolles scans his precious library "with an eye of scorn" upon discovering that teachings of the Church Fathers are "conspicuously ignorant of life" (119). Making straight for his gentleman's club, he craves practical advice about how to sell a stolen diamond. A club member recommends the writings of one Gaboriau. An intertextual joke alludes to detective fiction by one of the originators of the genre, Émile Gaboriau.[7] Unfortunately, credulous Rolles cannot find in Gaboriau a manual of thievery. The corrupted reverend wanders into two subsequent stories bearing his diamond, unable to profit from his theft. Fortunately for him, he is drugged and his booty stolen. In the final tale, "Adventure of Prince Florizel and the Detective," Rolles is advised to leave holy orders and immigrate as a farm laborer to Australia where the pure air will cleanse him.

The third story, "The Story of the House with the Green Blinds," bears out an influence of Gaboriau's use of coincidence and introduces the third naïve but comely young man. Francis Scrymgeour, a model employee and devoted son of a man he thinks is his father, is transformed in *The Arabian Nights* manner by a mysterious endowment and the promise of marriage to a fair heiress whose father turns out to be the brother of Major Vandeleur, who turns out to be Francis's father. The innocent Francis knows nothing of diamonds, like Rolles and Hartley, and is untouched by the rajah's diamond because he only receives it wrapped up as a keepsake from his future wife. He later gazes at it with horror at its "monstrous bigness and extraordinary brilliancy" (138) before handing it over to Prince Florizel.

The Eye of Light corrupts those vulnerable to it until Prince Florizel of Bohemia reappears from a previous series of stories, "The Suicide Club." Florizel warns against Westerners' coveting of Indian diamonds. The Rajah's Diamond would be "better in the sea" than allowed to tempt the men of Europe (158). He addresses his remarks to the ex-dictator of Paraguay, John Vandeleur, brother of Sir Thomas, "who gloried in the appellation of the Diamond Hunter" (125). At the gentleman's club where Rolles coincidentally overhears the conversation, Florizel tells the dictator that Indian diamonds strike back at the Empire :

> Jewels so valuable should be reserved for the collection of a prince or the treasury of a great nation. To hand them about among the common sort of men is to set a price on Virtue's head; and if the Rajah of Kashgar . . . desired vengeance upon the men of Europe, he could hardly have gone more efficaciously about his purpose than by sending us this apple of discord. As for you, who are a diamond-hunter by taste and profession, I do not believe there is a crime in the calendar you would not perpetrate . . . and all this for what? Not to be richer, nor to have more comforts or more respect, but simply to call this diamond yours for a year or two until you die, and now and again to open a safe and look at it as one looks at a picture. (123)

Seeming like a munificent gift for dastardly deeds, the Eye of Light betokens revenge. Florizel interprets the diamond's fetish power in line with Indian lapidaries, its force also imbued with Christian morality.

After taking the diamond from Francis, Florizel believes himself chosen to save humanity from the corrupting Eye of Light:

> The manner in which it had come into his hands appeared manifestly providential; and as he took out the jewel and looked at it under the street lamps, its size and surprising brilliancy inclined him more and more to think of it as an unmixed and dangerous evil for the world.
> "God help me!" he thought; "if I look at it much oftener I shall begin to grow covetous myself." (213)

Prince Florizel's prayer is no mere casual locution. "The Satanic charm" (168) of this bloody diamond masks its evil with its beauty.

In line with Indian diamond fiction, "The Rajah's Diamond" identifies this gem as a primordial essence, an irresistible marker for the forbidden. Diamond love is universal and cursed: "The Rajah's Diamond was a wonder that explained itself; a village child, if he found it, would run screaming for the nearest cottage; and a savage would prostrate himself in adoration before so imposing a fetich" (117). The Eye of Light conquers rationality, compels devotion, spooks the savage and the child, and grips holy men with atavistic desire.

Prince Florizel's sermon to a credulous Parisian police officer delivers a pious message that recollects the biography of the Koh-i-noor:

> "We have spoken of corruption," said the Prince. "To me this nugget of bright crystal is as loathsome as though it were crawling with the worms of death; it is as shocking as though it were compacted out of innocent blood. I see it here in my hand, and I know it is shining with hell-fire. I have told you but a hundredth part of its story; what passed in former ages, to what crimes and treacheries it incited men of yore, the imagination trembles to conceive; for years and years it has faithfully served the powers of hell; enough, I say, of blood, enough of disgrace, enough of broken lives and friendships; all things come to an end, the evil like the good; pestilence as well as beautiful music; and as for this diamond, God forgive me if I do wrong, but its empire ends tonight." (168)

The bright crystal nugget burns with the implacable fire of a killing machine. Prince Florizel dispels the Eye of Light's diabolical magnetism by tossing it into the Seine. Drowning the Eye of Light performs a purification ritual that enables decent characters to lead pleasant lives.

The Rajah's Treasure in *The Sign of Four*

Conan Doyle, like Stevenson, showed little interest in learning about the properties of diamonds but used them for their demoniacal shine. Rather than devote his detective's arcane studies to gems, Holmes's research focuses on ephemeral phenomena, the dust of daily life. Were it not that Holmes's hands-on methods were eventually adopted by actual police, the detective's specialties might be interpreted as a satire on scientific minutiae, "the Science of Deduction" meticulously distinguishing kinds of mud on shoes, dents on a timepiece, and tobacco smoke, "the black ash of a Trichinopoly." That ash (perhaps wafting from the deposed Prince Florizel's tobacco shop; Doyle avidly read Stevenson) is the first allusion to India in *The Sign of Four* when Holmes cites one of his technical monographs, "Upon the Distinctions between the Ashes of the Various Tobaccos."[8] The detective's Science of Deduction often leads to foregone conclusions, cloaked in rational objectivity while a sleight of hand rearranges facts. With characters misshapen by the 1857 Indian "Mutiny," as the story refers to what is also called the Uprising, the Sepoy Rebellion, and the first battle for Indian independence, Doyle constructs an imitation India by setting *The Sign of Four* in London neighborhoods, in Agra, and in the Andaman Islands in the Bay of Bengal. Doyle's Indian stones carry a curse based on those Indian settings in reciprocal acts of wrongdoing.

Upon hearing Watson recount the fabulous story of intrigue and detection that constitutes the plot in *The Sign of Four* (1890), Mrs. Cecil Forrester, employer of Miss Mary Morstan, discerns the adventure's generic antecedents in romance, particularly in the quest romance: "'It is a romance!' cried Mrs. Forrester. 'An injured lady, half a million in treasure, a black cannibal, and a wooden-legged ruffian'" (111). Doyle distills the romance of Collins (also an admirer of Gaboriau) into stereotypical outlines of detective stories, and, according to Jaya Mehta, wrote merely a more conservative knock-off of Collins's novel.[9] Yet unlike Collins, Doyle includes connoisseur consumption as part of imperial romances. Moreover, his story is set explicitly in the midst of the Uprising, weighing down his gemstones with bad conscience. In addition, Doyle's tale, more vigorously than Collins's complex novel, distills the quest element that becomes a feature of the detective genre, a form that develops from romance. Like "two knights errant to the rescue" (111), Holmes and Watson mount iron horses and four-wheelers to scour the countryside in a quest for justice for an injured damsel. Miss Morstan, the distressed lady, bears six immense pearls from an unknown sender, imploring the chivalric duo at 221B Baker Street to regard them as clues to the mystery of her father's disappearance ten years earlier. Captain Morstan had served in an Indian regiment and seems linked to the pearls, which themselves boast an Indian provenance.

Doyle directly includes consequences of the Uprising and its continuing traumatic resonances in the British symbolic economy.[10] After 1857, India cannot be regarded as simply a gem-filled setting. Rather, the subcontinent carries with those glittering associations the consciousness of bad faith. Doyle has it both ways, revealing a deep invasion of the Uprising into the British imaginary while at the same time drawing on India's atmospheric glamor. Doyle's frequent allusions to India in London bring consequences of the Uprising into pacific domestic settings as a tainted consumption of Indian goods, what men smoke and women wear.

Miss Morstan seeks Holmes's services, bearing both the Indian pearls and fashionable signs of imitation India. A "blonde young lady" of limited means, she works as a governess, but Watson discerns good breeding, evidenced by her dressing in "most perfect taste" (57). In a "sombre grayish beige" dress, Miss Morstan wears a matching colored "small turban . . . relieved only by a suspicion of white feather in the side" (59). The suspicion of a feather on a turban betokens a hint of nobility and quotes Sikh and Mughal style, adapting Indian male garb to a fashionable, petite, and blue-eyed blond. Turbaned Miss Morstan costumes herself in an echo of India, evidencing British democratization, dilution, and dispersal of Indian grandeur.

Intensifying allusions to imperial lands, the three arrive at an imitation India enclosed in the modest dwelling of Thaddeus Sholto, one of strange-looking twins. Part of the "monster tentacles" thrown out to house new wealth, Sholto's brick villa stands in a sparsely occupied terrace, a gentrifying development in a "questionable and forbidding neighbourhood" (66). There, the questers hear Indian words that foretell a Raj connection: The yellow-turbaned Indian servant who greets them refers to his employer as "sahib," and his employer calls him "khitmutgar," meaning "butler" in Persian and Hindi. The interior design of Sholto's inner sanctum, "an oasis of art in the howling desert of South London" (67), displays souvenirs of Anglo-Indian residence. Porcelain vases enrich the décor, tiger skins bestrew the furniture, and Thaddeus takes up a hookah to sooth his hypochondriacal nerves. Perfumed tobacco fills the room with aromas of the East. Here, the visitors' senses become acclimated for the next opulent setting, which brings the adventurers closer to spoils of empire, mementos for ordinary imperialists. In the deep of night, they arrive at a simulacrum of a Raj residence arising grandly in the respectable, but somehow tainted, newly developing London suburb of Upper Norwood.

Bartholomew Sholto, the other twin, inherits his father's Pondicherry Lodge, its name honoring a debt to Indian wealth. Pondicherry was the outpost of the French East India Company, with control of the region alternating between France and Britain, though it is not clear whether Doyle meant any significance to be read into the name, any more than Kashgar for Stevenson. Thaddeus explains that their father, Major John Sholto, had returned to London with "a considerable sum of money, a large collection of valuable curiosities, and a staff of native servants" (70). As the Holmes party ascends a staircase only to discover Bartholomew's corpse, they pass "a great picture in Indian tapestry" (80), only one instance in Doyle's inventory as evidence of how fully India had occupied domestic settings. Earlier, when the twins attend their father's deathbed, they observe signs of imperial consequences.

Major Sholto had contracted an incurable case of malaria and an urgent need for constant vigilance. In a nice juxtaposition betokening the wages of Empire, the great pearl chaplet, source of Miss Morstan's pearls, sat next to a quinine bottle on the dying major's nightstand. Pondicherry Lodge thus represents imperial India displaced to a London suburb, with disease, treachery, and treasures as its legacy. Major Sholto traveled always with bodyguards, terrorized by his own greed overlaid by a constant sense of transgression. He suffers from no mere paranoia, because one of the servants turns out to spy for the Four. When Jonathan Small hunts Sholto down to his imitation India villa, his malevolent glance through a window administers the final death blow to the major.

Mrs. Forrester identifies the invaders who cause the major's and his son's death as two figures from romance, here pointedly racialized. Tonga, an Andaman native, models contemporary ethnographic descriptions; he cannot be domesticated, save for his dogged loyalty to Small who had nursed him to health and then brings him to England. Jonathan wants only the treasure, but Tonga's savagery becomes unmanageable, and he blows his poison dart into the relatively innocent Bartholomew.[11] For a quest romance figure and one of the Four, Jonathan Small, the wooden-legged ruffian, could be a variant of Robert Browning's first figure in his quest romance "Childe Roland to the Dark Tower Came" (1855): "My first thought was, he lied in every word, / That hoary cripple with malicious eye" (1–2). A first view of Small mirrors such deformed malice, according to the Sholto twins, who were just about to learn from their father where the treasure was hidden when the major sees Small: "A face was looking in at us out of the darkness. We could see the whitening of the nose where it was pressed against the glass. It was a bearded, hairy face, with wild cruel eyes and an expression of concentrated malevolence" (73). The face scares Major Sholto to death.

Browning's ravaged landscape transforms to the Andaman Islands' "fever-ridden swamp" (133), the setting of a penal colony established to house convicts from the Uprising, including the Four. British-owned Indigo plantations dot the Islands, cultivated by forced native laborers.[12] Andaman plantations suggest a further cause of the Uprising in the workers' brutal treatment. In addition to that injustice, the indigenous Andaman population had nearly been exterminated; thus, Small's sidekick Tonga represents a remnant, an aftermath of conquest. The Four of the title—Jonathan Small, Mahomet Singh, Abdullah Khan, and Dost Akbar—have been rightly convicted of murdering the merchant in charge of a rajah's treasure. Doyle cares little about ethnic particularity in those Asian names or about his attribution of their religions as

"Hindoos or Mohammadans" (97) without differentiating the Sikhs, though he labels the "Punjabees" under Small's command as Sikhs and Mahomet Singh's name conflates Muslim with Sikh.[13] The gang of four steals the rajah's gems when he sends them to the fort that served as a refuge for the British during the Uprising. The men justify their appropriation of the rajah's wealth for two reasons: first, that he had been on the Sepoy side of the Rebellion but hedges by sending half his treasure to be protected by the British; and second, that he had been deposed, so "his property becomes the due of those who have been true to their salt" (141). Like Duleep Singh's jewels, his treasure is part of the spoils of war.

The three Asians who enlist Small voice a cynical attitude about imperialism: "We only ask you to do that which your countrymen come to this land for. We ask you to be rich.... We will swear to you upon the naked knife, and by the threefold oath which no Sikh was ever known to breathe, that you shall have your fair share of the loot" (140). Doyle here alludes to the unsheathed knife of Sikh ritual, by then a recognized sign of the Sikh religion. Perhaps Doyle meant all three to be Sikhs; at any rate the four, including Jonathan Small, the man from Pershore in Worcestershire, are true to the Sikh threefold oath, whereas the officers' code overrides the Sikh principle of honoring oaths to inferiors.

In Small's telling, there are no good guys in his sordid story. With casual, entitled imperialism, Sholto and Morstan do not report the Four's stolen treasure to the governor-general but instead sign a pact with them to divide the loot. Defying that agreement, Major Sholto decamps with the iron treasure box, and Morstan traces him to Pondicherry Lodge to split the booty in half. After an argument, Morstan's weak heart seizes and he dies, appropriately gashing his head on the Indian iron treasure chest. Protecting the damsel's father, the story does not condemn the two Raj officers, though there is ample evidence of their systemic implication in the ransacking of India. If the Four are true to their salt, the two British officers exist in a class and race category beyond salt that the story cannot overtly recognize without compromising the damsel. The story thus conveys unassimilated knowledge, an imperial unconscious, of transgression. The narrative offers evidence of British bad faith but slides over it in agreeing with Major Sholto that "half at least" and not one-sixth—or none—of the rajah's treasure belonged rightfully to Miss Morstan.

The rajah's treasure lies at the heart of Doyle's tale, and like other stories about Indian diamonds, it contains a curse. Small confesses his part: "It was an evil day for me when first I clapped eyes upon the merchant Achmet and had to do with the Agra Treasure, which never brought anything but a curse yet upon the man who owned it. To him it brought murder, to Major Sholto it brought fear and guilt, to me it has meant slavery for life" (128). Vedic wisdom lies behind the curse-bearing gems.

Doyle describes the setting as a place of religious extremism, particularly those in league with the devil: "The city of Agra is a great place, swarming with fanatics and fierce devil-worshippers of all sorts" (137). Worshippers of gems join others in their fanaticism, as Jonathan Small makes explicit in describing all human senses being engaged in gem worship: "The light of the lantern gleamed upon a collection of gems such as I have read of and thought about when I was a little lad at Pershore. It was blinding to look upon them.... When we had feasted our eyes we took them all out and made a list of them. There were one hundred and forty-three diamonds of the first water, including one which has been called, I believe, 'the Great Mogul,' and is said to be the second largest stone in existence. There were ninety-seven very fine emeralds, and one hundred and seventy rubies.... There were forty carbuncles, two hundred and ten sapphires, sixty-one agates, and a great quantity of beryls, onyxes, cats'-eyes, turquoises, and other stones" (145). Young Small in Pershore probably read bejeweled tales from *The Arabian Nights* such as the one about Sinbad the Sailor with his pockets stuffed with gems from the Valley of Diamonds.[14] Small casts his eyes on the second largest in the world, takes inventory of the loot, and fulfills the promise of his boyhood readings.

The legend of the Great Mogul diamond is more mysterious than that of the Koh-i-noor because the diamond itself has disappeared. Some speculate that the Koh-i-noor was cut down from the Great Mogul. Recently, using sophisticated computer models, the alleged connection between the two legendary Indian diamonds has been proven wrong.[15] Another generally discredited version has the Great Mogul appear disguised, re-faceted, and renamed the Orloff, one of Collins's models.[16] Stevenson also described the Eye of Light as egg-shaped. As part of generic features, the Great Mogul and the Koh-i-noor share similar biographies. When the Great Mogul is first described in the mid-seventeenth century as the largest stone ever found in India, taken from the Kollur mine near Golconda, it is about 787 carats and shaped, as Tavernier described it, as an egg cut in the middle, a great sparkling mound. Shah Jehan received it as a gift. When Shah Jehan's son, Aurangzeb, displayed the Great Mogul to Tavernier in 1665, the diamond (diminished by a hapless Venetian cutter) weighed in at 280 carats and could still enchant the eye. Soon after Nadir Shah sacked Delhi and returned to Isphahan with the

Great Mogul, he was assassinated. The Great Mogul disappeared. Affirming its celebrity status, the amazing diamond enjoys a cameo disappearing act in Doyle's story.

Like Florizel's aqueous solution to the Rajah of Kashgar's diamond, Small opens the Indian box to scatter its contents into the Thames. The Great Mogul and its precious companions sink to a muddy grave, along with Tonga, who has been described in the story as barely human and exaggeratedly tiny, an anti-jewel similarly imported from military invasions into India.

Holmes asserts about Tonga, "He lifts the case from the regions of the commonplace. I fancy that this ally breaks fresh ground in the annals of crime in this country" (84). The detective purportedly learns about the Andaman native from an ethnographic text that compares Terra del Fuegians with the Andaman tiny savage, delivering a conventional, imperial position about the nearly extinct Andaman native population, mischaracterizing their size and customs. Tonga's animality gains prestige for Holmes and inspires awe in Watson: "Never have I seen features so deeply marked with all bestiality and cruelty. His small eyes glowed and burned with a sombre light, and his thick lips were writhed back from his teeth, which grinned and chattered at us with half animal fury" (125).

The Indian gems and the Indian savage both glow and undergo the same fate. The reader's final view of this man flips the coin about irremediable loss of fabulous gems: "the unhallowed dwarf with his hideous face, and his strong yellow teeth gnashing at us" presents a horrible death as warranted. Watson describes the poor devil as he drowns: "I caught one glimpse of his venomous, menacing eyes amid the white swirl of the waters. . . . Somewhere in the dark ooze at the bottom of the Thames lie the bones of that strange visitor to our shores" (125–26). Doyle's vilification of the four-foot-tall Tonga associates the Andaman native with unredeemable evil, as does the author's solution for the treasure. "Unhallowed" Tonga exists beyond hope of salvation. The Great Mogul, also "a stranger to our shores" and linked symbolically to devil worship, lies in the muddy bottom of the Thames. The spirit of Bala, Hindu demon, inhabits the disavowed human Tonga as well as the fetishized gem.

The putative heroes—Holmes and Watson—solve overt misdeeds and murders while seeming to stand apart from imperial transgressions. In line with romance features, Dr. Watson falls for the maiden and properly marries her. In that function, the physician resembles Franklin Blake, who marries after justice is done for the Moonstone and for romance endings. Watson avers he could not have fulfilled this domestic romance function were Miss

Morstan heiress of the treasure. Watson narrates the story as a credulous participant without plumbing the depths of his own heart. Perhaps he is what he is: a loyal soldier and squire to Holmes, with conventional prejudices and gullibility. Yet his military past in Afghanistan leaves him with a limp, a shadow of Smart's repeatedly mentioned wooden leg.

Watson's knight, Sherlock, apparently remains on the side of justice despite some dents in his armor. First and last, he unheroically reaches for the cocaine bottle and needle.[17] A disapproving Watson at the outset of the story asks Holmes whether today he will choose opium or cocaine, both legally used as painkillers, both in the Holmes medicine chest. Though cocaine from the cocoa plant arrives from South America and not India, its identification with opium and the blur between cocaine as a stimulant and opium as a soporific also conflates the two drugs as imperial Others. Christopher Keep and Don Randall lay out connections between addiction and empire to show how the two very different substances became linked: "Watson's pairing of cocaine with morphine, the idea that the addict might use the one as easily as the other, was part and parcel of the 'orientalization' of the coca plant: though technically a stimulant, medical textbooks of the turn of the century classified it as a narcotic and thus relegated it to a sub-category of opium, a move which not only elided the biochemical differences between the drugs, but the cultural and historical differences as well. . . . The term 'narcotic' effectively effaced the distinction between a drug that traced its origins to a Spanish colony in South America and one that came from British colonies in Asia and India."[18]

Holmes's desire for Orientalized drugs, an addict's imperial urges, resembles a fatal, irresistible lure of gems. Doyle ascribes Holmes's cocaine addiction to his need for "mental exaltation." With similar avidity, Small describes the attraction to gems as an irresistible thrill, as do Stevenson's characters in "The Rajah's Diamond." And, sensationally, *The Moonstone* depends for its crime and solution upon addictions to tobacco, opium, and the Moonstone. Drugs and gems both satisfy emotional demands, described in Stevenson's story as cravings that exceed common social decency. Hence, Indian diamond stories are crowded with a mixed humanity, all seemingly caught in webs of desire for exaltation. Diamonds and drugs corrupt, addict, and weaken body and soul. From that perspective, Sherlock Holmes is an imperial victim. The Empire writes on his arms scarred with hypodermic punctures, imperial tracks. As for the gems, a fictional solution involves taking them out of reach, out of circulation, banishing them to swirling waters. For that, the wooden-legged ruffian serves the purpose.

Satanic Lures and Purveyor to the Gallows

A missing blue carbuncle in Doyle's story "The Adventure of the Blue Carbuncle," found in a fictional river in China and recently grown there—despite dawning recognition that real diamonds are very old—provides a gloss to the tales involving the curse of Indian diamonds discussed in this chapter. Doyle gives the carbuncle some diamondiferous properties to attest to its prominence. That is, without knowing much about diamond chemistry, Doyle knows he needs the most precious gem to earn credibility, interest, and distinction for his tale. Further, its color and phosphorescence link it to a notorious and fabulous named blue diamond that had been followed in Victorian periodical literature: the Hope Diamond, discussed in the epilogue of this book. Holmes characterizes the blue stone as "crystallized charcoal," mineralogically incorrect were it a carbuncle. What is more, Victorian fiction does not attribute to gems other than diamonds a power to exalt and corrupt. Modified by its unpleasant association with large boils, the blue carbuncle carries its curse in its designation. Like a bodily excrescence, the blue stone infects human relationships. Disease also connects the blue carbuncle to misfortunes following incorrect use of stones in Vedic lore. Echoing a moral message similar to Prince Florizel's, Holmes meditates on the perfect evil promised by a "good stone": "Holmes took up the stone and held it against the light. 'It's a bonny thing,' said he. 'Just see how it glints and sparkles. Of course it is a nucleus and focus of crime. Every good stone is. They are the devil's pet baits. In the larger and older jewels every facet may stand for a bloody deed. . . . There have been two murders, a vitriol-throwing, a suicide, and several robberies brought about for the sake of this forty-grain weight of crystallized charcoal. Who would think that so pretty a toy would be a purveyor to the gallows and the prison?'"[19] Although only about fourteen carats, the diamond-like carbuncle's power outweighs its size.

With its anomalous diamond qualities, the blue carbuncle belongs among legends about Asian diamonds tagged with diamond characteristics and beliefs. Satanic lures in Stevenson's metaphor become pictured in Doyle's adventure as the devil fishing for souls with diamonds. The power to curse gleaned from Indian lapidaries converts to a Christian register as "the devil's pet baits" that retain a fetish spirit as a greedy exchange between foreign cultures.

Fictional Indian diamonds charm and curse. In the tales discussed in this chapter, they are all stolen and are legacies of bad British conscience. Stevenson's Eye of Light, like other diamonds with a shady past, belies its contaminated spirit with brilliance, beauty, and value. Like Collins's Moonstone, the

Eye of Light gleams with acts of military cowardice, the Mutiny reflected as a mineralized scar on the British unconscious. Animated by a Hindu spirit that punishes their misuse, the Eye of Light, the Agra treasure, and the blue carbuncle not only ethically compromise those who take them up but damn them with a religious judgment that both Christian and Hindu could recognize. The Indian diamond inspires English fictions, bearing a Hindu curse organized according to Christian tenets. In imitating India, the authors disclose a horrified fascination with cursed, imported stones. In its attribution of carbuncle, Doyle's fictitious stone is an imperial disease, an apt diagnosis of diamonds discussed in this chapter.

4

Kim as Jewel and Crown

Certain things are not known to those who eat with forks. It is better to eat with both hands for a while.

—Rudyard Kipling, *Kim*

In 1867, well before Robert Louis Stevenson's Arabian-inspired stories, two Englishmen separately traveled to Kashgar, site of the rajah's bloody diamond, to establish with Yakub Beg the geographical survey that is the foundation for the Great Game in Rudyard Kipling's *Kim* (1901).[1] A Great Game connection between Stevenson's story and Rudyard Kipling's novel lies in their depiction of abandoned British troops as another effect of the Uprising. Soldiers form anonymous British victims in both imperial adventure tales, one of whom was Kim's father, a remnant from the army in India. Kim, a forgotten boy converted to a Hindu urchin, is both by-product of and opportunity for the British side in the Great Game, which forms an enlarged context for the British plucking Kim from his Indian ground and attempting to make him identify with his biological origins. Interpreting *Kim* with "The Rajah's Diamond" in mind forges connections among Indian diamond fiction, including *The Sign of Four* with its Uprising backdrop.

Kipling links Kim to a character from one of the tales that also inspired Stevenson: "He lived in a life wild as that of the Arabian Nights, but missionaries and secretaries of charitable societies could not see the beauty of it."[2] In alluding to *The Arabian Nights,* Kipling places his novel with Stevenson's as endowing diamonds with political, imperial reflections. In contrast to the other authors in this part, Kipling's birth in the heart of the Raj secures him local geographical authority. Unlike Indian diamond fictions discussed in earlier chapters, jewels in *Kim* may seem incidental, but they are fraught with Indian essence. Native women jingle with jewelry, and non-British men deal in jewels. The Raj is looking.

Jewels in *Kim* make up threads of India's very fabric. Diamonds are India when Kipling reaches for an image to capture its scintillating essence: "The diamond-bright dawn woke men and crows and bullocks together. Kim sat up and yawned, shook himself, and thrilled with delight" (193). Kim's discovery of his selfhood in the diamond-bedazzled air allies who he is with India. Kipling rhymes "diamond-bright" with "delight." The rhyme constitutes an affective shift from prose to poetry. It flags subconscious expression of alliance with India in the very core of the author's prose and points to a delightful escape into pleasure that occurs in other rhapsodic passages about the Indian scene.[3] Awakening to the diamond air, Kim knows his place, though experiences tame his vision of the world, or try to, and compromise his agency to choose his life that would be guided by India's diamond air to see its "real truth": "This was seeing the world in real truth; this was life as he would have it" (193). Kipling's diamond-bright dawn irradiates the country; diamonds so much define India that they constitute its surround. The diamond air adds a fairy-tale feature to the novel that, along with other poetic passages, indicates that this is a fable of a Neverland that Kipling made from his love of India. Kim, that shape-changing, identity-shifting boy, can be understood as a jewel faceted by the radiant land.

Kim's biography resembles a diamond legend woven from India's tapestry of values. Seen in the light of the entwined story of the Punjabi prince and his diamond in chapter 1, *Kim* builds a legend of a hero, a romance like other romance fiction. The novel opens with the image of an unnamed boy on the great Zam-Zammah, a cannon cast in Lahore in the Punjab, captured in battles, hauled off, and then returned. The boy's pose reproduces the cannon's political history: "He sat, in defiance of municipal order, astride the gun Zam-Zammah on her brick platform.... Who hold Zam-Zammah, that 'fire-breathing dragon', hold the Punjab, for the great green-bronze piece is always first of the conqueror's loot. There was some justification for Kim—he had kicked Lala Dinanath's boy off the trunnions—since the English held the Punjab and Kim was English" (3). The cannon was cast in 1757 during the reign of an Afghan ruler, and after many battles, Ranjit Singh, Duleep Singh's father, seized it in the beginning of the nineteenth century and used it in various sieges. Who knows but that he was also wearing his Koh-i-noor during some of his late forays? Remaining in Lahore to this day, the cannon retains its Asian identity through its lavish inscriptions in swirling Persian verses. At the outset of the novel, it is a sign of British dominance and of Kim's biological identity.

Kim's formation into the many-faceted treasure he becomes involves an education involving British indoctrination that shapes and reforms him—or misshapes and deforms him. It is true that Kipling asserts that Kim is English; he is Irish; he is white; he is poor—yet the author allows the boy continually to resist those categories.[4] Tied with love for al-Hind, the Persian name for India, Kim's development to the point where he might begin to frame his reiterated question "Who is Kim?" involves many challenges to discover an identity congruent with his Irish blood yet bound to the stuff that constitutes his place and its peoples, "the Irish and the Oriental in his soul" (201). Kim's body leaves no visible trace of whiteness when we first meet him, though the narrator asserts his identity as white: "Though he was burned black as any native ... Kim was white—a poor white of the very poorest" (3). The reader is enjoined to see beyond skin color to whiteness, though at the same time to see a little black boy.[5] The ambiguity of self-identity fills the boy's assertions about his race with double (or more) meanings. For instance, in one of his first conversations with Father Vincent and Bennett, British men who "rescue" him for his educational good, Kim decides to astonish his interlocutors, thinking to himself, "If the Sahibs were to be impressed, he would do his best to impress them. He too was a white man" (82). Given the context of identity seeking, Kim means not only that he, like the other two, is racially white but also that he is not *only* a black-skinned low-caste Hindu street urchin who identifies himself with Punjabis but is white as well. He possesses the double vision of his identity. The job of the English is to bring out the whiteness while enabling him to pass as a native. That aspect of Kim's story could be regarded as an attempted conversion narrative.

Yet, as in the example of Duleep Singh, conversions, always incomplete, disclose traces of what has been turned away from. In the attempt to turn him into a cog in the imperial wheel of the Great Game, Kim learns British ways of thinking in the *madrassah,* lovingly paid for by the Tibetan Teshoo Lama. Western education provides more cards to Kim's deck; he enfolds his treasured local knowledge and resourceful skills in the mantle of the sahib, whereas his identity always overflows that costume. Kim skillfully performs as a pawn in a British game, a prize specimen made for imperial purposes. And it is as a specimen that he is picked up by the Game's players, who lack a sufficient sense of his vital native being. He seems precisely a case, written up by someone such as the anthropologist Colonel Creighton, whose current position in the Ethnological Survey authorizes attempts to circumscribe identities into bounded and measured races in order to render publishable scientific reports. In the colonel's competitive zeal to protect his case study for his own renown, he reveals to Father Vincent as they plot Kim's training not only that he wants this boy for his own credit but that he wants to obscure the Indian element in Kim's makeup that he knows is there: "Well, don't say a word, directly or indirectly, about the Asiatic side of the boy's character" (97). Though Creighton knows, even values, Kim's Asiatic side, he confidently articulates the sahibs' goals for the boy but may overestimate their success. Kipling shows a ground of the boy's character not dependent upon genes, and that is what Creighton dimly knows. Contradictions between "race" and "character" expose the mélange of Kim's being. The identity war is waged on the political battlefield, including the Great Game.

The narrative proceeds in the direction of Kim's learning to play the Game, with powerful forces attempting to mold him. But, given the nature of a subjectivity that may experience an inward autonomy, the bildungsroman features of the novel allow Kim to believe that he has choice: "He could escape into great, grey, formless India, beyond tents and padres and colonels" (82). The text does not suggest that the boy forgets or is wrong about his conviction. The novel's ending cannot bear an unambiguous direction to a singular authority; rather, it leaves room in the narrative unconscious for renegade identities to be preserved.[6] In this way, the narrative follows in a direction similar to Duleep Singh's process as fundamentally a political pawn. Like his, Kim's conversion betrays signs of his Asiatic—more precisely, Punjabi—soul.[7] Because it is not history but romance, Kim's is a happier ending.

Unlike the little maharajah at the same age, Kim stays in the Punjab, centering and defining the imperial identity conflict from that contested land, whereas Duleep Singh wandered the world; then, politicized and disaffected, in 1887 appealed to the Russians for support against the British and unsuccessfully tried to be enlisted as a player in the Great Game.[8] As in the path to British identity only marginally achieved by the Punjabi exile, Kim undergoes a traditional British education, learning some version of Christianity that he translates into local knowledge, significantly alluding more to the "Goddess called Mary" or "Bibi Miriam" (100) than to the Father and the Son. His being drawn to female spirituality foretells his salvation, though eventually it arrives in a Hindu form. In addition to a garbled Christianity, Kim learns the three R's and some militaristic discipline. But he is unfinished, like a rough gem.

Creighton and Mahbub Ali (or C25 1B), both players on the British team, agree that Kim needs training that Lurgan Sahib uniquely can provide. "It is time," opines Mahbub Ali to Colonel Creighton, "the healer of pearls took him in hand" (110). Again later, when Kim regales Mahbub Ali with the story of how he escaped by having his skin darkened as a "Mohammedan" and was further disguised with a red turban by a woman of the night who jingles with native jewelry on her wrists and ankles, Mahbub Ali delightedly exclaims, "What will the healer of turquoises say to this?" (112). To appreciate that Lurgan Sahib restores faded gems such as pearls and turquoises to a marketable luster intimates the jeweler's role in evaluating the young boy. First, two players offer Kim to the jeweler, himself a player in the Game, as a gem to be healed and then finished for the sahibs' purpose. Figurative patterns that coalesce in Lurgan Sahib's shop confirm Kim's gemlike identity. The gem to be tested enters the shop, where he receives a jeweler's appraisal and a certificate of value. The jeweler evaluates the rough-cut gem and then delivers his report.

Lurgan's own shadowy credentials require interpretative efforts to confirm his importance as a jeweler to Kim's being a jewel. Like Kim, Lurgan juggles multiple identities; like Lurgan, Kim evaluates people. Kim issues an uncertain report on Lurgan's ethnic category: "Kim looked him over out of the corners of his eyes. He was a Sahib in that he wore Sahib's clothes: the accent of his Urdu, the intonation of his English, showed that he was anything but a Sahib. He seemed to understand what moved in Kim's mind ere the boy opened his mouth. . . . Sweetest of all—he treated Kim as an equal on the Asiatic side" (128). Lurgan Sahib treats the boy as an Asiatic equal, undermining Kim's decision as he approaches the shop that "he would be a Sahib for a while" (125). Despite his resolve, he finds himself "speaking in the vernacular," the redolent floral and spiced air that is Lurgan's atmosphere wafting away Kim's sahib identity. Lurgan Sahib, too, apparently accepts his own manifold selves. Kim's delight in Lurgan's respect for his Asiatic side confirms Kim as not entirely a white man. Lurgan may match Kim's identity with his own. He speaks more than one language fluently. Apparently, Kipling based Lurgan upon a real person, Alexander Jacob, a jeweler who was perhaps Muslim and who constructed ever more exotic life stories for himself.[9] As he transformed Jacob into Lurgan Sahib, Kipling makes clear that he is not "a genuine imported Sahib from England" (129).[10]

Though Mahbub Ali reports that "men say he does magic," the jeweler is not so much a magician as a craftsman, bringing out the best facets of the specimen brought to him. Lurgan's shop is filled with objects other than jewels that interest him in themselves, many of which will be enrolled to teach

Kim, already adept at disguises, to slip into personas as the need arises. In that sense, the shop contains fragments of Kim-ness. It is a Kim grab bag, needing Lurgan Sahib's healing to test and mold the boy's imperial mettle. Kim, aware that he has been handed over to a specialist, surveys the motley objects in the shop, trying to figure out what the jewel doctor will do to him:

> "These things are nothing," said his host, following Kim's glance. "I buy them because they are pretty, and sometimes I sell—if I like the buyer's look. My work is on the table—some of it."
>
> It blazed in the morning light—all red and blue and green flashes picked out with the vicious blue-white spurt of a diamond here and there. Kim opened his eyes. (129)

Kim's eyes open to diamond's nefarious possibilities. Confirming that Kim is not easily frightened by the disembodied voices issuing from a phonograph, Lurgan tests to see if the boy is a genuine jewel or merely a fine paste copy, his measuring instrument a heavy clay water jar. After Kim follows Lurgan's advice and flings the jar, breaking it into many pieces, Lurgan tries to hypnotize the boy into seeing the jar as coming back together to heal itself. Kim's successful resistance—by repeating some multiplication tables and using English words to ward off the spell—convinces Lurgan that Kim is the real thing, a jewel. The jeweler explains that he did no magic but rather used his gemological skills: "No, that was no magic. It was only to see if there was—a flaw in a jewel. Sometimes very fine jewels will fly all to pieces if a man holds them in his hand, and knows the proper way. That is why one must be careful before one sets them" (131). Lurgan explains that there are possible veins or inclusions that will shatter a diamond—in Kim's case, his blended identity. Kipling uses the jewel metaphor to represent Kim's marvelous character. Kim is an unset fine gem; his legend enables him to slip out of efforts to give him a permanent setting. Such success for Kim marks a difference between romance and history. Despite reconversion and failed efforts to join the Russian team in the Great Game, Duleep Singh's imperial setting proved to be a gilded cage.

Lurgan is amazed and satisfied that Kim is a better jewel than he suspected; then he trains him in the jewel game. Kim acquires a skill that many Indian boys learn as part of the jewel trade—to distinguish among different gems, evaluating and categorizing them. The sorting game is a synecdoche of his training to be a spy: to sort and discern various types. It is a game with bits of disparate kinds of stones that Indian boys learn to play for economic gain.

Kipling uses the "Play of the Jewels" in Lurgan's shop to place his hero in the context of Indian diamonds. The Little Game where the Hindu boy at first bests Kim and then teaches him is one parable about India as both a part of the British Empire and a place that cannot be circumscribed. Kim learns a skill demonstrated by the sullen Hindu child, who is understandably enraged—to the point of attempting to murder Lurgan—when the interloper takes over. The Play of Jewels becomes more than only a game with jewels, but with other objects as well, but it is called the Play of Jewels to retain its India-inflected name.

In the Play of Jewels, Kim learns a skill that had in fact characterized many Indian children's basic education. Tavernier's account of his inspection of the Indian diamond mines near Raolconda and Golconda describes the active role of youths of Kim's age in evaluating diamonds:

> It is very pleasant to see the young children of the merchants and other people of the country, from the age of ten to fifteen or sixteen years who seat themselves upon a tree . . . : Every one of them has his diamond-weights in a little bag. . . . If any person brings them a stone, they put it into the hands of the eldest boy among them, who is as it were their chief; who looks upon it, and after that gives it to him that is next him; by which means it goes from hand to hand till it return to him again, none of the rest speaking one word. After that he demands the price if possible; but if he buy it too dear, 'tis upon his own account. In the evening the children compute what they have laid out; then they look at their stones, and separate them according to their water, their weight, and clearness.[11]

It is somewhat true, as Philip Wegner asserts, that Kim can assume and discern multiple identities and acquire Indian skills, but that Indians can only approximate European skills.[12] At least such is the dynamic in Lurgan's shop, illustrated in Kim's ability to assume disguises: "The Hindu child played this game clumsily. That little mind, keen as an icicle where the tally of jewels was concerned, could not temper itself to enter another's soul" (134). Rather than Kim's chameleon abilities only belonging to his European side, his mixed identity better enables him to enter other souls, whereas the Hindu child is circumscribed by one, as his appellation attests. Kipling emphasizes Kim's Asiatic side as a kind of sensory knowledge gained from his character formation. Figuring the boy's multiple selves requires a letting go of bounded identities, as Teshoo Lama's Tibetan Buddhist teaching would recommend.[13] This episode in the shop establishes his symbolic meanings as both Indian jewel and British crown. As the crown, he represents the Raj as white sahib, but as a jewel, he reveals his affiliation with India's diamond air.

Kim's identity changes ally him symbolically with the shape-shifting of

Indian diamonds, particularly when they undergo European faceting. Those who write about the Manichean structure of colonialist literature, such as Abdul JanMohamed, argue that such a framework creates a story of civilizing the savage. JanMohamed's formulation more closely resembles the (failed) effort to tame Doyle's Andaman Tonga than it does the efforts to polish Kim. It is probably accidental though not inconsequential that a Manichean paradigm traces its origins of binary structures between light and darkness, good and evil, to a Persian prophet, although JanMohamed is not attentive to its Eastern roots. Such clear opposition, with no room for a middle ground, is rarely challenged in postcolonial literary criticism of Kipling's novel. In contrast, Jeffrey Franklin's study of Buddhism in English literature resists such foreclosures. The lama and his religion show that the search for enlightenment bypasses having to choose between the Buddhist search and the Great Game. The road comprises all, as Franklin shows; the Buddhist Middle Way "leaves Kim with the indeterminacy of continuous choice . . . with the uncertainty and excitement of becoming."[14] It is also the role of the diamond as symbol of Indian complexity. Though Mahbub Ali assumes that Kim will go on to serve an urgent need "as a scribe by the State" (236) or as a teacher, the ending finesses his confidence; Kipling's Kim would chafe at that role. The novel provides no end to Kim's becoming.

Kim's unfolding parallels that of Teshoo Lama, who submerges himself in the River of the Arrow, yet unlike purloined diamonds and Tonga, he does not remain submerged. Rather, he returns for Kim, as he says: "I pushed aside world upon world for thy sake" (234). The Lama is finished with his Search and sacrifices enlightenment for his *chela*. One cannot take that return lightly, nor can one ignore Kim's spiritual disease. Towards the end of the novel, he is exhausted with a sickened soul that is directly connected to his capturing the enemy's instruments as a consequence of himself being regarded as merely an instrument in the Great Game: "For some absurd reason their weight on his shoulders was nothing to their weight on his poor mind" (228).

His mind, heavy with implications of his imperial adventure and inextricable from his tired body, undergoes a similar kind of transformation as that of Teshoo Lama when he catches "a sickness uncommon in youth these days," (228) according to the Sahiba, or Hindu lady, who first purges him and then with "a cousin's widow" massages his entire body: "And the two of them, laying him east and west, that the mysterious earth-currents which thrill the clay of our bodies might help and not hinder, took him to pieces all one long afternoon—bone by bone, muscle by muscle, ligament by ligament, and lastly, nerve by nerve. Kneaded to irresponsible pulp, half hypnotized by the perpetual flick and readjustment of the uneasy *chudders* that veiled their eyes, Kim slid ten thousand miles into slumber—thirty-six hours of it—sleep that soaked like rain after drought" (229). Positioning him in line with what Kipling portrays as the primordial magnetic poles of the earth and then kneading his body, the women deliver him in a kind of rebirth, a female antidote to male attempts to shape Kim according to the anonymous and deadly political rules of the Great Game.[15]

The end of the novel does not resolve a question of Diamond Kim's identity, if that question is posed as a binary opposition. Rather, indeterminacy suggests an ending among the world's textures but also beyond them, a deliverance from ordained paths for both the holy man and his disciple.[16] Adults such as Creighton, who seems silly to local eyes, look at the youth as an abstraction without accounting for his consciousness. Healed by Hindu women, he hands over to Hurree Chunder Mookerjee (R17 on the payroll) the "whole bag of tricks—locks, stocks, and barrels" (231), extracted from the Russian and French opposition. This giving up represents the end of Kim's obligation *in the novel* to the Great Game, with R17 as witness to both the lama's and Kim's conversion. R17 returns to the Great Game.

Kim isn't quite reconstituted. Even after he hands over the results of the Russian survey, he feels as if his "soul was out of gear with its surroundings—a cog wheel unconnected with any machinery" (234). For a healing that contrasts with that of Lurgan Sahib's, he enters a trancelike state, chanting his name: "I am Kim. I am Kim. And what is Kim? His soul repeated it again and again" (234). Repeating his name as a mantra reconnects his soul to the "proper proportion," to place him in his Indian setting: "Roads were meant to be walked on, houses to be lived in, cattle to be driven, fields to be tilled, and men and women to be talked to" (234). Kim's vision does not mention any aspect of the Great Game, but rather earthly cycles of Indian life.[17] Falling to "Mother Earth" who holds him, he is in touch with the "hopeful dust that holds the seeds of all life. . . . Hour upon hour he lay deeper than sleep" (235). Mahbub Ali and Teshoo Lama, two poles of his being, neither of them British, discover him, yet Mahbub Ali departs, sure that Kim will return to the Game. He does not appreciate Kim's realignment, his being attuned in spiritual and fleshly restoration. Kipling leaves his brilliant hero on the threshold of adulthood, not diminished as Sara Suleri claims: "Kim is inexorably reduced to the sum of his utility."[18] On the contrary, Kipling allows a final view of the lama in the pose of a Buddha, smiling "as a man may who has won Salvation for himself and his beloved" (234). Kim recovers from his trances, following a familiar Victorian conversion narrative, awakened to his own truth. That truth is allied to the sacred nature of Indian gems.

For Kipling's starkly realist depictions of Lahore, consider a report from his early journalism, where the stench of cattle living among human filth led the journalist to jumbled squalid courtyards. Twenty-year-old Kipling followed a policeman through the narrow byways near the Delhi Gate, the very site that appears in the first chapter of *Kim* as part of the "wonderful walled city of Lahore" (5). The novel offers no scent near that very gate of the rotten odors from courtyards where cows, knee-deep in composting manure, share toilets with their human caretakers and cohabiters:

> Here and there side drains from the neighbouring houses added to the sluggish currents, or spread themselves aimlessly over the interstices of the worn and broken brick pavement . . . giving access to dark courtyards . . . beyond the reach of the sunlight. . . . But the dead wall, the barred and grated windows, and the high storeyed houses, were throbbing and humming with human life . . . and it seemed as if, at any moment, the tide of unclean humanity might burst through its dam of rotten brickwork and filth-smeared wood. . . . By unclean corners of walls; on each step of ruinous staircases; on the roofs of low out-houses; by window, and housetop, or stretched amid garbage unutterable, this section of Lahore was awakening to another day's life.[19]

Unlike such aromatic scenes, the novel does not reek with manure or stinking human masses cohabiting with horses, bullocks, and sacred cows. "Fragrant deodar logs" (5) scent the city. *Kim*'s Indian diamond air surrounds the youth through his city, towns, highways, and railroads.

Kipling's refusal to write beyond a beatific ending has provided many critics of different aims and ideologies a text to focus on what William Blake called "single vision"—political, ideological, cultural, or psychological, to name a few.[20] Confidently writing his own ending, Edward Said asserts, "As the novel ends, Kim returns to the Great Game, and in effect enters the British colonial service full-time."[21] Such assurance assumes that Kipling's mixed sympathies and the novel's freighted political background could not permit an ending such as the one Kipling wrote. Yet what we have is a sophisticated youth who does not grow up to be a certified Englishman; he's an imperial Peter Pan. Placing Kipling's novel in the context of English diamond fictions about Indian-denominated gems demonstrates its generic ties to the romance, allying Kipling's novel with Collins's romance, with Stevenson's *New Arabian Nights,* and with Doyle's quest romances.

As a singular diamond, Kim is reshaped but mainly escapes many consequences of re-faceting, of brutalizing, of converting. Two of his many names, "Little Friend of All the World" and "Friend of the Stars," encompass earth and sky. The epigraph above asserts in Kim's voice that eating with both hands offers knowledge unavailable to those who eat with one hand, holding a distancing implement. Confirming Eastern world practices, near the beginning of the novel, the lama and Kim hear a Buddhist mantra chanted in the background, *Om mane pudme hum!* (31); its meaning conveys vatic prophecy: "The jewel is in the lotus." The lotus flower, floating above muddy waters yet springing from them, a complex Buddhist symbol for purity and birth, finally beckons to Kim to seize wisdom that he heeds in the final image of Teshoo Lama and his *chela*. At its ending, Kipling reaches for a diamond out of time.

Kipling's is a poetic fantasy about a superhumanly elastic youth. A diamond has been reshaped to exist in company with other Indian diamonds in this section. Kipling's spiritual vision lends a mysterious ending to his picaresque bildungsromance. Multifaceted, all is absorbed into diamond's white light.

Kim's ending recalls *The Moonstone's* ecstatic religious gathering that eludes Western comprehension and that elevates a diamond to a holiness considered outside the fold. Yet and still, given the Western representation of diamonds, fictions about them are rarely untainted by intimations of global wickedness. That they carry a curse betrays unconscious knowledge of transgression, of evil along with glory. That diamonds addict is one overt figure of that knowledge, a return in symbolic form of what has been repressed. Indian diamonds reflect what Marx predicted in 1853: "England has broken down the entire framework of Indian society, without any symptoms of reconstitution yet appearing. This loss of his old world, with no gain of a new one, imparts a particular kind of melancholy to the present misery of the Hindoo, and separates Hindostan, ruled by Britain, from all its ancient traditions, and from the whole of its past history."[22] England, he believed and stated only a few years before the Uprising, would devastate the ancient society while creating a social structure modeled on a Western pattern. Re-faceting Indian diamonds according to Western standards is emblematic of that process. Ancient Persian and Arabian wisdom saw great power both to benefit and to kill in the potentially vicious diamond. Translated into British literary forms, the wisdom is there, disguised in English accents and colonized almost beyond recognition. In the meantime, traces of that Asiatic world haunt English fictions about Indian diamonds, dismantled by a process that included the licit and illicit diamond trade and its symbolic richness as satanic lure and sacred glory.

II
England

Diamond Metropole

> As I am writing a book on Jewels, not for the year 1777, but for a century later, and in London, the greatest emporium and market of Gems and Precious Stones in the world, I do not follow the topographical order of my predecessors.
>
> —Edwin Streeter, *Precious Stones and Gems*

English diamonds attain their national identity from their economic dominance in London. Never an English natural resource, diamonds *become* English in the world's "greatest emporium." They represent social and cultural concerns contributing to nation building and fortune making. Diamonds written about in an English context represent insecure familial status. Embedded in an imperial capital, they serve as deceptive symbols for a tumultuous gender revolution and a changing national formation. In addition, they are racially marked. To deflect attention from incomprehensible social alterations that shake a culture's sense of stability, diamonds in English nineteenth-century writings come to symbolize those very changes that their adamantine structure might promise to deny.

By the late nineteenth century, a jeweler, Edwin Streeter, in his popular lapidary quoted in the epigraph above, airily dismissed topography to celebrate London's supremacy in the diamond trade. To locate the diamond empire in "London" employs the city name as a label blanketing over differences among London areas, old parishes and newly created boroughs, enclosing two cities, the City and Westminster. Extolling his 1888 London map, George Bacon boasted in familiar imperial terms, "London is something more even than the metropolis of an empire on which the sun never sets—it is the largest, most populous, and wealthy city in the world; it is the financial centre of the world." In reissuing the map, Ralph Hyde glossed Bacon's observation with both ethnic and religious distinctions: "Living within its bounds were more Scots than in Edinburgh, more Irish than in Dublin, and, a bit surprising this one, more Catholics than in Rome."[1] To Hyde's list, one would add an increasing population of Jews, Indians, and Chinese. Owing to such diversity, Londoners could regard their neighbors as differing as much from themselves as the Saxon from the Semite, a cockney from a duchess.[2] London's mosaic was a source of its wealth, poverty, and chauvinistic terror.

Percy Fitzgerald in 1890 recognized that the area encompassing London on a recent map disguised its significant differences: "We are told of the 'growth of London' . . . ; but London has never become one homogenous mass. Yet, despite all, it remains 'London City,' with London Suburbs attached to it; and a continued familiarity prevents us observing how all these annexed districts retain marked characteristics of their own. . . . This individuality has been not a little fostered by the erection of Town Halls, which suggest an idea of municipal independence, and which tend to concentrate all the local energies. . . . London City, like British rule in India, has drawn all."[3] Fitzgerald associated London with imperial India to characterize metropolitan London's multitudinous shapelessness as a microcosm of the British Empire, formed this way and that, with "annexed districts," differing populations, political authorities, and relations to the center. "Heterogeneous compartmentalization," in Saree Makdisi's words, like the diamond empire itself, enabled "London" to own diamond as its mineral, overlooking how it got there and who controlled its fame and fortunes.[4]

In fact, Jews ruled London's diamond empire. Through ancient trade routes, they were ascendant in the diamond trade, eventually affiliating with the English East India Company. Jews could not directly influence the company management or policies, but a seventeenth-century decision of the East India Company to abandon diamond trading provided the basis on which the Anglo-Indian diamond trade was to be carried on for the next 150 years.[5] Jewish diamond traders arrived in England from Holland and Portugal, and later from Italy and Germany. After they had settled in London, Jewish merchants maintained their former business connections, with Holland on the one hand and with Goa on the other.[6]

In 1874, when the diamond trade was undergoing global shifts, the East India Company disbanded. With the transfer of Indian territories to the Crown and the ascendancy of the London diamond trade, diamonds assumed a firmer English identity, without losing their Jewish cast. The diamond discovery in 1867 in South African territories that the British soon annexed solidified

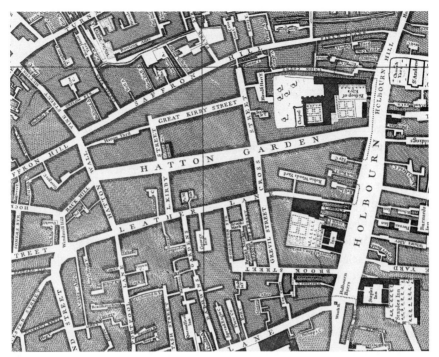

Figure 4. Hatton Garden, detail, in John Roque, *Survey of the Cities of London and Westminster,* 1746. (Lionel Pincus and Princess Firyal Map Division, New York Public Library)

diamond's English ties. Topographical alteration was central to the evolution of England becoming an empire and to the signification of diamond.

The diamond district in Hatton Garden, an area of about one square mile, was diamond's imperial center (figure 4), occupied largely by Jewish gem dealers, some recent immigrants who went to Africa to buy diamonds for "about a dozen London houses."[7] Located in Holborn, it is approximately in the center of the London metropolitan map. By the end of the century, its diamond empire radiated from there. Three types of Jewish dealers plied their diamond trade in the Hatton Garden area. Importers sold the stones to big dealers, who were the wholesale merchants of the trade. They had the stones cut and polished locally or sent them for cutting to Amsterdam or Antwerp. The third class consisted of jewelers who bought finished stones or polished them to manufacture jewelry.[8] Diamonds in retail shops passed first through Hatton Garden. Before World War II there were no retailers there.[9] Elite jewelry shops in Mayfair and criminal dens in Saffron Hill (just north of Hatton Garden) and St. Giles drew sustenance from Hatton Garden diamonds.

Troubling an exotic identity derived from original Indian dominance, however, Jews' established diamond trade with India adds a less enticing, yet still Oriental, aspect to diamonds. Makdisi points out that Henry Mayhew divided the peoples of the world into the wanderers and the settlers.[10] Neither he nor Mayhew mention that Jews are the archetypal group notorious for wandering. Forming worldwide webs, they traded in central London, often living in northern suburbs, while less wealthy Jews—pawnbrokers, storekeepers, and peddlers—lived in the East End, some in the Walworth area.[11] Those diamonds are cleansed of distasteful origins when they appear in prepossessing shops such as the House of Garrod, established in 1735 in Panton Street, Soho, and purveyor to royalty. This wandering, displaced aspect often colors diamonds that Jews sell, which also wander in English fiction from rich English families with their inherited inventories or impecunious sons and daughters back to Jewish jewelers and pawnbrokers—from the English West (End) to the Oriental East (End).

Diamonds assume meanings particular to English national concerns. As articles of exchange within and between families, they promise to solidify, even mandate, communities of mutual interest. But they also represent conflict within those groups. Diamonds variously serve as emblems of family identity, trophies of a manly nation, badges of wealth, and marks of a disavowed race. In line with customs of the country, men give English diamonds to women, the exchange itself expressing gender relations at the very moment that Victorian gender conventions are under siege.

Describing his own social milieu at the end of the nineteenth century, sociologist and economist Thorstein Veblen pointed out that a significant problem in understanding industrial societies is not so much how goods are made (Marx's main concern) but how they take on meanings.[12] In the context of a new order built on commercial values, where women bear most of the moral weight and display tangible results of commerce, diamonds, glittering and dangerous, assume multiple meanings to characterize a freighted exchange between striving men as captains of industry and beautiful women as trophy wives. What is more, these executives assume a diffused identity, a corporate one. About Romantic writing earlier in the century, Daniel Stout proposes the category of "corporate persons" to describe a configuration that emphasized "corporate actors" as opposed to what had been celebrated as individual agency, an Enlightenment construct. Abstraction of people from direct financial responsibility produces "complex collectivities" under a corporate shield.[13] Later in the century, in Victorian times, such diffused identity in the context of governmental and business structures grows more distanced from individual persons, who themselves seem abstractions, almost personifications, according to the settings in which they operate. What happens in the social world is reflected in a kind of fictional character, constructed from ways of conceiving the individual in general terms, women as well as men. Whereas fictions about Indian diamonds discussed in part 1 symbolize the gem as having spiritual, moral agency and fall into the romance genre, diamonds considered in fictions about English social life represent this distancing of agency from consequences, often in realist novels. In general, English diamonds present a glittering façade to distract from ideological structures that fail to steady the march of time. Their very value, solidity, and brilliance, so the texts in part 2 tell, blind devotees to their dependence upon crumbling ancient institutions and the ascendance of a new kind of human who hides behind corporate shields, mainly in London, the new Camelot.

5

Diamond Games for a Dead Man

> These jewels, whereupon I chanced Divinely, are the kingdom's, not the King's.
>
> —King Arthur, "Lancelot and Elaine"

Two literary works, one an epic allegorical poem, the other a socially committed novel placed in dialogue—Alfred Tennyson's *Idylls of the King* (1856–74) and Charles Dickens's *Little Dorrit* (1857)— use diamonds as tropes for a developing social/political/economic system. The system is increasingly anonymous, with the person at the top deeding his enterprise to others in a structure that yields unanticipated outcomes.[1] Individuals of good intent and grand visions are prey to the very diffusion they themselves promote. Tennyson's dark imperial kingdom and Dickens's dark imperial marketplace portray corrupting systems that alienate people from each other and from themselves. In both works, a newly forming fashion system displays, disguises, indeed constructs, social realities. The visuality of fashion brings unresolved issues into material forms—embodying them in costumes that seem to confirm social positions but that, like fashions, confound formerly distinct classes.

Lord Alfred Tennyson's allegorical narratives with epic features chart the founding and collapse of an empire with an urban center that measures its worth in diamonds. These royal diamonds come to represent consequences of increased distance in human interactions. In a work written over decades, diamonds symbolize immense social changes in the very structures that represent reality. At the time of the poem's setting, the late Middle Ages, a fashion system developed in which gender rather than class determined attire.[2] Tennyson located his allegorical epic during that period, echoing concerns at his own moment about ways in which fashion blurs social boundaries. Likewise, Dickens portrays a realm in which an abstract Society shaped by its adherence to fashion mandates identities. In Society, characters seem pale shadows whose inner lives are often inscrutable. Government and business structures support incompetence and corruption, often with disastrous consequences. One cannot discern trustworthy minions from fakes. Within developing consumer economies built upon display, both authors offer figurations of the social world comparable to a fashion show in which the parade itself defines its members. Diamonds sparkle in the gloom of an alienating corporatized economy.

Tennyson dedicated the *Idylls* to Prince Albert's memory, then concluded the finished work with lines "To the Queen." Dedication and conclusion serve as parentheses, as if the royal couple embraced the laureate's work and provided solace for its portrayal of failing efforts to maintain conjugal and political contracts in the context of an empire where areas in it already possessed differing assumptions about the nature of reality itself. Homage to the royal couple sets the poet's epic panorama in her "ocean-empire with her boundless homes."[3] The phrase reinforces the work's concerns about building an empire without defined boundaries. Tennyson's gloomy prognostication, "You must not be surprised at anything that comes to pass in the next fifty years. All ages are ages of transition, but this is an awful moment of transition," expresses apprehension about changing times, one figure for which is Queen Victoria.[4]

The *Idylls* allegorize Victorian cultural revolutions in all areas—scientific, technological, religious, economic, and social—in the protracted wake of the Industrial Revolution.[5] Tennyson filtered his chief executive through medieval legends as a way of supplying middle-class empire builders with a fabricated pedigree that would seem to secure their positions. However, King Arthur seems more antiquated than newly minted because he voices Victorian values filtered through inherited legends. What is more, the medieval setting with its aristocratic characters requires a conceptual shift to picture them as referring to Victorian class and economic changes, most obviously increasing middle-class power and prominence, along with altering business and political structures.[6]

Arthur's formation includes conquering territories conceived as a civilizing mission while gathering them under his banner.[7] His justifications for empire echo imperial rationalizations, explained as civilizing the savage. Arthurian legends transfer contemporary anxieties about a boundless empire into a timeless realm.

Tennyson's apocalyptic vision, as in the Book of Revelation, is concerned with contemporary social conditions centered on a city. Camelot, initially comparable to the New Jerusalem, is a city of newcomers, chosen immigrants who pledge allegiance to a moral order. Tennyson's son Hallam explained that his father aimed to bring old legends up-to-date, "infus[ing] into them a spirit of modern thought and an ethical significance . . . as indeed otherwise these archaic stories . . . would not have appealed to the modern world."[8] Much of the poem concerns matters of power that might indeed seem modern once the archaic settings, rituals, and characters are scraped of medieval veneer to reveal concerns typifying a cosmopolitan, urban realm. Victorian medievalism provided a façade for the poet's concerns rooted in Victorian earth where altered textures of daily life contributed to his vision of a new order that he foresaw with fear, loathing, and horrible fascination. The poem responds to consequences of the social upheavals of its industrial, commercial moment: depersonalization in society and interlopers as leaders. In *Lancelot and Elaine,* a supernatural voice authorizes the hero. Further, this idyll fabricates a diamond myth, proclaiming the diffusion of male power and the gendered dynamic that the poem exposes as idealistic but empty. Diamonds, miraculously discovered, answer the poet's conceptual prayers, concentrating meaning in one symbol that could appear as both providential and crass.

Leading to *Lancelot and Elaine,* the idyll concerned with establishing Arthur's empire as a diamond one, earlier idylls lay out a Victorian gender dynamic that participates in empire building. In addition to an imperial mission that the poem places in a timeless realm, the perfidy of women—a theme running throughout the *Idylls*—seems also eternally true. Imperial misogyny universalizes Victorian adjustments between the sexes, known in the era's shorthand as the Woman Question. The poem casts the Woman Question as an imperial exogamous project with the knights—including King Arthur—venturing to outer territories to acquire mates. Chance encounters with eligible beauties occur in the context of alliances within a developing empire. To achieve his ambitions, Arthur desires a woman who not only affirms his success but enables it: "for saving I be joined / To her that is the fairest under heaven, / I seem as nothing in the mighty world."[9] When Arthur voices his sense of nothingness without Guinevere, he confesses not simply to an inferiority complex. Powerful people doubt his legitimacy and question his origins. A charismatic arriviste with impressive organizational capabilities, he cannot depend on merit alone to become acceptable as a leader. He needs the *bona fides* of King Leodogran's daughter, Guinevere. His accurate sense of insecurity prevents him from acknowledging that he shops for a great woman in a socially vetted marketplace. A seeker for the best article opens himself to speculative values, risking bad bargains and fatal contracts. King Arthur's sense that he is socially nothing in the realm he wishes to lead renders the fairest woman a badge, a credential. The market drains woman's individuality. The woman in question gains social prominence as she loses personhood. She herself remains generic, a modern trophy resembling other trophies.

Tennyson's chronicle of the rise and fall of an empire that centers on a city references the war economy of classical epic where women are awarded as trophies. Three words, *trophy, trope,* and *tournament,* share a common etymology in the Greek root *tropaion,* meaning "turn," and organize the following discussion. In ancient Greece, trophy referred to the place on a battlefield for a victory monument composed of captured arms—spears, battle-axes, and so forth—that marked the spot where the enemy turned and fled. By extension, a trophy is a status object awarded in a competition to make concrete the victor's preeminence. Stories about women awarded as trophies initiate a Western literary tradition, *The Iliad* its most familiar epic example and Helen its most familiar trophy. After years of fighting for Helen, the *Iliad*'s action culminates in Achilles's murderous pursuit of Hector around the battlefield. Homer's epic simile likens that chase to a chariot race at a warrior's funeral: "when chariot-teams around a course go wheeling swiftly, for the prize is great, a tripod or a woman, in the games held for a dead man."[10] The funeral games memorialize cultural values in which a worthy warrior collects tributes and values heroic death above family and community and who views war as competition. In a miming of the war that required them, games for a dead man play out the heroic war system, with trophies lending substance to that kind of male valor.

Women gained as trophies eventually seem to contain the spirit enabling victory, a short step from trophy to fetish. The avatar of such trophy women, Helen of Troy, is born into literature. Although Paris abducts her rather than wins her in battle, the Trojan War launches her as the figurehead for the deadly system that establishes beautiful women as rewards for men's success. No author has described Helen's looks, thus ensuring her universal reputation for beauty. Then too, the beautiful woman might find her own beauty troublesome. For instance, Euripides's Helen blames her beauty for preempting her accomplishments: "Would God I could rub my beauty out like a picture, and assume hereafter in its stead a form less comely."[11] Self-alienating, as if she were an artist's rendering (which she always is), Helen regrets that people reverence her looks and not her "career of honor."[12] Of little interest as virtuous Helen of Sparta, she is correct in her self-estimation. No woman becomes a trophy because of her good deeds or exemplary career, particularly in a form less comely.

Euripides directs attention to another root of "turn": *trope,* a turning of language through substitution. The playwright makes literal the Helen trope by employing a version of the myth where Helen herself was transported for safekeeping to Egypt while Paris carried off to Troy an eidolon, an image composed of male belief in the embodiment of his desires. Helen explains this phenomenon: "Hera . . . gave the Trojan prince not the real me but a living likeness, conjured out of air, so that believing he possesses me he possesses only his belief."[13] The living likeness exists insofar as the system conjures her, prefiguring how commodification affects the creation of the nineteenth-century trophy wife. As a trope for Victorian capitalism's eroticized business success, she indeed could seem as merely an emanation of a corporate entity's self-image — a logo. Airy and replaceable, she exists as an animated spirit, a cultural fetish made for display. "He possesses only his belief" also describes the relationship of the couple, the man believing in her as an objectification of his success. With the new business structures (rather than birth into a land economy, or personal relationships in the exchange of goods, for instance), it is hard to know who is authentic. Potentially anyone can pass himself off in an executive costume, his trophy merely an eidolon.

King Arthur, like other mid-century striving male upstarts, is besieged by Victorian revaluations of who or what counts. He rises to eminence through hard work, an inspirational message, and an imperial strategy. The *Idylls* builds on the ambiguity of his parentage from earlier Arthurian chronicles that offer modern interpretative possibilities. Tennyson's *The Coming of Arthur* describes his birth out of a ninth flaming ocean wave, caught by Merlin. Who could authenticate such parentage? Elementally thrown up from nowhere, he is a new kind of king who conceives of reigning as "work" and forms a corporate entity to represent his realm. The king embodies values of an imperial middle-class culture (including religious concerns), earning his eminence and then consigning his work to an executive board, the knights of the Round Table.

Ambiguities in assessing worthiness for a seat at the table cast doubt on the coin of the realm. The monk Ambrosius in *The Holy Grail* uses a money metaphor to compare counterfeit coins with Arthurian methods of dubbing new knights, the flaws of the process revealing vulnerabilities in the merit system of advancement:

> For good ye are and bad, and like to coins,
> Some true, some light, but every one of you
> Stamp'd with the image of the King. (*HG,* 25–27)

New knights bear Arthur's corporate seal. Guinevere describes this same system that places pressure on the knights who want to be stamped with Arthur's ambition: "No keener hunter after glory breathes. / He loves it in his knights more than himself: / They prove to him his work" (*LE,* 155–57). Rather than consolidate symbolic meaning uniquely in his own person (already composite with his wife), the Victorian leader radiates his code outward to his emissaries. In reframing chivalric behavior, the realm is a society ordained yet mediated by the leader's permission for knights to act in his stead. Arthur authorizes quests and jousts to authenticate a new order characterized by corporate sovereignty. That diffusion potentially produces light coins. The knights often operate as persons with portfolios, for instance, in *The Holy Grail,* where they weaken Arthur's realm in their misguided quest for a vision.

For their part, the ladies often resist traditional gendered behavior, aware of an ability to coin independent values. Arthur's need to harness his consort's source of energy expresses an element of that cultural change. The Victorian wife enlarged her domestic functions to become a force in an economy of consumption, one that the new empire depended upon for prosperity, growth, and well-being. Hers is a moment of increased economic power when political economists turn attention from production to distribution, consumption, and circulation.[14] Department stores, consolidated from individual specialty shops, offer social events as well as merchandise and open women to chance encounters. Women shop for pleasure, not necessarily need. To put it differently, need might be more variable, flexible, externally produced, and ungoverned by a shopping list. New magazines solicit women's patronage and curate their lives. In a consumer culture, women become the means of showing forth—of turning economic power into spectacle. Being bought in the market and buying in the market, this trophy carries heavy cultural weight.[15]

Arthur's hard work and his desire to embody its success in a woman characterizes Tennyson's response to nineteenth-century economic developments in the context of the Protestant ethic and the spirit of capitalism, a translation of Max Weber's inspired phrase.[16] Weber described the capitalist spirit as blessing limitless profit and the Protestant ethic as condemning the enjoyment of those gains. Following his paradigm, striving men fulfill the work ethic while women consumers exhibit its profits—and are blamed for it. The combination results in cultural fetishism, in which the stuff and the one buying it are on a par with spiritual practices—the Victorian angel in the house hovers over the department store.

The capitalist spirit is poured into a woman's body; she embodies an economy based on commerce and what Veblen called "emulation." Veblen offers a reason to produce trophies as "desire of the successful men to put their prowess in evidence by exhibiting some durable result of their exploits."[17] Such is the trophy wife, a thing composed out of the breath of heaven who bodies forth newly acquired male wealth and power: the spirit of capitalism as a living likeness. Diamonds sparkle with that spirit. Distracted by empire building, King Arthur interacts with his queen as if she were a thing, not a person.[18] Unfortunately, unlike things, wives must fail as the durable goods of Veblen's paradigm. In addition to their inevitable aging, women's emerging consciousness fights for subjectivity; wives' desires often emerge independent of husbands' mandates.

With adultery as a moral judgment against wives and a scapegoat for political failure, the *Idylls* reveal an uneasy consciousness of women's voices, often heard as wicked. For instance, in Tennyson's largely original story of Merlin and Vivien, the young femme fatale tries but fails to entrance Arthur, then successfully seduces a vulnerable old wizard. In an idyll filled with sexual gossip between Merlin and Vivien, the magician reminisces to her, "Full many a love in loving youth was mine; / I needed then no charm to keep them mine" (*MV*, 545–46). To rhyme "mine" with "mine" stresses Merlin's nostalgic self-absorption; his well-guarded charm desired by Vivien harbors an erotic spirit. Inspiring recollection of virile days sowing wild oats, the young woman touches Merlin's vulnerability.

Resorting to the old man after she fails with more potent ones, Vivien seeks power traditionally deeded to men. Born on the battlefield from a father who died fighting "against the King," (*MV*, 40) Vivien describes herself as "born from death was I / Among the dead and sown among the wind" (*MV*, 44–46). She survives on beauty, wits, and lies, appealing to Guinevere's mercy by altering her story:

> My father died in battle for thy King,
> My mother on his corpse—in open field,
> The sad sea-sounding wastes of Lyonnesse. (*MV*, 71–73)

Born in a cursed setting that merits attention, Vivien arrives in court on a mission from the Cornish King Mark whose kingdom abuts Lyonnesse.[19]

Successful only with an old man, Vivien is an easy mark for vituperative judgment, as in Algernon Charles Swinburne's vilification of her as "about the most base and repulsive person ever set forth in serious literature."[20] Base she is and a liar as well, though a turn of an evaluative prism finds Vivien's rage ignited by rejection as an outsider and hunger for classified information. In need of security and social acceptance, she wants to learn spells that allow access to male traditions; in bewitching Merlin, she wants to increase her control in a system stacked against women.

With more secure lineage than Vivien but with a similar disability, Guinevere feels alienated from the partner she is supposed to complete. The first idyll opens by describing Guinevere's value in men's political marketplace, as the "one delight" of her father, King Leodogran. Her father hands her over after he accepts Arthur's murky pedigree as good enough.[21] Guinevere suffers from the premise upon which her marriage was founded. The princess did not notice Arthur when he passed Leodogran's castle walls, gazed upon her, and wanted to possess her. Having bargained for Guinevere and in line with diffusion of his power, Arthur foolishly or arrogantly sends his favorite knight to fetch his trophy. While stabilizing this amorous triangle, Guinevere inevitably fails the diplomatic contract of which she is a pawn.[22] Her adultery grows contagious as it spreads throughout the land.

Attention to Guinevere's notoriously failed marriage has eclipsed notice of her kindly treatment of younger women—Vivien, Enid, and other ladies-in-waiting. When Guinevere retreats to a nunnery, she has permanently fled her degradation as a shamed adulteress in the Round Table games. Joining a women's religious order, she eventually receives recognition "for her good deeds and her pure life / And for the power of ministration in her" (*G,* 686–87) to become a successful abbess, running the convent for three years until she dies. No longer trophy wife and clad in a nun's habit, a form less comely, she achieves a career of honor denied Helen of Sparta.

Fashioning Imperial Accessories

Though the penitent queen thrives as an abbess, her success is ignominious. A nun's uniform deliberately resists elegant fashion pageantry of an imperial nation that follows fashion's dictates. Enid, a newcomer to the modern society in Camelot, thus takes her place as a mannequin for imperial politics in *The Marriage of Geraint* and *Enid.*[23] The only two idylls not taken from Malory, they confirm the poet's project of Anglicizing the Welsh legend for nationalist aims filtered through fashion imagery.[24] The politics of dressing and undressing Enid uncovers ways of knowing who counts and how in the project of empire building.

The Idylls echoed fashion concerns of its medieval source, the Welsh Arthurian sections of the prose *Mabinogion*. Both works reflect the emergence of fashion as a dominant social phenomenon. Fashion's ascendancy appears along with mercantile capitalism when there are increased chances for social mobility. Fashion theorist Joanne Entwhistle explains such attention to fashioning the body: "The medieval courts demanded increasingly elaborate codes of behavior and instilled in individuals the need to monitor their bodies to produce themselves as 'well mannered' and 'civil.'"[25] For social philosopher Gilles Lipovetsky, fashion's "instability is rooted in the social transformations that began to occur in the late Middle Ages.... We find the growth in economic power on the part of the bourgeoisie, a growth that facilitated both the bourgeoisie's increased desire for social recognition and its increased tendency to imitate the nobility."[26] In telling of Enid's family attire, the *Mabinogion* reflected fashion's expanding signifying power in about the mid-fourteenth to early fifteenth centuries. *Idylls of the King* reflects a comparable nineteenth-century turn to fashion in the face of social transformations, again following the growth of middle-class power. Fashion forms part of a mercantile capitalist ideology, exemplifying the claim of fashion theorist Elizabeth Wilson: "its function to resolve formally, at the imaginary level, social contradictions that cannot be resolved."[27]

Fashion opens society to those who emulate its appearance, not necessarily its core precepts. Sociologist Georg Simmel describes how fashion organizes social membership, suggesting similarities between the codes of fashion and those of chivalry: "Fashion is ... a product of class division and operates—like a number of other forms, honour especially—the double function of holding a given social circles together and at the same time closing it off from others.... Thus, on the one hand, fashion signifies a union with those of the same status, the uniformity of a social circle characterized by it, and, in so doing, the closure of this group against those standing in a lower position which the higher group characterizes as not belonging to it."[28] Simmel's social circle, however, cannot be impermeable. Subject to imitation, it cannot copyright its designs. The Round Table, apt image of a social circle, depends upon the entry of new members who try to prove their worthiness—in appearance as well as in the field, in their own attire as well as that of their partners.

Fashion imagery shapes the poem's medieval surface to its modern significance. Sexual, economic, political, and imperial anxieties parade in elegant robes. As fashion journalist Colin McDowell observes, "Fashion became political in the nineteenth century when the battle for social power was joined between the upper and middle classes."[29] Fashion, with its disposable economy predicated upon constant change, becomes emblematic of an age of diffusion of authority and power—represented in England politically by the Reform Acts and economically by new ways of conducting business.[30] Lipovetsky's antithetical definition of fashion as "durable organization of the ephemeral" could also describe Arthur's effort to organize and civilize a social order.[31] Tennyson's friend Julia Margaret Cameron, the photographer of the *Idylls,* conveyed the importance of fashion in the poem when she posed Enid in a bridal gown and veil, opening a wardrobe (see plate 7).

Literary critics have not matched Cameron's acuity, often agreeing with reviewers' objections to Tennyson's fashion consciousness. J. M. Gray, for instance, quotes a disdainful Victorian review to turn the comment to good account: "To our modern taste, Tennyson's emphasis on dress is apt to become wearisome. Our immediate feeling is to sympathise with the Victorian critic who declared: 'And here we are treated to an amount of millinery against which not all our reverence for Tennyson's genius shall stay us from protesting.' At the same time, we must keep in view Tennyson's own intention: apparel plays an essential part in the drama of appearances."[32] Clothing often signifies differences between appearance and reality, and the poem reveals a complex fashion dynamic: clothing can represent authentic social position or its canny emulation. And isn't that the point of fashion? Misidentification of surface captures a modern problem exemplified by the prominence of fashion in a politicized social system. In her study of Victorian women's magazines, Margaret Beecham shows that fashion writing had it both ways, insisting "that a woman should dress appropriately to her situation and income" but also helping "to create a mass fashion industry in which all such codes would eventually break down."[33]

Fashion journalism becomes an occupation, expanding meanings given to dress.[34] Clothes, as a Victorian fashion reporter could confidently assert, constitute a "symbolical language . . . the study of which would be madness to neglect."[35] The gorgeous raiment parades in cultural fetishism's symbolical language. Raiment forms a building block of Camelot, that ephemeral "city built / To music" (*GL,* 272–73).[36] Elegant Tennysonian evocations of fabrics worn with panache impart fashion information to readers habituated to assessing fashionable worth. Characters in the *Idylls* swathe themselves in samite, a heavy silk fabric interwoven with precious metallic threads. In *Morte D'Arthur,* the Lady of the Lake wears "white samite, mystic, wonderful" (30). "Robed in crimson samite" (*LE,* 430) with an embroidered or woven golden dragon writhing down its silken fabric, King Arthur presides over the last diamond tournament.[37] Given the duplicity of fashion, samite cannot measure status or respectability. Vivien also wears it to exhibit her physical charms:

> ... a robe
> Of samite without price, that more exprest
> Than hid her, clung about her lissome limbs
> In color like the satin-shining palm. (*MV*, 219–22).

At times the color of samite signifies moral fiber: the Holy Grail is "Clothed in white samite" (*HG*, 513) in Galahad's vision or shrouded in crimson samite in Lancelot's. Fashion marks Tennyson's moment—its appetite for change, its sense of time rushing on, and its concern with sorting out authentic people from deceivers.[38]

Prince Geraint of Devon, a newcomer to the Round Table, and Enid, his bride from the periphery, prove fashion's centrality in certifying membership in its circle.[39] They arrive in Camelot as celebrity newlyweds. In a flashback that is also a fashion alert, the reader learns how they met. Arriving late to observe a hunt, Geraint encounters Guinevere with her lady-in-waiting. His luxurious afternoon attire "in summer suit and silks of holiday" (*MG*, 174) meets Guinevere's approving eye. Then, during a chivalric mission to avenge a sexual assault on the queen's lady, Geraint discovers his bride-to-be and her mother in old but fine dresses, signaling Enid as a likely candidate for a makeover, her mother wearing "dim brocade" and her daughter "all in faded silk" (*MG*, 363; 366).

Geraint enters the lists of a tournament, first borrowing rusty arms from Enid's father, Earl Yniol, whose "suit of frayed magnificence" identifies him as a noble in need of a champion. But Geraint cannot enter without being pledged to a woman. Close at hand and lovely, Enid appears sent by God as the "one voice for me" (344) and "the one maid for me" (368). The proof of divinely sent manliness and a trophy wife come together in the description of the tournament field:

> Two forks are fixed into the meadow ground,
> And over these is placed a silver wand.
> And over that a golden sparrow-hawk,
> The prize of beauty for the fairest there. (*MG*, 482–85)

The marks of the tournament fixed into the ground, found also in the *Mabinogion*, recall the Greek meaning of trophy as a turning place on the battlefield marked with captured weapons.

With Enid as passport to the games, Geraint wins back her father's realm, including the family's elegant clothes. Tennyson sews together Yniol's realm with the language of tailoring. When the people learn of Yniol's restoration, they return plundered stuff, one of which is Enid's dream dress: "All branched and flowered with gold" (*MG,* 630). Enid's mother equates it with their "mended fortunes" (*MG,* 718). Glossing the dress with values of the fashion marketplace, she affirms: "Let never maiden think, however fair, / She is not fairer in new clothes than old" (*MG,* 721–22). Contemporary fashion journalists could not have said it better.

Sumptuary practices that encode national issues prevent Enid from wearing her reclaimed dress. In the *Mabinogion* and Tennyson's adaptation, the party in power clothes the maiden.[40] Enid's dress and dressing fit into common nationalistic practice, in this significant context of a nation-making epic erasing Enid's Celtic origins. Enid's concerns about dressing confirm the fashion spectacle as part of nationalized cultural fetishism. Here is self-abnegating Enid, who shops, cooks, and serves everyone else, wishing for a nice dress for herself.[41] So she should. In presenting a girl from a shabby realm to Camelot society, it is Geraint's concern as well. However, the gilded dress is the wrong dress from the wrong place put on her by the wrong person. Enid's mother wants her stamp on Enid's robing, imagining her daughter entering Arthur's court "Clothed with my gift" (*MG,* 753). But Geraint explains that Guinevere claims her right to enrobe his wife:

> . . . and the Queen herself
> Grateful to Prince Geraint for service done,
> Loved her, and often with her own white hands
> Array'd and deck'd her, as the loveliest,
> Next after her own self, in all the court. (*MG,* 5–19)

Guinevere participates in Enid's displays of cultural fetishism. Fashion sense underpins Geraint and Enid's relationship, expressing both love and power. He enjoys clothing her each day "[i]n crimsons and in purples and in gems" while she enjoys displaying herself to him "[i]n some fresh splendour" (*MG,* 5; 8). Some reviewers disapproved. *Blackwood's* reviewer sniffed, "We should humbly beg the Laureate for the future to tell us more of the maiden and less of her clothes—more of her wedding . . . and less of the trousseau."[42] Denigrating fashion's impact, the writer cannot see Enid's story as about a girl from a broken-down castle transformed into a Camelot lady by means of new clothes.[43]

Enid's dresses and gems both embrace and decry political market values.

Touched by the queen, her dresses stir suspicion that Enid has caught a court blight. Hearing rumors of Guinevere's perfidy, Geraint interprets his wife's new clothing as deceptive, their fashion knowledge covering loose moral undergarments. He forces Enid to clad herself in her faded silk and sulks back to his realm to prove his manliness and his wife's chastity. His retreat signifies his effort to return to a pre-fashionable, hierarchically transparent society. Dreading Fashion's sway, the *Idylls* reflect appreciation for fashion's power but apprehension about people becoming mass-produced. In that arena, fetishized diamonds play gendered games for a dead man.

Nine Diamonds for Public Use

When Gawain delivers Lancelot's ninth and largest trophy diamond to a reluctant Elaine, he urges her to take it without question. After all, "A diamond is a diamond" (*LE*, 691). Gawain cynically affirms that anyone should grab diamond for what it demonstrably is: a glittering fortune. What more appropriate fetish object for Camelot's fashionable economy? Used as trophies in tournaments, diamonds represent what the most masculine man pledges to a woman as a sign of his virility. To "infuse [his epic] with the spirit of modern thought," the poet enlarged to nine tournaments the one he found in Malory.[44]

Extending fashion's precincts to games for a dead man, the poet fabricated an elaborate myth of origin for diamond tournaments. Arthur comes upon a diamond crown as if guided by an invisible hand:

> For Arthur, long before they crowned him King,
> Roving the trackless realms of Lyonnesse,
> Had found a glen, gray boulder and black tarn.
> . . . .
> For here two brothers, one a king, had met
> And fought together; but their names were lost;
> And each had slain his brother at a blow;
> . . . .
> And he, that once was king, had on a crown
> Of diamonds, one in front, and four aside.
> And Arthur came, and labouring up the pass,
> All in a misty moonshine, unawares
> Had trodden that crowned skeleton, and the skull
> Brake from the nape, and from the skull the crown

> Rolled into light, and turning on its rims
> Fled like a glittering rivulet to the tarn:
> And down the shingly scaur he plunged, and caught,
> And set it on his head, and in his heart
> Heard murmurs, "Lo, thou likewise shalt be King." (*LE,* 34–55)

Attesting to the new realm's anonymity, the dead king remains nameless.

Arthur's glittering crown emanates from the Victorian diamond empire. Medieval crowns, which have been melted down with only illustrations to serve as evidence, are not diamond-encrusted; many have nary a diamond on them. Some were gold without gems; some were set with pearls, emeralds, rubies, and other stones. The last Anglo-Saxon king, Harold II, perches on the eleventh-century Bayeux Tapestry, wearing a trefoil gold crown; jewels in William the Conqueror's gold crowns are typically set in a simple row, some within a rosette, with pearls, emeralds, and other colored stones. In Victoria's coronation crown, diamonds set off colored stones. But midway in her reign a small, all-diamond crown featured large round diamonds in four fleurs-de-lys around its base (see plate 8).[45] The 1870 crown was so identified with her that it eventually lay on her coffin. Designed at the very moment of the South African diamond rush, the crown affirms a connection between the empire of diamonds and the British Empire.

The Lyonnesse diamond crown's gory provenance emerges as a parable about the wages of empire. The macabre scene of the tumbling skull with Arthur chasing it allegorizes royal desire. Arthur scrambles after the glittering rivulet—diamonds turned into water—its hypnotizing light blinding him to the crown's history. His diamond bewitchment signifies overreaching ambition. The moment is fraught with cultural baggage about patriarchal constructions of authority and concepts of heroism, all associated with death. Only Guinevere recognizes their lugubrious provenance: "from the skeleton of a brother-slayer." (*LT,* 47).

Arthur crowns himself, having internalized a voice that Jacques Lacan identified as the Law of the Father.[46] That voice murmurs a prophecy and blessing that comes from Arthur's desires, murmuring from "his heart." Providential discovery apparently frees the stones from a taint of imperialist looting or of crass commodity markets. "Unaware," Arthur stumbles on them, as if his aspirations do not require ambition, as if the diamond crown arrives sanctified for his use. Arthur overestimates his power to reframe the diamonds' murderous origins:

> Thereafter, when a King, he had the gems
> Plucked from the crown, and showed them to his knights,
> Saying, "These jewels, whereupon I chanced
> Divinely, are the kingdom's, not the King's
> For public use: henceforward let there be,
> Once every year, a joust for one of these:
> For so by nine year's proof we needs must learn
> Which is our mightiest, and ourselves shall grow
> In use of arms and manhood. (*LE,* 56–64)

In breaking up the singular crown indicative of monarchy, Arthur builds a model of "public use": dispersed power plucked from the diamond ground of kingliness and deeded to power achieved not by birth but through competition. Further, the dispersal of mightiness recasts ancient notions of majesty to national influence, a change that typifies Queen Victoria's realm. Moreover, given the anomalous power of a queen, the nine diamonds reflect and symbolize the power of the woman to bear children in a nine-month span, appropriated as symbols of manhood. Fortuitously, from 1840 to 1857, the Queen bore nine live children.

In the overdetermined number nine, the diamonds connect Arthur to his own mystical birth at the final and greatest of nine waves and to his birthright in Excalibur, his bejeweled arms. In an epic expansion of the nine months for human gestation, echoing the nine mighty waves, Arthur's sword was engendered by the Lady of the Lake during "nine mystic years" ("Morte d'Arthur," 104).[47] Nine mystic years along with nine mighty waves produce arms and the man, transferred from time and space. Such numerology confounds human biology with dynastic formations, culminating in a diamond symbolism that comprehends incommensurate models for social structures—a Victorian effort to understand itself.

In ascribing divine provenance to the diamonds, Arthur fetishizes them in the anthropological sense of attributing supernatural powers to objects. As psychoanalytic fetishes, they enable male potency, celebrated in the tournaments. And as Marxist fetishes, the labor required for their fashioning is invisible in their manifestation.[48] Each diamond represents little pieces of sovereign power (like the nine royal progeny), conceived as divinely anointed. Arthur recasts what must have been a disaster for Lyonnesse to reframe the stones as trophies in a game where knights mangle each other to test national superiority.

Trophy diamonds constitute Arthur's birthright of "arms and manhood," a freighted allusion to the founding of a nation in Virgil's *Aeneid,* where Aeneas murders Turnus to confirm his own virility. Lancelot plays the game, pledging his trophies to her who is already someone else's trophy. In conceiving an additional myth of Camelot's organizing principles, "Lancelot and Elaine" elucidates Tennyson's parable as if the realm were ordained by a magically numbered nine-diamond crown.

Crystalizing earlier meanings of Arthur's heritage in waves and sword, the nine tournaments culminate in the final tournament, for "the central diamond and the last and largest" in "Lancelot and Elaine" (*LE,* 73–74), the only diamond tournament described in the poem. Barbara Johnson's discussion of visuality and the Thing in Freud and Lacan clarifies the national stakes in Arthur's tournaments and suggests the fuel for their repetitive urgency: "If the phallus is the salient thing that organizes desire, the Thing is what is lost and has thereby created the feeling of lack. It also organizes desire, but around something missing: the 'navel of the dream,' Freud called it; the inaccessible woman in courtly love, says Lacan."[49] Diamond and woman reveal that the circuit of desire cannot be closed; rather the woman, Lacan's "hole in the real," describes the trophy woman, an eidolon fashioned from male desire.[50] The central Lyonnesse diamond sucks up life-giving elements. With what may be his last living gasps, Lancelot belatedly and only fleetingly rejects the chivalric system that has suffocated him: "Diamond me no diamonds / for God's sake a little air" (*LE,* 502–3). The largest diamond acts as a black hole in the real, negating tournaments as models for nation-shaping manhood; indeed, diamonds invoke the dead man whose ghostly presence cannot be vanquished in the circle of desire: that dead Lyonnesse king.

Lyonnesse again. The setting infects the poem. A mythical kingdom, Lyonnesse, in the west of England bordering Cornwall, sank into the sea, a particularly apt representation of repressed material. Mighty consequences ensue from Arthur's finding the crown in Lyonnesse. In addition to Vivien's origins, Lyonnesse is the birthplace of Tristram, whose adulterous adventures and ax murder appear in "The Last Tournament." Tristram's love for Queen Isolt parallels Lancelot's for Guinevere, a connection suggested by Dagonet, the Fool in "The Last Tournament," when he refuses to dance to Tristram's music because his adultery makes "broken music" with his bride and by extension with "Arthur's music too" (*LT,* 266). Tristram and Isolt's adultery in Lyonnesse is vividly rendered, more so than any meeting between Lancelot and Guinevere, bringing together the physicality of sex—"just as the lips had touch'd" (*LT,*

746)—and slaughter—"'Mark's way,' said Mark, and clove him through the brain" (*LT,* 748). Tristram's severed skull recalls the feuding Lyonnesse brothers of the diamond crown.

Modred, Arthur's slayer, also hails from Lyonnesse, the setting for their final battle. The villain is also the hero's son, part of a story about the "blameless king" seducing his own sister, Margause, wife of King Lot. To be fair, Arthur did not know she was his sister, but he knew she was married. Modred was the child of adulterous, incestuous mating. Tennyson's Arthur hears the imputation that Modred is one of his clan and denies it, significant because the poet allows a whiff of Arthur's immorality to linger in Lyonnesse air.[51] Nine diamonds represent those traces of Arthur's adultery at the very setting of his finding the crown, a sign that the tournaments confirm in awarding the trophy diamonds to Lancelot, chief knight and adulterer. Both mythical and submerged, Lyonnesse is lost to time and space yet saturated with wrongdoing. The disappeared kingdom endows a grim legacy to the newly forming realm where the king intends to instill humanistic values in tribal peoples, to end cycles of reciprocal violence, and to unite all under his banner. The repressed returns in another family slaughter. Nine bloody diamonds triumph over efforts to repurpose them.

Diamond as fetish represents *all* the terms of Camelot's organization: it represents what the flawed Guinevere also represents. Arthur blames the queen for the fall of Camelot, but she alone clearly articulates the system's contribution to her wrongdoing. Her interpretation of Camelot's sexual politics resembles Helen's perception of the Greek war economy:

"He cares not for me . . .
. . . .
Rapt in this fancy of his Table Round,
And swearing men to vows impossible,
To make them like himself. . . ." (*LE,* 126; 129–31)

Guinevere recognizes her role as a trophy for eroticized, narcissistic games among men. In her revulsion at the system that has cast her as a sparkling mineral, she throws all nine diamonds into the river.

Guinevere flings the diamonds in a fit of jealousy of a young, beautiful, and virginal girl, whose arms and neck are not yet "haggard" (*LE,* 1220). Aging Guinevere rages against being supplanted as a trophy, despite resenting that position. She recognizes diamonds as trophies of complicity in corporatized games for a dead man. And although she misinterprets Lancelot's wistful loyalty to her, she is not wrong about the pattern of serial trophy women. Once Guinevere breaks her connection to the diamonds, she has no place in the homosocial economy of the Round Table. Tossing over representational authority, she retreats from the sexual arrangements that color the poem.[52]

Neither does Lancelot's contrition purify the realm. When the wounded knight contrasts his trophies with the oxygen essence of life itself, he supports the system that has bound him by oath. Whatever recognition Lancelot arrives at in his disgust for diamonds and the tournaments that awarded them fails to banish his fantasies about a woman's potential salvific power. For Guinevere, he substitutes a young, isolated, overprotected, and virginal "Elaine, the fair, Elaine the loveable / Elaine, the lily maid of Astolat" (*LE,* 1–2). As the *Idyll*'s trophy-in-training, she exists primarily in relation to her devotion to Lancelot. Adoring him without knowing his name, she guards his shield and spends her days sewing an elaborate cover for it while he goes off to "tilt for the great diamond in the diamond jousts" (*LE,* 30–31). Lancelot in disguise wears Elaine's favor, a red sleeve embroidered with pearls, but he must present the final diamond to Guinevere.[53] Nearly aware of his fealty to a deadly system, the knight cannot imagine an exit strategy but rather fantasizes that this young, pearly virgin rather than his aging, married diamond one might have made a difference:

> And peradventure had he seen her first
> She might have made this and that other world
> Another world for the sick man; but now
> The shackles of an old love straitened him, (*LE,* 867–70)

Lancelot voices a familiar fantasy that a younger woman will restore a jaded, aging executive. It is the fantasy of the fashion system where new objects—dresses and persons—are better than old ones. The March of Time eventually must displace an older trophy. In Camelot, being a trophy and being dead unite.

Elaine's body floats down the river to Camelot, crossing the diamonds in the river and connecting diamonds and women with death and depersonalization. This diamond burial in conjunction with Elaine's funereal journey does not resolve the ideological constructs of the new social order but rather marks a stage in its dissolution. Enmeshed in their palace games, Camelot society is incapable of regarding the young, dead beauty now merged with the diamonds as symptomatic of their social disease. Society does not know her name. Nine trophy diamonds empty out the real.

The Capital World of *Little Dorrit*

Another Arthur, Arthur Clennam in *Little Dorrit,* arrives at a similarly ambiguous fate as his namesake owing to a comparable political and economic system that produced him. Though in other ways an anti-Arthur, Clennam, like the king, attempts to establish an ethically responsible organization in his partnership with Daniel Doyce, an inventor who cannot negotiate the Circumlocution Office, center of obfuscating bureaucracy. Like King Arthur as well, Arthur Clennam's birth is shrouded in secrecy; he does not know that he does not know his real mother. Dickens often calls him a Nobody as an expression of psychic emptiness. He himself feels as if he is nothing in the mighty economic world, and, in confirmation, he is thrown into the Marshalsea Prison for debt.

Set in London, *Little Dorrit* tackles crises endemic to the capitalist system and its concomitant consumerism. That system attenuates characters to the extent that they seem to act automatically, serving the Society that imprisons them. In seeking a corrective to the idea that making money comes first in social values, the plot produces instead a figure to bear the blame.[54] Though at least as early as Adam Smith, man's attempt at augmenting his income—not enlarging his humane sympathy—was admired as self-improvement. Institutions established to support fiscal ambitions, nefarious schemes, and government complicity mask direct agency and responsibility for deeds.[55] In his preface, Dickens alluded to the fiscal events that inspired him, naming general "enterprises," not persons: "I would hint that it originated after the Railroad-share epoch, in the times of a certain Irish bank, and of one or two other equally laudable enterprises."[56] Reported on regularly, deplored, forgotten, displaced by another fiscal scandal, such corruption at the heart of an economic system—that "capital world," as Henry Gowan, a feckless hanger-on, describes it—is textually resolved with the suicide of Mr. Merdle, a diseased person whose inner life remains mysterious.

The novel connects business enterprise with marriage in a similar way the *Idylls* connected nation-building with heterosexual partnerships, a displacement that allows illumination without action. In his interview with Mrs. Gowan at Hampton Court, a location that makes fiscal and governmental congruence explicit, "Clennam learned for the first time what little pivots this great world goes round upon" (261). The novel sets its characters in a society built on a rotating capitalist foundation and exposes the nooks and dungeons imprisoning characters, from corporate entities, to lords of government, to convicts in debtor's prison containing failures of the money system.[57] The capital world is a world of delusion, based on falsified numbers, rumor, and display; the novel represents varied consequences of corporate entities masquerading as people, including a representation of a trophy wife.[58]

Mr. Merdle and his trophy wife perch atop the capitalist pedestal. Though the king and queen of capitalism have moved out of the plot's center, this decentering enables some sort of positive resolution for the novel's two main characters. Both self-effacing and kind, Amy Dorrit and Arthur Clennam are drawn together, having similarly deprived childhoods and narcissistic parents who depend in different ways on a global consumer economy. Arthur's father leaves behind a disgraceful legacy from his business in China, where he dies.[59] Amy's father's narcissism prevents him from comprehending the economic system that serially raises and crushes him. He embodies economic cycles of capitalism. Resistant to commodified depersonalization, Amy and Arthur exit clutching each other's hands. The final scene shows them as virtuous flotsam and jetsam in the pivoting world, counterparts to an exploitative financier and his unfeeling wife.

Mrs. Merdle personifies a modern businessman's trophy, a Victorian capitalist Helen. Mr. Merdle acquires her after he has accumulated the heroic trappings of a captain of capital expansion. Sham investments entice those who buy into speculative ventures, making themselves sitting ducks for chicanery. Dickens denounces the new corporate trophy, presenting Society that prefers such signs — imitations, eidolons, phantoms made of air — over whatever animates, vivifies, and responds. Society, a judgmental gatekeeper allowing entry into London's Camelot, diffuses identity more than King Arthur's court. Mrs. Merdle joins the company of other trophy wives in Dickens: diamond-bedecked Edith Dombey of *Dombey and Son* and Lady Dedlock of *Bleak House,* whose name and history captures fashion's constant appetite for celebrity in a vicious metropole. Memorialized in Divinities of Albion, or Galaxy Gallery of British Beauty, Lady Dedlock, like Edith Dombey but more pitiably and secretly, offers herself independent of her volition to be hung on walls as poster girl for a new social order. A Divinity of Albion resembles a trophy woman under a national name, her sacred role to celebrate the fashion system's patriotic ability to hide the past. Mrs. Merdle, more opportunistic and stereotyped than Dickens's two other British Beauties, deploys fashion sense as the façade of fictitious capital, of fraud made possible by stock issues, aptly termed derivatives, and paper money.[60] She is more mechanical than the other two, whose capacity for shame and suffering humanizes them.

Merdle's trophy first appears on the scene as an adornment, thereafter anatomized in fetishized body parts. Thrusting forth her bejeweled hand, she makes a theatrical entrance: "The curtain shook next moment, and a lady, raising it with a heavily ringed hand, dropped it behind her as she entered" (233). The parlor curtain furnishes the stage set for the trophy wife, whose personal coldness represents both the jewels for which her body serves as mannequin and the death associated with the commodity culture she embodies. Dickens locates cultural fetishism in a woman crafted as an object for display: "The lady was not young and fresh from the hand of Nature, but was young and fresh from the hand of her maid. She had large unfeeling handsome eyes, and dark unfeeling handsome hair, and a broad unfeeling handsome bosom, and was made the most of in every particular" (233). Her maid manufactures the trophy according to Society's fashion dictates, occluding Merdle's financial diseases that produced her. Mr. Merdle suffers from some unnamed inner rot that gemstones hide: "There was no shadow of Mr. Merdle's complaint on the bosom now displaying precious stones in rivalry with many similar superb jewel-stands" (212). Mrs. Merdle is a fitting jewel-stand for the flamboyant, dehumanizing Society that her (second) husband lords over as king of its epicenter: "Mr. Merdle was immensely rich; a man of prodigious enterprise; a Midas without the ears, who turned all he touched to gold. He was in everything good, from banking to building. He was in Parliament, of course. He was in the City, necessarily. He was Chairman of this, Trustee of that, President of the other" (241). Disseminated, like the capital world he represents, he is too good to be true.

With needs of completion resembling King Arthur's, Mr. Merdle requires a trophy wife. Punning on the emerging economic system of which Mr. Merdle is regent, Dickens describes Mrs. Merdle's valuable part as symbolic equivalent of the "capital world" that Mrs. Gowan's son Henry celebrated with the pun that Dickens plays upon: "It was not a bosom to repose upon, but it was a capital bosom to hang jewels upon. Mr. Merdle wanted something to hang jewels upon, and he bought it for the purpose. . . . The jewels showed to the richest advantage. The bosom moving in Society with the jewels displayed upon it, attracted general admiration. Society approving, Mr. Merdle was satisfied. He was the most disinterested of men,—did everything for Society, and got as little for himself, out of all his gain and care, as a man might" (241). Displays of valuables constitute King Arthur's and Mr. Merdle's form of manifesting power, while they themselves recede to a background. They maintain a disinterested distance, have their hearts in their ambitions, yet stamp their followers with their images. They produce a market for counterfeit coins of their realms. Not for themselves do they work their work. Like King Arthur presenting the diamonds from the anonymous king, Merdle presents the bejeweled bosom to Society, classing it proudly yet defensively with his other signifying stuff: "Who does more for Society than I do? Do you see these premises, Mrs. Merdle? Do you see this furniture, Mrs. Merdle? Do you look in the glass and see yourself, Mrs. Merdle? Do you know the cost of all this, and who it's all provided for? And yet will you tell me that I oughtn't to go into Society? I, who shower money upon it in this way? I, who might be almost said—to—to—to harness myself to a watering-cart of money, and go about, saturating Society, every day of my life?" (332). Merdle's ambition to build an empire resembles King Arthur's though in economic dress. The capitalist represents himself as a slave to fashion. Dickens's satiric tone masks the truth of Merdle's self-characterization; he is as accurate in his sense of working for a system as King Arthur—and as unaware of the forces that have constructed him in that way. Mr. Merdle describes himself as a tethered mule that fertilizes this denatured fashionable Society, whereas Mrs. Merdle knows she is the fetish disavowing his mule-drawn cart.

The psychoanalytic fetish employs disavowal as a defense: I know but I don't know.[61] Mrs. Merdle exhibits that disavowed knowledge: "I know that you move in the whole Society of the country. And I believe I know (indeed, not to make any ridiculous pretense about it, I know I know) who sustains you in it, Mr. Merdle" (446). Such knowledge impels her actively to create the set upon which cultural fetishism performs an illusion as if without effort. Mrs. Merdle recognizes what ruffles the social façade: "'You ought to make yourself fit for it by being more *dégagé,* and less pre-occupied. There is a positive vulgarity in carrying your business affairs about with you as you do . . . instead of leaving them in the City, or wherever else they belong to,' said Mrs. Merdle. 'Or seeming to. Seeming would be quite enough: I ask no more'" (333). The Merdle marriage contract expresses their social contract: "You supply manner," Mr. Merdle explains, "I supply money" (447). Sparkling on the Bosom, Mr. Merdle's money enters Society cleaned up, though the sparklers are carbonized merde.[62]

Society resembles the nightmare hypocrisies of Tennyson's dark idylls where simulacra replace ideals. As in the Camelot of *The Last Tournament,* so in London Society. Mr. Merdle's business affairs exchange legitimacy for counterfeit—forgery, fraud, and embezzlement—fitting crimes in a Society characterized by cultural fetishism. Flaunted on the Bosom, jewels embody ostentatious sham, making the sick system (indicated by Mr. Merdle's undiagnosed bodily complaint) sparkle.

Sparkle, a typical description of diamonds above other less sparkly gems, spreads as contagion.[63] Leaders of the New Corporate Order grace salons of Society. In such an order, Mrs. Merdle's offspring properly occupies a position in the Circumlocution Office, where mere activity replaces action, where the stakes in capital's games are rendered not merely inefficient but cruel and arbitrary. This government functionary is not Merdle's biological son, as the knights and pages of the Round Table are not Arthur's. "Not so much a man as a swelled boy," Mrs. Merdle's son "had given so few signs of reason that a byeword went among his companions that his brain had been frozen up in a mighty frost which prevailed at Saint John, New Brunswick, at the period of his birth there, and had never thawed from that hour. Another byeword represented him as having in his infancy, through the negligence of a nurse, fallen out of a high window on his head, which had been heard by responsible witnesses to crack" (242). Frozen and cracked, the boy cannot be thawed or glued. A product of empire, like Tennyson's knights from everywhere, the boy enters the urban imperial center in London from the Canadian periphery. The swelled boy exposes the inner child of modern life. Like King Arthur's, his birth is the occasion of mythmaking. His surname, "Sparkler," signifies his symbolic role, for he emanates from Mrs. Merdle's necklace, his name troping the gems for which her capital bosom exists and of which he is a somatic extension.[64] That the gem is only named by its effect conforms to the atmosphere of anonymity, as if hard diamonds had left behind only their simulacrum, their sparkle.

Along with other ethically deficient young men, Sparkler plays useless games in government offices. Dickens deplores the corporate fetishism represented by Mrs. Sparkler Merdle and her son, yet with Victorian melodrama to resolve the plot, he punishes the capitalist criminal, leaving the capital world to spin on. *Little Dorrit* ends like the indeterminate future at the end of the *Idylls*. To consider Tennyson's poem in tandem with Dickens's novel reveals their mutual concern with a world that seems to be rushing to catastrophe. In endowing women with gems as talismanic signs of masculinity, diamonds signify developing gender exchanges in a capitalist imperial market that supplants human community with crystalized carbon, chemical cousin to the coal that fuels its industries. Their notorious hardness belies the social system they trope, where all that is solid melts into air.

6

Ivanhoe's Racialized Legacy to English Diamond Novels

> In a country beset with such worthies as Front-de-Boeuf, Malvoisin, and the rest, Isaac the Jew could neither have grown rich, nor lived to old age; and no Rebecca could either have acquired her delicacy, or preserved her honour.
>
> —Francis Jeffrey, 1820 review of *Ivanhoe*

English diamonds carry a heavy symbolic load in simultaneously signifying both a gendered arrangement whereby women represent men's wealth and a challenge to the very idea of England as Anglo-Saxon. To conceive of a nation as a unity defined by the common blood of its peoples, disallowed ethnicities that Victorians called "races" threaten fragile, fiercely defended national formations.[1] Perturbing efforts to represent a racially circumscribed national identity, Jews associated with diamonds disturb the concept of a racially coherent nation. Jewish identity inhering in diamonds pervades the English fictions discussed in this chapter as symptomatic of a national problem grown more acute as the nation begins to encompass a global empire constituted of many-hued peoples. The Jewish Other is a familiar figure that differentiates—and elevates—the English considered as a race. Jewish fingerprints adhere to the diamonds Jews own, steal, and sell, lending a disavowed touch to symbolic meanings of diamonds in English settings. Victorian novels in this chapter form a tight cluster about Jews and diamonds with their progenitor in Sir Walter Scott's *Ivanhoe: A Romance* (1819). In struggling with race consciousness, *Ivanhoe*, Scott's first historical romance with an English, not Scottish, setting, explicitly influences subsequent novels set in England that link Jews with diamonds. This chapter follows narrative pathways whereby the light of the diamond rarely appears without the shadow of the Jew.

Ivanhoe is concerned with the aftermath of the Norman Conquest, a time when England is murderously and racially divided: "A whole race of Saxon princes and nobles had been extirpated or disinherited."[2] Extirpation or disinheritance describes what happened to both Saxons and Jews with contrasting solutions. The nation imagined in *Ivanhoe* reconciles aristocratic Saxon natives with their Norman oppressors to produce a composite English identity. This resolution contains an irony rooted in the very notion of race, because indigenous Saxons and French Normans regarded each other as different races. However, both were Christian, whereas a third term, the Jew, could not be admitted into the English club.[3] Scott banishes the Jewish maiden whose sexual appeal threatens miscegenation to a developing national configuration.[4] Ian Duncan points out that Scott founded the generic tradition "in which romance represents an allegory of historical and cultural formation."[5] Often mistakenly regarded as based on authentic history, *Ivanhoe* tells about the creation of Englishness.[6] In agreement, Lisa Lampert-Weissig's later postcolonial analysis asserts not only that "English identity and the birth of England as a nation are undeniably central concerns" but also that those concerns emerge through an unacknowledged desire for the Other.[7] Michael Ragussis explains Scott's inclusion of Jewish characters in *Ivanhoe* as a response to "a profound crisis in nineteenth-century English national identity."[8] Imagining a nation emerging from the persecution of upper-class native Saxons mirrors the oppression of Isaac and Rebecca of York. Scott's allegory concludes with the departure from England of Isaac with Rebecca, his marriageable daughter. Their emigration apparently answers the Jewish Question by foreclosing their legacy to Englishness. Perhaps mindful that all Jews will be expelled from England in 1290, Scott sends his two Jewish characters to Spain, anachronistically ruled by the fifteenth-century last Muslim ruler, "Mohammed Boabdil, King of Grenada" (45:497), where for a high ransom they might live in harmony with the Muslims—at least until their expulsion by the Catholics from Spain following Boabdil's reign. Telescoping three centuries of outcast Jews bracketed Scott's characters within two Jewish expulsions: from England and then from Spain.

In the course of synthesizing a new English race against the Jewish outsider, Scott also attempted to rationalize the Jew's negative portrayal in Early Modern drama, drawing on two plays that portrayed crassly materialistic Jewish merchants with enticing Jewish daughters.[9] Those paired characters appear in Christopher Marlowe's *The Jew of Malta* (c. 1589) and William Shakespeare's *The Merchant of Venice* (c. 1596–98), when economic activities associated with Jews occurred at a moment of redefining the economic basis of the nation.[10] Scott alluded to both plays in chapter epigraphs in *Ivanhoe*. He frequently quoted Shakespeare and was intimately familiar with Marlowe's play, having edited it as part of a collection, *The Ancient British Drama,* published in 1810 in London. Scott's novel aimed to deepen understanding of the Jewish character portrayed in the plays, not by denying that it was contemptible but by analyzing its formation.[11] The Jew, he explained, repels because of centuries of atrocities that deformed the "race." Scott follows Enlightenment views of the plasticity of human character, in which Jewish traits were thought to be formed by centuries of Christian oppression.[12]

The Jewish Question gained urgency in the nineteenth century.[13] That question parallels the novel's racialized romance, whereby the Norman conqueror and the Saxon conquered are brought to truth and reconciliation. Scott points out that a "whole race of Saxon princes and nobles had been extirpated or disinherited" after the Norman Conquest (1:408). Michael Ragussis explains Scott's Jewish characters in *Ivanhoe* as a response to "a profound crisis in nineteenth-century English national identity."[14] That English identity crisis seems personal for Scott himself when he turned from his Scottish Waverley novels to his English romance.[15] The renowned Scottish author used Shylock's famous defense to find commonality between Jews and his own clannish, rude progenitors.[16] In an extraordinary comparison of Jews with his forebears—whoever "our ancestors" might be—his "Dedicatory Epistle" quotes Shylock's defense, also in his epigraph to chapter 5: "Our ancestors were not more distinct from us, surely, than Jews are from Christians; they had 'eyes, hands, organs, dimension, senses affections and passions;' were 'fed with the same food, hurt with the same weapons, subject to the same disease, warmed and cooled by the same winter and summer,' as ourselves" (44:496). "Our ancestors" belong to a separate nation from Jews, however common their human traits.

Scott posed his own Jewish Question when he changed his setting from the First to the Third Crusade two centuries later when Richard I, known as Richard Coeur-de-Lion, returned to England in 1194, a return that made his York Jewish characters nearly incredible. The date required Scott to finesse two massacres of Jews, one at Richard's Coronation in 1189 and the other at York Castle in 1190. Because many richly clad Jews waiting to honor their new king after the coronation were murdered, Richard decreed before leaving for the Holy Land that Jews in his realm should be left alone. Less than a year later, the York Massacre proved such edicts unenforceable.[17] The Massacre effectively decimated the York Jews, in the process erasing the enormous Norman and Saxon indebtedness to them, while their properties reverted to the king. In the face of evidence about the Massacre that Scott read about in Sharon Turner's *History of England during the Middle Ages,* acknowledged in his Dedicatory Epistle, he created a Jewish merchant and moneylender, settling him in the very place of the Massacre. Prosperous Isaac of York could hardly have existed in 1194.

Isaac's abject fear of both Saxon and Norman anti-Semitism results not from recent massacres but to treatment of Jews throughout history. His obsequiousness and miserly materialism evolved over centuries of abuse, but it remains "unmanly" and despicable. He was slender and tall, though habitually stooped from groveling: "His features . . . would have been considered handsome, had they not been the marks of a physiognomy peculiar to a race, which, during those dark ages, was alike detested by the credulous and prejudiced vulgar, and persecuted by the greedy and rapacious nobility" (5:69). Extermination never far from his consciousness, Isaac falls to his knees in an "extremity of terror" when he fears "the rack, saws, harrows, and axes of iron." He displaces English torture and massacres onto the biblical treatment of "the men of Rabbah, and of the cities of the children of Ammon!" (6:82). The novel portrays the Jewish merchant both as an abject prey to Christians and as a patriarch attired in Oriental splendor rivaling the Three Kings.

Isaac's materialism derives from his racial inheritance, but that same pedigree breeds Rebecca's generosity. Liberal with money, she also volunteers her racially acquired medical skills—explicitly traced back to the Hebrew Miriam—and saves Ivanhoe's life. Not a wizened crone, the healer is inconveniently beautiful and virtuous. Norman Templar, Brian de Bois Guilbert, attempts to rape her, but when she threatens to leap from the Torquilstone castle tower, he offers to abandon rank and privilege to escape with her to Palestine. Lampert-Weissig believes that Rachel's threat alludes to the York Jews who killed their wives and children by tossing them from Clifford Tower of York Castle where they had fled for safety; then the men committed mass suicide, aided by their rabbi.[18] Provocatively alluding to the Massacre, Scott sexualizes it as an attempted rape, but then Brian, overcome by Rebecca's beauty and character, wants to break his vows of celibacy and abandon his career, all for her. In this scene, Rachel embodies the Jewish Question as one villain wants to solve it. At Scott's conclusion, Rebecca survives a witch trial to gain a definitive place in the novel's climax, where she leaves behind a trace of the

Jew embedded in the new English identity. Massacres live on symbolically in Isaac and Rebecca of York, first as memorials, then as minerals.

A Gift of Immense Value

When Rebecca offers the lustful Templar, Brian de Bois Guilbert, pearl and diamond jewelry as ransom, the bandit rejects them, conventionally comparing diamonds unfavorably to Rebecca's eyes: "Fair flower of Palestine . . . these pearls are orient, but they yield in whiteness to your teeth; the diamonds are brilliant, but they cannot match your eyes" (24:254). Scott had earlier established diamonds as a figure for his Jewess's body. He confirmed his diamond symbolism when Isaac and Rebecca appear in Oriental splendor at a tournament at Ashby convened by Prince John, where they pay tribute to the tyrannical prince, who is "even then in the act of negotiating a large loan from the Jews of York to be secured upon certain jewels and lands" (7:95). Amid those business dealings, Isaac, whose immense wealth is hidden in an underground crypt, flaunts his daughter to the eyes of his royal customer. Prince John's licentious gaze rests on Rebecca, "the very bride of the Canticles" (7:98). Business between Jewish Isaac of York and Norman John, also of York, is facilitated by John's attraction to Isaac's "terrified" daughter, "now hanging on her father's arm" (7:94):

> Her form was exquisitely symmetrical, and was shown to advantage by a sort of Eastern Dress, which she wore according to the fashion of the females of her nation. Her turban of yellow silk suited well with the darkness of her complexion.[19] The brilliancy of her eyes, the superb arch of her eyebrows, her well-formed aquiline nose, her teeth as white as pearl, and the profusion of her sable tresses, which each arranged in its own little spiral of twisted curls, fell down upon as much of a lovely neck and bosom as a simarre [Oriental robe] of the richest Persian silk, exhibiting flowers of their natural colours embossed upon a purple ground, permitted to be visible. . . . It is true that of the golden and pearl-studded clasps, which closed her vest from the throat to the waist, the three uppermost were left unfastened on account of the heat, which something enlarged the prospect to which we allude. A diamond necklace, with pendants of inestimable value, were by this means also made more conspicuous. (7:97–98)

There she glows in silk and diamonds, "heat" exposing the diamond necklace on her warm bosom, a location that charges Rebecca's diamonds with sexualized fervor.[20] Her fashion differentiates her as a female "of her nation." Directly bearing on their symbolic value, the diamonds as part of Rebecca's national attire sublimate the murder of Jews. Lampert-Weissig regards the tournament scene as alluding to the Jewish massacre at King Richard's coronation.[21]

At the end of the novel, Rebecca's diamonds as a sign of her body heat become also her legacy to Englishness. After Rowena's marriage to Ivanhoe at the very place of the York Massacre in "the most august of temples, the noble Minster of York" (44:495), Rebecca approaches the bride, insisting that Rowena remove her wedding veil, enabling the two beauties to face each other directly. Rebecca extends her arms, saying, "Accept this casket; startle not at its contents," as she proffers a "small silver-chased casket," which contains "a . . . necklace, with ear-jewels, of diamonds, which were obviously of immense value" (44:498). Rebecca has given jewels and money throughout *Ivanhoe* as both ransom and repayment of favors, but her final gift appears unforced, gratuitous, and symbolic. Her diamond treasure, charged with Jewish sexuality and death, emerges from the Ashby tournament and Torquilstone tower, scenes that alluded to the York Massacre. This culminating diamond exchange, no mere marriage plot ending, offers a climax to the novel's racial allegory by sublimating the Jewess's sexual body into gems.

Sublimation into diamonds transforms a forbidden attraction to Jews. A psychoanalytic defense, sublimation was inadequately theorized by Freud as a transformation of sexual drive into creativity and recently has been retheorized.[22] According to Giuseppe Civitarese, sublimated energy remains within the object. The name of that defense gains resonance by recollecting the chemical process used to purify a base metal, found in alchemy, in actual mineral purifications, and in the metaphor "the sublime." Scott purifies (sublimes) savage massacres of Jews into a gem that has been taken as a sublime symbol—as in Hopkins's immortal diamond discussed in the introduction. The transformation occurring in the *Ivanhoe* diamonds preserves the Jewish and sexualized substrate.[23] The Jewess survives, sublimated in her diamonds. Scott's Rebecca transmutes bloody, atrocious history into an irresistibly beautiful, virtuous, and jewel-owning Jewess; then the diamonds sublimate what she signifies into a treasure. By bedazzling all eyes, the gems thereby sublime their provenance in the extirpation that lives in locating Isaac and Rebecca in York. They also connect the Jewess to the Woman Question, idealized as a Jewess on a pedestal.[24] This creative alchemy, this subliming, achieves its climax at the end of *Ivanhoe,* when Scott draws on Early Modern plays to repair calumny upon Jewish daughters and fathers.

By drawing a parallel between Rebecca's silver casket and the silver container in *The Merchant of Venice* that is inscribed "Who chooseth me shall get as much as he deserves" (act 2, scene 7, line 7), Ragussis believes that Ivanhoe deserves the high-born, bland maiden.[25] There are no diamonds in Shakespeare's silver casket, but Christopher Marlowe's *The Jew of Malta* provides a Jew with a diamond daughter, enlarging the correlation between Jewish daughters and diamonds. Barabas, the Jewish governor of Malta, describes his daughter as an erotic diamond when he entices her Christian suitor (whose father had stripped the Jew of great wealth) to his death:

> Lodowick: Well, Barabas, canst help me to a diamond?
> Bar. O, sir, your father had my diamonds.
> Yet I have one left that will serve your turn. . . .
> Lod. What sparkle does it give without a foil?
> Bar. The diamond that I talk of ne'er was foiled. . . .
> Lod. How shows it by night?
> Bar. Outshines Cynthia's rays;
> You'll like it better far o'nights than days. (act 2, scene 3, lines 49–64)

By boasting that his diamond daughter delivers unearthly sexual delights, Barabas attests that no false props, such as foil backs, falsify her attractions.

Abigail, dark sister to Scott's chaste yet sensuous Jewish daughter, clarifies the family dynamics informing the diamond scene in *Ivanhoe*. That both Jessica and Abigail abandon their father and their religion, but Rebecca and her father leave together to remain Jewish, intensifies the diamond gift. Rebecca's gift sublimates the mutual desire of Rebecca and Wilfred that otherwise threatens to mongrelize the newly formed English race.[26] Wilfred sees Rebecca in the diamonds bedecking his handsome wife with a sublimated pleasure that enables him to relinquish Rebecca yet have her too, and the text comes close to admitting as much: "Yet it would be inquiring too curiously to ask whether the recollection of Rebecca's beauty and magnanimity did not recur to his mind more frequently than the fair descendant of Alfred [Rowena] might altogether have approved" (44:432). Ivanhoe rues his sacrifice to nation building; nonetheless, the diamonds provide some recompense.

Resisting readers wanted a fleshlier satisfaction, objecting to Scott's sending Rebecca off to permanent chastity as a nurse in Andalusia. Ten years after the initial publication, the author defended his choice, admitting that "the fair Jewess found so much favour in the eyes of some fair readers" who wondered why "he had not assigned the hand of Wilfred to Rebecca, rather than the less interesting Rowena" (Introduction, 14). Reminding women readers about the medieval prejudice against such a union, he did not allow that an equivalent marriage would unlikely be an occasion for rejoicing in his own times. The ardent controversy remained twenty years later when, in 1850, William Thackeray, writing a parodic sequel, *Rebecca and Rowena*, under the pseudonym of Mr. M. A. Titmarsh, fell in with readers' disappointment in Rowena: "that vapid, flaxen-headed creature . . . unworthy of her place as a heroine, . . . a frigid piece of propriety[,] . . . an icy, faultless, prim, niminy-piminy" creature who should have "gone off to a convent."[27] Nevertheless, Thackeray could only wed Rebecca to Ivanhoe by converting her to Christianity.

Neither did Scott content himself with a defense based on racialized marriage conventions alone. A further ethical reason with a Protestant cast compelled a spiritual renunciation. It is never seemly, Scott intoned, to reward virtue with "temporary prosperity" or with "the gratification of our passions, or attainment of our wishes." "Sacrifice" of passion to "high-minded discharge of duty" brings rewards of a higher nature (Introduction, 14). Wilfred must find his reward on earth and beyond it by closing his eyes and thinking of Englishness.

In his turn to disapproval of wholehearted bodily gratification and passionate love, where denial is cast as virtue, Scott evokes a stereotype of the sensual Jewess with her diamond attribute—like the Jew of Malta's boast about his daughter. A Calvinist-inflected rejection of sexual pleasure as indulgence charges the gift scene with religious and reproductive force. Saxon and Norman can merge their races and their language into a powerful whole, but such amalgamation can accommodate curly sable hair, warm bosoms, formidable intelligence, and cadences of an Oriental tongue, not to say considerable wealth, only when sublimated into diamonds. Rowena appreciates that indebtedness when she hesitates to take the gift.

Adding to the complexity of the scene, the diamonds enter a gift economy that is not essentially purer than commodity exchange but replaces the money market with a personal relation, implying reciprocity.[28] As a gift, the diamonds circumvent an economy that might rank humans on a scale with commodities, projecting those materialist values on to merchant Jews like Barabas who figured daughters and ducats with the same calculus.

Gems and gender, race and sex, frame the gift scene. What is more, a gift from a woman to a woman intensifies the diamond exchange as signifying a moment that anthropologist Marilyn Strathern would recognize as "symbolic behavior."[29] The mother of what will contribute to a consolidated English race ritually accepts a sign of the Jew—a diamond admixture—to otherwise pure Saxon progeny. Exchanged the "second morning" after Rowena and Wilfred's marriage and immediately before Isaac and Rebecca's departure, the gift identifies diamonds with church-authorized sexual congress.[30] This nuptial gift is fraught with finalities: the end of Rebecca and Wilfred's amorous potential and the end of the Jews' Englishness. Remaining in England, the gift unites marital and national identity. The diamond gift overflows finalities.

To perform its complex meanings, the text deconstructs the diamond gift's "obvious immense value." At first Rowena refuses: "'It is impossible,' she said, tendering back the casket. 'I dare not accept a gift of such consequence'" (44:498). The pun on consequence points beyond the gift's domestic implications to its national ones. Whereas Rowena refers to the diamonds' calculable value, the word includes awareness of being on the receiving end of an extraordinary wedding gift. Given the novel's nation-building subject, the consequence of accepting the diamonds signifies that the new-formed English race is marked by the Jew.

For her part, Rebecca's plea for Rowena to accept the diamonds includes her own stake in the gift exchange. Minimizing the gift's importance, she urges Rowena to take them, not because of their "obvious immense value" but because of their lack of it. For the Anglo-Saxons, "power, rank, command" ensures the enactment of "their slightest wish," with or without jewels. Diamonds permit nothing of consequence to earn Jews a shred of political power, and so Rebecca dismisses the diamonds as "toys": "To you, therefore," she concludes, "the gift is of little value; and to me, what I part with is of much less" (44:498–99). Diamonds—rhetorically reduced to a bagatelle—thus slip into the imaginary as a consequential Jewish legacy to Englishness. Thus, the Jewess's diamonds emerge from this last scene with biopolitical value. Their sublimated power contains Wilfred's barely suppressed passion, dangerous for Protestant virtue and Christian nation-making. This diamond offering—not pearls, not rubies, not emeralds—marks it as Jewish. Leaving England, Isaac and Rebecca endow the diamond gift with their own "immense value." Sublimating the Jewish Question into diamonds in the context of the British racial crisis, *Ivanhoe* poses unresolvable questions of ethnic exclusivity in British national identity. Rowena and Wilfred's progeny may seem to bear assured pedigrees in the new English nation, as will the amalgamation of Saxon and Norman in the English language, but around Rowena's neck and on her ears, she bears the sublimated sign of the Jew.[31]

Though diamonds in English novels influenced by Scott may seem merely fashionable adornments as evidence of high family standing, they bear the Jew's mark. The diamond dealers that people the novels might seem realistic descriptions of Hatton Garden's business denizens, but their diamonds also bear symbolic as well as actual Jewish fingerprints. Rebecca's diamonds leave their trace in Victorian diamond novels that present Jewish ethnicity in the context of uncertainties about national identity. Consequences of the Jewess's diamond gift persist in English diamond novels that embed Scott's concerns about racial purity in their very core.

The Pivot of Trollope's English World

Diamonds and Jews provide the pivot on which the world of *The Eustace Diamonds* turns. Those diamonds are indebted to *Ivanhoe,* a novel Trollope rated a close second to *Pride and Prejudice* as the greatest in the English language.[32] At one moment in his deeply intertextual novel, Trollope alludes to Saxon Ivanhoe's desire for Jewish Rebecca.: "The Ivanhoe that you know, did he not press Rebecca's hand?"[33] The fleshly metaphor of pressing a woman's hand affirms Scott's Jewish/diamond linkage in Trollope with the thread between Jew and diamond stringing together the novel's cultural concerns about property, territory, family, and race. The Married Women's Property Act of 1870 echoes in the novel as a question of what women and men can keep and what they can give away. That concern is linked with what Indian territories natives can claim.[34] Those cultural urgencies are distilled in the racializing of diamonds, finally residing not in Indian or English but in Jewish hands. Although Rebecca's gift sequestered Jewish diamonds from market values, connections between diamond and Jew return to financial calculations in Trollope, reinforcing a symbolic bondage of materialistic Jews to diamonds, a conjunction fitfully disavowed in Scott.

At first such an identity seems strictly business: Messrs. Harter and Benjamin, jewelers, moneylenders, and pawnbrokers, control all the diamonds—trinkets and treasures—in the plot. Legally and illegally, gemstones pass through those Jewish hands. Lizzie Greystock Eustace cannot do without the exchange, nor can one of her "Corsairs," Lord George Carruthers, who is suspected of collaborating with Benjamin to steal the diamond necklace that Lizzie receives from her new husband in a rare, sweet moment early in their marriage. Like Mr. Septimus Luker, the Judaized pawnbroker and fence in *The Moonstone,* Benjamin enjoys ties to all levels of the social order. Benjamin and Harter's two establishments map their ability to traverse elite consumer culture—in their fashionable Bond Street Mayfair location—and a parallel criminal consumer society—at their secret location, with vaults, in Minto Lane in the City. Jews game the economic and social system. As a pivotal figure in the novel, Jewish Mr. Benjamin will ultimately make Lizzie's choice of a converted Jew for a husband seem predictable. Non-Jews press the Jew's hand because that hand is both despised and indispensable.

Lizzie knows that jewels are legal and often illegal tender of those who need to scramble. They are a girl's way of getting what she needs. Trollope introduces her at her father's deathbed where he portrays debt-ridden Admiral Greystock's daughter as bearing a gem-ridden identity: "When she was little more than a child, [she] went about everywhere with jewels on her fingers, and red gems hanging round her neck, and yellow gems pendent from her ears, and white gems shining in her black hair."[35] Her father's example connects her fortunes with the jeweling Jews. That alliance will come to seem inevitable by the novel's ending with what otherwise seems like Lizzie's anticlimactic second marriage to a dissembling, converted Jew. Plotting strategy might stretch to the limit that early association of girl with gems and a pawnbroker Jew with her marriage to an underground Jew, but her fate follows that logic to make the marriage seem a matter of poetic justice.

The well-tailored, gray-haired Mr. Benjamin and the underage orphan Lizzie meet for business in which both agree on a relative truth for mutual benefit. Mr. Benjamin risks lending Lizzie her pawned trinkets so she will dazzle an immensely rich suitor, Sir Florian Eustace, a man both vicious and generous. Because the girl lies about her age, she and the jeweler well know that the note she signs guaranteeing repayment is not worth the paper it is written on. Benjamin returns the jewels to impecunious Elizabeth Greystock as a surety against her marriage, banking on the Eustace money to cover his risk. Thus, Benjamin helps to seal the match. With gems on Benjamin's sufferance, Lizzie wears the sign of the Jew. In the course of the novel, the diamonds gather meanings in multiple ways to extend beyond one desperate beauty on the marriage market to notions about family prominence measured in gems, to imperial ambiguities about the spoils of empire, and finally, again, to Jews.

Trollope's enticing title sets a dazzling trap whereby the ground of society gives way. Ultimately the trap ensnares domestic, foreign, and imperial matters in its revelation that almost nothing in the new world is really real. "Paste" Lizzie wears real diamonds as opposed to what Trollope deems the genuine gem in plain Lucy Morris, the honest and faithful governess, who, like our heroine, is also an orphan but who lives by her authenticity and not, as Lizzie, by her performances. Lizzie considers untruths circumstantial; gossip forms the substance of social reality. Politics is part of a fashionable game. An earlier scion of the Eustace family initiated the game for dead men that Society plays throughout the novel, with teams named for the star player—"Lizzieites and

Anti-Lizzieites"—depending on their opinion about who owns the trophy necklace.

Given their symbolic centrality, it is no surprise that diamonds should structure and deceptively name the novel. Lizzie, a dedicated liar, rarely knows when she's telling the truth but is inadvertently correct in asserting the diamonds cannot be Eustace diamonds.[36] The diamond necklace, called "Eustace," stands at the meandering boundary of nation and empire in Trollope's novel, a great imperial fiction that features diamonds to draw analogies between nation and family—as had Scott—and masculinity and empire—as did Tennyson. In its varied episodes, *The Eustace Diamonds* offers contentious evidence of the movement toward empire. W. J. McCormack observes in his compelling introduction to the novel, "In a manner which no other Victorian novel attempted, *The Eustace Diamonds* tosses off... insights into the immediacy with which England becomes Britain."[37] England moves in that imperial direction under the sign of a diamond necklace, either belonging to a securely English family or to a beauteous widow who lives by her clever but defective wits. Trollope's novel delineates dynamic webs in imperial England, lamenting the moment when England becomes Britain, when women can own property, and when the imagined English race shows increasing signs of mongrelizing. It is a moment when dusky Indian functionaries with strange titles object to appropriation and when squinting, imposter Jews pass as Christian clerics. Elizabeth Eustace née Greystock and the necklace embody that moment.

The novel's political world with its debates on the logic of coinage—Plantagenet Palliser's mission to decimalize the penny—shows that in finance and politics as well as in society the foundation seems spongy and relative rather than solid and certain. Society pays serious attention to the diamond controversy and yet ridicules governmental currency debates. The problem centers on a character who in a more rational world might be regarded merely as a silly, unprincipled girl. But she expands in importance as an unanticipated by-product of empire building, her valuable, burdensome, and ultimately useless necklace containing the provenance of its messy familial and imperial history.

Sir Florian's grandmother, the first Lady Eustace to wear the newly proclaimed Eustace diamonds, upheld her role as ornament of her husband's family. Daughter of a duke, she supported a class system that calculated prestige with family jewels: "'They are as well known as any family diamonds in England,' said Mr. Camperdown" (1.9:100), the lawyer who zealously attempts to protect the family jewels. Casting doubt on family heritage, Trollope presents dissonant voices, often within the very family. For instance, John Eustace, the infant heir's legal guardian, recognizes those diamonds as fungible. The little Sir Florian, he points out, can buy his own diamonds, if he should want and could afford them in whatever might constitute his sweet by and by. Further, the diamonds are not worth the bother or expense of reclaiming them. John's measured tones echo Lizzie's operatic complaints about burdens of such easily altered targets of envy, status, and theft.

Because diamonds can change shape and settings, they are metonyms for changing gendered arrangements within an English family. Trollope endows the necklace with a history that illustrates both why it cannot be an heirloom and why it can represent a time when old certitudes—Trollope alludes to many of them—no longer apply.[38] Expressed in gendered terms, the necklace poses a basic problem of possession, eventually not only personal but territorial. Lizzie Eustace claims that rebellion against patriarchal control forces her to claim the necklace as belonging to her: "After all, a necklace is only a necklace. I cared nothing for it,—except that I could not bear the idea that that man should dictate to me" (2.53:122–23). Mr. Dove, lawyer extraordinaire when questions of inheritance are concerned, acknowledges vulnerability on the very ground of entitled male possessions when he admits, "We none of us know, for instance what a man can, or what a man cannot, give away by a mere word" (2.68:358). Taking universal male ownership of diamonds, Englishmen place them on their women whom they also assume they possess. Thus, Sir Florian, Lizzie's dying husband, fulfilled a patrimonial role by clasping the fabulous necklace around Lizzie's white neck. That ceremony marks her not as heiress but as wife.

If only Sir Florian had been Indian, he would have put the necklace on himself. That difference provides the fuel of the plot as an illumination of a Victorian gender contract that extends to the present day. Fashionable for Englishwomen, necklaces are effeminate for Englishmen, so men proudly adorn their women with signs of their family's prominence, their masculinity. What a man can give away opposes what he can proclaim in perpetuity as a family foundation—what a family name can modify as a pronoun. The answer is: not diamonds.

Trollope follows how that adornment is constituted, how financed, and the aims of the paterfamilias in attempting to deed them permanently to the family. The earlier Sir Florian Eustace assembled the necklace as a gift to his bride. He sold "old family jewels" (1.16:149) and exchanged others to fashion his bridal gift. Doing so, he demonstrated that family jewels were not heirlooms. Nevertheless, his will proclaimed that the newly formed necklace was bound to each male heir. The diamond-necklace-making Sir Florian demonstrated a hubris regarding family inheritance similar to that of King Arthur in his diamond deeding to the realm.

Mr. Dove, a legal authority regarding heirlooms, opines that jewels cannot function as a stable indication of family possessions. In so ruling, he strikes a blow against the family fortress. English patriarchy holds itself together by an increasingly shaky ground of tradition. Though based on precedence, women, even harpy, lying, scheming, and basically ignorant ones such as Lizzie, demonstrate a disconcerting ability to toss carefully intertwined political, legal, and marital establishments to the winds.[39] Traditions fall apart by the wiles of a girl who has read too much Tennyson, Byron, Shelley, and other popular literature, interpreted through her self-regarding eyes. Formed by her reading, performative Lizzie applies literature to life, with unfortunate but also occasionally comic results. She prefers Lancelot to King Arthur; in that, as Frank Greystock mordantly observes, she resembles Guinevere. Lizzie's is a naughty misreading; given her circumstances, why not? She has read Romantic poets and novelists; she has read *The Arabian Nights,* glittering with gemstones. She knows that Rebecca is free to give her diamonds as she pleases.

So, the diamonds cannot stand as heirlooms but might as paraphernalia. The very term, odious to Mr. Camperdown, indicates a female gender. Paraphernalia are woman's property, independent of her dowry and regardless of how obtained.[40] They are gendered female, whereas a dowry passes from the bride's father to the bride's husband—like the bride. Unlike "heir" that allows a female "heiress," paraphernalia carries no male linguistic counterpart. Debates leading to the Married Women's Property Act of 1870 rendered the concept of paraphernalia somewhat obsolete, but the principle itself survived.[41] Outside the clutches of marital custom, jewels were passed from woman to woman, as with Rebecca and Rowena. Exhibiting the necklace to Society as if it were paraphernalia, the widow Eustace defies family claims and propriety. Those diamonds upend legal claims of diamonds in perpetuity as revered signs of family importance. Such objects harken back to those very aristocratic values that are weakening at Lizzie's moment, driven in part by Britain's emergent networks of wealth. The hardest of gems discloses the soft underbelly of family dynasties.

Imperial Possessions

When Mr. Camperdown offers the necklace's provenance, he also brags about their Indian origins: "No diamonds more real had ever come from Golconda"[42] (1.11:100). Taken apart as separate stones, acquired over generations, the notorious diamonds were sold in Golconda, a trading area near many diamond mines in India. Eustace gems thus bear upon the novel's imperial theme of Indian possessions.[43] In addition, the relationship of the Golconda diamonds to the Sawab of Mygawb, who is protesting the British grabbing of his lands, joins a political dispute to an amorous one, equating levels of concern about property in personal and geopolitical terms. Lucy's loyalty to her man, Frank, and by default to his political party sways her opinion about the poor Sawab against Lord Fawn of the India Office: "I think the Prince is being used very ill,—that he is being deprived his own property,—that he is kept out of his rights, just because he is weak" (1.7:65). Lizzie and the Sawab occupy parallel positions, with Lord Fawn at the time as Lizzie's fiancé believing that Lizzie has no viable claim on her necklace or the Sawab no viable case for his land or recompense for it.

When Trollope names his Indian petitioner a "Sawab" and names his territory "Mygawb," he mocks a narrative thread bearing on the movement from nation to empire. Trollope's made-up title, "Sawab," for the Indian prince minimizes his situation, and "Mygawb" seems a mispronounced profanity. Indian titles and places, it suggests, land on English ears as ridiculous. The Sawab of Mygawb would find a home among the grandees of Gilbert and Sullivan comic operas, though the serious question of India is central to the difference between English nation and British empire. Traces of the Sawab's dilemma find a way into those Golconda diamonds. Camperdown's reverence for Golconda diamonds contrasts to the demeaning attitude about the Mygawb place, sounding like Mysore. Its ruler's title resembles "Nawab," or "nabob," an honorary Mughal title, not a prince or rajah but a governor. An area in Deccan India, known as Arcot, was the "capital of the Nawabs" that included important diamond mines, fashioned and sold in Golconda.[44] Mysore is a location of many diamond fields.[45]

The Eustace Golconda diamonds gain interest in the context of diamond discoveries. Brazilian diamonds found in the eighteenth century do not share the cachet of Indian diamonds. A more relevant and recent diamond lode—and an imperial location that contrasts with India—was South Africa. From 1867, shortly before Trollope wrote his English diamond novel, a quantity of diamonds such as the world had never known were uncovered. Trollope journeyed to South Africa, publishing his two-volume work about that place in 1878. As discussed in part 3, he described conditions at the great diamond mine in Kimberley, where he observed diamond's gritty origins. In contrast, Golconda enhances the novel's nostalgia for a Merrie England when people could bank on words, real money, and white gems. It was a place where diamonds bedecked royals, aristocrats, and gentry without pesky Indians nagging the government about injustice. Not only indicating the novel's imperial theme, diamonds in Sir Florian's necklace predate Brazil and Africa, when India was the primary source of the world's diamonds.

Golconda is tied to magic carpets and genies, not to Brazilian slaves or grubbing Jews. Lizzie alludes to *The Arabian Nights* as the exotic place where fortunes are miraculously won and instantly vanish as a counterpart to a dirty origin for the empire's present and future diamond treasures. Holding in her hands the very necklace, she constructs a legend of their eventual fate in being valued less than paving stones: "'I do feel so like some naughty person in the "Arabian Nights,"' she said, 'who has got some great treasure that always brings him into trouble; but he can't get rid of it, because some spirit has given it to him. At last, some morning, it turns into slate stones, and he has to be a water-carrier, and is happy ever afterwards, and marries the king's daughter'" (1.31:287). Identifying with her Arabian, gem-owning male character, Lizzie's ending is not so happy; in the last lines of the novel, the ancient Duke of Omnium, whose blood has been kept circulating by tales of Lizzie's adventures, predicts, "I'm afraid, you know, that your friend hasn't what I call a good time before her, Glencora" (2.85:375). In place of the magical gem-strewn Orient, Trollope offers marriage to an imitation Anglican, an East European Jew.

A Jewish Solution for the Widow

Whereas Lizzie's moral laxity confounds and entertains society, John Eustace admires her untapped genius: "'She is a very great woman,' said John Eustace, '—a very great woman; and, if the sex could have its rights, would make an excellent lawyer'" (2.73:302). John points to career possibilities for women that would allow Lizzie not to marry but to shine at the bench, her ability to perform and to lie apparently no disadvantage for lawyers. But rather than a profession, Society offers her a disagreeable mate. A repellent kind of poetic justice—diamonds to the Jews, Lizzie to the Jew—Lizzie's marriage to Mr. Emilius, "the fashionable foreign ci-devant Jew preacher" (2.66:237) arrives as a last resort and a punishment in a social world that requires her to marry. Her British suitors have abandoned her. A woman who deals too much with Jews ends up with a particularly lowly one, called by Frank Greystock "once a Jew-boy in the streets" (2.53:128).

Mr. Emilius proclaims himself a racial aristocrat: "The blood that runs in my veins is as illustrious as your own, having descended to me from the great and ancient nobles of my native country" (2.73:313). Although Emilius claims

Magyar stock, he tells an inadvertent truth about the ancient lineage of Jews, older than any Christian, older by far than any Greystock, Fawn, or Eustace. It is the wrong kind of old—as in uncultured, tribal. Trollope quickly rewrites Mr. Emilius as a "nasty, greasy, lying, squinting Jew preacher, an imposter, over forty years of age" (2.73:314). The preacher comforts the widow for her loss by first reading her Scripture, then switching to Byron's "Childe Harold." Romantic poetry for a reader such as Lizzie paves the road to love for Jewish liars. His poetic ability to polish his greasiness to a shine renders Reverend Emilius more dangerous than an ordinary Jew.[46] His conversion opens society doors to a fashionable preacher—Christianity reduced to poetic phrases mouthed by a converted immigrant. In assuming an elite religion, hook-nosed Emilius pushes that spectacle occupying the center of social life to parody: a Hungarian Jew wrapped in Church of England clothing. Christian ladies in Mr. Emilius's London congregation find him physically attractive and worship eloquence more than conviction, preferring fashion to the churchy Bishop Eustace and Dean Greystock, stuck in their boring Bobsborough parish complacency. Worse, since Lizzie cannot truly love anyone, Emilius is as not as repellent to her as he should be: "She certainly liked the grease and nastiness. . . . She liked the lies" (2.73:310). Emilius, the paste Christian, weds Lizzie, the paste trophy.

Like Rachel Verinder's similarity to Queen Victoria, Lizzie's enchantment with Emilius resembles aspects of Victoria's flirtation with her prime minister, Benjamin Disraeli. Lauren Goodlad argues for the allusive connection between Trollope's depiction of the "cartoon villain" of Emilius, in fact as both Lizzie and Emilius resembling the performative Disraeli, poetic and dissimulating.[47] Worse than Disraeli, however, Emilius is a Hungarian immigrant, whereas Disraeli was born in Bloomsbury, was baptized along with his three siblings, and did not disguise his origins. Lizzie's physical attraction to the eloquent Jew emerges in the context of a queen with a foreign susceptibility, two widows who must make their way in a man's world.

Finally, Golconda diamonds glitter ominously as a sign of a world not merely upside down but scattering in all directions. Throughout the novel, their worth seems huge, repeatedly £10,000, but finally as property called "fictitious." Because the Eustace case did not settle even small issues of family property law, Mr. Dove declares them practically useless: "Thus, we have had to fight for six months about a lot of stones hardly so useful as the flags in the street, and then they vanish from us" (2.72:298). Dove narrates the legal version that Lizzie's Arabian Night tale foretold—but with marriage to a Jew not a king. "Annihilated" by robbery, re-setting, and foreign owner-

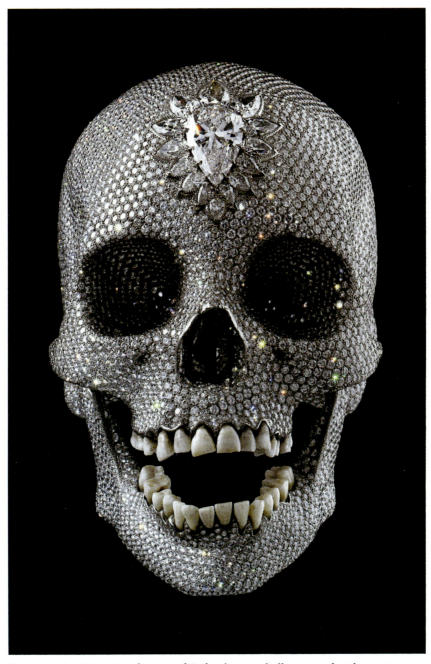

Plate 1. Damien Hirst, *For the Love of God*. A human skull encrusted with over 8,000 flawless diamonds represents a memento mori to instill consciousness of mortality, while its dazzling gems are regarded as eternal. (© Damien Hirst and Science Ltd. All rights reserved/DACS, London/ARS, NY 2019)

Plate 2 (*top*). *Durbar of Maharaja Dalip Singh,* c. 1845, watercolor miniature on paper, possibly by Hasan-al-din of the School of Lahore. Duleep Singh is about seven years old.

Plate 3 (*opposite*). George Duncan Beechey, *Portrait of Duleep Singh,* 1852, oil on canvas. Commissioned by Duleep Singh, the painting represents the fourteen-year-old prince as if he still rules the Punjab, with selected jewelry being returned to him as an eleventh birthday present. (Permission, Gurbani Centre)

Plate 4 (*bottom*). Paste replicas of the Koh-i-noor Diamond and its flanking diamonds in their original Punjabi bazuband as received by Queen Victoria. (Royal Collection Trust/© Her Majesty Queen Elizabeth II 2019)

Plate 5. Franz Xavier Winterhalter, *Portrait of Maharaja Duleep Singh,* 1854, oil on canvas. Elaborately costumed, Duleep Singh could be dressed for a tableau vivant, a Victorian entertainment enjoyed by the royal family and household. (Royal Collection Trust/© Her Majesty Queen Elizabeth II 2019)

Plate 6. Detail of Queen Alexandra coronation photograph, 1902. Alexandra's crown shows the Koh-i-noor Diamond in the center, the first English crown to exhibit its glory. Alexandra's bejeweled body emulates Indian princely array. (Royal Collection Trust/© Her Majesty Queen Elizabeth II 2019)

Plate 7. Julia Margaret Cameron, *Enid,* 1874. Cameron posed Enid opening a wardrobe, eyes modestly cast downward, an interpretative pose of Enid's fashion role in Tennyson's evocation of Camelot. (Metropolitan Museum of Art)

Plate 8 (*top*). Queen Victoria's small diamond crown, 1870. The diamond crown can be regarded as evidence that Victoria embraced a diamond empire. The crown was designed a few years after the Eureka Diamond legend was developing, during the years of the South African diamond rush. (Royal Collection Trust/© Her Majesty Queen Elizabeth II 2019)

Plate 9 (*bottom*). Eureka Diamond superimposed on a map of the Diamond Fields. (The Kimberley Diamonds, De Beers Consolidated Mines Limited, Kimberley Public Relations Department, Johannesburg, South Africa, 1969. J. Walter Thompson Diamond Information Center, Box 56, John W. Hartman Center for Sales, Advertising, and Marketing History, David M. Rubenstein Rare Book and Manuscript Library, Duke University)

Plate 10. Heart of the Ocean from the J. Peterman *Owner's Manual,* no. 68, Fall 1998, whose philosophy was "Clearly people want things that make their lives the way they wish they were." The statement illuminates the concept of "democratic desire" used here.

ship, miscalled Eustace for a few generations, the necklace represents a vanishing world.[48] Trollope throws Mr. Benjamin into jail, Lizzie to the "renegade Jew" (2.66:241), and the reformulated diamonds to the extreme boundaries of the civilized world, on the neck of an "enormously rich Russian princess" (2.78:353). Society will never be the same; it already is not the same. As the novel follows the diamonds into an oblivion accompanied by Jews, *The Eustace Diamonds* tells that its deceptive title is just and only that, of less value than paving stones, which are usually set upon a bed of sand. The diamonds disperse and expose the shifting social desert that fails to secure them.

Whispering Stones in *Daniel Deronda*

In *Daniel Deronda,* the ominous topography, Whispering Stones, "two tall conical blocks that leaned towards each other like gigantic grey-mantled figures," serves as a topographical metaphor for meanings of diamonds in the novel.[49] Walter Scott whispers that Eliot's interest in *Ivanhoe* includes the racialized diamond exchange at the end of his novel. Whispering stones carrying Scott's sublimated Jewish history disclose Eliot's central concerns about races within national borders. Among critics finding connections between Scott and Eliot, Bernard Semmel points out that *Daniel Deronda* is in part an inverted *Ivanhoe.*[50] Like Scott's, Eliot's diamonds come to symbolize both erotic and racial conflicts, absorbing concerns about race within English national identity during an imperial moment when Scott's solution of Saxon/Norman unity and Jewish emigration is inadequate. Eliot's multiple figurations of diamonds play on that final diamond exchange from Scott with its sundering of potential lovers, one Jewish, the other Christian, in tantalizing encounters between Gwendolen and Daniel, neither of whom enjoy a clear future at novel's end. In dialogue with Scott's closure, *Daniel Deronda*'s diamonds whisper challenges to resolution itself in fictions that address a problem about what peoples belong in a nation.[51] The Jewish Question deflects attention from the unmarked but equally vexing English Question.[52]

Though Eliot features jewels in many of her novels, *Daniel Deronda* is the only diamond novel among them, deriving from Scott and Trollope but using diamonds to symbolize gender and racial ambiguities, not sublimated solutions.[53] First, a diamond ring signifies a danger of Jewish assimilation, when some Jews cannot be differentiated from authenticated racial purity of inhabitants of English country manors. Assimilation allows for absorption into a national culture without the sexual reproduction assumed in miscegenation.[54] A nurtured, mimetic façade appears in the person of a lovely Jew who has successfully and unwittingly passed as English. Eliot's racialized portrayal of characters highlights the novelist's concern with national identity, assimilation challenging a conception of pure Englishness. In Daniel, character and upbringing forge ties that cannot be erased.[55] Though embracing his Jewish origins, Daniel could not credibly shed his English civility and his English clothes. He will not, despite his musical disposition and his musical wife, take on the eccentric garb of artistically attired Herr Klesmer, whose cosmopolitan Jewishness shows itself in his hairstyle, his costume, and his intonation. Habitus as an Englishman is part of Daniel's very being. Rather than accepting a Jew into the gentry as a challenge to English-authorized bloodlines, Eliot banishes the marriage of unassimilated Herr Klesmer and English heiress Catherine Arrowpoint to settle outside national borders rather than preside over an English estate to produce English progeny. A marriage of affinities but intermarriage of races, rejected in *Ivanhoe,* also cannot bear a national test in *Daniel Deronda.*

Daniel's assimilation covers its Jewish substrate that only seems to be resolved when the unknowing Jew discovers and embraces his origins and properly marries within his faith. Passing according to high standards of Englishness, Daniel is exposed sensationally as a Jew, so assimilated that for most of the novel only Sir Hugh knows that he is as Jewish as racializing theories type him—both parents are Jewish—and he's not telling.[56] Though Daniel's racialized marks are opaque even to those in the novel who assume his illegitimacy, some are familiar from English ethnology. For instance, though unlike Mr. Emilius in *The Eustace Diamonds,* he embraces his Jewish heritage and is free of telltale nose or lying tongue, both Jews attract English beauties such as Lizzie and Gwendolen with what seems like a genetic poetic soul.[57] Then again, Daniel's dark curly hair differentiates him from the flaxen-haired ancestors of Sir Hugo Mallinger's portrait gallery, the family pedigree framed on his walls. Daniel's upbringing, his dress, and his restrained manner are English, but he is drawn to Jewish thought, as if Eliot claims for him a Jewish intellect as a genetic component. His English upper-class attitude recoils from Sir Hugo's suggestion that he might pursue a vocation as a singer, but he has inherited some of his mother's talent, and he sails off to Palestine with his wife, a Jewish singer like his mother. It is as if an Oedipal attraction endures in the vocal cords and soul of this passing-as-English Jew.

Unlike *Ivanhoe* and *The Eustace Diamonds, Daniel Deronda* places diamonds on both its male and female protagonists to soften a boundary between men and women. Daniel and Gwendolen apparently belong to the English upper class, privileged and burdened by it. In describing assimilated

Daniel, Eliot emphasizes his upper-class English masculinity: "He was young, handsome, distinguished in appearance—not one of those ridiculous and dowdy Philistines" (1.1:7). Equally distinguished by her appearance, Gwendolyn suffers from it: "Her life moves strictly in the sphere of fashion; and if she wanders into a swamp, the pathos lies partly, so to speak in her having satin shoes" (1.6:47). Eliot rues Gwendolen's dysfunctional shoes, a mark of class wherein the dictates of fashion hobble and distract this unfortunately beautiful young Englishwoman. In jewelry, too, the two characters wear diamonds as scars as well as marks.

The novel multiplies instances of diamonds—almost litters the plot with them. Remembering Scott's legacy in the conjunction of Jews and diamonds, it is not surprising that once Eliot mentions Daniel's diamond ring, it is likely that he is not an Englishman but a Jew.[58] To complicate that identification between diamonds and Jews, diamonds do not disclose their origins by examination. As such they serve as a metonym for the racial disguise embodied in Daniel, whose appearance does not definitively reveal his. Eliot's disquieting solution to presenting and disposing of the Jew who doesn't know or show adds nurture to naturalized connections between Jews and diamonds in Victorian English diamond novels. Eliot's whispering stones follow Scott's symbolic paradigm and multiply its resonances.

Diamonds signify not only unacknowledged racialized, gendered tensions between Daniel and Gwendolen but also larger indeterminacies of national, racial, and moral communities. Diamonds as well as assumed names undermine apparent truths of identity. The Jewish Question resembles the English Question to pose that Victorian problem about national belonging, a similar concern in Trollope's diamonds as fictitious. Because of the possibility of assimilation, stones worn by Jews and English alike whisper about Englishness as a fiction. Unknowingly or unwittingly, characters wear their fate in their diamonds.

The narrative opens with Daniel observing a beautiful woman gambling at the roulette table whom he compares to a serpent and assumes she is evil. Linking a question about gender with one about race, it immediately offers a panorama of racialized types who are also playing roulette: "Those who were taking their pleasure at a higher strength ... showed very distant varieties of European type: Livonian and Spanish, Graeco-Italian and miscellaneous German, English aristocratic and English plebeian" (1.1:4). In this motley gambling crew, only the English are differentiated by class, identifying the narrative eye as judgmental and English. The novel often defines English character as expressed in English clothing, differentiating the English from darker

European men, whose clothing looks effeminate to the English narrator: "The strong point of the English gentleman pure is the easy style of his figure and clothing: he objects to marked ins and outs in his costume, and he also objects to looking inspired" (1.10:92). Englishness once more sets itself against other races when Grandcourt and Gwendolen arrive at the Genoa docks for their fateful sail with an imperial performance: "The scene was as good as a theatrical representation for all beholders. This handsome, fair-skinned English couple manifesting the usual eccentricity of their nation, both of them proud, pale, and calm, without a smile on their faces, moving like creatures who were fulfilling a supernatural destiny—it was a thing to go out and see, a thing to paint" (7.54:634). Italians' aesthetic eyes view the English couple as a painting or a tableau vivant. The scene performs racialized entitlement in national costumes. Racial types appear socially determined but not to be shed as easily as taking off a dress, or a pair of shoes, or a necklace, or a diamond ring.

To those eyes attuned to fashion as a racial marker, a Jewish trace colors all the novel's diamonds to differing degrees, troubling the certainty of racial and national identity. In those diamonds, the novel links the Woman Question and the Jewish Question to the English Question. Charisi (Daniel's father's name) and Grandcourt (Henleigh's mother's name) diamonds highlight questions of heritage. Fully assimilated, Daniel, who assumed Englishness as his birthright and asserts his desire to remain clearly English but with a yen to know more of the world, turns from his profoundly English nurturance to embrace his supposedly essential Jewish nature. In welcoming his ancient heritage, Daniel emerges from his English cocoon as a newly minted Jew, though with English markings. Diamond stones in this novel often, like Daniel, seem assimilated to Englishness. Their Jewish trace whispers of alternative realities as a challenge to racialized types. Whereas *Ivanhoe* diamonds sublimate the horrors of Jewish expulsion into pleasure, beauty, and national belonging, and in *The Eustace Diamonds* to an undermining of English family identity, diamonds in *Daniel Deronda* assimilate to satin shoes and well-cut coats but incompletely, challenging the very constitution of race and identity.

Mirah Lapidoth, a victim of paternal exploitation and Jewish homelessness, refers to Jews' practicing ritual suicide rather than converting to Christianity: "I know our fathers slew their children and then slew themselves to keep their souls pure" (2.17:176). Her comment recalls Scott's sexualizing the York Massacre in the confrontation between Brian and Rebecca. In an allusion to *Ivanhoe* that pinpoints the issue of conversion, Mrs. Meyrick compares Mirah's immovable faith to that of "Scott's Rebecca" (4.32:333). Though

Mirah flees her father, who is about to pimp her to a Christian, Mirah's allusion to self-slaughters like that at York in the context of Rebecca's threatened suicide foretells the sexual overtones of Daniel's preventing Mirah from killing herself. The moment of virginal Mirah's desire for death confirms both her racial purity shared with Rebecca and Scott's similar depiction of the Jewess as unassimilable to True Englishness. Those bedrock convictions placed in little Mirah's mouth challenge those like the Meyricks, who wish the petite Jewess—and her smallness is emphasized by gratuitous attention to her tiny feet—ripe for conversion or at least assimilation. Mirah's evocation of Jewish extirpation sets the terms for her departure with Daniel to Palestine. Daniel embraces his dead brother-in-law's urge to reach the Jewish homeland. Having studied Hebrew texts, Daniel then travels to their setting to recognize their message, and perhaps to discover a worthy mission.[59]

The other overtly Jewish characters fit Jewish types.[60] Little Mr. Meyer, the Jewish pawnbroker in Leubronn, profits from others' financial desperation. Like Mr. Benjamin enabling Lizzie Greystock's courtship, Gwendolen's jewelry handled by Mr. Meyer promotes a potentially amorous encounter. Daniel "redeems"—and Eliot chose the word carefully—Gwendolen's turquoise necklace.[61] Mordecai Cohen's intellectual intensity is no less a typifying mark of the Jew than is the pawnbroker Ezra Cohen's jovial materialism. Cohen's diamond-wearing, "vigorous" mother is not "repulsive" but she "presumably slept in her large earrings, if not in her rings and necklace" (4.30:351) without being overly fastidious about cleanliness. She is a not quite clean, if not a dirty, Jew. The Ezras' identical names place them in the same Cohen caste, though Mordecai's name is changed—as are other characters' names in the novel.[62] Daniel discovers he is a Charisi, distantly Deronda, but with a father in the same profession as Mr. Weiner and Mr. Cohen. His uncommon names disguise his association with that Jewish business, yet might be discerned in his diamond ring, which at first passes as English.

Race in the novel seems a matter of social conformity as well as of lineage; assimilation muddies the racial waters. Daniel appears English in demeanor and tailoring, manner and education. Assimilated, his diamond ring links him with English privilege odiously flaunted by Henleigh Mallinger Grandcourt, who, like Daniel, wears a diamond ring. Grandcourt's ring appears at a moment where he performs Englishness in Leubronn when he denies interest in "play": "'It's a confounded strain,' said Grandcourt, whose diamond ring and demeanour, as he moved along playing slightly with his whisker, were being a good deal stared at by rouged foreigners interested in a new milord" (2.15:145). Grandcourt's gesture (a melodramatic sign of the villain) draws eyes to his sparkling ring by those whose painted cheeks mark them as not English.

What are we to make of the two eligible young men who both wear diamonds rings? For his part, Grandcourt is a milord who values diamonds. His ring flashes with an indolent assumption of superiority that is part of his Englishness. Grandcourt wields diamonds as class weaponry, sending Gwendolen a fine diamond engagement ring. He endows her with this diamond pledge at a distance, in "a delicate little enameled casket, and inside was a splendid diamond ring with a letter . . . 'Pray wear this ring . . . in sign of our betrothal'" (4.28:286). The rest of his note contains instructions for a check to cover her mother's living expenses. That diamond engagement ring, splendid and contractual, highlights financial straits impelling Gwendolen to break her promise to Lydia Glasher. It announces class wealth and ownership in a gendered manner, though with a message similar to Grandcourt's own ring—admired for the lordliness of its provenance. This diamond engagement ring, not prescriptive at the time or place, foretells misfortune.

Beautiful Daniel's diamond ring might betoken the same mark of race, class, and privilege as Grandcourt's ring. Its paternity hidden, the ring assimilates to Englishness. Its owner wears it without knowing that he carries his father on his finger. The novel teases the reader with Daniel's ring by first using it as a ticket into a strange world. In seeking Mirah's family, Daniel lights upon the subterfuge of pawning his ring to Ezra Cohen, who coincidentally bears the same name as Mirah's brother and equally coincidentally employs that brother under a different name. A transgressive element colors apparently English Daniel's pawning the ring he does not know is Jewish and whose value is a bargaining point on the Jewish Sabbath when financial dealings are forbidden. A secretly Jewish tourist to the Oriental East End, "those parts of London which are most inhabited by common Jews" (4.33:351), Daniel inadvertently finds his people. His diamond ring draws together the Jews, used as a valuable to be pawned, as a passport to Daniel's Jewish mother who demands that Daniel bring his diamond ring to her unveiling of his past, and as an indication of the thieving ways of Jacob Lapidoth Cohen, Mirah's father.

In removing a sign of his parentage, Daniel relinquishes "my memorable" ring to Lapidoth's greedy eyes. He has been rejected by his converted Alcharisi mother, for whom the diamond bears an unspecified importance, as if it were a birth certificate. Daniel declares the ring is hot and "heavy" for a finger that is going to the sultry climate of Palestine (8.68:734). The ring must be shed in favor of a purer Jewish mission. Legacy of a pawnbroker father who gives up his profession to nurture his wife's career, it is tainted by the wrong kind of Jewishness and disappears with Jacob Lapidoth, the wrong kind of Jew.

The Grandcourt Diamonds

Grandcourt diamonds, possessed by Henleigh Mallinger Grandcourt, carry a curse that Eliot alludes to in referencing the Golconda diamond, Koh-i-noor, Mountain of Light: "These particular diamonds were not mountains of light; they were mere peas and haricots for the ears, neck, and hair; but they were worth some thousands, and Grandcourt necessarily wished to have them for his wife" (4.30:315). The allusion to the Koh-i-noor reminds readers of the reputed curse of that fabled stone and demonstrates how a curse effectively operates because of belief in it. More plangently, the Grandcourt diamonds reference Rebecca of York's diamonds and their Jewish legacy to Englishness. *Daniel Deronda* inverts the final scene in *Ivanhoe* in poisoning Gwendolen's wedding gift. First, the diamond parure is a family legacy, like the so-called Golconda Eustace diamonds, to declare a strong male family line. Grandcourt is more vicious and cannier than Sir Florian Eustace but their desire to honor the family name with diamonds is the same. With Henleigh Grandcourt's mistress wearing the Grandcourt diamonds for years, the diamonds assume a moral taint, resembling a gift to some demimonde.[63] In keeping with the dynamic of *Ivanhoe*'s final scene, the diamond suite passes from a dark-haired, outcast woman to a blonde bride.[64] Lydia stands in the place of Rebecca. In inverting Rebecca's gift, the Grandcourt diamonds pass from dark woman to blonde woman, transformed as a curse.

Lydia Glasher, mother of Grandcourt's four children, retains enough power over him that he allows her to send the diamonds to his bride without calculating the poison she expresses as a curse in a letter accompanying the bridal gift. Gwendolen believes in Lydia's diamond curse, founded both on her broken promise to Lydia that she would not marry Grandcourt and on a false assumption that Grandcourt intended to marry Lydia but for her, though Grandcourt first appears in the novel as a swain on the marriage market. Gwendolen cannot disconnect the stones that continually whisper her "willing wrong": "The words had nestled their venomous life within her, and stirred continually the vision of the scene at the Whispering Stones" (5.25:395). In the allusion to the setting where Gwendolen met her nemesis, this diamond exchange confirms connection of the Grandcourt diamonds to consequences of Rebecca's wedding gift. The diamond curse deepens Gwendolen's bondage. Lydia is Rebecca's demonic shadow.

Grandcourt's family standing derives from a custom of inheritance that encourages a name change, in this case from Mallinger to Grandcourt, his mother's family name. Eliot specifies that the diamonds belonged to Grandcourt's mother. The name change verifies a legal fiction enacted to enable male privilege by enabling the male heir to protect family inheritance from the mother's side. Throughout the novel, the English line reveals itself as not only a matter of performance but manipulated by inheritance law beyond primogeniture. Henleigh Grandcourt (Sir Hugh's younger brother) "had married Miss Grandcourt, and taken her name along with her estates" (2.16:150). Men can construct their lineage; inheritance tied to legitimacy can be declared: Grandcourt acknowledges his bastard son as his heir. This legal declaration parallels Grandcourt's own family history, thoroughly English according to precedent. Eliot exposes legal fictions that sustain family fortunes. Carrying with them their manipulations of birthright, Grandcourt diamonds are not thoroughly assimilated. Eliot continually troubles Englishness as she troubles the diamonds as racial markers. Deconstructing the Jewish/English binary, the text shows that Englishness is partly, though profoundly, a matter of fashion, of how people show themselves, a matter of legalism, of how people name themselves, and a matter of faith, of how people endow objects with moral agency.

The novel has often seemed dissatisfying because Eliot cannot definitively answer the nationalized race questions she explores in the course of her research into the Hebrews. Daniel's mother, like Mirah's father, is morally compromised. The Princess Halm-Eberstein, born as what she herself regards as an English Jew, gets to be a royal princess with five children, thanks to a moment, like writer's block, when she cannot sing. And Daniel gets to be a Jew, not needing to grovel because the history of his people's oppression did not form his self-image as a youth: upbringing replaced husbandry. In the novel's scheme, Daniel is the perfect Jew, pure in his genetic makeup but untainted by his people's persecution, manner, and speech. His Englishness endows him with an assurance that he can sail off to Palestine bringing enlightenment as he enlarges his own narrowly English experiences. It is an idealistic ambition, both modest and hubristic.

And the diamonds? Their futures, like the futures of the protagonists, are uncertain. Grandcourt's diamond ring is momentarily drowned, like those in other diamond fictions in this book, but it is not purified. Perchance his heir wears it. But that beautiful lad, though English, is shadowed by his out-of-wedlock conception, not entirely erasable by legal maneuvers. The fate of the Grandcourt diamonds is undetermined, like Gwendolen's future. And

Daniel's diamond ring disappears into the underworld of Mirah's father. Diamonds whisper that social constructions are subject to change, but surely it is better for Jew and Christian, man and woman, to face the future humbly and diamond-free.

Rebecca Returns

In *Reuben Sachs* (1888), Amy Levy responded to *Ivanhoe* and *Daniel Deronda* with skepticism about their characterizations of Jewish desires and a satirical eye on her fellow Jews that might seem to confirm antipathies toward Jews in English Protestant authors discussed above. Modern Jews, the topic of her novella, identify themselves as English but with tribal loyalties. About Eliot's novel, Levy remarks, "As a novel treating of modern Jews, *Daniel Deronda* cannot be regarded as a success."[65] While she objected to inadequacies of Eliot's diamond novel, her Sachs character displays her stones as a similar sign of the Jewess as Mrs. Cohen of Eliot's East End. Wearing diamond solitaires— diamonds with no other stone to detract from their dazzle—Adelaide, Mrs. Montague Sachs Cohen, the sister of the title character, wears diamonds as if they were a religious badge of otherness: "She was richly and very fashionably dressed in an unbecoming gown of green shot silk, and wore big diamond solitaires in her ears. She and her mother indeed were never seen without such jewels, which seemed to bear the same relation to their owners as his pigtail does to the Chinaman" (57). Levy's gloss on her character's fashion sense denigrates Jewish Orientalized Englishness, connecting Adelaide to Eliot's East End Jews.

Living in the prosperous West End, Mrs. Montague Cohen takes the given name and patronymic names of East End Adelaide Cohen, Ezra Cohen's daughter in *Daniel Deronda*. Little Adelaide's inadequately washed grandmother, like Mrs. Montague Cohen's mother and herself, wears her diamonds night and day. Like Eliot's Mrs. Cohen, diamonds mark Levy's Mrs. Cohen with flagrant taste and Jewish identity, no matter how careful her ablutions or fashionable her dress and address. Referencing the vulgarity of Ezra Cohen's family, Levy yet disapproves of Eliot's similar view. In turn, Eliot gives Adelaide Rebekah Cohen the middle name of Scott's Rebecca, the diamond influence in all novels of this chapter. In *Reuben Sachs,* Rebecca returns through the lens of an English Jewish woman writer.

Levy's comparison of Adelaide Cohen's diamonds to the Chinaman's pigtail links her to Asian signs: pigtails, the mark of a Chinese worker; and silk, a fabric associated with Asia. Levy's characterization of Adelaide builds on border slippages during centuries of Jewish diamond merchants plying their trade between Asia and Europe. Jews thus cross representational boundaries between the familiar West and the amorphous East with the result that they seem familiar foreigners everywhere. Levy moved her pen with a trace of irony to link the forbidden food for Jews to the Chinaman's hairstyle. She gathered silk, diamonds, and Jews into an Asian cluster, national accuracy irrelevant to Jewish Orientalism.[66]

Levy refers to London Jews as "English," as did Daniel Deronda's mother, though unlike her they are intentionally unassimilated. The author adopted race-conscious language, sometimes echoing attitudes about Jewish stereotypes, sometimes challenging them.[67] She asserted that *Ivanhoe*'s Jewess might not have been attracted to the Saxon: "Generally speaking, the race instincts of Rebecca of York are strong, and she is less apt to give her heart to Ivanhoe, the Saxon knight than might be imagined" (95). Levy's remarks would cover almost every reader to the present moment. Her observation exposes the almost universal, racially inflected assumption that the sable-haired Jewess *must* find the blond Christian knight irresistible. Given a preference for her own kind, Rebecca might have kept her own diamonds as possessions of a thoroughly English Jew. Englishness might have been hers as well as Rowena's. Neither did Levy admire Eliot's Jewish characters. She regarded Daniel, Mirah, and Mordecai as "no picture of Jewish contemporary life" but created by "a noble spirit" ("The Jew in Fiction," 176). She was skeptical about Eliot's solution in Daniel's idealistic departure for Palestine. Her often negative race consciousness produced Adelaide Cohen, echoing the name of Eliot's pawnbroker family. Cohen diamonds shine with intertextual spotlights, Levy questioning Daniel's need to leave his native land and Rebecca's inevitable desire for the Christian Saxon.

Levy's portrait of Anglo-Jews embeds her Jewish protagonist among a segregated group that may not live in the same London area but are related by religious and family ties, some prosperous and some struggling. Unlike Daniel, Reuben could never pass as a Gentile. The woman who silently loves him is a poorer member of the Jewish community, Judith Quixano. When Reuben dies of a weak, overworked heart (a stereotypical characteristic of Jewish constitutions), Judith marries Bertie Lee-Harrison, a convert to Judaism who regards Judaism with a dilettante's aestheticism. Judith does not love him, but like Gwendolen Harleth, she marries for money. In a reversal of the more common pattern of Jews converting, Levy offers a prosperous Christian convert to Judaism. At the end of the novel, Judith (meaning Jewess) expects a baby, which according to Jewish practice would trace its lineage to its mother. The Jewish fetus embodies possibilities avoided in the other works of this chapter.[68]

Commemorating the rich matrix of English diamond novels, Levy placed Eliot's perpetual Cohen diamonds on her rich Cohen Jewess's ears. Rebecca's diamonds return as English but still sullied by those English Jews, whom Levy refers to as "the ill-made sons and daughters of Shem," a deformed tribal identity (114). The child in Judith's womb does not promise full national membership. Neither would a marriage between Ivanhoe and Rebecca, Levy suggests, answer the Jewish Question. Diamonds remain as diversions from English Questions that also seem constantly asked, eternally unanswerable.

III
South Africa

The Karoo Setting

It was his distinction to be the first of the new Dynasty of Money Kings which has been evolved in these later days as the real rulers of the modern world.

—W. T. Stead on Cecil Rhodes

A book about mining is a book about money.
A book about South Africa is a book about race.
—Geoffrey Wheatcroft, *The Randlords*

Value does not exist objectively at all in the absolute sense, but only by virtue of the fact that the human will desires the object in question.
—Georg Simmel, "On Money"

The Cape Colony was languishing economically when Richard Southey, its colonial secretary and then Britain's first governor-general of Griqualand West, echoed Jesus to Peter in comparing a diamond rock to the rock of empire building: "This diamond, gentlemen, is the rock upon which the future success of South Africa will be built."[1] With a melodramatic flourish, he reputedly delivered his prophecy to legislators as he placed before their eyes a perfect eight-carat diamond he had acquired from a man he identified as an African shaman. His often-quoted words are probably fanciful, repeated because they bless the location with providential fortune. Southey's aphorism promised material success to all, including natives. Britain had recently annexed the strip of land that Thomas Boyle in *To the Cape for Diamonds* (1873) described as uniquely unattractive: "Her Majesty possesses not, in all her empire, another strip of land so unlovely."[2] The land was a desertlike area, called "karoo," north of what was known at the time as the Cape Colony, the tip of southern Africa, a trading post set up in 1652 at the Cape of Good Hope. The area above, Griqualand West, was named after a mixed tribe who no longer controlled the territory and whose name disappeared from new maps (figure 5). Such name changes in South Africa affirm Robbie McLaughlan's contention that colonial mapmakers' topographical project was itself actively imperialist. It "eradicated indigenous place names steeped in a rich linguistic and cultural history, replacing them with a dizzying array of coordinates and signifiers designed to reconnect the colonizer with terrain that had been left behind."[3] Officials and other newcomers often renamed places after themselves.

On the face of it, the karoo was an unlikely place to answer aspirational prayers. Yet it is not hyperbolic to claim that the diamond discovery in the karoo was cataclysmic, altered the map, and assembled immigrant seekers jostling side by side. Questers tell stories about common people's dreams for adventure, comfort, and wealth. Their experiences regard diamond as raw material, cloudy stones wrested from dangerous, often death-ridden pits. Natives and prospectors alike contracted diseases, animals bit or ate them, fresh food was hard to obtain. Uncontrolled, fluctuating diamond prices bestowed destitution or fortune on its seekers.[4] Heaven and Hell lived together.

To outsiders, the landscape resembled nothing seen before and was viewed as uninhabited. An earlier settler, Captain Augustus Lindley, expressed territorial possessiveness, regarding the discovery with modified alarm. The title of his book conveys his own colonialist attitude: *Adamantia, The Truth About the South African Diamond Fields: or, A vindication of the right of the Orange Free State to that territory, and an analysis of British Diplomacy and Aggression which has resulted in its illegal seizure by the Governor of the Cape of Good Hope.*[5] Lindley expresses his mixed feelings about a British land grab: "These silent desolate wastes, untrodden, in the east, save at very rare and distant intervals by some wretched, wandering bushman, scarcely more akin to humanity than the great herds of wild animals around him . . . now echo incessantly the noise of a great multitude. And where at a few widely-separated spots, along the course of the far-apart rivers, or at the occasional fountains, *Boer,* or farmer; there now exists the greatest population, the greatest gathering of both whites and blacks in South Africa! The region which has experienced this sudden and stupendous change is, however, none other than that known as Adamantia, or the South African Diamond Fields."[6] Despite territorial disputes that boded further disaster to indigenous Africans by likening them

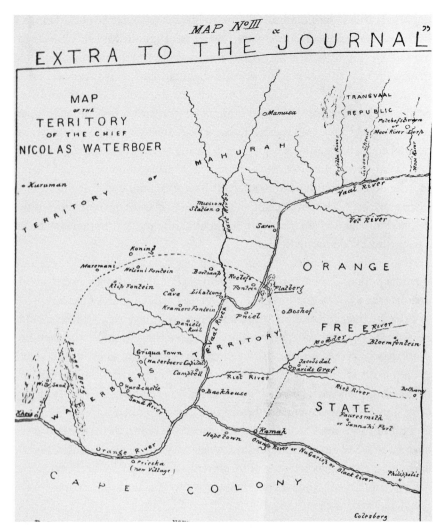

Figure 5. Map of Griqualand West, indicating its control by Chief Nicholas Waterboer. This fold-out map appears in *The Land Question of Griqualand West* by Francis H. S. Orpen and David Arnot in 1875, during the Diamond Rush. The area near the Vaal and the Orange Rivers is where the first diamonds were discovered. It was thought diamonds grew in the water. Because the kopjes were found to be diamond pipes, the Diamond Fields were then called dry diggings. (New York Public Library)

to animals, Lindley marvels at a magnetic pull that Adamantia exerted on wandering human herds.

The 1867 South African diamond discovery arrived as a perfect storm. It fed an expanding print culture, avid to fill pages with information about diamonds and diamond mining before an increasingly literate public, hungry both for science and adventure tales. Old stories about history and famous diamonds were rehearsed, along with accounts about strange peoples in unique places. Photographs brought diamond digging to popular scrutiny. Earlier diamond mines had been closed to public view, controlled by regal and governmental decrees. South African mines, many on farms, were uniquely open to the skies. Anyone who wanted to see actual mining could go to look. Prospectors could bring minimal supplies, a bit of cash, and start to dig on small claims. Moreover, the discovery occurred when new technologies could figure out the heretofore unknown source of diamonds and devise new means of extracting them. Moreover, changing gender and class etiquette increased the demand for the African diamonds inundating the market. Imperial eyes saw Africa through diamond lights.

The unprecedented South African diamond discovery quickly became legendary. Tales drew upon facts regarding the upheaval with global implications when South Africa began uncovering tons of diamonds, too many to preserve their inflated price or their reputation for rarity. Different kinds of writing—history, memoir, fiction, and journalism—mingle and blend to produce stories, often taken as fact, introducing readers to insider accounts about far-off Diamond Fields.[7] The writings describe varieties of people arriving from everywhere who aimed to extract a fortune from a resisting terrain, supplied the demand for basic goods, or bargained to buy the stones in a tumultuous market. Even those prospectors rising above the masses to become rich and famous did not shed royal glory on the developing diamond enterprise, coming as they did from unrefined origins. The immediacy, the intimacy, and the incongruity of the setting brought to the gem's meanings a distinctly earthy aspect.

Such nearly unimaginable consequences of the South African diamond discovery add further complexity to literary meanings of diamonds. The setting for diamond tales moved to this imperial land, which, unlike India, was considered both savage and empty. Literature drew new meanings from new kinds of diamond mines. What might it mean when rough diamonds offered themselves to anyone's pick and shovel? Diamonds took on a rough-and-ready aspect, ripe for male adventure genres that often merged with domestic novels. South African fiction creates networks of rough and polished men finding diamonds, with respectable and unrespectable women wearing them. The market grew to entice buyers in order to unload unpredictable piles of stones.

Stimulated by fashion writings, middle-class women were permitted and could afford to wear real gems.[8] Emulating their superiors in diamond display, they provided an essential market for small gemstones. Not distantly sparkling on a royal crown or a privileged bosom, African diamonds became up close and personal, extracted for profit by individual diggers, worn by prosperous husbands' wives. Rather than Indian objects of sacred power or English signs of national and familial status, diamonds in South African writing depict a scramble for wealth, a marvel at racial diversity, an exposé of business dealings, and a sense of the human cost. Fictions bred in Africa typically do not cleanse diamond from its myriad forms of dirt and the ordinary people, explicitly raced, who found them, sold them, and often died for them. African diamonds emerge from their messy setting, uncut and ready for imperial markets and meanings.

7

True Stories on the Diamond Fields

I have paid my first visit to the Colesberg Kopje, the well-known New Rush, now re-christened "Kimberley," and I feel inclined to call it the greatest wonder of the age.

— M. E. London, *Life on the Diamonds Fields*

In 1930, Erasmus Stephanus Jacobs, who pocketed an unusual pebble when he was sixteen years old, lent credence to a legend about the chance happening that initiated the southern African Diamond Rush. The sixty-three-year-old Boer, a farmer's son, told a journalist, Mr. Beet, about his attraction to a pretty stone. In clearing a water pipe for his father two hundred yards from the banks of the Orange River, he sat down for a rest under a tree when something flashing caught his eye. "It blinker," he explained. He brought it to his baby sister to play with.[1] The rest is history.

Commonplace details about the discovery took the shape of a folk tale with variants. Here is an amalgamation. One day, a trader named Schalk van Niekerk, in passing to the west of Hopetown, happened to see the children of a Boer farmer, Daniel Jacobs, playing a game called "Five Stones." Struck with the appearance of one gaming pebble, Niekerk told their mother, a Dutch Reformed Church member, that it reminded him of the white shining stones mentioned in the Bible. As he breathed the reverential words, an ostrich hunter named John O'Reilly chanced to pass the doorway of the house. He overheard, entered, and joined the debate. The three envisioned a diamond — which none of them had ever seen. Although Vrouw Jacobs refused their offer of real money for a replaceable toy, visions of diamonds danced in their heads. In other versions, the three are not together in the Jacobs house, where they allegedly agreed to split the proceeds.

O'Reilly took the stone to Hope Town for evaluation, where the idea of its being a diamond met with such ridicule that he nearly threw it away. Persevering, he went on to Colesberg, and from there he sent the stone to Grahamstown for the inspection of an amateur mineralogist, Dr. William Guybon Atherstone, who confirmed it as a diamond. Of a light brownish-yellow color, it weighed approximately 21.25 carats. Sir P. W. Wodehouse, then governor, apparently bought it for £500. In line with an Indian custom of naming big diamonds, it was dubbed "Eureka" (see plate 9). As a faceted 10.75-carat brilliant, it was auctioned off by Christie's in 1946 for £5,700. To mark the centennial of its 1867 discovery, De Beers diamond company bought the Eureka and gave it to South Africa. Visitors can gaze at it when they visit the Kimberley museum, near where the Jacobs lad picked it up.[2]

There were doubts. Skeptics questioned whether the Eureka signified a trove. In 1868, a Hatton Garden merchant sent Professor James R. Gregory, a mineralogist at London University, to the Cape.[3] Ignorant at the time about the kind of soil that signaled diamonds and suspicious that the land had been salted to inflate values, Gregory asserted that "no diamonds have, nor ever will be, found in the Cape Colony—saving such as are deposited there for a purpose."[4] Becoming a common noun, "gregory" signified egregiously wrong expert opinion.

Suspicion turned to elation when a larger, blue-white diamond achieved notoriety. At first called the "Star of South Africa," the stone was sold to a white man early in 1869. In many accounts, the discoverer of the diamond was either a Griqua or a Hottentot shepherd, apparently called "Swartboy" or "Swartbooi," Afrikaans for "black boy."[5] This second diamond legend suggests spirituality of a simple, religiously guided shepherd. Here is a biased telling: "The first known owner of this gem, which weighed 83½ carats, and will, it is believed, be cut into a brilliant of the finest class, was a Kafir witch doctor, or sorcerer. This savage conjuror was with some difficulty induced to sell it to the same Schalk van Niekerk, who was the quasi-discoverer of the Eureka. The 'Star of South Africa,' in the rough, was of an irregular shape, and about the size of a small walnut. After being exhibited at Port Elizabeth and at Cape Town, and visited by crowds of people, it was finally forwarded to England, where . . . it passed into the possession of Messrs. Hunt and Roskell, and was valued at 25,000*l.*"[6] This account by a manager of the De Beers Consolidated Mines misrepresents the man's resistance to the sale. It also gestures to the uncivilized religious vocation of the "Kaffir," a term variously spelled that became a disparaging label for all blacks.⁷ According to most accounts, Van Niekerk offered the shepherd what some reported as his entire estate: five hundred sheep, ten oxen, and a horse. To part with a rock, however interesting, for lifetime security in movable stock was no doubt the shepherd's intent. What better use could he make of a stone? And why else did he offer it up? Another version describes the shepherd taking his discovery to a store owner, Mr. Gers, who then reached Niekerk. Curiously ignored in all accounts is that ordinary people were on the lookout for diamonds. The shepherd knew to pick it up and knew where to sell it. Niekerk might have collected £11,200. The Star of South Africa is also known as the Dudley Diamond, after William Ward, Lord Dudley, who paid either £25,000 or £30,000 for it, then hung it from a diamond necklace.⁸ His English title erased the diamond's African origin, matching its family identity with other renowned English family diamonds. Its size, the ease of its attainment, and calculations of its worth fired the Diamond Rush.

Preserving an impression of utter surprise, no teller of either story owned up to a preexisting expectation that diamonds could be found in that place. They were not as naïve as they are depicted. One of them must have been primed to hope for their pebble. Before the English takeover of the Cape Colony, a mission map of the mid-eighteenth century proclaimed "Here be diamonds" across Griqualand West.⁹ Boers characteristically were uninterested in diamonds, and, though native peoples used rough diamonds for their spears, they would not have wasted time to secure them. In his travelogue, Thomas Boyle mentions Bushmen, Korannas, and "other tribes of low condition" who used the stones "mechanically . . . to bore their weighing stones."¹⁰ Interest in diamond grew even among those groups when some joined the mining enterprise for the wages. Given loss of territories, cutting of forests, parching of grazing lands, devastation of flora and fauna used for food and shelter, plus "economic destruction followed from trading," native blacks had little choice.¹¹ And Boers could either move or join. Confirmed by discoveries of two diamonds, "Here be diamonds" provided impetus for imperial invasions.

Kimberley, Diamond City of the Big Hole

Soon after the African diamond discovery in the Vaal and Orange Rivers area, prospectors learned that diamonds did not originate in rivers, but neither did they recognize true diamondiferous dirt. Many abandoned claims after reaching the bottom of loose yellow soil, ignoring the harder blue substrate, kimberlite, sign of greater riches beneath. In "dry diggings" diamonds lay deep in kimberlite pipes. That geological discovery brought prospectors pocking up Boer farmland. Consequently, the name most closely associated with African diamonds and the global diamond trade is of two Boer brothers, Johannes and Dietrich De Beer, owners of a 16,400-acre farm they named "Vooruitzict," Afrikaans for "perspective, outlook, chance, or expectation." Little did they know. After confirmation of the shepherd's discovery on land instead of near rivers, farming appeared imperially irrelevant and inconvenient. At first, pestered by diggers, the De Beers let out their diggings themselves in individual claims. The plots were small: the claims were split up by concessions, bargains, and sales, until there were at least 1,600 separate holdings of claims, and fractional parts running as small as one-sixteenth, or about seven square yards.[12] Individuals could rent a claim for a minimum of a week and start digging by hand. After finding claim administration aggravating and disruptive, in 1871 the brothers gave in to badgering and "sold out for £6,300 to a syndicate of Port Elizabeth financiers. It was not a bad profit they at first believed, for the farm had initially cost them only £40."[13]

Referring to Vooruitzict's squalid condition, Richard Murray, editor of the *Cape Argus,* offers an account of the place: "The uninhabited farm had changed as if by magic into a crowded and busy camp. . . . This poor and wretched farm of two years ago is now a mine of wealth. The very mud of which the old hut walls were made by Boer are diamondiferous. After Mr. Webb came to live in the hut, diamonds were seen sparkling in the mud walls, and were picked out from them and sold."[14] First called Colesberg Kopje (*kopje* is an Afrikaans word for a small hill), then New Rush, the area was named Kimberley after a British colonial secretary who could not pronounce the De Beer farm name.[15] Kimberlite soil (figure 6) bears the name of that same British peer who had not been to Africa. The farmers who rejected profit from diamonds gave their name as a synonym for the global diamond business. Groundwork was laid for apartheid as a business practice, then, in the twentieth century, as government policy.[16] Kimberley became site for the largest hand-dug mine in the world.

Vooruitzict was only the beginning. Once blue-tinged earth was identified as the source for kimberlite pipes that indicated a volcanic explosion to the surface from the earth's core, possibilities for the region seemed endless. "The extent of the diamondiferous region it is at present impossible to say, but, so far back as 1870, it was stated by Dr. Shaw, of Colesberg, . . . to be at least one thousand square miles in area. The same gentleman, writing in the *Cape*

Figure 6. A piece of kimberlite, showing an embedded diamond on the top. (Williams, *Diamond Mines of South Africa*, 2: facing 124)

Monthly Magazine of December 1870 says that it seems to him that every day the extent of the Diamond Fields enlarges, and that every week a new diamond farm is found in the Free State. Glittering pebbles of every form and colour glisten at his feet, and he feels indeed that he is in a new region."[17] Prospector Charles Payton marvels at uncharted possibilities in South Africa: "It is currently reported that a diamond mine will shortly be opened on the farm of a Mr. Jan Steyn, close to the village of Cronstad. . . . parties are begining (*sic*) to go there at once. This 'new rush,' being situated over 100 miles from the centre of the locality hitherto recognized as diamondiferous, would seem to indicate that we have considerably underestimated the vast extent of land on which diamonds may be found. Many are now bold enough to affirm their conviction that the whole of the Orange Free State is diamondiferous."[18] An immense state stuffed with diamonds surely pixilated the imperial imagination.

By 1870, diamond fever became an epidemic. What was imagined as civilization transformed the karoo. In Dutoitspan in the Orange Free State, Payton's census cannot keep up with daily increases: June 18, 1871: 10,000 people; June 20, not far from 20,000 people.[19] All this silence, this earth changed utterly from agriculture to diamond culture in weeks, even days:

> Three months after the rush began, the Colesberg Kopje was the centre of an immense encampment in whose heart streets were irregularly laid out, and neat stores built of iron and brick. In December 1871, there

were ... on the lower street of Kimberley, six stores, four hotels, and several butcher and shoemaker shops, besides a billiard room and saloon. On the upper main street there were three hotels, several diamond merchants' offices, a wholesale spirit and provision store, a bakery and confectioner's shop, a drug dispensary, butchers' shops, eating houses, bars, club and billiard rooms, and other miscellaneous shops and resorts. On the edge of these white-walled cities, and on the slopes of all the neighboring hills, were scattered the huts of wood or dirty canvas or mud-plastered stones, where the native blacks huddled together. When even this cover was lacking, some slept in tents, or in burrows scraped in the hillsides.[20]

Other accounts mention the stench of rotting dead animals, garbage, and open latrines. The smell of dust mingled with that of fly droppings. Nevertheless, by 1877, six years after the start of the dry diggings, "Kimberley (Colesberg Kopje) had become the second largest town in South Africa. Census figures ... show the ... population of the Kimberley district (including De Beers, Dutoitspan and Bulfontien) to have been 18,000: 8,000 whites and 10,000 'non-whites.'"[21] Four mines supported the town.[22]

The new settlement, unlike those of the American Gold Rush, acquired middle-class appearance, if not middle-class morality. Global immigrants brought gambling parlors, bars, and brothels to an area where the dominant religion resisted such pastimes. An early account specifies the "honesty and sobriety of the community." There is honor among diggers: "Everybody's things are at the disposal of the rest, and the opportunities of being dishonest frequent, but never taken advantage of; there seems to be a total absence of selfishness; and an apparent willingness to aid and assist one another prevails."[23] Diamonds were mailed by post; no Jesse James figures populate diamond reports, fictional or factual. Theft is quieter, less violent. Murray might be writing a travel brochure when he described the Diamond Fields as an idyllic community, with "a river running through it, where the bathing is free and an island provides an ideal picnic spot."[24] He was not alone in describing the pleasant setting.

A magnet for such growth was the Kimberley Mine, familiarly called the Big Hole. The largest hand-dug excavation in the world, the mine had a surface area of 42 acres and a depth of 2,625 feet. By 1914, 22.5 million tons of earth had been excavated, yielding 2.7 tons of diamonds. Eventually, because of the steepness of the diggings, walls would cave in, burying African worker and his employer alike. "A mine accident," explains a character in J. R. Couper's novel *Mixed Humanity* (1892): "Every day nearly there are two or

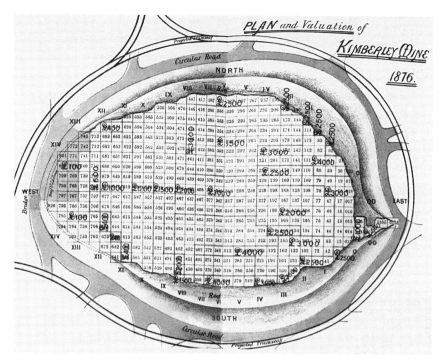

Figure 7. Kimberley Mine, or the "Big Hole," from an 1876 map in Anthony Trollope's *South Africa* (1878) showing the size of the claims and their valuation.

Figure 8. Colesburg Kopje, Kimberley Mine, 1873, showing the cables. (Williams, *Diamond Mines of South Africa*, 1:225)

three niggers killed."²⁵ Morally, the Big Hole offered a special vision of hell. Psychologically, the pit could be conceived as horror at the feminine, a place where men enter, never to emerge.²⁶ Anthony Trollope's two-volume *South Africa* (1878) featured only one illustration, a map of the Kimberley Mine, whose shape could be viewed as encompassing both meanings (figure 7).²⁷ Before wiring, miners clambered up the slopes by foot.

The hole was dangerous, unsanitary, chaotic. "The four diamond mines at Kimberley differed from alluvial diggings in Brazil or India.... Consequently, an entirely new method of mining was developed at Kimberley.... a far riskier undertaking.... Sorting inside the mine obstructed digging as debris mounds were left upon productive soil. To encourage diggers to take soil out of the mines ... a road system was adopted on a grand scale.... But the roadway system could not last. Diggers undermined the roadways in their search for diamonds and by April 1872 the system had developed into a death trap."²⁸

Like a manufactured Grand Canyon, the mine's very excess informs symbolic terms for imagining South African diamonds on the karoo. The gaze to the depths reminds men of their own fragility, as London explained: "The first glance down into the heart of the Kopje itself is so dazzling to the eyes, that one requires some time to get over the first sensation of giddiness and insecurity ... the top is encircled by a close row of windlasses, erected upon a high wood staging, and hundreds upon hundreds of wire ropes run from these stagings to the different claims, so that the Kopje looks like a huge spider's web [figure 8], and the bluish hue of the crossing and recrossing wires gives a misty indistinctness to the whole scene."²⁹

Viewing the mining operation, Trollope cannot decide which insect the workers at the Big Hole most resemble—ants or flies—but his description of their climbing out of the mine might be likened to bats or demons: "They come as flies come up a wall, only capering as flies never caper,—and shouting as they come. In endless strings, as ants follow each other, they move, passing along ways which seem to offer no hold to a human foot" (175). The depiction of African miners as manic insects connects them to a figurative as well as literal underworld.

8

The Scramble and the Scramblers

If a hundred towers of Babel had been brought within one man's hearing, the noise could not have been more deafening. There is here every type of man under Heaven.
—William Murray, *The Diamond Field Keepsake*, 1879

Let us hope that the days of Kaffir wars, cattle sickness and bad crops are over, and that as each digger stops rocking his cradle for the last time to pack up his things and returns to his mother country, he at least may have full and substantial assurance of the fact that diamonds have turned up trumps.
—G. F. Harris, *Belgravia*, 1871

What in political terms came to be called "the scramble for Africa" captures a difficulty in untangling transformations that seemed instantaneous. Referring to unruly European imperialism, the jolly phrase first may have been circulated in print by an Irish-born aristocrat, the British colonial governor in South Africa, the well-named Sir Hercules Robinson.[1] In the *Times* of November 7, 1893, he described the consequences of discoveries of diamonds and then gold a few years later in southern Africa: "A scramble for the interior of Africa had set in at all sides."[2] In 1919 Sir Wilfred Scawen Blunt echoed the phrase in the title of part 1 of his diaries; subsequently, the metaphor has become a tag phrase and a title for many books.[3] The term conjures a disorderly, though not aimless, free-for-all in a continent conceived as dark, despite its iconic sun. And, not by the way, there were wars, skirmishes, and basic hatred among interest groups: Zulu Wars, Boer Wars, wars among native peoples—intensifications of scrambles on a governmental and political level.[4] Observing potential ruthlessness and violence in scrambles, Blunt denounces "the British Empire" as "the great engine of evil for the weak races now existing in the world."[5] By "weak races," Blunt referred to African native groups, though his label could also be applied to the lower ranks of so-considered strong races—seekers after riches, buying, selling, scamming, and hoodwinking that constituted an on-the-ground daily tussle. Lured by refurbished fables of easy wealth and entrepreneurial enterprise tweaked to fit the African map, a cross-section of the globe's human variety voyaged to the karoo. These men and women tell their personal adventures, an ant's rather than a mogul's view. Diverse people, diversely they spoke.

True, European adventurers and hunters had already endangered animal and vegetable species, degrading the environment. Then came the Scramblers who constituted a change in number and kind. Appropriating "the Scramble" to indicate the struggle for diamonds signals a focus here on what has been labeled "history from below," referring to individual exploitation, rather than on wars or the well-documented, colorful characters who eventually corporatized the mines and, with diggers' communal rules first, organized black native servitude. Much has been written about those men, such as East End London Jew Barney Barnato; middle-class English Cecil Rhodes; Alfred Beit, a German Jewish mathematical whiz; German Ludwig Breitmeyer, a cartel consolidator and head of the syndicate; and bankers such as the English Rothschilds.[6] Barney Barnato enjoys a colorful reputation as a boxer turned canny investor; he eventually merged his company with Rhodes's to form the De Beers Mining Company. Much has been written and filmed about Cecil Rhodes, an imperial capitalist of intense ambition, who had a country named after himself during his lifetime. Corporate organization brought consolidation, syndication, and then cartel structure absolutely to control diamond marketing, including mandatory packets of diamonds, called "sights," to manufacturers and retailers. Rather than rehearse accounts of political, economic, and business histories of these individuals who eventually controlled diamonds from production to marketing, this chapter introduces direct accounts of seekers, not all of them prospectors, throngs initiating the Scramble in southern Africa to give that imperialist phenomenon an intimate habitation and a name.

Once over the ocean and on to the land, the trip to the Diamond Fields was arduous. Jack Senior, the English/Irish main character in *Mixed Human-*

ity, describes author J. R. Couper's own experience traveling to the diamond diggings on tracks barely a road: "The coach took six days to Kimberley. What a dreary journey it was! What a desolate, barren, monotonous country they passed through! Plain after plain, with only here and there a flat-topped kopje dotting the arid wastes. The only vegetation visible was the karoo bush, which forced itself up between the sharp stones, everywhere plentiful" (18). Accounts of individuals convey a perspective from the ground, adding up to a seismic shift in meanings of the Dark Continent.

This human stampede heading for the Diamond Fields included large numbers of Jews from everywhere in the Diaspora who in their diversity seemed to forge a closed fraternity, a guild that not only dealt in diamonds, but, in a familiar metaphoric cluster, were identified with them.[7] Once again, Jews are used to embody capital forces otherwise hard to conceive. Zine Magubane explains, "The urge to anthropomorphize capital by making it Jewish was inextricably related to the inherent difficulty of representing class power."[8] What is more, the Diamond Fields provided occasion to portray an unholy partnership between Jew and African, adding to the sinister symbolism of racial representations and meanings of African diamonds. Jews and Africans, whatever the many differences carefully delineated among and between them by nineteenth-century ethnographers and social theorists, cast crudely raced shadows on the vaunted purest of gems. In addition, a specifically South African viewpoint served the missionary project in bringing capitalism to Africa, converting Africans to miners and Christians, while casting the Jew variously as a money-grubbing necessity, an engine of commerce, or an enticing exotic.[9]

By the time in 1872 when Louis Cohen embarked from London for the South African Diamond Fields on the aptly named "good ship *European,*" equipped with minimal mining gear, modest cash, and a seventeen-year-old's thirst for adventure, what he called the "Diamond City of the Plains" teemed with people of differing tribes, including a reassuring abundance of his own.[10] Cohen marked the all-too recognizable Hebrews as beings of questionable lineage:

> A few, a very few, appeared well bred, but most of them postured like pilfering tinkers who had got their best clothes out of pawn. They were, as a rule, smoking large cigars. On driving up the Main Street, I had noticed the self-same species of gentlemen standing in front of their framed canvas habitations, and when I read on the signs displayed outside these tented offices that Abraham, Isaac, and Jacob had recovered from their long celestial sleep, and gone in for earthly diamond buying, "at the very

highest prices for the European market," I felt a real glow of hope as I inwardly ejaculated, "Thank the Lord I'm with my own people—and it's not Jerusalem!" But they certainly looked as if they had come from the Sublime East—of London.[11]

Cohen's mordant vision of patriarchal resurrection in a land of riches offered hope for the Jews but recognized that they were again delivered to a land already chock full of other claimants: "Upon each mound I saw I climbed and accosted the workers. They were of all nations, Englishmen, Irishmen, Scotchmen, Africanders [sic], Germans, Boers, &c." Despite racial diversity, he discovers that the claims are mostly held by "this breed of miners, Anglo-Saxon to the core . . . big, brawny, fine-made fellows."[12] On the other end of the European spectrum from Jews, brawny Anglo-Saxons dig but they do not wear or broker diamonds; they hire natives, but they are not pictured as in league with them. Cohen amplifies the symbolic economy discussed in chapter 6 that associates jewel with Jew and furthermore with shady dealing, with sin, with death.[13] The Diamond Fields recall Sodom and Gomorrah. A paradox is born: diamonds are tainted with their origins in South African diamond literature, yet readers remained avid for gory details and bloody diamonds.

In contrast to the European invasion of the New World, where imagery evoked the New Jerusalem and the Garden of Eden, Cohen portrays the diverse tribes in the Diamond Fields as descendants of the sinful Cities of the Plains; if Jews are the Chosen People of the Diamond, this association condemns more than it honors. But his adventurous gaze is not parochial as he scans the human panorama; he marvels at "such a cosmopolitan and heterogeneous population."[14] His racial survey, a tendency of Diamond Fields writing in general, categorizes humanity with the fine precision of nineteenth-century ethnographic texts—not only kinds of Jews, but kinds of Africans, differences among Celts, and varieties of Asians. In *Mixed Humanity,* Couper also offers racial taxonomies, describing the Diamond Fields as a human potpourri.[15] He mentions a rarely mentioned Asian group, the Malays, who briefly appear in some fiction, notably that of Olive Schreiner: "Malays and Capeboys . . . Men of all nations, colours, and complexions thronged the thoroughfares—Indians, Arabs, Kaffirs of all tribes, Europeans, from the swarthy Italian to the fair, blue-eyed Scandinavian; and those of the Hebrew race seemed very numerous. . . . The majority of the dealers were Jews, who, though from all parts of the world, retained the characteristics of their own race, resembling in a marked manner the inhabitants of the different countries they hailed from" (20). To Cohen's localizing of a certain kind of Jew, Couper adds a paradox, an ability to resemble non-Jewish compatriots—Jews as both internationally recognizable and nationally distinct. This Jewish chameleon nature enables them to tilt their identities to "the different countries they hailed from," thereby muting and diffusing their Jewishness.[16] The combination of clearly marked Jews with those of more ambiguous identity, yet all engaged in diamond scrambling, produces an impression that Jews dominate the town. As in other fantasies about the Jews, their numbers and powers seem a monopoly providing cover for other ethnicities engaged variously in legal, financial, or nefarious dealing.

African Diggers

Although they did not value diamonds in their life practices, Africans well understood the stakes in maintaining control of diamondiferous soil (figure 9). As early as 1869, they organized searches over lands then known as Griqualand West. However, according to Robert Turrell, "by October 1871, African chiefs had lost control of the 'river diggings' and the Vaal/Harts region had been annexed by Britain."[17] Griqualand West lost its Griqua label along with native power over invading prospectors.

After losing control of oversight, native people freely came and left the Diamond Fields; in the dry diggings, a black man could stake a claim, but not for long. As early as 1871, resistance to native ownership became policy, then law.

Figure 9. Africans traveled to the Diamond Fields for months of work before returning home with a bride price and a gun. (Williams, *Diamond Mines of South Africa*, 1:188)

Responding to what Boyle termed *"le spectre noir,"* proprietors of the Hopetown Diamond Company were fined £5 "for granting a respectable black man a license to dig on that kopie [*sic*].... The diggers were, and are, determined black men shall not share their privileges; the English Government refused to make distinctions."[18] Fearing black natives on their own claims foreclosed financial stakes to black inhabitants of the land. Payton opposed integration in the diggings when the British took over: "But if it is a fact that under the new government 'niggers' are allowed to work for themselves, this is indeed a grave abuse, and one against which every digger, be he Boer, colonist, or Englishman, will join in protest. Our only security against constant robbery by our servants, was the difficulty they found in disposing of the diamonds which they could not legally hold.... But if we are to have the utterly impracticable doctrine of black and white equality proclaimed, and if niggers can dig for themselves, and sell diamonds unquestioned, the employment of native labour becomes practically useless."[19] A black man with a diamond became by law a crook. He might sell a stolen diamond to a fence on the cheap. Cheating the native was insufficient for the diamond enterprise. They were sometimes whipped, occasionally to death. They must carry identification called pass cards; Diamond Fields apartheid became government policy in the next century.

Africans traveled to the Diamond Fields to work as laborers. With disproportionate attention to San people, called Bushmen, often mentioned as nearly exterminated, Diamond Rush writings describe native peoples from all over Africa.[20] African men traveled great distances to earn enough to buy an inexpensive gun and purchase livestock for a bride price. Whatever the condescending attitude to their diversity and energy, they upset European conventions of modesty, dress, and pleasure. No one arriving in the area could lump African peoples into one group. Writing a memoir while convalescing from his South African sojourn, Sir Charles Payton introduced potential English prospectors to varieties of African peoples, regarding them as inferior though of ethnological and touristic fascination: "You have them of all tribes and all colours, from sickly yellow to jetty black; Kafirs and Hottentots, Korannas, Griquas, Fingoes, and many more are here, helping the all-powerful white man to turn up the bright gems which so long lay hidden in the soil. Not a little do they contribute to the picturesqueness of the scene, though truth compels me to say they are sometimes more picturesque than decent."[21] Payton capitalized on his experience, soft-pedaling its physical consequence to him to cast his experience as a travelogue that included colorful African peoples.

Gardner Williams, a supervisor in the De Beers Consolidated Mining Company, portrayed ebullient African workers:

The flocking in of the native African tribes... made a compound of color, feature, and character never before assembled in any mines on the face of the earth. The sinewy negroes proved themselves such willing and sturdy workers in the dust and heat of the sun-scorched quarries, that the claim-holders were glad to hire them and confine their own work to the task of overseers.... No blaze of the sun and no whirl of the dust could subdue their bubbling spirits, breaking out in wild whoops and chants, and yelling in pack when any big diamond was found, reveling in every chance diversion,—the fall of a bucket, the slip of a ladder, the tumble of a climber, and convulsed with laughter whenever they could set mules capering, or bullocks shying or balking by shrill whistles and screams, and mimicry of a driver's call.[22]

Natives' color, customs, and costumes reminded people of their own otherness: "Many wear merely a parti-coloured bunch of rags before and behind, barely sufficient for purposes of decency. One will strut about with nothing on but a hat and a loin-cloth; another with an old shako and red coat, formerly the property of a private in the 20th; another with hat, jacket, and shirt, but both totally innocent of trousers.... These semi-barbarian, half-naked negroes are said to be the most honest and best workers. Educated, and consequently fully-clad, natives are looked upon with distrust."[23] The educated native apparently acquired bargaining canniness that emulated white men, some of whom taught them to smuggle. Workers secreted diamonds on—or in—their bodies, selling them to illicit diamond buyers, called IDBs.

The major crime on the diamond fields was surreptitious diamond theft, rather than holdups and criminal gangs. As in India, the laboring employees found creative ways to secrete diamonds on their persons, causing yet more elaborate surveillance methods. One method of stealing diamonds has a scatological provenance: "The Kaffirs were bribed to swallow the 'booty' before leaving the mines.... A meeting place was arranged, but in what circumstances they passed on the 'precious' stones to the purchaser of stolen property history leaves us to conjecture. It would not be incorrect to assume that many of the sparkling ornaments which at this moment adorn the neck of a beauty have been subjected to this procedure. If they could speak!"[24] As early as 1875, an elected committee of diggers addressed the Native Question. It "recommended compulsory registration of labour at a depot, enforcement of passes, confinement of workers to employers' camps and compounds, penal sanctions with lashes and fines to prevent desertion.... Purchases of firearms... were to be made subject to labour services by African buyers."[25] With corporate consolidation came policies for native theft control.[26] After their contract expired, Africans were interred for a week to allow any swallowed diamonds to complete their intestinal journey, inspectors using high-powered hoses to sift their excrement. Natives were also required to wear finger-inhibiting gloves to prevent them from reaching into body holes and crevices to remove inserted diamonds.[27] To occlude this digestive progress in the African diamond story requires an erasure at the imperial gut.

Justification for treatment of black miners argued that Africans benefited from the Diamond Fields, not as claimants or shareholders but neither uniformly as thieves. They first needed orienting to a radically new life. Bushmen and Korannas reputedly never wash; pyramids of hardened dirt hang from their elbows like immense tassels.[28] Once lucky enough to be selected for work in the mines, they are washed, organized, and (after mine consolidation) penned. Constructing a conversion narrative about the native population in his book *In the Early Days: The Reminiscences of Pioneer Life on the South African Diamond Fields (1910)*, John Angove, an Englishman, writes:

> If we go back to the early days, say, 1871–73, and compare the raw Natives then arriving from their kraals in the wild regions beyond the Transvaal with those who now travel most of the distance from their kraals by rail, we shall be forced to exclaim: "What a contrast!" Whilst the South African statesmen of the Union Parliament will have the Native Question to discuss and the Native Problem to solve, they will have to admit that there is no civilising influence to which the Natives are so much indebted for having raised them above the degraded state of their fathers as the manual labour taught them when working in the diamond mines. . . . The condition of the Natives arriving on the Fields from their country was most deplorable: besides their emaciation, they were overrun with vermin, and their only covering was often nothing more than a well-worn kaross.[29]

According to those such as Angove, the colonial encounter improved the native; his experience of digging domesticated a stinking savage to a hardy worker. Cleaned up, the native becomes Christian and joins the capitalist system. The Scramble promised salvation to both the body and soul of black folk.

Trollope acerbically shared the view with Angove that the pursuit of diamonds improved the native as other methods did not: "I regard Kimberley as one of the most interesting places on the face of the earth. I know no other spot on which the work of civilizing the Savage is being carried on with so signal a success. The Savages whom we have encountered in our great task of populating the world have for the most part eluded our grasp by perishing while we have been considering how we might best deal with them. Here, in South Africa, a healthy nation remains and assures us by its prolific tendency that when protected from self-destruction by our fostering care it will spread and increase beneath our hands."[30] Apart from killing African natives or allowing them to die, turning them into diggers seemed to offer mutual rewards. Nevertheless, the Africans' health did not always improve. Dutoitspan, a diamond mining compound, housed 2,900 workers. They could not pay for fresh food. Overcrowding, poor clothing, and malnourishment led to typhoid and influenza epidemics and dysentery. One way of making a profit on excess diamonds was to cut wages. Using convict labor also cut costs.[31] Gradual improvement by the mid-twentieth century provided food and medical treatment. At that time, the De Beers Consolidated Mining Corporation portrayed the joy to the native of employment in the mines as part of their pride in the civilizing of South Africa. Africans were taken from tents and ditches and were billeted in fenced camps, eventually netted atop to prevent lobbing stolen diamonds out of the compound. In corporate mines, native diggers arrived for a limited term (often three months), which prevented them from forming stable criminal organizations.

Global Scramblers

Then there were the European and American Scramblers, some down on their luck, some outcasts, and some excessed by primogeniture. Imperial writing noted not only wealth but spiritual conversion for them as well. Prosperity and good jobs promise to transform the sinner to the citizen, the disaffected to the contented. As a piece in *The Diamond Field Keepsake* reported, diamonds could reform the wretched to productive members of the capitalist enterprise:

> This is traceable to the ease with which men found remunerative labour, and there are thousands of examples which might be quoted to show that the majority of men prefer living by means of honest labour than by dishonest gain. There are hundreds and hundreds of men who, before that time, were decided to be irreclaimable, and confirmed in vices of various kinds beyond all powers of redemption, who have found their way back to their own positions of life, who have regained their self-respect, and who will live to do good work for the world. It was wonderful to see men which for a long time before had loafed about in rags, and had regarded themselves as lost to the world, grown rich in pecuniary means and ready to lend helping hands to those who needed them.[32]

Figure 10. A digger's camp, New Rush, probably 1871 or 1872. This early camp shows African diggers and sorters, the sorting tables on the right, the owner of the claim in the foreground, simple shovels and hand tools. (Williams, *Diamond Mines of South Africa*, 1:168)

Many prospectors' own words described less sunny perspectives (figure 10). They might wonder at the flowering of civilization in the middle of nowhere, but then, with dust stinging throat and eyes, or malaria and dysentery felling them, seek desperately for a viable exit.

In 1879 a Hendrie family of Albany sent James, their twenty-year-old son, in pursuit of an American dream unreachable at home. Hendrie described the White Man's plenty: "Dear Father and Mother: I am well pleased with the place it has turned out better than I hoped it would, there is 1001 ways of making money there is not a white man on the 'Feilds' (*sic*) who cannot do well if he is steady. . . . . We have in all 23 Boys & good horses, and two carts. I have 16 at the claim and 5 at the machine, . . . I like the work very well, the only fault I find is there is not enough to do. White men get paid here for walking around. . . . [Home] is a pretty little place and furnished equal to any house in 'Albany' of the same size. . . . The table . . . lacks nothing in the way of eatables of all kinds. There is nothing under the 'Sun' that you cannot get here 'if you have got enough to pay for it'" (To: Mr. and Mrs. George Hendrie, Dutoits Pan, June 29th/79). Hendrie moved from one mine to another, with no notable success, eventually going into groceries and supplies, then to selling water in response to the municipal supply "saturated with dead cats, Kafirs, or dogs"[33] (Cecil Rhodes, too, who disliked digging, sold water, ice, and ice cream with satisfying profit[34]), each move signifying a financial disappointment. He changes from delight to revulsion: "No man was ever more disgusted with the country, the People and the Climate, than I am with Africa and the Afrikanders, give them the country I say, this part at least. It is only fit the Koffirs. I would not stop a lifetime here, for all the money there is in the country. What is the use of it where you can't buy Comforts for Love or Money.... The sun is 'red hot' and we are anxiously looking for rain.... I am thankful I am out of the Claims, we have a cool store, which is better than standing in the sun all day.... This is my first day of my 27 years, 'Old Age'" (10/21/81). After trying and giving up the "Lemonade business" (Nov. 20th, 1882), James Hendrie turned to working as a bookbinder on the Diamond Fields, where his correspondence ends.

Another American Scrambler escaped with some bounty, returning to the midwestern plains of Cleveland, Ohio. J. P. Kower Jr. stakes a claim, hires Zulu boys, "knowing and must be watched." Like the common dream of prospectors, he believes he will gain easy wealth: "This morning took 2 kaffirs down in order to trim and square off the walls and do a little picking. Had been at work but half an hour when I picked a stone of seven and a half carats from the wall in trimming—a nearly pure cape white, good shape, but worth now only about Three pounds per carat. Quite a lucky beginning, surely, and it augurs well for the future."[35] Soon, however, with his eyes swollen from dust at his sorting table and "severe illness . . . nothing less than camp fever,"[36] despondent and gloomy, he sought to sell his ground in a buyer's market: "What makes, or helps to make things depressed, is the great rush to the gold fields at Leydenburgh just now. Hundreds and hundreds are going from here."[37] Kower's diary records fluctuations in both his moods and diamond prices, consequently in prices of claims: "Everything seems to combine Just now to try to crush me." After losing eight hundred pounds in gold selling his claim, fortuitously helped in the sale by discovery of a four-carat stone by "one of the boys", he is "happy as a lark"; in the process of striking his camp, he finds another half-dozen diamonds and another stone rolls out from his final sorting table. His heart leaping up at the thought of "home.—Home!" he delivers a valedictory: "I bid final farewell to the diamond fields, providence permitting—so then, goodbye ye clouds of dust! Goodbye ye vast armies of fleas! Adieu to ye million, aye, myriads of pestiferous flies. No longer will our throats, our nostrils, our mouthes [sic], our very food be filled with and our stomaches [sic] be disgusted . . . no longer will the flies dispute with us 'the right of way' over our plates at meal times; no longer shall our slumbers be disturbed by the countless thousands of fleas with which we have constantly been compelled mightily, to do battle. Thank Heaven, a few hours more and we shall be 'at peace' once more."[38] Deliverance arrived with bodily cost and fifty diamonds worth selling. He does not name a diamond "Peace."

Earnings for Scramblers were uncertain because independent diggers and buyers subjected the market to daily price fluctuations. "Made my first sale of diamonds . . . today," reported Kower in 1870, "nine and a half carats at 'Two-Ten' per carat. Three weeks ago, before the last great 'smash' in the diamonds market, these same stones were worth 'Three-Ten,' so that I got one pound per carat less" (22–23). Resolving never to go back to the mines, Hendrie ponders economic instability and arrives at a local explanation: "The Glut in the Diamond Market is not caused so much by over production as Illicit trade. . . . Hanging could not stop it. Fancy the lowest of 'Petticoat lane' Jews refusing a Diamond! The sun will stand still first" (March 1st/85). He concludes that "Amalgamation, and the Compound System will reduce the stealing to a few inside men and give more scope for detection. It is slowly coming to the fore in Kimberley and De Beers" (March 1st/'85 Beaconsfield).

Hendrie was correct about systems to control theft. At the end of the century, "purging and search resulted in 190,000 carats in 1897–98, and the annual recovery rate remained at about 100,00 carats till 1901. White workers who surrendered diamonds earned about £3,000 a year in bonuses, compared with £11,000 for blacks."[39] Foreseeing the unification of claims and the compound system for blacks, Hendrie accurately analyzed the fate of the Scramblers: "Kimberley is very quiet at present. 'Unification' of mining Interests has frightened what little life there was away. . . . Of course . . . it means Ruin to many, but fortunes to many more, overproduction means slow starvation, amalgamation, sudden death" (Kimberley Mch 7/85). By 1889, the London board of De Beers pledged to sell their diamonds only to a syndicate and to limit sales.[40]

Many global prospectors went home. They left a legacy of writings, a scramble of genres which combines to create a story from a personal perspective, a unique blending of news and fancy. And the mines? They were consolidated—an often-recounted history—by corporatization and syndication to centralize the diamond business from extraction to distribution. Diamonds again became rare and expensive.

9

Domestic Romance Adventures on the Diamond Fields

The dinner was served by a black dwarf named Bela, who in his fantastic proportions resembled a heathen idol in bronze.
—Louise Vescelius-Sheldon, *An I.D.B. in South Africa*

... the little weazened old yellow man crouched there watching beside him on that rocky ledge, so faithfully, so lovingly. His comrade—the white man—his friend and equal—had deserted him—had left him alone in that desert waste to die, and this runaway servant of his—the degraded and heathen savage—clung to him in his extremity, watched by his side ready to defend him if necessary at the cost of his own life.
—Bertrand Mitford, *Renshaw Fanning's Quest*

Adventure blends with romance in Diamond Fields fiction. Novelists manipulated ideology and racial attitudes, while the setting fulfilled their dreams. Characters encountered and reported in periodicals and memoirs appear ready-made to be slipped into novel pages. Kimberley open-pit mines offered their symbolic treasure along with diamonds but not without ideological complexities. The treasure bears a dark message. At the very lip of the awesome mine, literary diamonds do not appear independent of degraded conditions of production and commercial motives of buying and selling. African diamonds began their history mired in impurity—in mucky probing and crass bargaining with Jews in dusty tents. The karoo setting presented special difficulties in signifying a diamond as pure, valuable beyond cost, a sacred amulet to the highest reaches of society, of what nineteenth-century Western culture destined for women's or royal adornment. Vicissitudes of diamonds in South African novels chart their meanings—as the ultimate jewel of romance, as the ultimate commodity, as the ultimate material sign of the Jew.[1] Combining these functions, the jewel/Jew stands at the center of contested meanings in South African diamond field novels. Shadowing its Jewish center with a darker aura, native Africans leave a trace on diamond that is more difficult to discern, figuring on the margins in its symbolic system. Whereas Jews often taint meanings of the diamonds they buy and sell—a function of projection—Africans disappear from meanings of the diamonds they mine—a function of repression. Actual native miners return to kraals; in fiction, they help their masters steal, or they rescue their masters from death or prison, often at risk to their lives, and then they disappear.

Novelists inspired by the promise of a glittering story in an exotic locale confront a troubling symbolic economy that wrestles with the Jewish Question, the Native Question, and the Woman Question. Can Kimberley diamonds sustain refined meanings independent of the terrible mine, diamond-dealing Jews, and unclad African laborers? Linkages of diamonds to dark, despised peoples shape plots and problems in South Africa Diamond Fields novels where the source of diamonds is their setting.

Five South African novels confront the "problem" of the Jew in the jewel, the "problem" of the erased African, and the "problem" of the white woman.[2] The first three novels discussed in this chapter feature plots centering on the heroine. Such a focus categorizes them as a type of domestic novel, a feminine genre that in South African settings often merges with the adventure novel, thought of as manly reading. This South African form adapts to the karoo by encompassing bourgeois domesticity as an aspect of imperial escapades. Beauteous heroines frequently assume names reminiscent of bodice rippers—Dainty Laure in American Louise Vescelius-Sheldon's *An I.D.B. in South Africa* (1888) and Loraine Loree Temple in South African Cynthia Stockley's *Pink Gods and Blue Demons* (1920)—where both heroines succumb to irresistible Jews. Their counterpart in *Mixed Humanity,* May Sinclair, a sexy and diamond-dealing Jew, opens a window on functions of both Jews and heroines in African colonial domestic novels. May expresses sexual knowledge prohibited from those Christian heroines, whose hearts are nevertheless fluttered by Jewish lotharios.[3]

The last two novels examined in this chapter are adventure novels, Rider Haggard's *King Solomon's Mines,* which has often been considered a historically accurate rendering of a biblical character's enterprises in Africa, and

Bertrand Mitford's *Renshaw Fanning's Quest,* a tale generically comparable to Haggard's best seller although including a romance plot with the quest. Both involve penetrating a dark continent filled with hostile natives to find diamonds sequestered from Western markets. As in other novels in this chapter and the next, loyal natives enable the manly explorers to succeed. All the novels introduce intricacies of diamond-mining life to far-off readers.

Couper's *Mixed Humanity*—bildungsroman, domestic novel, adventure tale, and detective story—tells the story of Jack Senior, a fine blue-eyed Irish/English lad, prospector and boxer, while a subplot follows May Sinclair, mistress of IDB Ikey Mosetenstine.[4] Mixed humanity assembles at the mine, filled with nearly naked African workers, digging, shoveling, and inspiring metaphors of insects as it had for Trollope: "Kaffirs, like swarms of ants, were to be seen working at the bottom of the mine.... Senior thought of the Kaffir whom he had seen carried along on the stretcher, and the many lives lost in trying to unearth these stones held in so much value simply for ornaments; then, thinking of those of whom he had heard so much, the illicit diamond buyers, more generally known as the I.D.B., he wondered how many of them had forfeited the best years of their lives by being tempted to buy stolen diamonds from the Kaffir workmen" (20–21). Almost condemning the human cost of diamond mania, Couper pulls his punch and allows his character to skirt ethical judgment. African swarms are crucial in the illicit trade: "Senior had now become well experienced in the tricks of the wily African. Every dodge had been tried on him in the concealing of stolen diamonds.... All parts of the body they used for this purpose—ears, nose, stomach, hair—and they even made cuts in their legs to hide the precious stones" (45). Illegal possession of diamonds reveals Africans as figures sequestered from the symbolic diamond economy, as apartheid mining policy cordoned them from their birth land. Uncannily present, a scent of something rotten lingers as knowledge about their repression in maintaining the white stone's value.

As they were characterized as fences in English diamond novels, so here Jews appear as foundational to the underground diamond economy. Receivers of the Africans' looted stones were identified in memoirs, newspapers, and novels as Jews, the typical IDB.[5] Couper describes IDB Fagantsine: "His face was long and thin, his eyes bloodshot, his head was nearly bald. He had side-whiskers and moustache, dark in colour. He was rather well dressed, had on a long-tail coat and spotless white waistcoat, which, being low cut, allowed a broad expanse of white shirt to be seen. The cast of his features was decidedly Hebraic" (25). Fagantsine's formal outfit resembles descriptions of Bram Stoker's Dracula, while his name echoes Charles Dickens's Fagin.

In fact, the Kimberley air could not sustain Faganstine's pristine attire for more than two minutes. Trollope evoked an infernal atmosphere that clarifies the symbolic function of the IDB's shirt front: "dust so thick that the sufferer fears to remove it lest the raising of it may aggravate the evil, and of flies so numerous that one hardly dares to slaughter them by the ordinary means.... A gust of wind would bring the dust in a cloud hiding everything, a cloud so thick that it would seem that the solid surface of the earth had risen diluted into the air" (190–91). Because the sky rains dirt, whiteness at the center of Faganstine's body appears sinister. This is the white of stolen diamonds. The IDB's unsavory trade and spotless shirt link dirty dealing with Jews, along with the Africans who serve them.

If Africans in mines resemble insects, the good black natives as servants resemble loyal dogs as another answer to the Native Question. They die, as in *King Solomon's Mines,* when Khiva, the Zulu boy torn apart by an elephant, sacrifices himself to save his master. Or they support unsavory business: talented Basutos in Couper organize the thieves and shield Jewish crooks. For instance, Ikey Mosetenstine, the wealthiest and most successful of the IDBs, earned the undying loyalty of a brilliant and talented Basuto, Charlie, who acts as his agent and trains newly arrived native miners to steal.[6] Fictions rely on the trope of the trusty, self-sacrificing, yet often devious native.

Ikey represents the stereotypical materialistic corpulent Jew, with a Yiddish accent ("Zometimes I tink I go, and zometimes I tink I stay" [110]), luxurious home, and loyal Basuto gem runners, whereas May Sinclair, his mistress, blends features of lovely Christian heroines and irresistible Jewish heroes. A temptress, she is also an illicit diamond dealer. A renegade Jewess (like Marlowe's Abigail and Shakespeare's Jessica), she offers her treasure to a Christian man, in this case Searight, a scoundrel whose apparent charms are his forthright Christian good looks and a taste for brutality.

May's appearance and use of Yiddish phrases (*mozel* for luck) confirm her origins. From ages fifteen to nineteen she enjoyed a short, successful career as an actress, recalling celebrated nineteenth-century Jewish actresses Rachel and Sarah Bernhardt. Couper's delineation includes the canniness, beauty, sexuality, and emotionality of the stereotypical Jewess: "May Leslie, now nineteen years of age, was of medium height, of slender and exceedingly graceful build.... Her complexion was of a dark olive tint, yet delicate and transparent. She had large bright eyes, the blue of which contrasted strangely with the darkness of her hair, eyebrows, and complexion; her teeth also perfect in shape, shone with a dazzling whiteness against the dark skin. The lines and expression of her face bespoke a curious mixture of passion and shrewd intelligence, of pathos and strength of character; and the somewhat thick rosy lips of her small pouting mouth gave her a faint suggestion of sensuality" (70). Sensual lips are a giveaway to ethnicity, both Jewish and African.

Hoarding jewelry as portable, personal riches places May in the literary tradition of Jewish merchants, characters such as Barabas from *The Jew of Malta* and Shylock from *The Merchant of Venice,* recapitulated in Haggard's King Solomon, with May as these characters' lineal descendant: "From her childhood she had shown a strange fondness for jewellery, though curiously she wore but little. She was always buying some ornament, which, together with her numerous presents, she hoarded up, and like a miser brought forth in secret, to look at and feel with her light fingers.... Leading the way into her room, she went to . . . an empty box . . . and lifting the cover exposed a small safe . . . and produced gem after gem, jewel after jewel, ring after ring, ladies' tiny watches, tiaras, pendants, charms, lockets, gentlemen's pins, childish baubles she had stored up almost from her infancy.... She gazed fondly at her treasures, the hoarding of which had been the greatest pleasure of her life" (70). Here is Dickens's Fagin caressing his illicit treasure, Haggard's Solomon storing his hoard. Moreover, May's prototypes appear in such pornography as "The Beautiful Jewess in the Boudoir."[7] Combining the female porn star with economic savvy—the sexual connection between May's jewel box and the Kimberley Mine—produces a creature born and bred in the colonial, salaciously racist imagination.

On the other side of the domestic coin, innocent and Protestant Loraine Loree Temple, the heroine in *Pink Gods and Blue Demons,* never yearned for diamonds, apparently content with her diligent Scots husband's serial gifts to an add-a-pearl necklace. When she encounters the diamond mine and the Jew, erotic knowledge and sophistication awaken her; she falls into the romance plot: "It was only since she came to Kimberley that the romance had taken hold of her imagination. It was seeing 'the biggest hole in the world' that started it. She had gone by herself and gazed long into the vast excavation delved by the hands of men in search for those strange little cadres of imprisoned light.... She wondered what became of diamonds. They seemed indestructible, yet where were all the millions of them that had been taken from this one great hole alone—that, down there, out of the light, were still being dug and groped and sweated for? And it was all for women! That gave her a thrill she had never felt before."[8] Stockley evokes an established symbolic pattern about gemstones. Diamond has been divorced from the market economy, wedded to durable love rather than durable goods. Yet in the teeming presence of the Big Hole, Loree should more accurately have exclaimed about the delving miners, "And it was all for money!" Loree's substitution of lust for greed eroticizes the diamond. Her meditation assumes diamonds' economic value while suspending them from market exchange, instead indicating the immense worth placed on the beloved. The heroine's romance fantasy recasts the dangerous scene of production as a chivalric tale—conflating (mostly black) miners' miserable deaths with the love tokens of white knights and whiter ladies.

Lorraine Loree's racial profile—a "Jersey Lily with French blood"—alludes to Lily Langtry, a notorious mistress of Queen Victoria's Bertie, Prince of Wales, and suggests Loree's potential. Pat Temple's erotic torpidity matches his occupation: he sells cold storage plants along with beef and mutton—what the author calls "corpses." Though unromantic, his occupation was crucial to life on the Diamond Fields. According to mine supervisor Williams's account, "To supply the urgent demand for cheaper meat, the De Beers Company has erected large cold-storage plants at Cape Town and Kimberley, and is now importing meat for sale to butchers at Kimberley."[9] In earlier days, animal corpses would decompose for the delectation of buzzards, and—some averred—Bushmen, who were deemed able to incorporate rot without harm. The corpse-dealer's name, Temple, suggests colonial commercialization of religion.

Living with Protestant Temple, Loree's passionate register remains unmeasured until she sees the Big Hole and meets mine owner Hazeltine Quelch—sensual, fiscally sharp, and irresistible. In him, the affinity between Jews and diamonds appears somatic, even genetic. Credulous Loree eventually grasps Quelch's open secret: "This strange Eastern man with his gentle un-English eyes while she stood considering him—how un-English he was to have tears running down his cheeks like that; that he *must* be a Jew (as she had often supposed) to be so emotional, so unreserved, so piercingly sapient—the truth came to her like an arrow" (187). Loree requires an insight because Quelch differs from Cohen's crassly masculine East End Jews with big cigars. This gentleman Jew joins Thomas Carlyle's Captains of Industry in colonial form. Though his son attends an English public school, Quelch, without a specified national origin, appears as an Orientalized exotic. And although he owns a diamond mine, his financial dealings are shrouded. Rather, he lavishes diamonds on women. More than Couper's May Sinclair, Quelch gives himself when he gives diamonds. May craves diamonds; Quelch is a diamond—aphrodisiac and addictive.

At the novel's outset, Loree languishes alone in a comfortable hotel that had once housed a men's club where Kimberley mining princes retreated when tired of domesticity, a place imbued with the aura of illicit sex and diamonds. In the suggestive setting, Quelch casts his un-English eyes upon our heroine: "Immediately Loree experienced the same odd prickling in her blood as the rays of the diamond seemed to cause her. Only she no longer felt that she was missing something or that life was passing her by. . . . He was a dark, gracefully-built man with thick dark hair brushed back smoothly on his well-shaped head. Everything was right about him, from his hair to his shoes. He was the kind of man who could not make any mistake about dress, and gave distinction to anything he wore. His name was Quelch, and Loree was aware that he was a power in the hotel and in Kimberley" (12–13). When Loree tucks a rose from Quelch in the "V of her gown, her hands trembled a little and her veins thrilled again as if in answer to some magnetic current which, whether it came from a magic stone or from a man's eyes, made her feel curiously alive and daring. . . . His voice held a melancholy cadence; the dark beauty of his face suggested the East where women are addressed with a caressing softness" (15–17). The Jew's diamond carries its sexual charge from its donor, as it did with Rebecca's gift in *Ivanhoe*.

Quelch romances Loree with stories of famous Indian stones, bringing their exoticism to diamonds of more recent pedigree: "It was wonderful to hear Quelch speak of them. It seemed to Loree that his words were like the gems themselves sparkling and rippling and tumbling in cascades" (21). The gem-inflected voice materializes in Loree's room—one magnificent rose-pink diamond, "a little pink god smiled and sparkled" and a "chain of diamonds, two blue diamonds on each side of the clasp, and one of these diamonds has three dots or defects in it that, held in a certain light give the impression of a tiny death's head grinning at you" (109). Emerging in the Diamond City of the Plains, this diamond gift from the Jew warns against the wages of sin, the tiny death's head, like Damien Hirst's huge one discussed in the introduction to this book, a memento mori.

Pink Gods differentiates this enticing Jew from his low-born brethren while assigning them all intimate relationships to diamonds. Whereas diamonds associated with Quelch glitter in an exotic light cast by the harem, other Jewish diamonds mark conspicuous consumption. Mercantile Jews share with Quelch possessive, enveloping passions, unnamable sorrows, and glorious diamonds, but their lives and their diamonds result from greed more than lust. Mrs. Solano, a plump and still beautiful high-spirited Jewess, with her husband, Mikey, had been IDBs until Mrs. Solano inadvertently choked their infant son to death when he sucked down his tiny throat a huge yellow diamond hidden in his sugar bag. Because she has killed her baby while dirty dealing, the widow wears the stone on her forehead as a mark of her transgression, a grotesque imitation of an Indian goddess. And although Loree enhances her Paris frock with the glorious death's head diamond chain, Quelch keeps her name out of the society pages to protect her reputation. Only Jewish jewels are identified: "Mrs. Ikey Mosenthal's famous tiara; Mrs. Solly Moses' wreath of Jagersfontein roses. Miss Rebecca Isaac's magnificent necklace and pendant of water white stones. Lady von Gugenheim's priceless plaque of black diamonds" (123–24). Stockley's list enforces a linkage between Jewesses and jewels.

Loree's devil-head necklace is doubly illicit. Mrs. Solano had sold it but was never paid, so Loree indirectly receives her demon-marked jewelry from an IDB funneled through her Jewish lover who had liquidated the debt. The blue demon warns that this glorious jewel cannot be separated from its provenance. There is nothing left for Loree but reluctantly to escape her relationship with them—the Jew, the pink god, and the blue demon. With the help of the Irish Mrs. Cork, Quelch's former lover, she disguises herself as a boy, escaping to her cold-storage meat salesman and bourgeois respectability, where she will wear her pearl necklace-in-progress. The plot ends primly by giving up the Jew and his diamonds in favor of a Protestant ethic that preaches domestic simplicity and sanctifies industriousness, chastity, and discreetly modest wealth, while disapproving of stimulation, display, and ecstasy.[10]

Whereas Stockley alludes to a diamond in an Indian deity's forehead, American-born Louise Vescelius-Sheldon's *An I.D.B. in South Africa* places a huge stolen diamond in a Bushman's eye. With its sensational features, a secret African and a hidden Jew form one romance plot that reflects on European couples in the novel. Giving up a great diamond to the Jew and the African maintains British purity, a pious comfort.

The title announces its illicit theme, its economic motive, and its relation to crime fiction. The first character caught as an IDB, Count Telphus, commits suicide when he is apprehended. Other traders identify with him, while observing his lack of élan: "'Father Abraham,' exclaimed a sympathizing Israelite, 'how could he be so careless with such a blazer?'" (8). The count's companion, Herr Schwatka, represents a trace of the Jew and shares characteristics with Hazeltine Quelch as a passionate, sapient seducer.

The plot centers on domesticated Dainty Laure, who does not know that her husband, Donald, an "impulsive Scotchman from the cold North," is an IDB.[11] Dainty's home decoration mirrors her African/English blood: "Her home seemed a part of herself—a bright light creature, glorifying the materialities about her with a certain radiance."[12] Certain radiance pairs the heroine with diamonds, both of African origins. "Materialities," aesthetic objects deployed in the romance of domestic space, disclose the influence of the veld and its peoples and mingle with the European culture that has colonized an African landscape—the Scramble for Africa in a Kimberley parlor. The novel answers Anne McClintock's call for a "theory" of domestic imperialism by offering a concrete example that links African women, African goods, and an English-styled parlor:[13] "Within rifle-shot of the 'ninth wonder of the world' the great Kimberley Mine stood a pretty one-story cottage nestling among a mass of creepers.... The walls were artistically hung with shields, assagares, spears, and knob-kerries and in either corner stood a large elephant's tusk, mounted on a pedestal of ebony. A small horned head of the beautiful Hessebok hung over a door—India matting over which was strewn karosses of rarest fur, a piano stood in one corner, while costly furniture, rich lace and satin hangings were arranged with an artistic sense befitting the mistress of it all" (12). Decorative African animal body parts form the backdrop to display the African princess: "Bracelets of dewdrop diamonds encircled her wrists, and with the rubies and diamonds at throat and ear completed a toilet which might have vied with that of some semi-barbaric Eastern princess. Such was the woman in whose veins ran the blood of European and African races" (14–15). Rubies—primarily an Asian, not African, gemstone—add to her symbolic representation. Her racial profile conjures postcolonial descriptions of Orientalism, as if Dainty's mixed blood has produced a "semi-barbaric Eastern princess" resembling Quelch, an Eastern prince.

In line with similar fantasies about the native saving the white man, the author draws on a fable about all great men in a confederacy of the chosen: "Captain Montgomery wounded and dying in one of the Zulu Wars, makes a sign, the sign known to the elect of all nations. The sign was recognized—understood—by that savage in the wilderness. There, in that natural temple of the Father of all good, stood one to whom had descended from the ages the mystic token of brotherhood" (16). The African elect saves the English Captain who reciprocates by captivating and marrying the African princess; they produce beautiful Dainty. Danger lies in the proximity of handsome white man and gorgeous black woman. The author diagnoses racial mixing as enticing but pathological: "But the union of European with African produces, in their descendants, beings endowed with strange and inconsistent natures. These two bloods mingle but will not blend; more prominently are these idiosyncrasies developed where the Zulu parentage can be traced, and naturally so, for the Zulus are the most intelligent of the African tribes. Now they are all love, tenderness and devotion, ready to make any sacrifice for those on whom their affections are placed; again revengeful, jealous, and vindictive" (3).[14] However, Vescelius Sheldon conveys some sense of injustice for the Zulus when she questions what has been gained by civilization. She cites the Zulu chief's visit to Queen Victoria in England, when "old King Cetewayo innocently asked: 'When Queen Victoria has all this, why does she want my poor little corner of the earth?'" (61).

Nonetheless, the Zulu character remains an enticing Other. Dainty's unconscious sexuality and dormant primitivism betray her racial heritage: "On a divan, the upholstering of which was hidden by a karosse of leopard skins, reclined Dainty Laure.... Her eyes were closed ..., but for the occasional motion of a fan of three ostrich feathers.... The lids slowly unveiled those dark languorous eyes, which seemed like hidden founts of love.... Should occasion come, she could smile with her eyes, while her mouth looked cruel" (13–14). Dainty's racial mix accords with Western fantasies about Oriental royalty—ostrich fan, feline quiescence, and latent but stunning sexual force. However, the feline native sleeps. Like virginal Loraine Loree before Quelch, Dainty preserves a Victorian virginity owing to the Scots' low sexual registers: "She was, as yet, unconscious of the powers that lay dormant in her; under her child-like exterior was a soul of which even her husband knew nothing... the strange truth of which she herself was entirely oblivious, that the great pulsating power of Love had not yet inspired her.... Born of the English soldier and the daughter of a savage warrior, there slumbered in her soul a possibility of passion that needed only to be aroused to burst into flame" (32–33). The ability to kindle Dainty's flame lies in a dashing Jew, careless of the soupçon of sadism revealed in the sensual cruelty of Dainty's Zulu mouth.

Seductive like Quelch, Herr Schwatka exudes compelling sexuality. Like Quelch, too, he differs from ethnographic descriptions of the Semite. He is "a fair-haired Austrian of distinguished appearance and engaging manners, a cool-headed, strong-willed materialist whose spirit of determination dominated most of those with whom he came in contact" (34). Schwatka adopts physical characteristics of his birth country without shedding a Jewish essence. Bryan Cheyette reminds us that such people represent the double nature of the Jew, whose ability to blend in threatens traditional delineations of race.[15] Unspoken otherness quickens alien hearts; Dainty and Schwatka recognize the Other in each other. This affinity links Jew to African—their ability to "pass" and to taint European racial purity. Racial taxonomies move to the fore in South African diamond novels, where characters' racial composition menaces English identity. To pair off Schwatka and Dainty prevents dilution of the "races of Britain."[16]

Dainty discovers that her husband will be sent to jail for illicit diamond buying. With the cooperation of her Bushman servant Bela, "who in his fantastic proportions resembled a heathen idol in bronze" (29), she hides a great diamond in his eye socket, behind the adoring servant's glass eye. Here, sensationally, the ancient African icon incorporates the illicit diamond, like a jewel embedded in an Indian god's forehead. Resembling a strange god akin to the pink god and blue demon of Stockley's novel, Bela serves as guardian angel to Dainty, his eye accident rendering him uniquely qualified to save her. Inserted by a half-African into an African body, the hidden blazer darkly recalls practices of African miners to hide illicit diamonds in body cavities or wounds created to harbor them. Vescelius-Sheldon carefully delineates his race: "Bela was a 'Bosjesman' or Bushman, with features of the Negro type, and short, crispy black hair. He was about four feet in height, being one of the race of pygmies, nearly extinct. They are the oldest race known in Africa. . . . Their traditions tell of a mighty nation who dwelt in caves and holes in the ground, who were great elephant hunters, and who used poisoned arrows in warfare" (82). Hereditary cunning enables Bela to slip into neutral territory and return the eyeball-sized diamond to fleeing Dainty, Donald, and Schwatka. Inserting into Bela's description a generally accepted habit of Boers killing the once mighty San people supplements other narrative effacements of Bushman identity.[17] His selfless duty done, he exits the plot.

Escaping from the law, Donald, not only a thief but a bigamist, is revealed to have a wife in Scotland. The Scotsman regretfully hands over the diamond to Dainty; she falls into Schwatka's arms; they disappear with their huge gemstone, probably to America. The melodramatic finale of *An I.D.B. in South Africa* proposes a solution to miscegenation. The Scot returns to his racially pure spouse and his cold north country's frigid conjugality. Balancing the racial economy, tainted matter, including the gem, escapes to a shore where mixed breeds enjoy pleasures endemic to their kind.

Diamond in both novels carries that fetish spirit proposed in psychoanalytic theory as a sexual enabler. Such promise is taboo for cold Scotsmen. In both South African domestic novels, the heroine awakens through diamond's fetish power. Quelch and Schwatka contain the sexual spirit whose counterpart is the diamond. Loraine Loree renounces with difficulty that intense pleasure in the name of virtue, but Dainty's African blood enables her to enjoy it. According to cultural stereotypes, the Jew and the African take to sex and diamonds that are marked with their sensuality. In transferring sex to a moral register, the taint of death and the illicit cling to intensely desirable and envied diamonds. Beautiful Jews and Africans in these South African domestic diamond novels stand for this aspect of the diamond—yearned for but associated with what must be sacrificed to maintain middle-class respectability, the Protestant ethic, and Anglo-Saxon purity.

Bloody Diamonds in Quest Tales of Haggard and Mitford

The two historically enhanced legends of the Eureka and the Star of South Africa described in chapter 7 tell about finding only one notable stone, discovered by chance. In contrast to legends about common people seizing a single precious pebble, H. Rider Haggard's *King Solomon's Mines* tells of unmeasured tons, three huge chests of stones possessed by a genuine biblical king. Haggard's imaginary account of King Solomon's African diamond mine has slipped into the historical record. Despite its fabrication, his gems add a venerable lineage to the otherwise harum-scarum diamond discovery. Haggard's mine draws both from the author's own experiences in Africa and from Victorian biblical exegesis. Haggard's novel has been regarded as based on biblical and historical fact. African adventurers in the novel resemble actual characters introduced in chapter 8. In addition, the tale confirms imperial adventure stories and locates the fruits of diamond adventures solidly in London. Thus, the work exemplifies the blending of genres, history, journalism, diary, and adventure novel to present diamond mines as a centerpiece of British imperial might.

Haggard's tale earns additional credulity because its historical information is based on biblical authority. One Victorian assessment of Solomon's character revered him as the author of wisdom literature, Ecclesiastes, the Song of Solomon, and Proverbs, presiding over his people with humane understanding. He is John Ruskin's Solomon, an evangelical touchstone based on a literal reading of 1 Kings.[18] Ruskin regarded Solomon's proverbs as a type for which Jesus's parables were the fulfillment. Even Ruskin, however, opens the king's character to a less exalted interpretation, calling him "a Jew merchant, largely engaged in business on the Gold Coast."[19] Perhaps his own father's mercantile prosperity removes a tad of the derisive tone from casting the great king as being in trade. Solomon emerges from the Victorian era with mixed credentials. Interpreters influenced by the New Biblical Criticism selectively read scriptural passages to portray him as licentious, a liar, and a builder of an ostentatious, inferior temple, with inflated figures regarding its gold and silver ornamentation. Adding to his low character, he was a bad ruler, promoting his interests before his people's well-being. Hence, Victorian Solomon with his

Victorian diamond mine appears in this account of diamond scrambling as an influential African-Jewish-Victorian diamond legend, taken like the Eureka and Star of South Africa legends as actual history.

All was not glory for Victorian Solomon. On Sunday evenings in 1861, freethinking Christians gathered for a series of lectures at South Place Chapel in Finsbury, London, to learn from P. W. Perfitt, PhD, about King Solomon's dark side. Not only are the Proverbs "of low abstract or practical value," but perhaps he didn't write them. Covering himself with splendor, "the savage occasionally showed from beneath the purple robes."[20] There is worse:

> ... incapable of undertaking any important building operations without the architectural guidance and handicraft assistance of foreigners, [Solomon contravened Mosaic law to take an Egyptian wife]. ... Solomon's temple was Egyptian in design. ... We are led to conclude that in size and splendor it must have surpassed ... all ancient temples; whereas ... when we come with rod and line to measure it, that in Egypt it was altogether too petty to have called it a temple. ... It would not have been possible for them to work so much wealth into such a small compass. Had the entire temple been built of solid gold, the alleged amount would not have been exhausted, and the silver would have built a wall round it.[21]

Like his ostentatious temple, trumpeted with misleading superlatives, Solomon enjoyed an inflated reputation, himself being self-involved, self-indulgent, and self-aggrandizing:

> I repudiate altogether the statement that God made Solomon wise above all other men, for, as his conduct showed, he was ignorant of the commonest principles of good government. He opened a large trade, but by this his people were neither improved nor enriched. He retained that trade in his own hands, and heavily taxed the commodities he supplied, so that by means of his profits he was enabled to live in luxury. This was to exhibit selfishness as a man, and folly as a king; for as a king, desiring his people to grow, he would have tried to clear away all the stumbling-blocks on the path of commerce, looking to his own profit rather as the outcome of their success than as the result of their being impoverished. ... His notions never went beyond the sensual indulgence of the moment, and the glory which has ever been so captivating to the Oriental mind.[22]

Sunken in Oriental stewpots, Perfitt's materialistic Solomon would fit a psychological profile of a destructive narcissist developing at the time of Haggard's novel.[23]

Perfitt was not the only biblical interpreter to represent Solomon as a political disaster. In *A History of the Jewish Nation,* Edward Palmer also condemned his violation of moral precepts. While ruling at the pinnacle of the Jewish nation, the twenty-year-old monarch's immorality laid the groundwork for its fall. Defying Moses's advice for prudence and simplicity, the king succumbed to corrupt influences: "Solomon's reign was the culminating point of the prosperity of Israel. . . . Incalculable wealth thus flowed into the country, and the magnificence of the Hebrew monarch exceeded that of the most opulent and luxurious courts of the ancient world . . . [reflecting the] king's own tastes for luxurious indulgence and oriental display. His military displays raised up against Israel many and formidable foes, his lavish expenditure laid heavy burdens upon his subjects, and his strange wives seduced him from the worship of God to follow the vain and filthy idols of the surrounding peoples."[24] Palmer and Perfitt limn a profile befitting modern rulers, perhaps with anxious eyes to their own empire's excesses, their own sovereign's amorous inclinations, and her growing store of gems.[25]

Biblical criticism became African history when H. Rider Haggard set his adventure tale at a grand site supposedly built by the Hebrew potentate. Cecil Rhodes, the English colonist closely associated with South African diamonds, imperialist ideals, and the De Beers Consolidated Mining Company, Ltd., funded the first archaeological expedition to the Great Ruins of Zimbabwe, led by Theodore Bent.[26] Because he thought the sophisticated buildings beyond native African capacity, Bent attributed the ruins to Phoenicians. Though Rhodes sought gold, not diamonds, the expedition offered Haggard a setting for his novel in a real place; Solomon's building of the Great Ruins has become part of what Robin Derricourt decries as a "blight" of fancy that merged with fact and religious belief to invent African history.[27] Blending biblical with fabricated modern history and real African mining, *King Solomon's Mines* endures as an account of "Ophir," the supposedly lost storehouse of Solomon's wealth.[28] Given Jewish domination of the London diamond trade, the association between Solomon and diamonds seems pre-scripted.[29] Like Scott's Isaac of York, Haggard's Solomon hid immense treasure in a crypt. While affirming Bent's premise that black Africans could not have built the monumental Zimbabwe structures, Haggard changed Bent's architects from Phoenician to Hebrew.[30]

In the novel, the site is discovered by three Englishmen, adventurers in search of a lost brother and Solomon's treasure. They get caught up in a political struggle involving an African tribe much like the Zulus, noble savages, particularly the men, admired for their great height and military prowess (figure 11). The sculpted white body of English adventurer Sir Henry and the equally statuesque black one of Umbopa, eventual king of the Kukuanas, are the yin and yang of masculinity. At their first meeting, Umbopa recounts his lineage and displays in a striptease his superlative physique: "I am of the Zulu people, yet not of them. . . . Sir Henry told him to stand up. Umbopa did

Figure 11. Zulu warrior, probably named Jim Caneel. The Zulus were considered the acme of African tribes, as Haggard's obsession with their tall stature and martial skills demonstrates. The background suggests a studio painted backdrop. (Williams, *Diamond Mines of South Africa*, 1:95)

so, at the same time slipping off the long military great coat he wore revealing himself naked except for the moocha round his centre and a necklace of lions' claws. He certainly was a magnificent-looking man; I never saw a finer native. Standing about six foot three high he was broad in proportion, and very shapely."[31]

Umbopa represents a towering figure for Haggard's nostalgia for the Zulus, an admiration that extended from his first published essay, "A Zulu War Dance," to his final trilogy of romances.[32] The three Englishmen sign on to defend the dignified Umbopa. After bloody battles, the fictionalized Zulu is restored to his realm on the very lands where lay Solomon's lost mines. Haggard believed in a biological and cultural link between Solomon and Zulu nobility, finding similar customs issuing from their putative common origin in the Fertile Crescent.[33] Hebrew and Zulu kings possess the treasure the Englishmen seek but claim not to desire. The Englishmen's projection displaces diamond lust on to the African and the Jew.

Given the author's linking ancient Zulus to ancient Hebrews, a connection between the Great Ruins of Zimbabwe and Solomon's site in Haggard's novel seems inevitable. Haggard's mine itself, however, describes both contemporary Kimberley mining technology and Victorian miners' equipment. Hired to guide Sir Henry and Good, the other adventurers, elephant hunter Allan Quatermain acquires "a solid, good quality used wagon. It was not quite a new one, having been to the Diamond Fields and back, but in my opinion it was all the better for that" (41). Used equipment of a prospector, the wagon knows its way. Haggard's African sojourn at the Diamond Fields becomes his basis for describing Solomon's mine; like the wagon, the writer had been to the Big Hole, as Quatermain describes it: "I pointed to a series of worn flat slabs of rock which were placed on a gentle slope below the level of a watercourse which had in some past age been cut out of the solid rock: 'If those are not tables once used to wash the 'stuff,' I'm a Dutchman.... At the edge of this vast hole, which was the pit marked on the old Don's map, the great road branched into two.... In many places this circumventing road was built entirely of vast blocks of stone, apparently with the object of supporting the edges of the pit and preventing falls of reef" (257). Haggard explains what was gradually understood about kimberlite pipes containing diamonds needing to be extracted from substrate; he adapts Kimberley washing practices to Solomon's natural watercourse with rock tables, attributing nineteenth-century technology to the Hebrews. In Kimberley mines, sand and gravel were brought up from the hole on cables, then separated at the top by a type of cradle that washed the material. This device was adapted from its use on the Australian gold fields by an American, J. L. Babe.[34] At first attempts to maintain stable roads in Kimberley mines were doomed to digging enthusiasm, but wise Solomon's vast blocks of stone for roads (demonstrating the architectural prowess in the Great Zimbabwe Ruins) prevented such calamities.

Haggard portrays Solomon's mine as many journalists, memoirists, and novelists describe the Big Hole: "a vast, circular hole with sloping sides, three hundred feet or more in depth, and quite half a mile round" (257). Confirming the Big Hole as model, Quatermain remarks to the two adventurers, "It is clear that you have never seen the diamond mines at Kimberley. You may depend on it that this is Solomon's Diamond Mine; look there, I said, pointing to the stiff blue clay… the formation is the same" (257). Solomon's miners apparently knew about kimberlite, the "stiff blue clay," as diamond dirt only recognized in Haggard's time. Quatermain delivers an authoritative mineralogical lecture that seemed to authenticate Haggard's romance as actual history. Before the Big Hole, there had never been a diamond mine such as the South African ones. The South African entrepreneur is imagined as a Hebrew king.

Victorian imperialism is written into the symbolic cluster of Jew and African who lost to the British in Haggard's account of the race for diamonds and racial supremacy.[35] Heidi Kaufman argues for the Jewish attribution to Solomon's Victorian diamonds and the novel's rationale for what she regards as the adventurers' "theft" of them: "Haggard's production of masculine Jewish space in Africa not only enables the three English adventurers to prove themselves racially superior to Jews and Africans but also imaginatively secures the British imperial project by aligning it with Solomon's earlier one."[36] That the adventurers steal the riches, however, is a murky legal matter. Who would own them? Haggard regards the English not as raiders but as rightful inheritors, seeming to have a license to steal. In celebrating their discovery, the Englishmen exult that they, neither the Hebrews nor the Portuguese, are the Chosen People. Quatermain underscores a providential delivery of riches to the superior race of man: "There we stood and shrieked with laughter over the gems which were ours, which had been found for *us* thousands of years ago by the patient delvers in the great hole yonder, and stored for *us* by Solomon's long-dead overseer.… Solomon never got them, nor David, nor Da Silvestra, nor anybody else. *We* had got them; there before us were millions of pounds' worth of diamonds…, only waiting to be taken away" (author's emphasis; 279). As mentioned above, diamond hoarding was consequent on an excess of South African diamonds, the practice Haggard backdated to the biblical king. The hidden chamber of riches, unessential to Solomon's daily indulgences, stores his leftovers as security, worship of hoarded wealth in the cathedral devoted to it.

Writing a Victorian allegory of material aspiration as God-blessed, Haggard links Solomon's great treasure cave to a cathedral: "Let the reader picture to himself the hall of the vastest cathedral he ever stood in, windowless indeed, but dimly lighted from above (presumably by shafts connected with the outer air and driven in the roof, which arched away a hundred feet above our head), and he will get some idea of the size of the enormous cave in which we stood, with the difference that this cathedral designed of nature was loftier and wider than any built by men" (262). Haggard makes virtual history, a good evangelical story constructed from alternative facts.[37]

Despite Haggard's claim that the tale is without women, their symbolic presence informs the core and outcome of the adventure.[38] There would be no adventure without the ancient map outlining a topographical woman with mountains called Sheba's breasts complete with nipples and a pubic triangle, "the Place of Death" that is loaded with diamonds. An unnamed woman accompanying the unfortunate Da Silvestra apparently betrayed him, leaving in the cave a womblike goat-skin intended for food but weighted down with diamonds: "Good stooped down and lifted it. It was heavy and jingled. 'By Jove! I believe it's full of diamonds,' he said in an awed whisper; and, indeed, the idea of a small goat-skin full of diamonds is enough to awe anybody" (275). To underscore the glory of it, Haggard italicizes the sentence of the goat-bag discovery, the first time the men run across diamonds. These gems in the pouch have not fully transformed from Solomon's gold coins stamped with Hebrew lettering to Solomon's diamonds. Pebbles, even diamond ones, do not jingle. Haggard's adventure tale competed with R. L. Stevenson's *Treasure Island,* a boy's quest romance about lost treasure and piracy.[39] Jingling diamonds recall *Treasure Island* with its musical pouch of foreign gold coins, "a canvas bag that gave forth, at a touch, the jingle of gold."[40]

Penetrating the Place of Death, the three discover a womblike alcove with three stone chests: "the chest was three-parts full of uncut diamonds, most of them of considerable size . . . 'We are the richest men in the whole word,' I said" (278). Jubilation over incalculable wealth trumps the men's denial of fiscal motives. While the other two try to find an escape route, Quatermain calculates gains: "I may as well pocket a few in case we ever should get out of this ghastly hole. So I just stuck my fist into the first chest and filled all the available pockets of my old shooting coat, topping up—this was a happy thought—with a couple of handfuls of big ones out of the third chest" (292).

The muse of money inspires happy thoughts and regrets for tons of lost wealth: "Somehow I seem to feel that the millions of pounds' worth of gems that lie in the three stone coffers will never shine round the neck of an earthly beauty" (302). Though Quatermain projects regret for lost jewelry on to women as jewel stands, money is his game.

As the diamond discovery created unintended, uncalculated economic challenges, so King Solomon's diamonds, even a miniscule fraction could depress profits. Good warns of real financial consequences of selling their South African diamonds: "We shall flood the market with diamonds" (278). The fictional characters seek counsel and profit from an actual diamond expert, Edward Streeter, according to Sir Henry: "Good and I took the diamonds to Streeter's to be valued … and I am really afraid to tell you what they put them at, it seems so enormous. They say that of course it is more or less guess-work, as such stones have never to their knowledge been put on the market in anything like such quantities.... I asked then, if they would buy them, but they said that it was beyond their power to do so, and recommended us to sell by degrees, for fear we should flood the market. They offer, however, a hundred and eighty thousand for a small portion of them" (318–19). The considerable English pounds proposed for a small proportion of slowly released diamonds preserves high prices in novel and London market alike.[41]

Testimony of the diamond adventure, trophies, such as the "axe with which I chopped off Twala's head" (320), ornament Sir Henry's home. Twala, the hideous, evil ruler, first appears in his regal garb; "bound on his forehead … a single and enormous uncut diamond" (141), rough like the savage. Haggard's yarn does not enlighten the reader about the state of Solomon's diamonds, but they are also likely in the rough. *King Solomon's Mines* forges strong links between Jews, Africans, and diamonds. Native Question joins Jewish Question in sequestering diamond's pure white splendor from the taint of despised races. Victorian Solomon's diamonds fill worthy British pockets as a fulfillment of imperial diamond dreams.

Vicious Bushmen and an Evil Eye Diamond

Without mentioning Jews or diamond mines, Bertrand Mitford's African diamond novel *Renshaw Fanning's Quest* (1894) banishes an African diamond closely associated with Bushmen. Mitford echoes common denigration of Bushmen, or San peoples, such as the more vicious evaluation of Robert Moffat: "With the exception of the Troglodytes … no tribe or people are surely more brutish, ignorant, and miserable than the Bushmen of the interior of

Southern Africa."[42] The novel combines the country manor genre with the adventure novel to create a fantasy of both domestic contentment and racial superiority.[43]

Renshaw Fanning, an unmaterialistic, overly trusting geologist, is obsessed by a seven- or eight-hundred-carat unmined diamond, called the Eye, that gleams by moonlight in a territory controlled by Bushmen. The quest novel includes two African peoples—yellow Basutos and blackest Bushmen—and two Englishmen of opposing moral character. Mitford projects on to the Bushmen diabolical diamond worship.[44] Why not wrest the diamond from its savage substrate? Why, after all that questing, give it up?

Geologist Fanning wants the diamond, but his recurring malaria leaves him gasping in a dirt-floored room in his parched karoo farm, blanketed with insects: "The swarming flies buzz around. The windows are black with them; the table is black with them; the air is thick with them.... They light on the diner's head, crawl about his face, crowd over plates and dishes and tablecloth—mix themselves up with the food, drown themselves in the drink."[45] Flies accumulate on Fanning's dying sheep: "The veldt was studded with the shriveled, rotting carcasses of dead animals" (48). Ill and weak, Fanning had persisted in this terrible terrain to launch four times in pursuit of the Eye. He wears a leather pouch around his neck hiding a map deeded him, as in Haggard, by a European man. Mitford had explained that the tribe had earlier rescued, fed, and restored the white man who willed the map to Fanning, but the text disregards this Samaritan behavior by savages. Renshaw finally embarks on his fifth quest for the stone, this time accompanied by a rascally English stranger, Maurice Sellon, whom Fanning trusts because the adventurer, straying to the farm in need, sat by him during the geologist's delirium.

All is not karoo in this South African diamond novel. Sunningdale, a farm owned by Christopher Selwood, an English settler, seems a new Eden: "A wild, deep, romantic valley ... melodious with the piping of birds ... where the stream winds and curves through a green fertile bottom" (24) offers a productive settlement, enabled by loyal black servants. Agriculture supports family values on the one hand, karoo promises manly quests for treasure on the other. Narrative structure balances domestic comfort against the lure of great material wealth, crystallized in the huge, primitive diamond.

Because Bushmen hold the Eye "greenish, but brilliant as a star" (134) in sacred dread, it is inextricable from the "filthy devils." Suffused with the diamond's infernal light, the Valley of the Eye "was a demon-haunted place," the diamond "a devil's eye that would scorch up whoever looked at it too long" (134). Fear of raising the devil impels hideous natives to defend the place and to shoot poisoned arrows at invaders. They are incredibly small, unlike statuesque Zulus, about whom Mitford wrote in a travelogue.[46] After generic dangers, Fanning and Sellon finally gaze with epiphanic rapture at the stone that promises moral and material conversion:

> "HERE IT IS! THE EYE!"
>
> Well might they be struck speechless. To one the retrospect of a hard, lonely life, sacrificed ... to the good of others, a struggling against wind and tide, a constant battle against the very stars in their courses—rose up and passed before his eyes in a lightning flash at that moment. To the other what experience of soured hopes, of reckless shifts, of a so far marred life, of failure, and confidence misplaced and unrequited—of gradual cutting loose from all principles—a confusion between the sense of right and wrong, and following immediately upon all, a golden glow of hope no longer deferred, a sunny ideal of abundant consolation; of love and happiness! But to both comfort, ease, wealth. (191)

Money promises abundant consolation in this manifesto of South African diamond power. As financial security, the Eye promises reform to both men along with scientific credentials to Fanning. Who could argue against middle-class values grafted on to imperial escapades? Were it not for its setting, the perilous diamond discovery could compare to a Samuel Smiles profile about rewards of hard work. Both characters might clean up good. But the diamond's green light, its association with primitive religion, and its disproportionate value indicate that it is incompatible with middle-class morality. The novel finally neutralizes the evil Eye.

Unmined, the Eye is inextricable from the soil where it had been imbedded for millennia and from the people associated with that soil. Without denying the Eye's glory, Mitford cannot abandon it to devil-fearing natives. Neither can he taint the good geologist with it. Sellon can have it. Although Fanning had twice saved the irredeemable Sellon from death and has shared the secret map with him, the scoundrel abandons Fanning who collapses when he's hit by a Bushman's poisoned arrow. Sellon pockets the diamond, cashes it in for immoral pleasures, and though already married, escapes with a narcissistic English beauty. Bigamy, as in *An I.D.B. in South Africa,* adds another sensational feature. The bad Brits go off together with the huge devilish diamond, dangerous not only to credulous Bushmen but to Anglo-Saxon virtue.

Meanwhile Fanning's Koranna servant, Dirk, who abandoned the farm to hunt, discovers his former master on the brink of death. Dirk saves the good

Englishman, finding that Fanning's boot prevented no more than superficial penetration of the arrow. Dirk kills the tiger about to attack his unconscious master, cures him with native medicine, and, after watching over him until he can be transported, lugs him home. Fanning survives to live well because of faithful Dirk and because his geologist's knowledge enables his bare hands to cull enough diamonds from the loose soil in the Valley of the Eye to be sold at a bargain price in England "nearly seventeen thousand pounds" (240). Again, the African novel calculates the financial worth as an obvious meaning of diamonds. Though he could have negotiated for a higher payment, unmaterialistic Fanning takes away enough to make him sufficiently rich to marry silently faithful Marion Sellwood and to buy a flourishing farm near her brother, Fanning's best friend. Better yet, the domestic life triumphs over the karoo with its cursed diamonds and infectious dust.

Most imperial diamond novels find a way, however convoluted as in the five discussed in this chapter, both to dazzle the reader with diamond's allure yet to restore a moral universe by snatching the stones away, or better, cashing them in. Diamond fortune transforms to middle-class comfort rather than flamboyance. The successful quest is revealed not for that demonic diamond but for a monogamous, loving life of fruitful labor. The Eye remains on the side of the devil when it becomes British. Bushmen were right.

10

Disavowed, Dispossessed Boers in Charlotte Mansfield and Olive Schreiner

> The farmers of South Africa had managed to live before gold and diamonds brought the riff-raff of the world into the country.... Diamonds are no good to no one, no, not under or over the earth. Men lose their lives and their characters to get 'em, and then sluts wear 'em...
> —Charlotte Mansfield, *Gloria*

> The Boer, like our plumbagos, our silver-trees, and our kudos, is peculiar to South Africa.
> —Olive Schreiner, "The Boer"

Boers settled in southern Africa in the mid-seventeenth century, sponsored by the Dutch East India Company. Somewhat later, the Company encouraged settlement of the French Huguenots fleeing from persecution, whose religion appeared compatible with the Dutch Reformed Church and whose children were taught only the local Dutch dialect. Dutch and French farmers merged through marriage and culture. Their religious convictions preached dominion over African natives. Hence, they became at odds with the British abolition movement and with urbanized settlements organized around mining and commerce. They lived at a pastoral pace opposed to urbanization and overvaluation of material goods. To escape British laws that forbade them to keep slaves or inflict corporal punishment on servants and to maintain their agrarian way of life, the Boers trekked eastward to the Transvaal. Along the way, they battled Zulu troops and were ambushed by them. The trek helped to produce a strong Afrikaner nationalist mythology centered on persecution and a sense of divine protection. Later, during the Anglo-Boer War of 1899–1902, 30,000 Boer women and children died of disease in British concentration camps, which further contributed to a developing Afrikaner nationalism.

Boers generally regarded diamond prospectors as invading hordes. True, promises of financial security encouraged some to join the diamond rush. With the notable exception of Olive Schreiner's later essays, Boers are reviled as an embarrassment to the white race—ignorant, ugly, fat, and filthy. As prospector Boyle found the karoo unlovely, so he regarded the Boer:

> About every twenty miles, one reaches what we are pleased to call a farm, some nasty hut, . . . inhabited by a filthy race of savages—the Boer. Such unutterably dirty dens are most of them . . . that even men colonial born . . . will sit outside in the shadow of their carts . . . rather than enter them. Poverty is not an excuse for the farmers' beastly habits. Wretched though the country looks, it is well liked by sheep; and the man whose family all pig together in two cabins, with stinking skins piled in each corner, raw flesh drying on the rafters, every disgusting parasite in heaps upon the floor, shears perhaps five thousand fleeces in the year, and owns some hundred head of horses and cattle. It would be an unmerited insult to the Basuto Kaffir . . . to compare him at least in all that concerns decent and cleanly living.[1]

Boer wives fit into their domestic scene. Complacent and fat, they are loyal to family, religion, and ethnic group. In *The Story of an African Farm* (1883), the serially marrying, waddling, Boer hausfrau, Tant' Sannie, is wily, materialistic, and sadistic, with pity for neither child nor black. In essays, Schreiner admired the Boers' lack of sentimentality regarding marriage, praising them for remarrying as soon as possible to preserve social stability.[2] Such is Sannie, who courts a younger widower whose wife has just died, but her eagerness to marry resembles Chaucer's lusty Wife of Bath more than a prim defense of morality.

Mansfield and Schreiner are notable for their inclusion of Boer main characters. Both find the karoo awesome and condemn its monetization. They mourn its transformation in works haunted by the incalculable cost incurred by the scramble for Africa. Mansfield writes as a settler. Olive Schreiner, with the karoo as her earliest memory and born in Africa from missionary parents, describes an unforgiving karoo in which diamond has erupted into a setting that she often celebrates in the wake of its destruction. Her literary use of diamond is idiosyncratic; her Diamond Fields settings ignore the mines to focus on ancillary laborers, not even on diggers, though her brother was one of them. Her work serves as a multivalent riposte to other Diamond Fields writing.

Charlotte Mansfield writes with more sympathy than Schreiner in portraying central Boer characters who honor marriage, family, and land. Mansfield's *Gloria: A Girl of the South African Veld* (1916) features a beauty born from an English father and Huguenot Boer mother. Her mother, though generous, affectionate, and fiercely attached to her heritage, fits the Boer stereotype. Aletta Dutoit (a venerable African Huguenot name, as in Dutoitspan, location of a former farm, then a diamond mine) conforms to the stereotype: "Her fat chin seemed able to rest upon her fat chest, for her short neck appeared to be rapidly disappearing and though in years not much over forty, she had long settled down into the stout contented vrouw of the South African born farmer's wife, who lose their beauty when quite young and never cultivate the grace and deportment which may hide middle age and postpone the so often hideous spectre of old age" (10).

English novelist and poet Mansfield lived with her husband in Johannesburg. She allows her Boers a history and offers significant vignettes of Africans in their kraals, having lives and desires of their own. *Gloria* begins in praise to the sun that blesses the karoo: "Many have been the arguments as to whether the sunsets the renowned artist Turner painted were ever really seen by human eyes . . . but any one who has watched the sun rise in South Africa, or reveled in its gorgeous passing, will admit that there are beauties which even Turner knew not of" (5). Holding out his hands towards the west "where the glory of the setting sun was greatest," (6) William Fairbain, the English farmer married to Aletta, names his daughter Gloria, after this radiant South African sun. Mingling English beauty and Boer love for the land, Gloria is born into a transformed karoo where pleasant towns and lovely farms vie with corporate diamond mines.

Written when the individual prospectors had given way to corporate organization, syndication, and cartel business structures, *Gloria* portrays the pursuit of diamonds as endemic to foreign capitalists and their singular pursuit of money.[3] Invading the veld, the diamond mine's "powerful arc lights" dim the stars. Enchantment dims judgment as well: "seeming as an enchanted city, the Vuurklip diamond Mine [*sic*] . . . was uncanny to come upon such a place in the middle of the open veld, so far from other habitations, a village in itself. . . .

Thus for many miles on a dark night, one could... know that through all the hours, the row of machinery would continue, and hundreds of white men and thousands of black, work away, for ever bringing up the earth out of the great hole, and washing it and searching it for diamonds" (43). Corporate mining spawns parasitic lawyers, boards of directors with tentacles into devious speculators, and Jewish corporate crooks.

Gloria casts the karoo as hallowed ground, not only to native Africans but to those Boers, such as Aletta, who revere the rocky earth suffused with ancestral bones and diamonds: "I found the diamonds... there on the veld where the graves of my people lie... I found one near where grandfather lay, and another where my father had just been buried... I showed them to my mother... and she said 'Aletta, promise no one shall ever dig for stones'" (288). Grandmother Dutoit's implicit curse on diamond mining pervades the novel, linking the gem with death as in other writings in this book.

Mansfield contrasts domestic and rural values to the mining operation: "the stones so sought after by men who want to make money, and worn too often by the women least merited to spend it. Stones, precious, yes, for their price is often one of loss of life in the getting, and loss of virtue in the wearing. Was it God or the devil who first named diamond precious?" (43). In the belly of the beast, the narrator articulates the conflict subtending diamond novels written in the face of the diamond discovery. Johannesburg, city built to gold and diamond dealing, creates political and business structures to harbor corruption. In the dominating ambiance, where talk is only of money and women as commodities, honesty seems naïve. For her part, Gloria wonders at such delving: "But how dreadful to think that anyone should ever get hurt, and all because women wear jewellery" (137). Mansfield places a judgment in a veld girl's mouth that is unarticulated in other novels discussed in this book; in *Gloria* no one concedes the mineral's beauty. Diamond shreds moral fabrics.

Gloria depicts a panorama of cast-offs from the mines. The utterly materialistic characters represent unsavory leftovers, detritus from gold and diamond mining. "His Satanic Majesty" has made his capital in Johannesburg, the "city of the golden calf" (45), founded on entrepreneurial thievery. "Two of the devil's special favourites" (45), the city their base, fan out to the karoo when opportunity presents. Though Snyman is a Boer name, King Snyman echoes King Solomon, but this wicked creature rose up from nowhere, having been a lowly "machine man on the Fanny Margaret Diamond mine" (46). After the mine fails, Snyman lurks around Johannesburg, "cesspool of the financial world" (48), as an IDB. The second demon, the lawyer Mr. A. Vancohn aka Abraham Cohen, "had given up being an area sneak thief, and promoted himself to the more exalted position of a financial burglar" (48), serving on the corporate board of Vuurklip. Another Jew who has ineffectively changed his name and married a stylish Gentile, Mr. McGreedy, managing director of the Vuurklip mine, cannot hide his stripes: "Though his name sounded Scotch, his religion was certainly not of that order. . . . Certain it was that North of the Tweed had seen very little of Mr. McGreedy. His body was not only small, but hunched together, as though his shoulders were constantly in fear of a hearty slap. . . . His head was of the style known as bullet, he had very little hair and that grey, his eyes were blue-grey and just escaped a squint, and his hands were large and out of proportion to the rest of his growth. . . . He had a thick ugly voice, and talked with his hands as well as his mouth. Yet he was not French in gesture any more than he was Scotch by blood" (108).[4] McGreedy joins the other two demons to bilk the Fairbains of their farm, with the assistance of Gloria's bad uncle, Petrus, who sells out his own family after illegally prospecting on their land for diamondiferous soil.

Resembling a *Moby Dick* of diamond mining, Mansfield details contemporary mining techniques. She includes policies about the "boys" employed for restricted contracts, identifying corporate structures that place the compound manager controlling native African workers.[5] Her mine is modeled on the Big Hole, by the time of her novel corporatized and no longer hand dug but extracted with explosives: "The Vuurklip mine was an open mine, which means that so far it had not been necessary to make underground passages and workings. The mine itself resembled what the earth would probably be like, if a mountain had grown downwards instead of upwards and then been dug out! Thus, the hugeness of the size of the hole can be imagined. It was worked in different levels 150 feet and 190; these levels were like enormous ledges in the sides of the hole. Some 3.000 natives worked there loading the trucks after the miners had blasted the sides of the mine" (251). Washing machinery and the pulsator beside it, "the most interesting sight at a diamond mine" (252), receive the precise description of a technical manual, including measurements of the pan and the rotator blades. The plot involving stolen diamonds depends on explaining "test stones," stones with distinctive inclusions that ensure the proper control of washing and sorting machinery. Because Snyman steals one of the identifiable test stones, his exposure can be technically credible. Moreover, unlike earlier pell-mell scrambling, corporate officers keep elaborate written records of test stones and sorting results.

In contrast to Vuurklip's mechanized city, the Clevedon plantation nurtures its natives. Corneels, a young, unmarried worker, lives in a farm hut and courts a woman living in the kraal; he catches sight of Petrus Dutoit digging in the moonlight. Gathering some of the yellow ground for his girlfriend's safekeeping, Corneels suspects its value, perhaps for medicine. Gloria describes this loyal servant: "He is devoted to us; besides mother is going to give them both a home when he is married, and his mother was born on grandmother's farm. He wouldn't work for anyone else. There are not many faithful boys, but Corneels is one" (211). In the nick of time, Corneels hands Gloria his box of Clevedon soil as evidence of Petrus's crime. Giving the lie to the rarity of faithful boys, Gloria testifies to another good-as-gold boy: "Quite the best boy . . . old Claas. He used to work on Clevedon . . . he and all his family, and his father before him. Mother was good to his wife and little ones when they were ill" (275). Claas spies on IDBs in the mine, befriends a fellow tribesman, and produces exculpatory information for a contrived trial involving Gloria's fiancé. Claas also exposes Snyman and Vancohn's part in the distressed sale of Clevedon.

Promised one cow for his service, the Fairbain family rewards Claas with two, paid from the £75,000 they receive from the prospecting rights of their diamondiferous farm. The Native Question answered with two cows, Mansfield addresses the Woman Question by recourse to the marriage plot. Gloria's courageous, momentary defiance of propriety enables her to hire an honest lawyer to gain security for her family and justice for her beloved. This diamond novel challenged a developing symbolic system that will in the next decade equate diamonds with everlasting heterosexual fidelity: "She was clad in a simple white gown of soft material, her only ornament a string of pearls, the gift of her mother, for she had said that she would never wear diamonds, the cruel glittering stones of avarice and betrayal" (363). Mansfield's novel was a lonely, obscure voice against what would become the commercial association of diamonds with marriage.

Unlike other writers, including those like Mansfield who are antagonistic to diamond's symbolic value, Schreiner utterly ignores diamond's potency. Drafting three of her major novels in her late teens when she lived in 1870s New Rush, her karoo settings never mention the diamondiferous reason for the settlement. She rejects diamond fever, a disease reluctantly caught by her brother Theo as a means of providing what their improvident parents could not. Schreiner's attitude overlooks the mineral with such willed inattention that its absence creates an avenging specter. She does not mystify it but disembodies it, offering instead a disturbed nostalgia for a place already alienated.[6]

Schreiner published only one of the three novels in her lifetime, *The Story of an African Farm,* though they all were conceived during her teenage years on the Diamond Fields. The first, *Undine,* introduces the novelist's convictions about the subjection of women that she returns to in her canonical *African Farm* and then narrates at length in her favorite, *From Man to Man.* Diamond in all three novels symbolizes the oppression of women and the rape of the karoo.[7] Life is intolerable to her heroines. who welcome death as an ultimate protest against materialism and women's bondage to men and money. An allegory equating land with women's bodies comes to a tragic union in her fiction. In face of its truth, the early death of a beautiful heroine is the only way out.[8]

Schreiner occupies a parallel position to Kipling's as a native writer, leaving and returning to a setting generating diamond meanings. But Schreiner does not equate African air with diamonds. Tied to the land as Kipling was to his, her passionate vision desires the karoo at the same time as it denies a satisfying union with its rocky, red ground. She produces fierce yet docile heroines who do not know how to rebel or do not have resources matching their ideology. How different is Undine, Lyall, and Baby-Bertie and the abused Waldo in *African Farm* from Kim, who can slip through ideological fissures in his complex society and savor his existence in a beloved country. Schreiner's characters may strain against their oppression, but finally, with their characterological, existential emptiness, give up the ghost.

"Karoo." This first word in *Undine* echoes in an unfamiliar ear like a call of the wild. The first paragraph surveys its blasted, deformed setting: "red sand, great mounds of round iron stones, and bushes never very beautiful to look at and now almost burned into the ground by the blazing summer's sun."[9] "Dirty and benighted" ducks delude themselves that the "thick red fluid" is pond water. Its redness like a wound, the harsh setting doles out similar torments as the severe Dutch Reformed worshippers: "An old Dutch farmhouse built of the brightest red brick to match the ground and stones . . ." (13). Those stones are not diamonds.

After a sadistically religious upbringing, orphaned Undine is sent to family in London. Undine's transfer polishes her without easing her sense of being irredeemable. She harbors unconscious rage against the evangelical severity that spawned her masochism. The beautiful heroine represents Schreiner's view of marriage as an economic exchange akin to prostitution; to worsen the character's subjection, she shows that female masochism at once submits and rebels, creating debilitating splits in the woman's very self. Pursued by Blair men, two sons and a father, but despite loving sadistic, narcissistic son Arthur, Undine enters a marriage compact with George, the repellent father, agreeing to marry him for an unrestricted £50,000. Fifty-one-year-old George Blair, with "bloated face and bags of money" (127–28), vows to marry Undine: "It made him swear in the fatty depths of his inmost heart that come what would, he should yet have her as his wife. He drew the little scarlet cloak that was slipping back lightly over her shoulder, and fastened it with a brooch formed of diamond-studded flowers which he drew from his pocket" (128). The diamond brooch of imitation flowers serves as Undine's fetters, her sumptuous home, her prison cell: "In a richly furnished apartment, enveloped in a soft cloud of white lace and delicate azure ribbons, sat Undine Blair. Diamonds glittered in her hair and her little jeweled fingers" (190). Undine's diamonds dramatize Schreiner's equation of marriage and concubinage. Pinned to her, pinning her down, Undine's English diamonds signify the husband's money and lust and the wife's abjection. Undine's London jewelry, the unspoken end point for those African diamonds, confirms Magubane's analysis of the replacement of economics with aesthetics in portraying "civilized" women's bodies in a colonial context. Marriage to a loathsome creature replicates her isolated, punitive childhood; her premature, dying baby that "aint much bigger nor your hand, and more like a rat than a baby" (141), "a puny shriveled thing" (142), expires after she talks herself into loving it, cradles the hopeless lump, and names it Violet.

Fire smolders under Undine's ice. Cousin Jonathan is a married cleric whose erotic feelings for Undine responded to the young woman's untapped sexual energy: "He knew of that power of passion that lay dead and unawakened beneath the cold, feelingless shell; and he knew as surely that the day would come when it would be called into wild life" (92). He is optimistic. Wild life transformed to self-destruction. If bloated George's diamonds contain a fetishized charge, it is a deadly one. Her powerful passion kills rather than enlivens her.

When George dies, Widow Blair takes only ten pounds to support her return to the Diamond Fields in a denial of the necessity of money. Schreiner's description of New Rush focuses on its filth. Her contemptuous description of native miners takes the reader inside the tent city, but with a racist tone that might surprise admirers of Schreiner's politics: "Alone, though the street was so thronged with the streaming crowd of niggers and diggers . . . that they kicked up the red sand into a lurid cloud over their heads—stark-naked savages from the interior, with their bent spindle legs and their big-jawed foreheadless monkey-faces, who, though they were going home to fire and meals, could hardly get out of their habitual crawl—colonial niggers half dressed not half civilized, and with some hundred percent more of evil in their black countenances than in those of their wilder brethren—great muscular fellows, almost taller and stronger than their masters" (193–94). Settling her among workers spawned by miners' needs, Schreiner deposits the beautiful young woman in the "poorest and most wretched part of the camp" (195) where she finds "a dark, bright-eyed Malay woman" (195), a laundress supporting too many children who employs her but quickly absconds with the remainder of Undine's belongings.[10] Willfully isolated and anonymous, Undine takes in ironing, her only friend an unnamed "broken-backed" little girl whom she comforts with harsh stories. Laboring to keep a puny rose bush alive, the nameless girl sprawls on the red dirt until she finds an empty tub and lives in it with her rose bush. Schreiner's allegorical propensity finds its expression, depicting in the deformed girl an image of white African women's deformed, sterile subjection.[11]

At the opportune masochistic moment, a diamond ring sparkles amid squalor. Unmentioned, it has been on Undine's finger not from a man but from her London Aunt Margaret, a tender woman who goes mad when her fiancé, Undine's brother Frank, drowns. The diamond surfaces only to be sacrificed. Undine has reencountered a man she had seen on the passage to Africa, now penurious and fevered. A man who will not survive in this blasted atmosphere offers further opportunity for Undine to be "utterly alone" (156). She has already given half her ten pounds to a woman on the ship whose story moves her; she has given half her bread to a dog in the streets; and now she can give up her diamond to a man after her own damaged heart: "He had bonny light curls like some she had cared for long ago, and he had broken boots and stockings so old that the red flesh showed through. She hardly knew which drew her to him most, the curls or the boots, for there is something achingly pitiable in broken boots. When a gentleman who has called himself a gentleman falls to that, he can fall no lower" (227). Low is perfect for our heroine, who moves his small tent next to hers. When Bill Brown, if that is his name, only mentioned once, will die unless he can return to England, Undine sells her diamond ring that is preternaturally filled with sentiment for one who has given up all material possessions. "She had worn it till it seemed to have grown a part of herself.... It had whispered to her that truth and love were possibilities" (232). She silences the final whispered essence of her being when she sells it, for the unlikely high and specified price of £100. Undine's ensuing melodramatic death brings together attachments from her English past—cruel Arthur Blair who dies on the Fields, apparently from its toxic atmosphere, and his dog Prince, who remembers loving Undine in England. Undine kisses Albert's cold lips and crawls back to her tent, faithful Prince curled up on her deathbed to attend her.

They all die young and beautiful. Lyndall, a main character in *African Farm,* dies after childbirth, falling ill after extravagantly mourning her dead infant in a raging karoo storm. The baby's father, called "Lyndall's stranger," gives her a ring that expresses ambivalence about attachment to a man: "Sometimes I wear it; then I take it off and wish to throw it into the fire; the next day I put it on again, and sometimes I kiss it" (227). Lyndall accepted the heavy ring from the stranger as a sign of men's power: "a massive ring upon her forefinger—a ring more suitable for the hand of a man, and noticeable in design—a diamond cross let into gold, with the initials 'R.R.' below it" (181). R.R.'s male ring, with its reminder of patriarchal religion on Lyndall's index finger, points to her ambivalent fight against male oppression. Neither a sign of Africa nor love, the diamond-cross ring represents a religion that endorses men possessing women.

That message entitles Schreiner's last nearly finished novel, *From Man to Man,* begun on the Diamond Fields in 1873 and worked on passionately on and off throughout the 1880s, up to her death.[12] At times, the book effaces her: "Just now I do not exist; my book exists";[13] her love devours all else: "I love my new book a hundred times better than I ever loved *An African Farm . . . From Man to Man* will be quite different from any other book that was ever written. . . . I love it more than I love anything in the world, more than any place or person" (n.p.). Loving her women characters, she first contrasts their fate but then shows they are comparable: two sisters, one married to a philanderer, the other mistress to a Jew, becoming a prostitute and dying of venereal disease. Woman, the unwritten term in the title, always serves as the object of exchange between men. One, called only "the Jew," returns to England from the Diamond Fields. Schreiner describes him in terms familiar from other Diamond Fields novels: "He was a small man of about fifty, with slightly bent shoulder and thin, small limbs. His face was of a dull Oriental pallor, and his piercing dark eyes and marked nose proclaimed him at once a Jew . . . with a strong foreign accent . . . He was a money-lender and diamond speculator" (306–7). Like Ikey Mosetenstine in *Mixed Humanity,* the accent is Eastern European. "Vitch zinks she is the best now?" (309) he asks Bertie of a mound of diamonds he produces from a pocket. The Jew's grammar genders diamond as female. By giving her the fine diamond of her choice, the Jew seems to reward Bertie's diamond acuity, though his generosity serves as down payment on the beautiful woman, not as a wife, because "Jews don't marry Christians" (313), a partial truth even in Victorian novels. Poor Bertie, who had been seduced and abandoned by her tutor, is damaged goods with no respectable options, so goes along with the Jew rather than retreat to her sister on the veld. The Christian girl cannot marry the man she loves, having "given herself" in the words of her true love, who rejects her as totally as the Jew finally will. The Jew furnishes his mansion for her but kicks her into the streets when he wrongly suspects her of enticing his nephew.[14] She dies from a venereal disease, passing herself her entire life from man to man.

Schreiner cannot comfortably occupy a firm ideological position, attacking conventional gender relations, racial relations, and economic relations, her opinions, in Anne McClintock's kind phrase, "crisscrossed with contradiction."[15] Her essays claimed great sympathy with the Boers to the point of her being detained by the British during the first Boer War. Her fiction portrays no sympathetic Boers, but rather offers Sannie, whose jealous regret in treating a servant is that "she had never broke a churn stick on a maid's head" (199). Similarly inconsistent, her essay "A Letter on the Jew," about Russian persecution, welcomes to South Africa members of "that great Jewish race" who "whenever he has been given even a limited measure of protection and liberty ... has blossomed out into the noblest forms."[16] Yet her portrayal of "the Jew" in *From Man to Man* repeats the very anti-Semitic opinions she found painful. Caught up in cultural contradiction, Schreiner took up one position or another; one can see in her extremism a passionate inconsistency indicating there was for her no firm subject position.

Schreiner's brutal upbringing informs the profound depersonalization in her novels.[17] Death of creatures, humans, babies, animals makes concrete a dark emptiness at the core of her creativity. Her characters have been emptied out, and the karoo often becomes an equivalent, or in other terms, an objective correlative, of desolation, however sublime it seems. It is the romantic sublimity that excludes without comfort. Her karoo is shocking and awesome.

Significant characters lack names—the stranger in *African Farm,* the Jew in *From Man to Man,* for instance. "Depersonalization" identifies a process in Schreiner's characters that refuses them selfhood. Characters depersonalize as an effect of abuse. Those damaged children empty themselves out as the child Undine habitually does during harsh, religiously based denigration when she suffers severe sense of sin without hope of redemption: "She seemed in a wide void in which there was only endless space and blackness, and she had not even two hands, the one of which might touch the other and in touching might find fellowship; and when she cried aloud her voice fell dead upon the air. There was only emptiness and black space, above, around, below, and she was one alone" (17–18). Loneliness and exclusion suffuse novels with ominous despair, whether located in humans or countryside; her four main woman characters' devotion to place or persons ends in betrayal and isolation. They suffer existential and physical loneliness and then they die, without a trace or legacy, two having borne shriveled, dying babies, and Bertie, one of twins, the other of whom gradually dies in infancy. *From Man to Man* is dedicated to "My Only Daughter, Born on the 30th April, and died the 1st May." Schreiner turns dead babies into allegories of emptiness.

Schreiner depersonalizes diamonds as well. She rejects diamond except as commodity bespeaking the male traffic in women. Undine works in the Diamond Fields, but the novel barely alludes to the diamond industry. The novel briefly mentions its pull: "She was attracted, like all others who were near enough to feel its influence, by the great magnet that draws to itself all who are good-for-nothing vagabonds, wanderers, or homeless—the Diamond Fields" (249). Perhaps magnet puns on "Adamantia." Writing on the very site of the mines, Schreiner's ostentatious disregard of them may indicate a fear that their very mention would replicate their magnetic, degrading attraction.

The same is true of her nonfiction. Diamond hardly merits attention in *Thoughts on South Africa*. Curiously passive, her reference to the city of mines regards it as hopelessly oppressed by influence, of Jews, Englishmen, and others, who live outside Africa while enriching themselves "in a town called Kimberley."[18] Schreiner abstains from engaging for more than a passionate paragraph on the oppression of mine workers. Because the black miners cannot save themselves, the "fierce and indomitable love of freedom" of the Boer farmers might save the country from purely financial values of the "Jew and Speculator, and foreign Shareholder."[19] Her inattention to native peoples conspicuously ignores Boer racism and their murder of Bushmen; she turns away from native peoples in a profoundly ironic vision of the Boer saving Africa for freedom.

Without openly declaring her position about diamond itself, Schreiner could not separate the mineral from its mythology, indeed from her own family name. Supporting the spiritual aspect of diamond and its connection with prayer and the female spirit, George Beet, the journalist who had interviewed Erasmus Jacobs, invokes Schreiner's literary fame: "The very large stone known as the 'Faith' diamond, was unearthed there [the Diamond Fields] by Mr. Schreiner, a brother of the celebrated South African novelist, Olive Schreiner. The name 'Faith' was expressly chosen for it as it was in answer to a prayer of that lady or her sister that the find was attributed."[20] Lacking the author's own observations on diamond itself, Beet's hype or hokum could take Olive's name in vain. In a black space, her writing hands cannot touch the subject.

Beet's blurring of whether the Schreiner sisters' imagined prayer was for salvation or fortune points to correlations between spiritual ecstasy and financial reward. To promulgate pedigrees, stories, or promises to signify satisfaction, the jewel from South Africa parts from its origins, in the classical Marxist sense that the African fetish of the commodity appears independent of its conditions of production.[21] In a related formulation, diamond gleams like Walter Benjamin's phantasmagoria, where the reified object signifies unconscious desire, magically free, a thing in itself, swathed in myth.[22] Yet the setting at the South African mines continually threatens to expose the magic trick, its thing embedded in diamondiferous soil. With a sleight of literary pen, the African disappears into the dark continent or dies in the big hole. And the Jew, a white hole of representation, like diamond, glitters and gleams somewhere else.

Captain Lindley optimistically prophesied that the karoo would settle back into indigenous dust: "The expense of trying to govern the diamond fields absorbs whatever revenue is derived from them. The diamonds, too, are becoming exhausted, and it may not be long before the migratory digging population retires to whence it came, leaving only the barren plains of Adamantia."[23] Nearly a century after his prophecy, Kimberley, the Big Hole recently abandoned, remains a dusty city, its mine a museum.

Lindley was right about the Scramblers and the Big Hole but wrong about diamondiferous Africa. After thirty years or so of Scramblers, their hopes for abundant diamond consolation became corporate recompense; in 1905, Frederick Welles, a supervisor in the Premier mine at Pretoria, plucked from a mine wall an enormous rough diamond of 3,106.75 carats, the largest uncut diamond ever reported. Legend says that when he brought it to the managers, they threw it out the window, claiming it was glass. Welles fetched it back. At slightly over 530 carats, the Star of Africa, also known as Cullinan I, only one of nine perfect faceted stones taken from this pure white lump, was the largest white diamond in the world at that time, the mine a corporation, the Star of Africa now part of the crown jewels, the anonymous Scramblers unknown once more.

And the unlovely land they abandoned? Spent mines in the karoo remain pits with water at the bottom. Tons upon tons of diamond-free kimberlite heaps add man-made trash to the red dirt they cover. Kimberlite itself is unusually useless. If diamond has been hugely overvalued, no value at all can be found for the junk brought to the surface in its pursuit. According to David Koskoff, "Kimberlite wastes may be the world's most useless substance . . . prone to expand, contract, and disintegrate, so that it cannot be used as a substitute for either sand or gravel in the construction industry. It is useless even for fill. About all that kimberlite is good for is yielding diamonds, haunting landscapes—and being reprocessed at some later time when improved recovery techniques may make it profitable to sift through it all again."[24] In exploring consequences of the South African diamond discovery, kimberlite waste haunts this setting, like the lives Kimberley absorbed for a while, then tossed away.

EPILOGUE

America — A Diamond Is for Everyone

Cal Hockley, American industrialist in James Cameron's blockbuster, Academy Award–winning *Titanic* (1997), holds aloft a huge blue heart-shaped diamond encircled by small white diamonds, dangling from a white-diamond necklace. As he's about to perform an act reminiscent of Trollope's Sir Florian Eustace and clasp it around the neck of his fiancée, Rose DeWitt Bukater, who objected to the piece's grandiosity, he responds, "It's for royalty. We are royalty, Rose." Although antidemocratic, he is correct. By 1912, the year of the *Titanic*'s sinking, the diamond empire had made its way to the United States with its treasures, jewelers, and newly rich who harbored *toshkhanas* a rajah could envy. As a harbinger of the diamond empire's transatlantic passage, Tiffany Jewelers bought at auction most of the French crown jewels in 1887.[1] Not only did the French need the money after the fall of Napoleon III in 1871 but also royal jewels symbolized the overthrown regime, inappropriate for a democratic republic. The irony of the move to a retail jewelry store in the land of the free seems obvious and commonplace. Never mind the Declaration of Independence; arriviste royalty crowned itself in the United States of America, where diamonds were mostly purchased rather than killed for or inherited. As the film portrays it, the blue diamond carried a message for men making fortunes and women liberating themselves.

Central to Cameron's film, the blue diamond named "Heart of the Ocean" (see plate 10) is modeled after the Hope Diamond, a stone with a troublesome past that makes a ghostly appearance in the Sherlock Holmes tale "The Blue

Carbuncle," mentioned in chapter 3. The Hope is an Indian diamond whose appearance in the West has been traced to the annals of crime.[2] When Tavernier bought a bluish-purple gem and carried it out of the reach of the Indian rulers who decreed that all diamonds over ten carats belonged to them, the Tavernier Violet, as it was sometimes called, was an impressive 112.75 carats. The West's premier diamond addict, Louis XIV, bought it and Europeanized its faceting, producing a scintillating 67.25-carat jewel. Now called the French Blue, it was stolen from the French crown jewels in 1792. Twenty years later a much smaller, though still hefty, diamond of the same rare color and purity surfaced in England. Though no definitive chemical analysis could determine its identity as a diminished French Blue, the dates, the color of the stone, and its mysterious emergence have tied it to the French diamond. This large chip off the Blue was evidently recut and smuggled to England where it appeared in a jeweler's shop as a 45.52-carat brilliant-cut blue-grey diamond.[3] In the tradition of exalted but perhaps fictive provenance, George IV may have bought it around 1830 and then sold it to pay off debts. Certainly, Henry Philip Hope, heir to merchant bankers, bought the blue stone. His 1839 catalogue, published the year he died, boasts of its incomparable color, rarer than any diamond in any royal collection. Court cases over ownership covered in the press were finally resolved in favor of Henry Thomas Hope, the eldest of three disagreeable nephews. Henry Thomas displayed it at the Great Exhibition of 1851, directly down an aisle from the Koh-i-noor, but looking more impressive in the white light of the Crystal Palace.

That celebrity blue stone now rests in the Hall of Gems in the Smithsonian Institution in Washington. The most visited exhibit in the sprawling museum, it is the glory among what passes as the American crown jewels. Its donor, Harry Winston, jeweler to the rich, wanted the United States to have a gem collection comparable to but surpassing the royal treasuries of Europe. Bought from Europe by Americans, then by an exclusive jeweler, and then moved to a national museum, the Hope became a sign not only that the seat of diamond power had moved from Europe to the United States but also that the great jewel commerce had migrated to America. Nouveau royalty emulated anointed monarchs.

In the following interpretation of the film and its American setting, "democratic desire" refers to an irresolvable ideological contradiction in its holding both a belief in equality among citizens and admiration for the very rich.[4] In America, democratic desire is grafted on to an imperial story to demonstrate that diamonds carry with them those earlier values while adding a mixed American message about the importance of wealth and great comfort yet the need to deny that class values, particularly monarchical ones, inflect American culture.

Though the film, of course, is based on a true event and expands on many earlier films, its main characters, including the diamond, are fictional. Treasure hunter Brock Lovett links the blue diamond to the legend that preceded the Hope's mysterious appearance in England. According to him, the Heart of the Ocean was once part of the great French Blue, owned by Louis XIV. He likens the jewel design to that of the Hope when it was owned by an American heiress, Evalyn Walsh McLean. Magnifying United States ascendancy, the fictional 75-carat rock weighs considerably more than that putative French stone, which weighed over 67 carats and also more than the Hope, which is, according to recent calculations, only 45.52 modern metric carats.[5] Oversized like the movie, the big blue diamond is the primary object of Lovett's salvage operation to recover the *Titanic* wreckage where he wrongly expects to find the gem secure in Hockley's stateroom safe. The treasure hunt frame belongs to the diamond quest genre, joining other diamond stories featured in this book.

McLean not only wore the diamond but sometimes fastened it around her dog's neck.[6] In a deleted part of the script, Rose remarks that the necklace feels like a dog collar. At its unveiling in an upper-class cabin on the *Titanic*, the Heart of the Ocean stands for the rigid gender and class laws, enforced on the upper deck. We watch as a servant and then Rose's mother lace her tightly into a corset. Escaping those strictures, the big blue stone comes to support women's liberation from corsets and class inhibitions. Rose unlaces her stays, then removes her clothes but not the diamond for Jack Dawson, an American artist returning from Paris.

Jack, who belongs on the lower deck, can live an artist's life, win his ticket on the *Titanic* in a card game, and defy class-bound strictures on propriety. Then, in a performance of democratic desire, Jack can "shine up like a new penny," as the unsinkable Molly Brown, the real-life American socialite and *Titanic* survivor Margaret Brown, proclaims while dressing Jack in a tuxedo for dining on the upper deck. Jack is an artistically gifted middle-class Wisconsin youth with a cultural hunger that drove generations of students to Europe for a sense of a history and fewer puritanical restrictions. Under Rose's commission, Jack draws her wearing only the Heart of the Ocean, should we miss the blue stone's meaning at that moment when it migrates from Cal's possessiveness to Jack's less materialistic masculinity. Rose takes charge of her body and future when she arranges her own pose and flips Jack a coin to draw the diamond perched on her nude chest.

The remarkable treatment of Rose's eye at the close of this scene, where the camera moves into an extreme close-up of young Rose's deep blue iris and emerges from old Rose's eye, affirms personal memory as history. The moment captures centenarian Rose recounting her experience of the sinking to a rapt audience of the crew on the recovery vessel, the *Keldysh*. Viewers peep through the tiny porthole of Rose's eye to secrets of the past.

Rose herself is salvaged by Jack, whose dying words license her to live an adventurous middle-class life. As shown by framed photos in her cabin on the *Keldysh,* Rose rides horses astride, not feminine sidesaddle; she stands next to a plane wearing pilot's garb; she rides a roller coaster in homage to Jack's promise to teach her to ride horses and roller coasters. Wearing handmade jewelry, she fulfills an American middle-class dream: we watch old Rose's clayey fingers form pots on a wheel in a nice home with the TV blaring in the background, by coincidence mentioning the *Titanic* salvage operation. Although the audience does not know it, Rose harbors her enormous diamond as an amulet throughout the long film and her long life. She boards the *Keldysh* to tell her story.

Heart of the Ocean comes to symbolize nearly absolute liberation from diamond values. In its inflated incarnation, a diamond symbolized family prestige based on money, governed by men (like the Eustace and Grandcourt necklaces), and then performs feminist time travel to symbolize the power of democratic eternal love. The penultimate scene may have shocked viewers in its profligate abandonment of a fortune, whereas the action will not surprise readers of this book. Rose slips out onto the deck, clothed only in a white nightgown, brushed nostalgically by those same ocean breezes that, eighty-four years earlier, wafted her dress when Jack Dawson encircled her in his arms. Climbing deliberately onto the rails in the stern of the vessel, she opens her hand to reveal the blue diamond and tenderly watches as it falls into the deep blue heart of the ocean. The sinking stone is shot both from below and above, allowing the audience—hundreds of millions of us—secretly to witness its gentle merging with its namesake.

The gesture resembles the tossing of great diamonds into the brink in earlier chapters as a rejection of imperial symbols: Guinevere's challenge to imperial sexual politics; Lizzie Eustace's repeated threats to drown family prestige ("I used to think I would throw them into the sea" [2.62:210]); Jonathan Small's revenge on imperial class structures; Prince Florizel's deliverance of humankind from diamond covetousness. Here, the blue diamond sinks at the very spot where Jack Dawson drowned, a tribute to love removed from cupidity at the root of all evil. Trophy diamonds must be rejected to attain heaven. But one cannot cast them off if one never had them. In all instances in this book, flinging diamond into the water cleanses its performer while it reminds readers of the vanity of worshipping earthly stuff. *Titanic*'s diamond constructs democratic desire as obtainable both when we have it and when we give it up.

Having turned the gem into a sign of remembrance and rejection of materialistic classed values, Rose's act prepares her for her death. The final frames show her young and translated to heaven, ascending a sweeping grand staircase to the upper-deck dining room where under a heavenly white-leaded glass dome, Jack Dawson, waiting in front of a clock, enfolds her in his arms. Amid the applause of all the resurrected souls from all the decks, the kiss lasts forever in that solid portrayal of eternity. Heaven is the upper deck.

A Diamond Engagement Ring

Is it a ring vs. a honeymoon? Take the ring: Niagara Falls has been falling for 50,000 years.
—"Lines and Logic on the Solitaire"

Even your diamond engagement ring may be washed with gentle Ivory Flakes.
—"Diamonds in Advertisements for Other Products"

Diamond meaning reweaves its web, translated into an American accent. Cal not only placed his huge stone around Rose's neck as a betrothal token but slipped a large white diamond ring on the third finger of her left hand, which she displays in a familiar gesture of the newly engaged. Well after 1912, the requisite indicator of love and marriage had become a diamond engagement ring. A recent tradition, the uneven progress to that shining pinnacle extends at least as far back as the fifteenth century in Europe, when Marie of Burgundy received a diamond ring in 1477 as a sign of her impending marriage to the Austrian Archduke Maximillian.[7] Though Marie's ring did not start a trend, it is generally cited as initiating diamond engagement ring history. That putative origin has become legend. Centuries later, Victorian suitors were not obliged to bestow a diamond ring on their fiancées. Henleigh Grandcourt in *Daniel Deronda* is somewhat of an outlier, his diamond engagement gift a sign, as with Cal Hockley, that betrays his controlling, abusive masculinity. His diamond engagement ring to Gwendolen did not signify an established English custom.

Although London has been the center of diamond marketing, a diamond engagement ring is not requisite in Britain, as the royal House of Windsor indicates. After Edward VIII's abdication for love of her, the Duchess of Windsor received an emerald engagement ring. Elizabeth II wears a three-carat diamond engagement ring, repurposed from her mother-in-law's tiara. A twelve-carat oval sapphire surrounded by round white diamonds, though purchased from Garrard's regular designs, has become a sacred icon because Diana, Princess of Wales, chose it. The Duchess of York (Fergie) received a large ruby, starting a trend. Prince William gave Kate Middleton his mother's sapphire ring. When Prince Harry became engaged to marry the American actress Meghan Markle, he replicated the country customs of his wife's citizenship. The large diamond, often called huge, but not by the standards of diamonds featured in this book, is estimated as between three and a half and four carats, flanked by two stones from Diana. Like diamonds discussed in this book, the central stone receives an estimate in money: "Grant Mobley, a gemologist and Director at Pluczenik, one of the world's leading diamantaires, estimates the ring would be worth around £122,500."[8]

Prince Harry and Meghan Markle along with their diamond engagement ring merge the first diamond empire and the second. They embody ethnographies that tag diamond identity. She is biracial, with an African American mother, and he passes as Anglo-Saxon—although with German, Greek, and Danish genes that confound Walter Scott's construction of Anglo-Saxon Englishness, discussed in chapter 6. Hence the ring might seem to settle and even bless its custom, encircling and uniting two or three continents. Yet and still, mined in Botswana, Prince Harry's ring adds a further complication to trouble ring-finger politics. One does not know if he has visited diamond mines there, owned by a transformed De Beers corporation, which shares profits with the government and promotes its Botswanan mining enterprise as bringing prosperity to a floundering country.[9] The reformed De Beers mining company controlling Botswana's diamonds enforces equitable conditions and has apparently exonerated the royal diamond engagement ring from any taint of being a "blood diamond," those that finance African wars. Their stone has thus been conceived of as philanthropic.

Engagement rings differ from wedding rings in that they are not a requirement, are less binding, but cost more. Worn on a woman's hand with a wedding band, now on the third finger of the left hand "because the ancients believed that a special vein of love ran from it, direct to the heart," the ring has associations with possession of the woman, some early ones having a pendant key.[10] But its symbolism with the diamond on it as an emblem of eternity develops into a slogan seemingly without end.[11] This diamond-selling custom waits for America and the twentieth century to set in diamond what has become a requirement for many in "all walks of life." Advertisement copywriter Dorothy Dignam, or Dorothy Dig as she often signed her name, used that last cliché to purvey the word "diamond" like a mantra to everyone: Do not say engagement ring, she insisted; always say *diamond* engagement ring. She probably wrote the epigraphs in this section as strategies to sell the solitaire.

One of the most familiar and successful advertising slogans, "A diamond is forever," draws not only from mineralogy but also from diamond lore that this book has explored. It plays a secular variation on Hopkins's ecstatic metaphor in its promise of eternal love. Its origins in a kind of optimism seem quintessentially American of a certain time. In 1938 the South African De Beers Mining Company inquired of executives at the New York advertising agency N. W. Ayers whether they believed a De Beers advertising campaign made sense. After all, they were not in the retail business, nor did they wholesale faceted diamonds but only gem-quality rough. Moreover, the Sherman Antitrust Act of 1890 prevented the syndicate controlling most of the world's diamonds from doing business in the United States. Authorized dealers, or "sightholders," had to travel to De Beers in London for their allocated share of uncut gems, called a "sight." In this instance, the diamond monopoly made the reverse journey to deliver a tale of profit woe. Diamond sales had been steadily falling even before the Roaring Twenties; they were not fashionable. The Depression and World War II further weakened sales. Gilded Age Diamond Jim Brady with his immense appetite for food appeared too fleshly, too materialistic, even old-fashioned and vulgar. More boring than racy, portly dowagers, diamond brooches on their bosoms, deadened the diamond market. A Diamond Is Forever answered diamond industry prayers.

The motto was a late-night inspiration in 1947 of the advertising copywriter Margaret Gerety, who never married. The article "a" of the motto exalts the singular, *a* solitaire, signifying a couple's unique love. The slogan confirmed a faith in holy matrimony. Even in depressed diamond times, diamond engagement rings were the backbone of sales; in the 1930s, 70 percent of diamond sales were engagement rings. American lovers believed that a diamond engagement ring exalted their commitment. After the two relentless Misses at Ayers persisted, the belief turned into a requirement. Jewelers in the 1950s declared that "a girl is not engaged unless she has a diamond engagement ring."[12] That is what Margaret Gerety did to America, seemingly forever, or at least into the twenty-first century.

American Diamond Jubilees, Seven Crowns of England, and Philip Roth's *Everyman*

From one vantage, De Beers approached N. W. Ayers at a difficult moment because changes in fashion and values suggested that an advertisement campaign would be fighting against a cultural tide. Married women after World War II, according to Ayers market research, preferred a washing machine or a new car. In another sense, though, the timing was auspicious for the founding of American towns, industries, and cultural institutions in a country that was relatively young. Dorothy Dignam's diamond researches turned up Queen Victoria's Diamond Jubilee in 1897 celebrating her sixty years on the throne. She counted out the towns across America that were approaching sixty or seventy-five years of incorporation and, as the country developed westward, calculated department stores, banks, manufacturers—any organization that would be having "diamond" anniversaries. But, she warned, these occasions are limited. Make the most of it and mention diamond constantly. Dorothy Dig saw that they could, with her detailed instructions. A Jubilee Ball, lectures, TV appearances, quiz shows, all of the answers related to diamonds, replicas of world-famous diamonds, Jubilee lapel buttons with a diamond chip (for male department store employees), exhibits of heirloom jewelry, and most relevant for the meanings traced in this book, replicas of English crown jewels: "A spectacular exhibit of crowns, scepters and diamonds from the Tower of London, all in Authentic British-made replicas, may be rented from Famous syndicates, Inc., 507 Fifth Avenue, New York, 17, N.Y.," Dignam promised in a memo entitled "Make the Most of Your Diamond Jubilee."[13]

Dignam pointed out, "An anniversary is one day. Strictly speaking, 'jubilee' refers to a year." Figuring a jubilee could be at sixty or seventy-five years, she induced prestigious institutions to sign on: Metropolitan Opera (1943) at sixty years, the Metropolitan Museum of Art (1947) at seventy-five. Others followed suit. Kaufmann's Department Store in Pittsburgh featured a diamond cutter "right in the store"; replicas of the crown jewels; movie stars Jeanette McDonald as Madame Du Barry and Greer Garson as Lady Hamilton, represented by the costumes and jewels they wore in the movies; and a pageant or play representing the history of the Koh-i-noor. The list represents a fraction of diamond tie-ins.[14] "We also suggested a certain type of display to Kaufmann's department store in Pittsburgh in connection with their Diamond Jubilee, helped to prepare it and had the necessary material shipped from New York."[15]

Ayers Agency inspired a manic phase of diamond jubilees. Dignam revealed her calculations beyond logic, despite her claims for rationality: "A Diamond Jubilee offers an opportunity to associate diamonds logically with any product whatsoever, even though diamonds ordinarily have nothing to do with the business. For example, diamonds have recently been featured in the Jubilee celebrations of Grand Union Stores, Warner Brothers corsets and Walk-Over shoes."[16] Diamond carried its fetish charge to middle-class grocery stores, undergarments, and footwear.

Towns and cities climbed on the Jubilee bandwagon, one example being Passaic, New Jersey, in 1948 (figure 12). History, as is often the case, had to tinker with the dates. According to its website, Passaic was settled in 1678 by Dutch traders under a different name only to be named Passaic in the 1850s, incorporated as a village in 1871 and a city in 1873. That last date conformed to the surge of Diamond Jubilee campaigns. As Dorothy Dig announced, "For window and other displays, we can be of help through our contact with the diamond trade. . . . Our publicity work for De Beers Consolidated Mines, Ltd.

Figure 12. Diamond Jubilee banner, Passaic, New Jersey, 1948. (Photography Studio: Roger Terhune of Clifton, N.J., J. Walter Thompson Diamond Information Center Collection, Box 65, John W. Hartman Center for Sales, Advertising, and Marketing History, David M. Rubenstein Rare Book and Manuscript Library, Duke University)

Figure 13. Diamond Jubilee display at a bank in Passaic, New Jersey. The seven crowns of England appear on the top shelf, the medieval crown without diamonds. (Photography Studio: Roger Terhune of Clifton, N.J., J. Walter Thompson Diamond Information Center Collection, Box 65, John W. Hartman Center for Sales, Advertising, and Marketing History, David M. Rubenstein Rare Book and Manuscript Library, Duke University)

seeks to stimulate interest in diamonds among people in all walks of life. The 75th or Diamond Anniversary of the City of Passaic, N.J. offered a splendid opportunity to do this. By actively working with the Mayor's arrangements committee, we were able to make diamonds a feature of the civic jubilee. Through our arrangements, a New York wholesaler loaned a collection of more than a $1,000,000 in diamond jewelry in a display that became the focal point of the anniversary. The exhibit, placed in the city's largest bank, was viewed by thousands and featured by the local press."[17] Seven English crowns, pictured at the top of the display, connect US citizens to royalty (figure 13). They confirm Cal Hockley's fantasy while including lower classes in its monarchical calculus.

Diamonds were offered to the common man who could buy a diamond on the installment plan to fit the queen of his castle. Couching diamond language in an American idiom, Philip Roth's novel *Everyman* (2006) reframes in Jewish immigrant terms the diamond meanings explored in this book. Should readers fail to appreciate its allusion to venerable English literature known to English majors at least up to Roth's generation, the publisher, Houghton Mifflin, informs them, "*Everyman* takes its title from an anonymous fifteenth-century allegorical play . . . whose theme is the summoning of the living to death."¹⁸ In fact, death and diamonds come together in the title as they do in much of the fiction discussed in this book and including Damien Hirst's *For the Love of God,* discussed in the introduction, the legend of Bala, the biography of the Koh-i-noor, Collins's *The Moonstone,* Tennyson's Elaine, and Olive Schreiner's novels. One year after *Everyman* was published, Damien Hirst's work provided a gloss on Roth's book, with its reminder of our mortal clay. An American iteration presents Hopkins's poor potsherd Jack as Everyman (echoed in poor Jack Dawson's name). Hirst, Dawson, and Hopkins return here, not only because Roth makes concrete an association of diamonds with death but because his title is also about a jewelry store, not in Passaic but in Elizabeth, New Jersey, called Everyman: "The stroke of genius was to call the business not by his name but rather Everyman's Jewelry Store" (56). The novel offers an account of the owner's dead son, an everyman, never named and about to be buried in a dilapidated, vandalized, Jewish cemetery, located "at the butt end of the airport and . . . the steady din of the New Jersey Turnpike" (4). In his older brother's eulogy, the dead man is remembered as a nine-year-old proudly boarding a bus to Newark carrying a pocketful of diamonds to be polished and set.

As a sign of American diamond meanings, the protagonist's jeweler father sold rings to "Elizabeth's Irish and Germans and Slovaks and Italians and Poles, most of them working-class stiffs" (10). Roth recites ethnic origins in the context of Jewish diamonds, the word "stiff" an uncomfortable pun on the novel's attention to death. In the spirit of Everyman, immigrants, and diamonds, this dead man's life history is filled with details of a different kind of migration from that initially hoity-toity voyage of the Heart of the Ocean. Had they been unlucky, Roth's Jews might have been crammed in steerage with other drowned immigrants in the *Titanic.* Roth himself imports the fateful ship to his novel in an allusion to the nameless hero's too-young trophy wife, "the titanically ineffective cover girl" (46) who is not Jewish.

The novel evokes Isaac and Rebecca of York hastening to Spain, also ordinary Jews sailing to South Africa. Instead of those Kimberley dealers in tents who bought and sold diamonds, Roth portrays the immigrant receivers of small South African stones and brings us detailed close-ups at the heart of a small American diamond business that bears the mark of the Jew. Roth explains that the jeweler wanted to erase the Jew from his jewels. His store opened in 1933, a few years before De Beers traveled to America to launch their offensive on the American buyer.

Understanding his own Jewish shadow on diamond, the jeweler articulates the diamond legend sustaining the American capitalization on diamond allure: "'It's a big deal for working people to buy a diamond,' he told his sons, 'no matter how small. The wife can wear it for the beauty and she can wear it for the status. And when she does, this guy is not just a plumber—he's a man with a wife with a diamond. He wife owns something that is imperishable. Because beyond the beauty and the status and the value, the diamond is imperishable. A piece of earth that is imperishable, and a mere mortal is wearing it on her hand!'" (57). Whereas the Jewish jeweler universalizes and democratizes his jewelry store with his store name, in linking diamond to death, Roth's title also evokes every man's fate in contrast to diamond's legendary imperishability, his jeweler repeating the word three times. In making Everyman into a Jewish jeweler, Roth confirms ethnicity at the center of diamond identity. In the Everyman family, Roth's novel, like Gerety's slogan and Cameron's movie, articulates democratic desire. Everyman can own a chip of the rock of eternity. Diamonds are for everyone, forever.

Notes

Introduction

1. "Carats" is the word given to the measure of gemstones and gold. Carats were originally based on the carob seed. The measures fluctuated historically so that one cannot confidently know the precise size of legendary diamonds, unless they can be physically weighed.
2. Harlow, "What Is Diamond?," 5–22.
3. Tagore, *Mani-mālā*, 143.
4. King, *Natural History*, 27.
5. The current value of diamonds is reduced if they phosphoresce, but that glow has added to its symbolic uses.
6. Hazan, *Diamond Makers,* presents a history of the successful attempt at manufacturing diamonds. For a business account, see Sherman, "Will Lab-Grown Stones," about Diamond Foundry, a start-up producing diamonds. See also A. T. Collins, "Diamonds," 255–72.
7. http://www.bbc.co.uk/news/science-environment-14505109. Experiment reported in 2011.
8. Gregory, "Body of Work," 26–33.
9. Hart, *Diamond*, 23.
10. Kirkley, in "Origin of Diamonds," offers a brief account of when diamond arrived in the depths of the Earth (48).
11. "The alien planet, a so-called 'super-Earth,' is called 55 Cancri e and was discovered in 2004 around a nearby star in our Milky Way galaxy. After estimating the planet's mass and radius, and studying its host star's composition, scientists now say the rocky world is composed mainly of carbon (in the form of diamond and graphite), as well as iron, silicon carbide, and potentially silicates. At least a third of the planet's mass is likely pure diamond" (Clara Moscowitz, "Super-Earth Planet Likely Made of Diamond," SPACE.com, 11 October 2012, https://www.space.com/18011-super-earth-planet-diamond-world.html).
12. A. T. Collins, "Diamonds in Modern Technology," 225–26.
13. Hart, *Diamond;* Roberts, *Glitter and Greed.* Both books, and others, such as the earlier Kanfer, *Last Empire,* expose diamond marketing but do not stifle desires for diamonds or books about them.
14. A compact description of diamond as a mineral is found in Lenzen, *History of Diamond,* 8–11.

15. Epigraph from Geertz, *Interpretation of Culture,* 5. "Thick Description," 3–32, particularly what he calls "symbolic action" (10).
16. Koh-i-noor diamond, the most celebrated Indian diamond, has been the subject of many books. See Dalrymple and Annand, *Koh-i-Noor;* Amini, *Koh-i-noor;* and Rushby, *Chasing.*
17. Tagore, *Mani-mālā,* 1:150. Alluvial diamonds found there and by a company formed in 1867 were inferior in color and size. In the twentieth century, Australia produced distinctive pink diamonds, finding them in soil other than kimberlite
18. Paraphrased information from Swiecki's online article "Diamond in Brazil."
19. "Diamond mania" is a term used in an article about South African diamond fields in 1871: "The diamond mania has caused a ferment in our colonies among all sorts and conditions of men" ("South African Diamond Fields," 118).
20. MacDonald, *Language of Empire,* 2–3.
21. Tidrick, *Empire,* 1.
22. Cannadine, *Orientalism,* writes about social structures and social perceptions of empire, including subjective experiences and interconnectedness of its parts, and challenges grand narratives in earlier historical writings.
23. Weber, in *Protestant Ethic,* elaborates on Adam Smith's evaluation of success as material wealth and the paradox of being forbidden to exult in that success.
24. See Levine, *Forms.* See also Angus Brown, "Cultural Studies," 1187–93. Brown discusses how close reading in Levine's work connects the formalist practice of reading with sociopolitical concerns as a network.
25. Latour, *We Have Never Been Modern,* 1.
26. Latour, *We Have Never Been Modern,* 3–4.
27. Simmel, in *Philosophy of Money,* points this out, and Appadurai quotes Simmel, relevant to diamond: "We call those objects valuable that resist our desire to possess them" ("Introduction: Commodities and the Politics of Value," in *Social Life of Things,* 3). Simmel's essay might have been written about control of diamond prices: "For many people, the mere fact that the object can only be had for a certain price provides it with value. This frequently results in a circular determination of value: if the seller allows the price to decline, then the valuation of the commodity also declines, and this pushes the price even lower" ("Money and Commodity Culture," 241).
28. Cannadine, in *Ornamentalism,* insists that Britain itself be joined to considerations of empire: "There can be no satisfactory history of Britain without empire, and no satisfactory history of empire without Britain" (xx).
29. Proctor, "Anti-Agate," debunks diamond values, claims diamonds are racialized, the lowest black diamonds and the highest white. Whether they continue to pass as white may be explored in the adoption of bling of mid-twentieth-century to twenty-first-century America.
30. Pietz, "Fetish, I," 7.
31. Pietz, "Fetish, I," 7.
32. Diamonds move, quite literally, as in Plotz's chapter in *Portable Property.* Rather than Plotz's attention to portability, my emphasis is on their symbolic movements and their literal physical properties.

33. Pietz's three articles in *res* from 1985 to 1988 are starting points in all elaborations of fetishism. Other work on fetishism bearing on my thought includes Apter and Pietz, *Fetishism;* Krafft-Ebing, who uses "charm" to invoke a magical quality of the "fetich," and addressing how sexuality has become fetishized (*Psychopathia Sexualis,* 19); see also Gamman and Makinen, *Female Fetishism,* and Logan, *Victorian Fetishism.*
34. McCallum's effort to rehabilitate the concept for cultural uses, "not as a threat but as a promise," can extend not only to her attention to sexual discourses as a symptom but also to material, psychological, and anthropological concerns (*Object Lessons,* xii–xiii). Among the Victorians, Mary Kingsley is unique in her interest in the concept of fetish, which she expands beyond belief in objects to the interactions of a culture.
35. Marx, "Fetishism," 163; Freud, "Fetishism," 21:152–57.
36. Marx, "Fetishism," 167.
37. Stratton, *Desirable Body,* 1.
38. Hopkins, poem 72, 105–6. No line numbers.
39. Hopkins, *Poems,* poem 65 (probably 1885), 100.
40. He reportedly was about thirty-five years old, a European who died between 1720 and 1810. "The skull was purchased from a taxidermist shop . . . Get Stuffed in Islington, North London" (*For the Love,* 17). The shop resembles that of Mr. Venus in Dickens's *Our Mutual Friend* who sells bones and articulates skeletons.
41. The phrase comes from the title of Ray Brown's *Objects,* his book about fetishes.
42. Wilson's introduction to *New Imperial History* insists on coercive aspects of identity formation rather than its being solely a subjective process (5–16). Specifically, from the perspective of slavery, this new imperial history differs from what came before and what follows, which is post-1840, in the period under my scrutiny. Yet some of these elements of coercive identity apply to my consideration of Jewish and African ethnicities, considered in chapters 2 and 3.

1. India: Gems from the Gods

1. Murthy, *Gemmological Studies,* 1:iii. In 1993, Murthy extended his 1990 study to yet more texts in a short monograph, and there he limited required gemological knowledge to artisans rather than to everyone.
2. The cliché comes from Lenzen, *History of Diamond,* 26, though Babu's history also cites two millennia as the beginning of diamonds in India.
3. MacCarthy, *Fire,* cited in *Diamonds and Coral,* 72.
4. About Marco Polo's role in transmitting diamond lore to Europe, see Lenzen, *History,* 82.
5. Tagore, *Mani-Mālā,* 595.
6. Tagore, *Mani-mālā,* 2, 1039.
7. Translated roughly as the "science of governance," the influential treatise is authored by various hands over three centuries and it includes diamonds as a part of considerations of political economy. Including profit verifies its prominence into all aspects of life. The treatise was lost until the beginning of the twentieth century

when it was translated into English in 1915. Harlow's "Following the History of Diamonds" includes a different summary of its contents (117).
8. Murthy, *Gemmological Studies,* 1: 4.
9. Murthy, *Gemmological, Studies,* 2:iii.
10. Sacrifice is an essential element of Brahmin orthodoxy; see the *Bhagavad Gita* and any gloss on it.
11. For an authoritative account, with various sources, see McHugh, "Gemstones," in *Handbook,* 60–61; Harlow, "Following," 119.
12. In one collection of Vedic hymns, the *Garuda Maha Puranam* (about fifth century AD), Bala's bones become diamonds whereas every other part of his body becomes a different gem. Depending on where the bones fall, the color of the diamond differs. The sacrifice of Bala is part of a sacred task, discernable traces of that practice of sacrifice surfaces in Collins's representation of the three Brahmin trackers of the Moonstone discussed in chapter 2.
13. *Rasaratnasamuccaya;* Murthy, *Gemmological Studies,* 1:28.
14. RRS; Murthy, *Gemmological Studies,* 1:29.
15. Murthy, *Gemmological Studies,* 1:23.
16. Tagore, *Mani-Mālā,* 1:615.
17. Tagore, *Mani-Mālā,* 1:107.
18. Lenzen, *History of Diamond,* 31.
19. "History of the Diamond," *Eclectic Magazine,* 5.
20. Thakur, "Vernacular Objects," 557.

1. Conversions of the Last Maharajah of the Punjab and His Koh-i-noor Diamond

1. "Koh-i-Noor," *Chambers' Edinburgh Journal,* 49.
2. Rushby, *Chasing,* 234.
3. Many accounts exist of the Koh-i-noor. For brief contemporary analyses of its various histories, which summarize both "traditional" and "historical" versions, see Kinsey, "Koh-i-Noor," 391–419, and Amini, "Koh-i-noor."
4. Mersmann, "Diamonds," focusing on commodity exchanges, calls the diamond's process of change "acculturation" in the biography of the diamond.
5. Johnson, *Persons,* explores tropes that enable the transfers of persons to things and things to persons that bear upon my interpretations.
6. Bance, *Sovereign,* 19.
7. For a comment on "zones of flat art," see Peter Brown, "Magic Carpet," 27.
8. Cohn, "Cloth," 306–7.
9. Atwal, "Between," argues for Jind Kaur's close and responsible regency, protecting and raising her vulnerable son, until the English removed her. Atwal largely dismisses the slanders of the governors-general, who portrayed her with stereotypical accounts of promiscuity as reasons to remove her when her son was nine.
10. Aijazuddin, "Sikh," surveys European portraits of Sikhs, but none are seated on a throne-like chair.
11. Because of the politics that determined his life, Duleep Singh's actions are always monitored and therefore agency and choice are compromised, as in the case of

his commissioning the portrait (Alexander and Anand, *Queen Victoria's Maharajah*, 32).

12. In a later period and a different Indian region, but suggestive, see Sinha, *Colonial Masculinity*.
13. In a letter to his wife, Login writes, "I was installed . . . as the Governor of the Citadel and its contents, and have to make out a list in English for the Governor General of all the jewels and valuables belonging to the Sikh government, and now transferred to ours: among them is the Kohinoor. . . . I should like to show you the gorgeous state jewels arranged in the fine boxes I have had made for them. You would laugh to see how they were kept (and yet quite safely) by the native treasurers, all rolled up separately in little bits of rag" (quoted in Bance, *Sovereign*, 28).
14. Letter from Sir John Login to Lena Login, Lahore, 15 September 1849, in *Sir John Login and Duleep Singh*, 17. See also Bance, *Sovereign*, 29. One *lakh* is one hundred thousand, written in numerals.
15. Cohn, "Cloth," 315.
16. When Muslims invaded the Punjab (AD 1031), they "blended their own tenets of kingship with Hindu traditions they found there" (Adamson and Prior, *Maharajas' Jewels*, 16).
17. For a history of the feminization of India in English writing, see Rajan, *Under Western Eyes*. For a later interpretation of masculinities, see Sinha, *Colonial Masculinity*.
18. According to Alexander and Anand, Ranjit Singh could not have fathered that child, given his decrepit condition at the time (*Queen Victoria's Maharajah*, 2). As far as the miniature is concerned, the contemporary description indicates that it is the gifted miniature and is set in a star rather than an oval: "Lord Auckland's picture, set in a star of fine diamonds, suspended to a string of large pearls" (Osborne, Runjeet Sing, Journal Entry 28th May, 1838, n.p.).
19. In 1846, Duleep Singh apparently wore the miniature at the signing of the Treaty of Lahore after the first war of the Punjab. See Alexander and Anand, *Queen Victoria's Maharajah*, 5, and Bance, *Sovereign*, 38.
20. The portrait was probably painted by Emily Eden, the sister of the governor-general. For more about her, see Plotz, *Portable Property*.
21. Scarisbrick, *Portrait Jewels*, 224.
22. The "Peter Pan" theory regarding "Oriental" populations held that they were eternal adolescents, who would never grow up. See Darby, *Three Faces*.
23. Atwal, "Between the Courts," 189–85. Atwal cites Gil Anidjar, who argues that the idea of blood competed with and won over an idea of royal status.
24. Amini, *Koh-i-noor*, 212.
25. Tagore, *Mani-Mālā*, 1: 850.
26. A synopsis of a generally accepted version of the Koh-i-noor legend beginning only in the sixteenth century is found in Prior and Adamson, *Maharajas' Jewels*, 71–74. Dalrymple and Anand, in *Koh-i-Noor*, offer detailed descriptions of human slaughter as the Koh-i-noor traveled to different territories.
27. Amini, *Koh-i-noor*, 9. The East India Company claimed it was not Dalhousie's but theirs to grant.

28. Mersmann, in "Diamonds," also considers the Exhibition as a turning point in the Koh-i-noor's story, calling the change not acculturation, as he had earlier, but reinterpretation and translocation. Conversion encompasses these different concepts and contains the turning root, "version," which also opens the meanings signified by stories. Mersmann discusses the tensions located in the diamond by its placement outside the Indian Court, but he does not recognize that its very name maintains its otherness within the main exhibition space reserved for Great Britain (179–81).
29. Armstrong, "Victorian Prism," 55–83.
30. *Punch Magazine*, 5 July 1851.
31. *Illustrated Exhibitor*, no. 6 (12 July 1851): 94.
32. Mersmann, who describes the India Court in relation to the display in the British section of the Koh-i-noor in "Diamonds," also considers the diamond in light of commodities. Yet it is never only that. The nations wanting it back are not calculating its monetary value, which is partly why it cannot be divided into four and distributed among them. Nor is it kept by the Crown because of its commodity value.
33. Bance, in *Sovereign*, claims Duleep Singh later believed that this tutor, Bhajun Lal, a Brahmin, was hired to spy on him, and he noted in retrospect the incongruity of a Brahmin reading him the Bible. However, Bhajun Lal wrote a report in which he averred that the prince had requested the Bible readings, being curious about passages on Christianity in *The English Instructor,* one of his textbooks, 31.
34. Viswanathan, *Outside the Fold*, xii, xv.
35. Viswanathan calls for a historicization of conversion "not only as a spiritual but also a political activity" (*Outside the Fold,* xvii).
36. Duleep Singh to Login, 2 December 1850, in Alexander and Anand, *Queen Victoria's Maharajah*, 25.
37. The letter is to Dalhousie's friend, Sir George Couper, in 1851. Quoted in Alexander and Anand, *Queen Victoria's Maharajah*, 30.
38. Quoted from a letter from Lord Dalhousie to John Login in Bance, *Sovereign,* 34.
39. Lady Helen Mackenzie in her memoirs; see Bance, *Sovereign,* 28.
40. Alexander and Anand, *Queen Victoria's Maharajah*, 37.
41. The name itself continued to interest Orientalists as late as 1894. Debates featured a continuing conversation about the derivation of "Duleep Singh," first by Max Müller, which concerned the transliteration of his name and then a response by three other Orientalists not only about the spelling but the etymology of "Duleep," "Dallip" or "Dhulíp." In addition, they generally concluded that the etymology had nothing to do with Delhi ("Derivation of 'Duleep Singh,'" 188–89). Why this was still of interest at the end of the century suggests that the maharajah provoked conversation two years beyond the grave.
42. As recounted in a 2019 BBC documentary, *The Stolen Maharajah,* a lock of hair, resembling those given to Victorian loved ones, has been found in Lady Login's scrapbook, which also contains letters. I thank Pryia Atwal for sending me the documentary, in which she takes part.
43. Bance, *Sovereign,* 34.

44. Bance, *Sovereign*, 35. In his letter, Dalhousie refers to the Bible as containing "the secret to all happiness."
45. Using Victorian ethnographic theories, Cohn points out that the Indian present was considered the European past. Thus, the Indian had to move slowly out of their feudal present to preserve order. Cohn, "Cloth." In contrast, Atwal more recently argues for a more equal attitude embraced by Victoria that partly explains her favoring him. It is likely that both views color a mixed and unreconciled attitude to Duleep Singh. Victoria was smitten later by the son of an Indian apothecary Abdul Karim, as described in Munich, *Queen Victoria's Secrets*.
46. The curved sword in the Winterhalter painting looks like a talwar, not literally the required ceremonial sword or kirpan required to be worn always by Sikhs. See Cohn, "Cloth," 306.
47. Cohn, "Cloth," 308.
48. On the performance of costume as politically resonant messages in Victoria and Albert's fancy-dress balls, see Munich, *Queen Victoria's Secrets*, 27–35.
49. For an afterlife of the Winterhalter painting, see Gell, "Origins." The painting's subsequent iterations interpret the interchange between Sikh presentation and British notions of the Sikh.
50. Quoted from Victoria's journal, 11 July 1854, in Bance, *Sovereign*, 39. Dalhousie considered Duleep Singh's widely quoted speech as manipulative hokum.
51. Brown, "Tragedies," 52.
52. Amini, in *Koh-i-noor*, as have many before him, casts some doubt about whether Babur's diamond is the same as Ranjit Singh's. The legendary diamond in all its forms suffers diminution, and its being cut signifies only one aspect of its symbolic cutting. We might regard all the cuttings as indication that its owners needed to make it their own and that in having it, they came to see in its imperfections the gap that always exists between legend and reality.
53. "Koh-i-Noor," *Chambers' Edinburgh Journal*, 52.
54. Caroline Brown, "Tragedies," 58.
55. Kinsey, in "Koh-i-Noor," traces the Koh-i-noor's political history and the ideology of its most recent "refashioning," 392. Her argument is congruent with mine, with a different emphasis: "the Koh-i-Noor's refashioning was an attempt to reconstitute the stone as a gemological component of Britain's civilizing mission, where the weight of British science and machinery was literally brought to bear on the diamond's structure," 392.
56. Barker, *Symbols*, 79.
57. King, *Natural History*, 74.

2. The Moonstone's Sacred Masculinity

1. James Mill in *History* acknowledges Tipu's hostility to the English but nonetheless doubted the necessity of war against him. Mill saw some advantages of Tipu's reign, for the Mahrattas were more inclined to submit to the English against Tipu (63).
2. Cohn, *Colonialism*, 80. See also Goodlad's response to Cohn's discussion of later relationships of authority in Victorian India, in *Geopolitical*, 46–47.

3. James Mill's account of "Tipoo Sultan" focuses on his "eager desire to do mischief to the English." He describes the killing of Tipu by an English soldier, who then "pulled off the sword-belt of the Sultan, which was very rich" (96–100). Mill's account verifies that stripping the corpse of its jewels was part of the received story.
4. Mehta, in "English Romance/Indian Violence" (618–19), offers a useful survey of the utterly distorted British representation of Tipu Sultan as a "stereotypically cruel oriental despot" in text and images, particularly in Collins's relative David Wilkie's painting *Sir David Baird Discovering the Body of Sultawn Tippoo Sahib* (1839).
5. Goodlad, *Geopolitical*, 136–37.
6. W. Collins, *The Moonstone*, ed. Kemp, 12. Subsequent citations to this edition appear in parentheses in the text.
7. In *Dead Secrets*, Heller points out that "Collins differs from the response of most of his contemporaries by locating the source of violence in imperialism itself" (145).
8. For romance in relation to *The Moonstone*, see Duncan, "Imperial Panic." Mehta in "English Romance" also writes about the conjunction between violence and romance in Collins and Doyle.
9. Rajan, in *Western Eyes,* places Collins in the long tradition of British animus against Islam. However, the "Mohammadans" were admired by many English, including Queen Victoria, for their monotheism. See an account more admiring of Islam than Hinduism in James Mill's history.
10. Betteredge's attribution of devilish possession to the diamond expresses post–Sepoy Rebellion recasting of India from romantic and exotic to dark and devilish. Duncan draws on critics such as Brantlinger, Sharpe, and Heller for his interpretation of "imperialist panic" in the novel but does not mention the diamond as reflecting the newly imagined imperialist dangers of the Empire striking back ("Moonstone," 305).
11. King, *Natural History,* 74.
12. In *Mani-mālā,* Tagore reports on the Orloff's being in the forehead of an Indian deity and cites an English periodical, later than Collins's novel, as his source. It is likely that Collins found a reference to this same information. "The Russians have a very good Diamond known as the Orloff. It is about the size of a pigeon's egg, and one time formed the eye of an idol in the Temple of Brahma at Pondicherry. Brahma was robbed of it by a French deserter, from whom it found its way to a Greek merchant established somewhere on the shores of the Mediterranean, who sold it to Count Orloff, at that time in command of the Russian Mediterranean squadron, for half a million roubles, an annuity of 20,000 roubles and a patent of nobility" (1:849). Tagore cites the above information as taken from *Pall Mall Gazette,* 30 January 1880.
13. Roy, in "Imperialist Semiotic," discusses the occlusion of the Russian gem but is not relevant to my focus on the Britishness of the Moonstone. His argument is that the specificity of naming does not suggest more precariousness in the Russian use than in the security of the Koh-i-noor in Britain. The Koh-i-noor and its curse shadow the politics of the novel as much as the Orloff does. Goodlad, *Geopolitical,* summarizes interpretative disputes (134).

14. T. S. Eliot's labeling the novel as the "first detective novel" has influenced generic categories. *The Moonstone* is a romance with some detective generic features and contains more diverse features than most detective novels following it. To regard it as a romance, as the author labeled it in his title and thus asks readers to do, makes of the diamond more than a stolen object whose solution requires a detective. Collins read King's strong condemnation about cutting the Koh-i-noor (*Natural History*, 74). King suggests credulity about the curse.
15. Lonoff, *Wilkie Collins*, 175–76, cites the elements that Collins learned about diamonds and diamond lore from reading King and the eighth edition of the *Encyclopedia Britannica* as found in his preliminary notes to the novel.
16. Winterhalter painted Victoria in 1856 with her Koh-i-noor brooch sitting on her bosom almost in the center of the painting. It is a relatively inelegant adornment, despite or because of its immensity. It is no wonder that the bulbous brooch enjoyed a relatively short life.
17. Sutherland's notes to the 1999 Oxford World's Classics edition cite Sue Lonoff's researches into Collins's notebook (479).
18. Reed, in "English Imperialism," connects Ablewhite's murder by the Brahmins to the site of the East India Company's offices in 1849, torn down by the time of Collins's novel when the assets were transferred to the crown (287).
19. King, *Natural History*, 74.
20. Collins might have gleaned information about the Moon dynasty from Edward Balfour, *Cyclopedia of Indian and of Eastern and Southern Asia*, first published in 1857 and from the genealogical table found in "Essays in Indian Antiquities" (1858) by James Prinsep and Edward Thomas, the latter of which also indicates that Seringapatam, capital of the Mysore State, was ruled by descendants of the Lunar Dynasty. Perhaps he thought that Wyllie sufficiently supplemented his other researches, although Wyllie's published work does not mention the Lunar Dynasty but refers to Krishna as the "Lord of the Moon" (*Essays*, 325; hereafter cited parenthetically in the text).
21. Collins's notebook in the Princeton Library records his questions and Wyllie's answers. See Sutherland's note 463, which gives Collins's four questions (500–501).
22. Murthwaite may be wrong about Krishna's birthplace. It is Mathura, but for the purposes of the novel, Collins either got wrong information or wanted Krishna to be born, live, and die in the same place. Furthermore, he gleaned information about Somnath from Wyllie. In his notes, Sutherland quotes Anthea Trodd and Collins's notebook for Wyllie's input about the moon and Kattiawar.
23. Kemp's note 54 cites James Tod, a Victorian traveler, who describes the temple as a shrine to the sun god, but Shiva is described in the *Encyclopedia Britannica* as Lord of the Moon. Shiva is not portrayed as "four-handed" as Collins describes the "four-handed Indian god who typifies the Moon" (11). Somnath, variously spelled, is cited as the place where Krishna, the eighth incarnation of Vishnu—a four-armed god—died. Collins follows the moon mythology to end his novel about the Moonstone at a place of moon people. Wyllie alludes briefly to Tod without quoting him. Collins consulted the *Encyclopedia Britannica* as well, indicated in his notes and in Lonoff.

24. Roy, "Imperialist Semiotic," insists that *The Moonstone* establishes a semiotic system that favors British imperialism: "The Preface uses its synecdochic reference to idolatry to elucidate the position of the other in a pseudo-Manichean agon of good and bad empires" (661). Readers might not unequivocally condemn the Hindu mode of worship. To open a reader's eyes and to change his or her heart constitutes an aim of many Victorian novels. Needing an Englishman to convey the Hindu sacred ritual, Collins consulted Wyllie about the possibility of a European passing as a Hindu to participate in the ceremony.
25. Mehta, in "English Romance," offers a different perspective on Murthwaite, characterizing him as an "arch-rationalist" and "detective-like." But then she sees in Murthwaite's adventurous spirit, as she says, a romantic aspect, not only rational (632–33). On Collins consulting Wyllie, see Sutherland note, 501.
26. See Parry, *Delusions*, 49–50: "Anglo-Indians tended to find Moslems, Sikhs and Rajputs, the 'fighting races', more congenial than the 'passive, supine' Hindus, and they infinitely preferred villagers to literate Indians." The Rajputs in Collins's novel conform to such preferences and provide another reason for his restoring the diamond to this clan.

3. Imitation India in Robert Louis Stevenson and Arthur Conan Doyle

1. A year before Stevenson started publishing his tales, an 1877 edition by T. B. Dalziel "translated and arranged for family reading" was published.
2. "The Story of the Fisherman," number 215 of the 4,884 stories in *The Arabian Nights Entertainments Complete*, from the text of Dr. Jonathan Scott, in four volumes. Jonathan Scott, Oriental Professor, published his translation in 1811, revised and corrected from the Arabic (rather than the French translation by M. Galland, from which English translations were published in 1704).
3. Orientalists were tracing the *Arabian Nights* to India and Persia, though more recent scholarship indicates that many of the tales originate in the West.
4. Yakub Beg consolidated his power in Kashgar as part of the Great Game. See Sergeev, *Great Game*. His timeline of the Great Game is particularly useful.
5. *New Arabian Nights*, vol. 2 of *The Works of Robert Louis Stevenson* (Classic Library edition), 2:146. All references are to this edition and will be given in parentheses in the text.
6. Sudden transformations from wealth to poverty and back again characterize Sinbad's history. The General's story takes its shape from such tales that reward a favorite with a lovely woman as well as with a pot of gold and jewels.
7. Two years before Collins's *The Moonstone*, Émile Gaboriau (1832–73) began publishing detective fiction featuring an amateur detective and a policeman. His writing does not advise about how to fence stolen goods and contains nothing specifically about diamonds, although there are allusions to jewels as signs of women's wealth.
8. Doyle, *Sign of Four*, ed. Towheed, 52. All references to this edition will be given in parentheses in the text.

9. Mehta ignores important differences between the two texts, and Doyle's subtext of colonial transgression ("English Romance," 633).
10. In examining the "epochal impact" on the Victorian consciousness, Christopher Herbert, *War of No Pity*, considers the event as it infuses literary texts about India (3).
11. The text describes Tonga's weapons as a stone club and a blow pipe. Towheed points out that the Andamans did not use poisoned arrows or stone clubs. Nor did they worship gods they could carry around, as the text asserts. Tonga supposedly carries around his weapons and gods (153).
12. Towheed notes that the forced indigo laborers as well as the Sepoys were a factor in the Rebellion, so that the Uprising was not only about the grease in the rifles and other indignities visited upon the indigenous Raj troops but oppression of indigenous peoples more generally (153).
13. Towheed points out not only chronological discrepancies but in his notes to the text also indicates Doyle's inaccuracies in the names of the three.
14. The Tale of Sinbad is apparently a relatively late addition to the compilation.
15. Sucher and Carriere, *Gems and Gemology*, 124–41.
16. Dalrymple and Anand believe two claims, neither based on rigorous analysis, that the Great Mogul and the Orloff are the same (*Koh-i-Noor*, 59).
17. Keep and Randall, "Addiction," find that the fictions about addiction harbor the kind of bad faith about imperialism that I am extending to the "addiction" in diamond fictions: "But in their sheer multiplicity, in the compulsive need to reiterate the signal events of the empire's triumphant progress, such narratives also attest to the fundamental incapacity of British culture to expel from its unconscious that tincture or trace of the poisonous other upon which it had come so crucially to depend, not only for its economic well-being, but also in its claims to moral and racial superiority" (208).
18. Keep and Randall, "Addiction," 210.
19. Doyle, *Complete Sherlock Holmes*, 250–51.

4. Kim as Jewel and Crown

1. According to Sergeev in *Great Game*, Yakub Beg was a "risk-taker" who in the 1860s "appear[ed] in the forefront of the Great Game" (135–142).
2. Kipling, *Kim*, ed. Sullivan, 5. All citations from this edition will be given in parentheses in the text.
3. Suggestions here about a different linguistic register draw upon Julia Kristeva's description of the "chora" in *Revolution in Poetic Language*, useful for understanding the eruption of rhyme as semiotic within a symbolic or linguistic passage. Kim's vision originates in that process.
4. McBratney discusses Kim's purely Irish origins, which place him in the ethnographic mapping as close to the Indian and different from an Englishman; see *Imperial Subjects*, 106–7. He argues that Kim is not strictly white.
5. Walters, "A 'white boy,'" offers an interpretation of Kim's racializing.

6. Said's phrase "imperial unconscious" is constituted quite differently from my suggestion here because it does not allow for ambiguous alliances or repressed knowledge. The imperialist, in his powerful reading of the novel, is rational, racist, and realistic.
7. Kim refers to the Punjab as "my country" (59).
8. Sergeev, *Great Game,* 219–20.
9. For the failed quest to locate the real jeweler in his actual setting, see chapters 10 and 11 of Hopkirk, *Quest for Kim,* 169–99.
10. Lurgan's ability resembles the skill of Mr. Venus in Charles Dickens's *Our Mutual Friend* (1865) who assembles disparate bones to form of them a recognizable human skeleton. The "person" emerging from his skill is articulated through fragments. Furthermore, Mr. Venus's shop contains a "Hindoo baby" in a bottle, bringing the two shops in virtual dialogue.
11. Tavernier, quoted in "History of the Diamond," *North British Review,* reprinted in *Eclectic Magazine* 28 (January 1853): 3.
12. Wegner, "Invention of India," 154.
13. Franklin, *Lotus* argues that to fail to consider the perspective of Tibetan Buddhism offered in the novel has "predetermined the critical polarization" about Kim's identity (129–34; 146–61).
14. Franklin, *Lotus,* 161.
15. Earth's magnetic poles are north/south, and perhaps Kipling changed them to suggest an imperial paradigm.
16. In attempting to decide on a determinate ending, many interpretations refer to Kipling's conflicts. Some use the parallel between Mowgli in *The Jungle Book,* who must return to the man village. However, *Kim* redacts the earlier work.
17. McBratney, *Imperial Subjects,* argues that the return to the world signifies a return to the game, walking the paths of the Game, talking to informants (123). He argues against Mark Kinkead-Weekes, who finds that the ending commits Kim to the wheel of Buddhist iconography and instead believes the wheel as gear imagery refers to Western technology (123).
18. Suleri, *Rhetoric,* 127. Suleri also argues that Teshoo Lama is complicit in the Great Game and understands imperial dynamics well enough to support Kim's education and to agree to its terms. Franklin, *Lotus,* considers the lama's religion as a reason for his underwriting Kim's education.
19. Kipling, *Kipling's India,* ed. Pinney, 70–73.
20. As a summary of other critics in view of arguing that it is worth acknowledging Kipling's position without trying to resolve contradictions, see Hitchens, "Man of Permanent Contradictions," 289. Sullivan weaves biography with fiction to present a nuanced sense of Kipling's psychological and political sensibilities. Rickets, a relatively recent biographer, describes the author's "chameleon nature," celebrated in characters such as Mowgli and Kim, see *Rudyard Kipling,* xi. If one grants the chameleon changeable ideological positions, the metaphor is apt.
21. Said, *Culture and Imperialism,* 136. Said offers an illuminating account of the novel, but his reading beyond the ending also characterizes the work as a realistic novel, like "Scott, Austen, Dickens, and Eliot" (115). On the contrary, romance

features allow Kim and other characters escape into a mythical India, recognizable and yet benign and assisting Kim on his progress.
22. Marx, "The British Rule in India," *New York Daily Tribune,* 25 June 1853.

II. England: Diamond Metropole

1. *London Maps: The A to Z of Victorian London* (1987), with notes by Ralph Hyde, is a reprint of an 1888 Ordnance Atlas, edited and published by George W. Bacon.
2. In *Making England Western,* Makdisi deconstructs Occidental/Oriental. Victorians commonly anticipated Hyde's and Makdisi's characterization of London's heterogeneity.
3. Fitzgerald is quoted in *Village London Atlas* (1–3).
4. Makdisi, *Making England Western,* 47–48.
5. Yogev, *Diamonds and Coral,* 20.
6. Scott and Atkinson, *Short History of Diamond Cutting,* 1888, 83.
7. Newbury, *Diamond Ring,* 85. Newbury documents intersecting business operations; many diamond buyers and dealers in London became directors of mining companies as well as owners of London wholesale firms, which were in the Hatton Garden/High Holborn area. Newbury also provides information about the formation of diamond trading in the London/South African axis.
8. Yogev, *Diamonds and Coral,* 68.
9. Lichtenstein, *Diamond Street,* xviii.
10. Makdisi, *Making England Western,* 72–73.
11. There was an Orthodox synagogue, the Borough New Synagogue, on Heygate Street, Walworth Road, from 1867 to 1927, indicating that the congregants must have been able to walk there to worship. See Renton, *Lost Synagogues,* 196. The synagogue was in proximity to the Bermondsley Antiques Market, founded by Prince Albert in 1855, which developed a shady reputation for fenced goods.
12. Campbell, *Romantic Ethic,* outlined and described Veblen's process while adding the valuable insight about symbolic meanings of consumer products.
13. Stout, *Corporate Romanticism,* 13.

5. Diamond Games for a Dead Man

1. In *Corporate Romanticism,* Stout describes an earlier moment based on a model of corporate business, not "fully widespread until the 1860s," whereby the human individual does not bear singular responsibility, and instead "a transcendent, suprapersonal entity" (3) enables agency to be masked under its aegis. In line with Stout's analysis, Tennyson's Round Table and Dickens's Circumlocution Office protect its members' individual incompetence. It also traps those such as idealistic, "suprapersonal" Arthur into veiling his eyes and intelligence to the corruption of his knights and trusting Arthur Clennam to believe in the way finances are calculated.
2. In *Empire,* Lipovetsky claims that the Middle Ages instituted the ephemeral in dress as the beginning of the modern age, where fashion emphasized newly visible differences between men and women (21).

3. "To the Queen," line 29. All references, henceforth in parentheses in the text, are taken from *Complete Poems of Tennyson,* ed. Christopher Ricks.
4. Tennyson, *Alfred Tennyson,* 491. Munich, *Queen Victoria's Secrets;* Homans, *Royal Representations;* and Houston, *Royalties,* all explore complexities of a Victorian queen.
5. Tucker states that the "*Idylls* would in time prove one of Victorian Britain's fullest literary meditations on the terms of modern power" (*Epic,* 319).
6. Tidrick formulates empire in a way that Tennyson's poem conceptualizes as an evangelical revival of an ancient notion of government, profoundly extended "through the channels of institutional religion, to the middle classes" (*Empire,* 4). In appropriating to themselves hitherto supposedly aristocratic qualities, they asserted their fitness for political power. In her compelling class description "deceptively aristocratic appearance possessed by that generally very middle-class enterprise, the British empire," Tidrick's description accords with results of the developing fashion system (4).
7. In *Epic,* Tucker provides a comprehensive view of British uses of epic to affirm cultural unity while adjusting to historical relevance.
8. Hallam Tennyson, *Tennyson,* 2:122.
9. *CA,* 84–86. The abbreviated title of the Idyll and line numbers are hereafter given in the text.
10. Homer, *Iliad* 22.520.
11. Euripides, *Complete Greek Drama,* 2:14.
12. Euripides, *Helen,* 14.
13. This Michie and Leach translation captures the ultimately delicate system I trace here that exists only on the sufferance of belief based on male desire (22).
14. Campbell, *Romantic Ethic,* recasts Weber and writes about the circulation of goods, suggesting that the romantic ethic promoted both production and pleasure.
15. Stratton's concept of "cultural fetishism" is described in the introduction to this book.
16. See Weber's challenging, problematic uses of "spirit" in *The Protestant Ethic* to describe a political economy that captures the notion of a fetish as a spirit inhabiting an object.
17. Veblen, *Theory,* 24.
18. See Johnson's observations in *Persons and Things* about treating persons as things and her claim that "our real impossible dream is precisely to learn to live in a world where persons treat persons as persons" (2). Arthur's inability to do so leads to disaster.
19. The "land of Lyonnesse" is the first setting for the poem in the earliest (about 1833) prose sketch about Arthurian material that Hallam Tennyson found. See Ricks's introduction to the poem in the Longman's edition, 1460.
20. Swinburne, *Under the Microscope,* 40.
21. For Leodogran's efforts to verify Arthur's legitimacy as a more "general problem" of epistemology, see Kincaid, *Tennyson's Major Poems,* 158–65.
22. Sedgwick in *Between Men* offers a gloss on this kind of erotic triangle.
23. Pointing out the contemporary relevance of what was originally *Enid,* Ranum in

"An Adventure in Modern Marriage" attends to Tennyson's framing contemporary developments of marriage as testing male suitability to their domestic obligations. Rather than notice the increased prominence of fashion, Ranum focuses on Enid's dress in the context of ideological tensions about modern marriage.

24. Tennyson used an English translation of the 1830s and '40s by Charlotte Guest. In *Translation,* Drury shows how Britons moved from accepting a nation of mixed races to excluding the Celts as a savage race, 55. Tennyson not only made Arthur Saxon but did the same for Welsh Enid and Geraint.
25. Entwhistle, *Fashioned Body,* 13.
26. Lipovetsky, *Empire,* 40. Lipovetsky also claims that "far from emblematizing the supremacy of the nobility, fashion attests much more to its continuous weakening since the late Middle Ages, to its progressive metamorphosis into a 'spectacular' class that has self-advancement by sumptuary expense for display purposes as one of its major obligations" (45).
27. Wilson, *Adorned in Dreams,* 9.
28. Simmel, "Fashion, Adornment and Style," 189.
29. McDowell, *Dressed to Kill,* 55.
30. Lipovetsky points out that "fashion as we understand it today emerged during the latter half of the 19th century," (*Empire,* 55). Wilson asserts that "before the beginning of mercantile capitalism and the growth of cities in medieval Europe... fashion as we understand it hardly existed" (*Adorned in Dreams,* 16).
31. Lipovetsky, *Empire,* 55.
32. Quoted in Gray, *Thro' the Vision of the Night,* 17.
33. Beecham, *Magazine,* 78.
34. Tennyson's use of clothes contrasts with Thomas Carlyle's use of tailoring as a central metaphor for remaking the self in *Sartor Resartus* (1833), which, unlike *Idylls,* lacks sartorial description.
35. "Art of Dress," 373.
36. Glowka, in "Tennyson's Tailoring," pointed out that the Victorians interpreted the symbolic meaning of dress, citing articles about fashion and Carlyle's *Sartor Resartus.*
37. Richard Mallen notes the "unsettling presence" of the last diamond blazing in the canopy under which Arthur sits and its connection to "fratricidal strife" (l. 442) ("'Crowned Republic,'" 283).
38. Fashion theories often define the very notion of fashion as attention to time. Lipovetsky celebrates minute changes in fashion to mark the passing of time while Lehmann, in *Tigersprung,* shows how fashion is Janus-faced, taking fashion concepts from the past and making them markers of the present and future.
39. In *Fashioned Body,* Entwistle describes fashion's social function: "The ubiquitous nature of dress would seem to point to the fact that dress or adornment is one of the means by which bodies are made social and given meaning and identity.... Getting dressed is an ongoing practice, requiring knowledge, techniques and skills... [and] points to an important aspect of dress, namely its relation to social order" (7; 9).
40. Given her German-born mother and husband, Queen Victoria made known her choice of English lace and Spitalfields silk for her wedding gown.

41. Consider such analyses as Tucker on Enid's clothing anxieties: "This is the point of the most novelistic scene in all her story: the heavily domesticated, originally imagined, and thoroughly pathetic reverie and dialogue that are set in her boudoir and that center on the problem of how she will dress for her trip to Caerleon. Tormented to think what figure she will cut at court, she for once and in private indulges an uninhibited wish" (*Epic,* 450).
42. Quoted in Glowka, "Tennyson's Tailoring," 306.
43. Wilson, in *Adorned in Dreams,* points out the origin of fashion "in the early capitalist city" (9). Enid's clothing embodies conflicts about fashion as power.
44. Tennyson included the diamonds in his first draft of his retelling, as shown in the notebook for 1833–40. See *Complete Poems,* ed. Ricks, 668.
45. de Guitaut, *Diamonds,* 22–27. The book celebrating Elizabeth II's Diamond Jubilee featured the diamond crown on its cover.
46. Among the many articulations of Lacan's formulation of the law of the father, see Mitchell's introduction to *Feminine Sexuality* (particularly 23). Through the spectral voice, and then the voice's materialization in the diamonds, Tennyson's poetic myth exemplifies Lacan's Law of the Father. Also useful in Lacan is his formulation of language, not as fixed but as unstable. The periodic publication of the *Idylls* also indicates shifting perspectives; different characters receive and perceive the new order.
47. See Cooper, Munich, and Squier, *Arms and the Woman,* 12–13.
48. Marx, in "Fetishism of Commodities," section 4, uses diamond to exemplify a thing without use value.
49. Johnson, *Persons,* 212.
50. Johnson, *Persons,* 212, refers to Lacan's phrase from *Ethics of Psychoanalysis.*
51. That Tennyson suppressed the account of Modred's lineage as the adulterous, incestuous son of Arthur richly enhances this first setting of the crown as a Lyonnesse crown. In *To Strive,* Bachelor points out that Tennyson was aware of this story and had written about it as an undergraduate. The poet's decision to clean up Arthur's manly character makes of the nine diamonds an even more complex indication of the darker implications of proving a knight's worth in the diamond tournaments.
52. In acknowledging the centrality of gender in Victorian poetry, Armstrong in "The Dreaming Collection" observes that it is "unparalleled in its preoccupation with sexuality and what it is to love" (7). When viewed from that vantage, the *Idylls* filters so much life experience through the tissue of sexuality that it could serve as a prime instance of Armstrong's characterization.
53. See Markovits, "Form Things," 612, where she points to the difference in smooth pearls and faceted diamonds, given that Elaine's sleeve is embroidered with pearls.
54. For an elegant argument exploring how the crises of capitalism do not fit a recognition plot, and thus are mystified in the Merdle subplot, see Parker, "Recognition or Reification?," particularly: "The financial crash in the novel is not shown as systemic to the market, but as a freak "criminal" glitch therein . . . That is, the

reified logic of capital is kept separate from the full unfolding of Dickensian recognition" (135).
55. See Delany's "Introduction: The Peculiarities of the English" for the double-faced attitudes towards trade, making money, and the contempt for market forces that underlie Mr. Merdle's character—and his name.
56. Dickens, *Little Dorrit,* ed. Sucksmith, xxi. Subsequent references to this edition will be given in parentheses in the text.
57. Sucksmith's introduction mentions scandals, parliamentary bills, and political alliances that Dickens mythologizes and combines into an interconnected world. See particularly viii–ix, about two 1856 bank failures, railway share mania, mismanagement of the Crimean War, and other national betrayals of trust that form the context for Dickens's novel.
58. Stout's discussion of corporate identity in *Corporate Romanticism* throws light on how Merdle can imitate a corporate structure, "a legal fiction" to bilk investors (25–27).
59. Mr. Clennam may have participated in the opium trade. Other products of that trade were tea and porcelain. See Xu, "Opium Trade and *Little Dorrit.*"
60. For a wide-ranging discussion of relationships between fiction and finance, see the discussion of *Great Expectations* in Kornbluh, *Realizing Capital,* 45–64.
61. Freud, "Fetishism," 21:152–57.
62. For taboos about discussions of money and Merdle as excremental embodiment, see Christopher Herbert, "Filthy Lucre," 196–204.
63. Well into the twentieth century, "sparkle" referred idiomatically to diamonds. "One Word Led to Another" by Arthur "Bugs" Baer, *Los Angeles Examiner,* 18 October 1950, describes the 1910 movement of the "diamond mines" to the Bowery and calls the dealers "the sparkle profession."
64. That Dickens chose "Sparkler of Albion" as a nickname for himself complicates and affirms his diamond symbols. Used privately in letters, the self-aggrandizing but comically aware label for the English author evokes a mythic land that comments ironically on Edmund Sparkler's origins. As the author's anti-self, Sparkler possesses no talent whatsoever, is given no speaking lines, and functions as an emblem of a system that features sparkles devoid of worth.

6. Ivanhoe's Racialized Legacy to English Diamond Novels

1. In *Blood,* Anidjar offers a history of ideas of defining national identity according to racialized conceptions of blood.
2. Scott, *Ivanhoe (Dodd, Mead edition, 1930),* 1:408. Subsequent references to this edition will be given in parentheses in the text, with chapter number before the page.
3. In *The Jewess,* Valman cites scholarship about the Jew being unassimilable yet indispensable in European culture, true also about nation-building in England (see 4–5).
4. For an interpretation of the racial politics at the novel's end that sees the meta-

phoric union of Rowena and Ivanhoe but does not address the Jews' emigration, see Constantini, "Jews and Common Law," where "Rowena's marriage describes a metaphorical consummation of a prophetic wedding of the Norman and Saxon race, without entirely resolving the prospective place of the Jews" (477).
5. Duncan, "Imperial Panic," 298.
6. Simmons, in *Reversing the Conquest,* demonstrates how readers considered the novel historically accurate.
7. Lampert-Weissig, *Medieval Literature,* 58–59.
8. Ragussis, *Figures,* 8. By depicting the persecution of the Jews, including the attempt to convert them, at a critical moment in history—the founding of the English nation—*Ivanhoe* located "the Jewish question" at the heart of English national identity (2).
9. For analyses of Scott's racializing, see Ragussis, *Figures;* Lampert-Weissig, *Medieval Literature;* and Lewin, "'Distinction of the Beautiful Jewess,'" among others, although they do not mention diamonds, a peculiar omission on Lewin's part since she discusses earrings as a sign of the Jewess. Lewin and Lampert-Weissig attend to attire, claiming that Scott Orientalizes the Jew by anachronistically describing their clothing. Valman focuses on the Jewess as an empty signifier but both Jew and Jewess as "cyphers for broader cultural and political debates" (7).
10. Jews were only a handful of the population in England after their expulsion in 1290. The Jewish Emancipation Bill was not enacted until 1858, so the Jew's position was anomalous in Scott's time as well.
11. Shakespeare's merchant has posed a sticking point for literary critics. Mark Shell argues that Shylock's Jewishness is not as significant as his similarity to merchants in general at the time in their equating human flesh with money; yet Stephen Greenblatt points out that by criticizing materialistic merchant values in a specifically Jewish example, Shakespeare's Shylock reinforces the stereotype, taking the dominant group off the hook (Shell, "Wether and the Ewe," 48; Greenblatt, *Renaissance Self-Fashioning,* 292).
12. Francis Jeffries observed that "Isaac is but a milder Shylock, and by no means more natural than his original" (*Edinburgh Review,* 3).
13. For Victorian's habitual use of the interrogative mode, to refer to marginalized groups, see Alicia Carroll, "Race," 230. Todd Endelman, *Leaving,* provides the history of that question.
14. Ragussis, *Figures,* 8. By depicting the persecution of the Jews, including the attempt to convert them, at a critical moment in history—the founding of the English nation—*Ivanhoe* located "the Jewish question" at the heart of English national identity (12).
15. In his Preface, Scott explained his turn from Scotland to England. He can use his success of the *Waverley* novels, while boasting new expertise in a subject "purely English." *Ivanhoe* "display[s] his talent by a fresh discovery of untasted fountains" (6).
16. See Munich, *Queen Victoria's Secrets,* 44–45, for Scott's preferring an English audience in "The Lay of the Last Minstrel." Lampert-Weissig places Scott's racializing in a long perspective.

17. Essential information is found in Dobson, *Jewish Communities of Medieval England*. Brantlinger, "Nations and Novels," mentions the York Massacre in relation to *Ivanhoe*. Accounts differ about whether all York Jews were murdered. Dobson finds that Jews returned soon after the Massacre.
18. Lampert-Weissig shows that the massacres "haunt the edges" of Scott's novel (*Medieval Literature,* 61).
19. Perhaps Scott knew that a yellow circle worn on the chest or a yellow veil for women were required signs of Jews in various cities in Renaissance Italy. At the end of the fifteenth century, Recanati required Jewish women to "wind round their heads, from ear to ear, a band of yellow linen, a sign which in fourteenth-century Pisa and sixteenth-century Bologna, was required of prostitutes" (Hughes, "Distinguishing Signs," 30). The sign of the ear-ring is central to changing requirements (22).
20. Lewin, in "'Distinction of the Beautiful Jewess,'" asserts that Scott's Jewish costumes are Orientalized because medieval Jews wore the same clothes as Christians. In contrast, Spector's introduction to *British Romanticism and the Jews* claims that "between 1753, when the 'Jew Bill' was repealed and July 26, 1858, when Baron Lionel de Rothschild was permitted to assume his seat in the House without first having to swear an oath as a Christian . . . Jews learned how to speak and dress like Englishmen" (9).
21. Lampert-Weissig, *Medieval Literature,* 61–62.
22. Loewald, *Sublimation.*
23. Civitarese, "On Sublimation."
24. Valman, *Jewess,* calling Rebecca "nineteenth-century Britain's most celebrated Jewess," explores ways she is idealized (20). She is also sexualized and Orientalized, as Lewin argues. Lewin believes that portrayal of her garb is anti-Semitic, but Tennyson also pays great attention to medieval dressing of his knights and ladies, as demonstrated in chapter 5.
25. Greenblatt, in *Renaissance Self-Fashioning,* demonstrates that the play both undercuts yet reinforces stereotypes about Jews.
26. Civitarese quoting Conrotto: "*primary* sublimation, where it is not sexual contents which are excluded by sublimation, but 'it is the sexual enjoyment of the object that is substituted with an investment in the object" ("On Sublimation," 9).
27. Thackeray, *Rebecca and Rowena,* 5.
28. Arguing that a gift is not ethically superior to a commodity, Murphy, "Ethic of the Gift," also asserts, "The gift . . . carries with it personal attachments, obligations, and often a clearly articulated symbolism" (190).
29. Strathern, *Gender,* discusses customs in Melanesia, but her point that the gift itself is gendered can extend generally to implications of a gift between women (4).
30. Duby, *Knight,* illuminates the medieval dynamic between church-authorized marriage and political controls.
31. If it is true, as Lewin asserts in "'Distinction of the Beautiful Jewess'" that earrings in themselves are regarded as sexualized Jewish badges, Rowena confirms a mark of the Jew in her ears (36).
32. Glendinning, *Anthony Trollope,* 87.
33. The novel is structured intertextually, both by Lizzie's reading and by the narrator's

allusions. Critics sometimes treat it as a direct reworking of *The Moonstone,* but chapter 3 above demonstrates that the diamond in Collins functions in quite a different way, as do concerns about empire and Indians.

34. Goodlad, in *Victorian Geopolitical,* examines aspects of this question in relation to kinds of British sovereignty in India (45–56), expanding on an earlier published article, cited below.
35. Trollope, *Eustace Diamonds,* 2. Subsequent references to this edition will be given in parentheses in the text, with part and chapter number before the page.
36. Ben-Yishai, "Fact of a Rumor," most usefully distinguishes between two understandings of fact as a concept and way of knowing "an empirical, positive, objective understanding of fact (which is more contemporary), intertwined with an older, communal, intersubjective one" (94).
37. McCormack, Introduction to *Eustace Diamonds,* xxv.
38. Among others, Mrs. Hittaway voices that sentiment: "There used to be a sort of feeling that if a man behaved badly something would be done to him; but that's all over now" (1.60:182).
39. Ben-Yishai, "Trollope and the Law," discusses how "the jurisprudential upheavals and the legal reforms that characterized the British nineteenth century were in fact part of the ongoing cultural and social crisis facing Englishness itself" (155–56).
40. According to the *OED,* in English and Scottish Common Law, under which all personal or movable property of a wife was vested *ipso jure* in the husband, the *paraphernalia* became restricted to such purely personal belongings of a wife as dress, jewels, and the like. While the husband retained legal possession of these, the wife had free use of them and retained them on her husband's death. See "paraphernalia, n." Cohen, in *Sex Scandal,* discusses paraphernalia with an emphasis on the iron box and its contents sexualized (167–68; 188).
41. Though focused on the "tautological crime," Briefel, "Tautological Crimes," shows how the arguments around the Married Women's Property Act bear upon issues raised by the widow Eustace's arguments.
42. Golconda, usually referred to as a diamond mine, is a "fortress near Hyderabad which included a diamond storehouse" (Lenzen, *History,* 26).
43. Goodlad, "Anthony Trollope's *The Eustace Diamonds,*" points to relationships between Lucy Morris's reading of Burke to enable her to support her beloved Frank and the Sawab's situation in protesting a land grab as an exception to the author's characteristic reticence about Indian matters (100).
44. Haidar, "Diamonds of the Deccan," 329.
45. ". . . the Cuddapah group of diamond deposits on the Penner River, comprising the deposits in the catchment area of the Penner, which rises in the highlands of Mysore and reaches the Bay of Bengal north of Madras" (Lenzen, *History,* 26; see also Babu, *Diamonds,* 94).
46. According to Cheyette, "by the 1870s, however, an increasingly pessimistic Trollope began to lose faith in the capacity of 'the Jews' to regulate their worst excesses" (*Constructions,* 14). Cheyette further explains that "within Trollope's fiction, it was precisely the uncertainty caused by unknown, possibly 'semitic', *arrivistes*

that meant that the hidden 'reality' of his 'Jews' could not be assumed stereotypically" (27).

47. Goodlad, *Geopolitical,* 106–9.
48. In another context, see Plotz, *Portable,* on "fictitious" and the "risk of annihilation" as revealing diamond vulnerability, a tendency of things in general (33).
49. *Daniel Deronda,* ed. Graham Handley, 2.14:135. Subsequent references to the novel will be given as part, section, and page in parentheses in the text.
50. Semmel, *George Eliot,* suggests specific connections to *Ivanhoe,* such as the disinherited knight, the racial theme, and asks, "Can we regard the plot of *Daniel Deronda* as that of a somewhat inverted *Ivanhoe*?" (122–23).
51. Among criticism that finds Eliot's final novel inadequate, mistaken or wrong, see Preyer, "Beyond the Liberal Imagination"; Brantlinger, "Nations and Novels"; Law, "Transparency and Epistemology."
52. Endelman, *Leaving,* explains "the disproportionate amount of space of Jews in the Christian imagination," as a typical "screen" on which Christians project their fears and anxieties" (5).
53. Zimmerman, in "Radiant as a Diamond," mentions Grandcourt's diamonds but not that diamonds occur uniquely in this novel.
54. In "A Model Jew," Novak's conception of a model Jew, a composite in Daniel, like those of composite photos, argues that the hero is like a cipher of a Jew, perhaps a concept close to assimilation. However, Eliot's characterization does not so much settle any racial typing as present an English ideal for a Jew that might make the Jew conceivable as an Englishman. Daniel passes as English. Novak's examples of composite portraits of Jews show composite stereotypes, not able to pass as English.
55. Beer observes in *Darwin's Plots,* "But he does not cease to be an Englishman" (188).
56. Lesjak, "Labours," discusses the "ambivalent and contradictory negotiations over the frontiers of 'nation,'" pointing out that Daniel "cannot lose his English upbringing entirely" (724).
57. Scheinberg, "'The beloved ideas,'" examines Daniel's poetic nature and larger meanings of the poetic in Hebrew poetry.
58. Chase's deconstructive reading in "Decomposition" engages a similar logic regarding Daniel's Jewishness, with a different interest in its inevitability: "If whatever best is Jewish and Deronda happens to be best, then Deronda must be Jewish" (219).
59. For concerns about futurity and a secular messianic future for Daniel, see Beer, *Darwin's Plots,* 173–74.
60. For Eliot's anti-Semitism despite her philo-Semitic aims and ambitions, see Meyer, "Safely to Their Own Borders."
61. Eliot wavered between "redeemed" and "repurchased" and chose the possibility of redemption that Gwendolen eventually wishes from Daniel (*Daniel Deronda,* n. 1, 16).
62. Secret names and name-changing is a feature of the sensation novel, elements of which appear not only among the Jewish characters but also in Grandcourt.

63. Gallagher, in "George Eliot," includes the diamonds in her consideration of the illicitly marked exchanges in the novel (see particularly 52).
64. Slaugh-Sanford connects Lydia Glasher's appearance to Africa, thinking of Eliot's own family and investment connections with Africa at the time of the Diamond Rush. Dark-haired Lydia more convincingly alludes to Jews and their connection with diamonds, particularly if one regards *Daniel Deronda* as an inverted *Ivanhoe*.
65. Levy, "Jew in English Fiction," in *Reuben Sachs*, 175–78. Subsequent citations to this edition will be given in parentheses in the text.
66. Cheyette discusses Levy's groundbreaking effort neither to denigrate nor idealize Jews in fiction. See also Hunt, "Amy Levy."
67. Bernstein extrapolates W. E. B. du Bois's descriptions of "double consciousness" to describe the "hyphenated character" of Levy's depiction of Jews in her fine introduction to the Broadview edition of *Reuben Sachs*.
68. Beckman, *Amy Levy,* translates her name (174), hinting at a genetic solution of the Jewish Question that is also suggested and rejected in the other novels in this section. Apparently, Levy read *The Eustace Diamonds* in 1882 (172).

III. South Africa: The Karoo Setting

1. Scholars such as Zoellner in *Heartless* doubt the statement's veracity. Kanfer, *Last Empire,* disproves the anecdote by pointing out that the Star of South Africa had been shipped to London when the South African Parliament met on June 23, 1869. That may not be relevant, because some versions have Southey displaying an eight-carat stone. The anecdote exemplifies fables becoming touchstones of history.
2. Boyle, *To the Cape,* 218.
3. McLaughlan, *Re-imagining,* 101.
4. Newbury, *Diamond Ring,* points out that nineteenth-century discoveries of gold and diamonds "have been held to mark a 'new type' of rush to be rich[,] . . . one of the great adventures of the common man" (9).
5. For a brief history of land disputes and wars, see part 1, chapter 2, "Blue Ground," in Meredith, *Diamonds, Gold, and War.*
6. Lindley, *Adamantia,* 2.
7. See, for instance, Griffiths in *The New Journalism,* who focuses on the common imperialistic rhetoric of both journalism and fiction.
8. "Advertising had not taken over, though there was more than a touch of salesmanship in the articles inspired by London dealers for the *Pall Mall Gazette* in the early 1890s which extolled the brilliant as an item of female dress and as a mark of respectability among the middle classes" (Newbury, *Diamond Ring,* 143).

7. True Stories on the Diamond Fields

1. Ivor Herbert, *Diamond Diggers,* 10.
2. For contemporary sources, see Payton, *Diamond Diggings,* 1; Boyle, *To the Cape,* 85; Williams, *Diamond Mines,* much elaborated, with description of the farm-

house and Jacobs, who was "stolidly content with a bare and precarious living on the uncertain pasture lands of the veld." According to Williams, Niekerk heard of the stone, approached Vrouw Jacobs, who gave him the stone, which he took to O'Reilly, knowing he could find out more in Hopetown and Colesberg where "several Jews ... would not give a penny for it" (117–21).

3. See for example, Roberts, *Diamond*, 5.
4. *Diamond Discovery*, 23.
5. Leasor may have gotten the name from Boyle, *To the Cape*, 35. Kanfer gives the second spelling. "Hottentot" is a word constructed by Boers, based loosely on the sound of their language.
6. Williams, *Diamond Mines*, 2.
7. The word means "unbeliever" in Arabic.
8. The lower figure quoted by Williams, *Diamond Mines*, 125; the larger number by Roberts, *Diamond Magnates*, 5.
9. Boyle, *To the Cape*, 84.
10. Boyle, *To the Cape*, 85.
11. Pridmore, "Introduction," *Journal of William Clayton Humphereys*, ix.
12. Williams, *Diamond Mines*, 197.
13. Ivor Herbert, *Diamond Diggers*, 29. Some accounts peg the purchase price as £50. As an index of Boer values, when Johannes complained to his wife that he could have gotten as much as £63,000 for the farm, she apparently responded that the two of them together could not possibly need that much money.
14. Murray, *Diamond Field Keepsake*, 27. Murray was one of the founders of the *Cape Argus* in 1857.
15. Roberts, *Diamond Magnates*, 10.
16. For more about mine policy as root of apartheid in the twentieth century, see Meredith, *Diamonds, Gold and War*.
17. Payton, *Diamond Diggings*, 2.
18. Payton, *Diamond Diggings*, 205.
19. Payton, *Diamond Diggings*, 197.
20. Williams, *Diamond Mines*, 193–94.
21. Roberts, *Diamond Magnates*, 78.
22. "The abundant yield of Kimberley Mine made it the richest mine in the world, but it did not produce the finest diamonds. That honor went to the Dutoitspan mine, poor in geological quantity but compensated with quality. Bultfontein diamonds had nothing special to recommend them as they were mainly small and spotted, whereas De Beers diamonds were remarkable for their size. And, although Kimberley Mine had a rich yield, it produced 90 per cent of the industry's *boart*, the diamonds used for industrial purposes." See Turrell, *Capital and Labour*, 6.
23. Harris, "South African Diamonds," 227–28.
24. Murray, *Diamond Field Keepsake*, 18.
25. Couper, *Mixed Humanity*, 20. Subsequent page numbers to this edition will be given in parentheses in the text.
26. Jill Matus, in a private conversation, reported that South Africans referred to young women of loose morals by calling them Kimberley.

27. Trollope, *South Africa,* 2:178–79. Subsequent citations will be given in parentheses in the text.
28. Turrell, *Capital and Labour,* 6; 11.
29. London, *Life on the Diamond Fields,* 35.

8. The Scramble and the Scramblers

1. Cecil Rhodes offered Sir Hercules a board position in his mining corporation when he no longer held a governmental position.
2. Schreuder, *Scramble for Africa,* 209.
3. Among those scholars using the phrase as book title: Betts; Chamberlain; Schreuder; and Pakenham.
4. Newbury, *Diamond Ring,* points out that the Diamond Rush "completely altered the demographic and political balance between Boer, Briton, and African" (10).
5. Blunt, *My Diaries,* part 1, xv.
6. For some books about those figures, see Thomas, *Rhodes;* Leasor, *Rhodes and Barnato;* Kanfer, *Last Empire;* and Newbury, *Diamond Ring.*
7. Kanfer, *Last Empire,* 52.
8. Magubane creates a binary of Jew/African, but in literary texts, they are often confederates in illicit capitalist ventures. See Magubane, *Bringing,* 107.
9. Comaroff and Comaroff, *Of Revelation and Revolution,* describes connections between religious and economic effects: "The impact of Protestant evangelists as harbingers of industrial capitalism lay in the fact that their civilizing mission was simultaneously symbolic and practical, theological and temporal. The goods and techniques they brought with them to Africa presupposed the messages and meanings they proclaimed in the pulpit, and vice versa. Both were vehicles of a moral economy that celebrated the global spirit of commerce, the commodity, and the imperial marketplace" (8–9). See also Mudimbe, "Missionary's Discourse," for the missionary role in imperialism in Africa.
10. Cohen, *Reminiscences,* 12; 17.
11. Cohen, *Reminiscences,* 18.
12. Cohen, *Reminiscences,* 24; 26.
13. My use of the phrase "symbolic economy" draws on Goux, *Symbolic Economies,* in his broadening of economics to include psychological understandings of the unconscious.
14. Cohen, *Reminiscences,* 13.
15. Among many relevant British ethnographers, see Knox, *Races of Men;* Beddoe, *Races of Britain;* Taylor, *Origin of the Aryans;* Lagden, *Native Races.*
16. Cheyette, *Constructions of the Jew,* observes about the Jew in English representation, "'The Jew', like all 'doubles', is inherently ambivalent and can represent both the 'best' and the 'worst' of selves" (12). Jewish characters in South African novels offer a taxonomy of stereotypes.
17. Turrell, *Capital,* 1.
18. Boyle, *To the Cape,* 163.
19. Payton, *Diamond Diggings,* 160.

20. Brantlinger, *Dark Vanishings*, considers the case of the Bushman throughout his study and examines "extinction discourse" as a "specific branch of the dual ideologies of imperialism and racism" (2). The Boers are singled out for murdering Bushmen. Olive Schreiner exonerates them but with ambivalence using an evolutionary model in regard to the Boers and a racial one in regard to the Bushmen. See Krebs, *Gender*, 129; 132–36.
21. Payton, *Diamond Diggings*, 198.
22. Williams, *Diamond Mines*, 202–3.
23. Payton, *Diamond Diggings*, 196.
24. Quoted from "'I.D.B.' *The Winning Post*, a London racing scandal sheet" by Roberts, *Diamond Magnates*, 123.
25. Newbury, *Diamond Ring*, 39.
26. When corporate policy proposed an examination of white miners, they successfully went on strike.
27. The practice was not new; Indian miners swallowed them as well. See Newbury, *Diamond Ring*, 126–27.
28. Father-in-law of David Livingstone, Robert Moffat, *Missionary Labours*, describes the evangelical mission of civilizing such people. A useful discussion of Moffat's missionary biography is found in Comaroff, *Of Revelation and Revolution*, 1:83–84.
29. Angove, *Early Days*, 190.
30. Trollope, *South Africa*, 189.
31. Newbury provides charts and figures for the business end of diamond mining.
32. Murray, *Diamond Field Keepsake*, 30–31.
33. Newbury, *Diamond Ring*, p. 75.
34. Meredith, *Diamonds, Gold, and War*, 29.
35. Kower, Diary, 18.
36. Kower, Diary, 17.
37. Kower, Diary, 90.
38. Kower, Diary, 100.
39. Newbury, *Diamond Ring*, 127.
40. Breitmeyer instituted the practice of bulk transactions, sample parcels, early in 1894. This meant a further control to buyers as well as sellers. The practice of "sights" when buyers came to London and were given no choice in the packet of diamonds they were offered, ensured the sale of inferior stones, along with excellent ones. See, for example, Newbury, *Diamond Ring*, 132–34.

9. Domestic Romance Adventures on the Diamond Fields

1. See Freedman, *Temple*, on the 1870s Jew as a figure of simultaneous disgust and pleasure in capitalism.
2. Magubane, *Bringing*, analyzes interpenetration of imperial sexism and racism, including the attribution to Jews alone of economic motives. Her discussion extends to the Boer War and beyond, yet it is relevant to the portrayals of blacks, Jews, and women in Diamond Fields writings.

3. May conforms to Richard Burton's description in *The Jew* of the Jewish woman as superior in "grace and form" to their husbands and brothers. Unfortunately, Jewish women "are nowhere remarkably distinguished for chastity" (7).
4. That Couper knows how he (and others) use stereotypes of Jews to negotiate their world is demonstrated when he baits his sister-in-law by describing his close friend, Louis Leonard as a pawnbroker, and when she voices her disapproval, Senior exposes her prejudice: "I suppose you imagine, because you have really seen so little, that all Jews are pawnbrokers or money-lenders. Leonard, you will no doubt be relieved to hear, is a member of the Civil Service, and a gentleman, too, and a great deal better educated than either you or I" (*Mixed Humanity*, 201).
5. Barney Barnato, East End Jew, fortune seeker at the Diamond Fields, briefly a partner with Louis Cohen, and eventually a partner with Cecil Rhodes in the De Beers diamond company, final owner of the Kimberley Mine, was suspected of IDB. Cohen accuses Barnato of nefarious practices, but it is not clear if these charges are simply sensationalized for purposes of Cohen's memoir. James Leasor, *Rhodes*, describes the situation of Barnato's partner and nephew, Isaac (afterwards, Jack) Joel, who was accused of IDB.
6. Basutos are Bantu-speaking people, native to southern Africa for centuries.
7. "Beautiful Jewess," *Venus Schoolmistress*, 67–79.
8. Stockley, *Pink Gods and Blue Demons*, 8. Subsequent citations will be given in parentheses in the text.
9. Williams, *Diamond Mines*, 1:49.
10. For the provocative analysis of this Calvinist ethic and its ties to materialism, see Weber, *Protestant Ethic*. Weber links the Protestant ethic to Chapel more than to Church. Thus, Stockley giving her Scottish hero the name of Temple is suggestive of the enterprising, upwardly mobile, yet emotionally frigid and stingy capitalist.
11. Both Donald Laure and Pat Temple are Scottish, cold, and materialistic. Magubane, *Bringing*, discusses comparisons of the Scots with Africans.
12. Vescelius-Sheldon, *I.D.B. in South Africa*, 32. Subsequent citations will be given in parentheses in the text.
13. McClintock, *Imperial Leather, 17:* "The mass-marketing of empire as a global system was intimately wedded to the Western reinvention of domesticity, so that imperialism cannot be understood without a theory of domestic space and its relation to the market."
14. Olive Schreiner believes that African whites and blacks are "more or less sexually repellant to one another" but that marriage among Boer and Englishmen will erase differences between them; see foreword to reprint by Richard Rive, xviii.
15. "This particular 'Jew' is, above all, a sign of confusion or indeterminacy" (Cheyette, "Unanswered Questions," 4).
16. Thomas Beddoe's title of his ethnography of the British Isles. Although Vescelius-Sheldon is an American-born writer, Young's analysis in *Colonial Desire* of the entrancement and fear of the other in English fiction, "riven with its own alterity," applies to the racial configurations in her novel.
17. The San peoples, apparently not extinct but widespread, now accept the attribution of Bushmen, once considered a derogatory term. Brantlinger, *Dark Vanish-*

18. See Wheeler, *Ruskin's God.*
19. Ruskin, *Unto This Last,* 17:57. For Ruskin, the Gold Coast included the entire west coast of Africa, including South Africa.
20. Perfitt, "King Solomon," South Place Chapel Sunday evening lectures, *Pathfinder,* 125.
21. Perfitt, "King Solomon," 192.
22. Perfitt, "King Solomon," 238–39.
23. Freud had been developing his theory and published in 1914 his summarizing essay "On Narcissism." The essay only hints at destructive elements.
24. Palmer, *History,* 45–46.
25. See Munich, *Queen Victoria's Secrets,* for indications of the Queen's amorous engagements and her subjects' erotomania.
26. Bent published his work that Rhodes financed in 1892. In May 1895, the name was officially changed from the area known as Zambesia to Rhodesia.
27. Derricourt, *Inventing Africa,* on the blending that drew from desire, the bible, and fake archaeology to produce "outsiders" perception of Africa (22–23).
28. S. Carroll, "Solomonic Legend."
29. On Ophir, King Solomon, gold, and empire, see Alborn, "King Solomon's Gold."
30. Bent, *Ruined Cities,* and Hall, "Great Zimbabwe," 33.
31. Haggard, *King Solomon's Mines,* edited with an introduction and notes by Dennis Butts, 49. Subsequent references to this edition will appear in parentheses in the text.
32. Griffiths, *New Journalism,* 95. The novels that charted the decline and fall of the Zulu nation: *Marie, Child of Storm,* and *Finished.*
33. See McClintock's discussion of the Zulu/Hebrew connection in *Imperial Leather,* 247.
34. Beet, *Grand Old Days,* 28–29. The joke at the diggings was that he was the only Babe to rock his own cradle.
35. British ethnography had claimed Aryan supremacy, and Haggard's fiction was taken as a historical support for their racial and imperial ambitions. Beddoe, *Races of Britain;* Knox, *Races of Man,* among many others, indicate the inherent somatic superiority that subtends cultural attitudes explored in previous chapters of this book.
36. Kaufman, "'King Solomon's Mines?,'" 518.
37. Accepting the superiority of diamonds to gold, Chrisman observes that the entanglement of history, biblical support, and Haggard's replacing diamonds for gold contributed to the novel's endurance: "Haggard uses the Bible to add empirical foundation to his fiction; yet he also tampers with that source by adding to it the most established gem of the South African mineral industry." Chrisman, *Rereading,* 30.
38. McClintock, *Imperial Leather,* on the gendered landscape (240–43). Haggard's map of the route to King Solomon's mine resembles a woman (2).
39. Butts, "Introduction" to Haggard, *King Solomon's Mines,* viii.
40. Stevenson, *Treasure Island,* chapter 4, "The Sea Chest."

41. See Patteson, "*King Solomon's Mines.*"
42. Moffat, *Missionary Labours.*
43. Mitford (1855–1914), a member of the writing Mitford family, like the novelists above, was a "colonial" writer, having been born and dying in England.
44. Monsman, introduction to the Valancourt edition, xxi. Olive Schreiner, "Problem of Slavery," wrote about distinctions between the Hottentot and the Bushman, one eternally childlike, the other irredeemably savage, 106–8.
45. Mitford, *Renshaw Fanning's Quest*, 11. Subsequent page numbers of this edition will be given in parentheses in the text.
46. Mitford, *Through the Zulu Country.* Admiring Zulus, Mitford shared their low opinion of the Boer: "They are mean and liars—always on the look-out to steal our land" (250).

10. Disavowed, Dispossessed Boers in Charlotte Mansfield and Olive Schreiner

1. Boyle, *To the Cape,* 218–19.
2. Schreiner, "Boer Woman," 13.
3. Newbury, in *Diamond Ring,* charts the financial organization to syndication, when diamonds are strictly controlled in a single sale stream in 1920, four years after Mansfield published *Gloria.*
4. Barney Barnato, the diamond magnate suspected of IDB, was also described as having a bullet-shaped head, but photographs do not show that shape.
5. Starting around 1883, a position such as McGreedy's controlled access to the mine sites from the compounds, functioning as a detective controlling theft. He would have been supplier of labor by contractors. Knowledge of this system plays a part in Mansfield's plot. See Newbury, *Diamond Ring,* 72.
6. In her affectionate description of the karoo, Schreiner devotes only one short paragraph to Griqualand West and only one sentence to the diamond mines: "In it are situated the great Kimberley diamond-mines, the richest in the world." See Schreiner, *Thoughts on South Africa,* 44. Henceforth cited as *Thoughts.*
7. For equations between rape of land and body, see Monsman, "Olive Schreiner."
8. Kucich. *Imperial Masochism,* uses a relational psychoanalytic model to argue for Schreiner's social class (86–135).
9. Schreiner, *Undine,* 13. Further references to this edition are given in parentheses in the text.
10. Malays are mentioned in other African diamond novels, such as in Couper's ethnic list, quoted above. See Bickford-Smith, *Ethnic Pride,* 36, who offers a photo of prosperous Malay women; see 193 on Malay ethnicity. Muslims, considered as "Coloureds," formed an elite community in Cape Town.
11. With Havelock Ellis's help, Schreiner published in 1890 a collection of allegorical tales entitled *Dreams.*
12. In *Modernist Voyages,* Snaith argues that diamonds appear "obliquely" and through references to the Fields, but she does not recognize their effacement as a device. Mentioning "representative possibilities" of the setting, she does not point out that the possibilities are not realized (4).

13. To Havelock Ellis, 15 December 1884, "A Note on the Genesis of the Book," assembled by S. C. Cronwright-Schreiner, *Man to Man,* n.p. Future citations to this edition will be given in parentheses in the text.
14. For melodramatic features, the "melodrama of the karoo," see Hultgren, *Melodramatic,* 166–170.
15. McClintock, *Imperial Leather,* 260.
16. "A Letter on the Jew," 147.
17. "Undine, like Schreiner, is a 'queer' child" (Mizoguchi, "Colonizer," 12).
18. Schreiner, *Thoughts,* 314.
19. Schreiner, *Thoughts,* 316.
20. Beet, *Grand Old Days.*
21. Marx, "Fetishism."
22. See Benjamin, *Arcades Project.*
23. Lindley, *Adamantia,* ix.
24. Koskoff, *Diamond World,* 35–36.

Epilogue

1. Tiffany & Co. of New York bought the major share: twenty-two lots for $480,000, a sum greater than the combined purchases of the nine next-largest buyers. Janet Zapata, "Diamond Jewelry for Everyone," 186.
2. Among the many incomplete accounts of the Hope Diamond are Fowler, *Hope,* and Kurin, *Hope Diamond;* Patch, *Blue Mystery.*
3. Its weight is usually reported as 44.5 carats, but apparently when it was removed from its setting for study at the Smithsonian Institution, it was bigger, according to an evaluation by the Gemological Institute of America in 1996. See Patch, *Blue Mystery,* 89.
4. Inspired by Lipovetsky's argument regarding the democratic possibilities inherent in fashion, this concept first appears in Munich and Spiegel, in *Titanic,* 155–67.
5. Patch, *Blue Mystery,* 90.
6. Patch, *Blue Mystery,* 47.
7. William Jones, *Finger-Ring Lore,* 284. A recent report of this event, found also widely on the web, is Doniger, *Ring of Truth,* 264.
8. www.express.co.uk/life-style/life/906033/meghan-markle-prince-harry-engagement-ring-botswana.
9. http://www.nytimes.com/2008/08/09/business/worldbusiness/09nocera.html.
10. From a magazine article placed by Dorothy Dignam about 1940 (Hartman Center, Duke University Library, 730 PUB, 17). Jones, *Finger-Ring Lore,* 292, offers various examples of the ring as signifying servitude.
11. Tagore, in *Mani-mālā,* lays out ring symbolism: "The Greeks and Romans were so fully convinced of the intrinsic value attached to this finger, that it was called the medical or healing finger" (1:843).
12. Sullivan, "How Diamonds Became Forever."
13. Suggestion sheet, N. W. Ayer & Son, Inc., New York 20, New York, 1959.
14. Dignam, "Kaufmann's Famous 12 Points."

15. Dignam, "Diamond Jubilees," 3–4.
16. Dignam, "Diamond Jubilees," 1–2.
17. Dignam, "How to Celebrate a Diamond Jubilee," from "Why and How," 3.
18. Roth, *Everyman,* dustjacket left flap. Subsequent quotations from this edition appear in parentheses in the text.

Bibliography

Adamson, John, and Katherine Prior. *Maharajas' Jewels.* New York: Vendome Press, 2002.

Aijazuddin, F. S. *Sikh Portraits by European Artists.* New York: Oxford University Press, 1979.

Alborn, Timothy. "King Solomon's Gold: Ophir in an Age of Empire." *Journal of Victorian Culture* 20, no. 4 (2015): 491–508.

Alexander, Michael, and Sushila Anand. *Queen Victoria's Maharajah: Duleep Singh, 1838–93.* New York: Taplinger, 1980.

Amini, Iradj. *The Koh-i-noor Diamond.* New Delhi: Roli Books, 1994.

Angove, John. *In the Early Days: The Reminiscences of Pioneer Life on the South African Diamond Fields.* Kimberley, South Africa: Handel House, 1910.

Anidjar, Gil. *Blood: A Critique of Christianity.* New York: Columbia University Press, 2014.

Appadurai, Arjun. "Introduction: Commodities and the Politics of Value." In *The Social Life of Things: Commodities in Cultural Perspective,* edited by Arjun Appadurai, 3–63. Cambridge: Cambridge University Press, 1986.

Apter, Emily, and William Pietz, eds. *Fetishism as Cultural Discourse.* Ithaca, N.Y.: Cornell University Press, 1993.

The Arabian Nights Entertainments Complete. From the text of Dr. Jonathan Scott. The "Aldine" Edition. 4 vols. London: Pickering and Chatto, 1890.

Armstrong, Isobel. "The Dreaming Collection." In *Victorian Prism: Refractions of the Crystal Palace,* edited by James Buzard, Joseph Childers, and Eileen Gillooly, 55–82. Charlottesville: University of Virginia Press, 2007.

"Art of Dress." Review of *British Costume. A Complete History of the Dress of the Inhabitants of the British Islands* by J. R. Planché. *Quarterly Review* 79 (1847): 373.

Atwal, Rajpreet. "Between the Courts of Lahore and Windsor: Anglo-Indian Relations and the Re-making of Royalty in the Nineteenth Century." PhD diss., Oxford University, 2017.

Babu, T. M. *Diamonds in India.* Bangalore: Geological Society of India, 1998.

Baer, Arthur "Bugs." "One Word Led to Another." *Los Angeles Examiner,* 18 October 1950. J. Walter Thompson Diamond Information Center Collection. Box 35. John W. Hartman Center for Sales, Advertising, and Marketing History, David M. Rubenstein Rare Book and Manuscript Library, Duke University.

Balfour, Edward. *Cyclopedia of Indian and of Eastern and Southern Asia.* 2nd ed. London: Bernard Quaritch, 1857.

Bance, Peter. *Sovereign, Squire, and Rebel: Maharajah Duleep Singh.* London: Coronet House, 2009.
Barker, Brian OBE. *The Symbols of Sovereignty.* Totowa, N.J.: Rowman and Littlefield, 1979.
Batchelor, John. *Tennyson: To Strive, to Seek, to Find.* New York: Pegasus, 2012.
"The Beautiful Jewess in the Boudoir." In *Venus Schoolmistress: A Victorian Collection,* 67–79. Reprint, New York: Grove Press, 1984.
Beckman, Linda Hunt. *Amy Levy: Her Life and Letters.* Athens: Ohio University Press, 2000.
Beddoe, John. *The Races of Britain: A Contribution to the Anthropology of Western Europe.* Bristol, UK: J. W. Arrowsmith, 1885.
Beecham, Margaret. *A Magazine of Her Own?: Domesticity and Desire in the Woman's Magazine, 1800–1914.* London: Routledge, 1996.
Beer, Gillian. *Darwin's Plots: Evolutionary Narrative in Darwin, George Eliot and Nineteenth-Century Fiction.* 2nd ed. Cambridge: Cambridge University Press, 2000.
Beet, George. *The Grand Old Days of the Diamond Fields: Memories of Past Times with the Diggers of Diamondia.* Cape Town: Maskew Miller, n.d. (stamped "received at library, 1930").
Benjamin, Walter. *The Arcades Project.* Translated by Howard Eiland and Kevin McLaughlin. Cambridge: Belknap Press of Harvard University Press, 1999.
Ben-Yishai, Ayelet. "The Fact of a Rumor: Anthony Trollope's *The Eustace Diamonds.*" *Nineteenth-Century Literature* 62 (June 2007): 88–120.
———. "Trollope and the Law." In *The Cambridge Companion to Anthony Trollope,* edited by Carolyn Dever and Lisa Niles, 155–67. Cambridge: Cambridge University Press, 2011.
Bent, J. Theodore. *The Ruined Cities of Mashonaland.* London: Longmans, Green, 1892.
Betts, R. F. *The Scramble for Africa: Causes and Dimensions of Empire.* Lexington, Mass.: Heath, 1972.
Bickford-Smith, Vivian. *Ethnic Pride and Racial Prejudice in Victorian Cape Town.* Cambridge: Cambridge University Press, 1995.
Blunt, Wilfred Scawen. *My Diaries.* Part 1. London: M. Secker, 1919.
Boyle, Frederick. *To the Cape for Diamonds: A Story of Digging Experiences in South Africa.* London: Chapman and Hall, 1873.
Brantlinger, Patrick. *Dark Vanishings: Discourse on the Extinction of Primitive Races, 1800–1930.* Ithaca, N.Y.: Cornell University Press, 2003.
———. "Nations and Novels: Disraeli, George Eliot, and Orientalism." *Victorian Studies* 35 (1992): 255–75.
Briefel, Aviva. "Tautological Crimes: Why Women Can't Steal Jewels." *Novel* 37 (Fall 2003/Spring 2004): 135–57.
Brown, Angus Connell. "Cultural Studies and Close Reading." *PMLA* 132 (2017): 1187–93.
Brown, Caroline. "The Tragedies of the Kohinoor." *Cosmopolitan Magazine* 26 (1898–99): 52–59.
Brown, Peter. "On the Magic Carpet of the Met." *New York Review of Books* 58 (8 December 2011): 27.

Brown, Ray B. *Objects of Special Devotion: Fetishes and Fetishism in Popular Culture.* Madison: Popular Press, 1982.

Browning, Robert. "'Childe Roland to the Dark Tower Came.'" In vol. 1 of *The Poems,* edited by John Pettigrew, supplemented and completed by Thomas J. Collins, 585–92. New Haven, Conn.: Yale University Press, 1981.

Burton, Richard. *The Jew, the Gypsy and El Islam.* London: Hutchinson, 1898.

Campbell, Colin. *The Romantic Ethic and the Spirit of Modern Consumerism.* Oxford: Basil Blackwell, 1987.

Cannadine, David. *Ornamentalism: How the British Saw Their Empire.* New York: Oxford University Press, 2001.

Carlyle, Thomas. *Sartor Resartus: The Life and Opinions of Herr Teufelsdröckh.* 1836. Edited by Charles Frederick Harrold. New York: Odyssey Press, 1937.

———. "Signs of the Times." *Edinburgh Review* 49 (1829): 439–59.

Carroll, Alicia. "Race." In *George Eliot in Context,* edited by Margaret Harris, 230. Cambridge: Cambridge University Press, 2013.

Carroll, Scott T. "Solomonic Legend: The Muslims and the Great Zimbabwe." *International Journal of African Historical Studies* 21(1988): 233–47.

Chamberlain, Muriel Evelyn. *The Scramble for Africa.* New York: Barnes and Noble, 1974.

Chase, Cynthia. "The Decomposition of Elephants: Double-Reading *Daniel Deronda.*" *PMLA* 93 (1978): 215–39.

Cheyette, Bryan. *Constructions of the Jew in English Literature and Society: Racial Representations, 1885–1945.* Cambridge: Cambridge University Press, 1993.

———. "Unanswered Questions." In *Between Race and Culture: Representations of "the Jew" in English and American Culture,* edited by Bryan Cheyette, 1–15. Stanford, Calif.: Stanford University Press, 1996.

Chrisman, Laura. *Rereading the Imperial Romance: British Imperialism and South African Resistance in Haggard, Schreiner, and Plaatje.* Oxford: Clarendon Press, 2000.

Civitarese, Giuseppe. "On Sublimation." *International Journal of Psychoanalysis* 97 (2016): 1–24.

Cohen, Louis. *Reminiscences of Kimberley.* Facsimile reprint of 1911 edition. Kimberley, South Africa: Historical Society of Kimberley, 1990.

Cohen, William A. *Sex Scandal: The Private Parts of Victorian Fiction.* Durham, N.C.: Duke University Press, 1996.

Cohn, Bernard S. "Cloth, Clothes, and Colonialism in India." In *Cloth and Human Experience,* edited by Annette B. Weiner and Jane Schneider, 303–55. Washington, D.C.: Smithsonian Institution, 1989.

———. *Colonialism and Its Forms of Knowledge.* Princeton, N.J.: Princeton University Press, 1996.

Collins, Alan T. "Diamonds in Modern Technology: Synthesis and Applications." In *The Nature of Diamonds,* edited by George Harlow, 255–72. Cambridge: Cambridge University Press, 1998.

Collins, Wilkie. *The Moonstone.* Edited by Sandra Kemp. London: Penguin, 1998.

Comaroff, Jean, and John Comaroff. *Of Revelation and Revolution: Christianity, Colo-*

nialism, and Consciousness in South Africa. Vol. 1. Chicago: University of Chicago Press, 1991.

———. *Of Revelation and Revolution: The Dialectics of Modernity on a South African Frontier.* Vol. 2. Chicago: University of Chicago Press, 1997.

Constantini, Cristina. "The Jews and Common Law: A Question of Traditions and Jurisdictions. An Analysis through W. Scott's *Ivanhoe.*" *Textus* 21 (2008): 467–85.

Cooper, Helen, Adrienne Munich, and Susan Merrill Squier. "Arms and the Woman: The Con[tra]ception of the War Text." In *Arms and the Woman: War, Gender, and Literary Representation,* edited by Helen Cooper, Adrienne Munich, and Susan Merrill Squier, 9–24. Chapel Hill: University of North Carolina Press, 1989.

Couper, J. R. *Mixed Humanity: A Story of Camp Life in South Africa.* Cape Colony, South Africa: J. C. Juta, 1892.

Craufurd, Quintin. *Sketches Chiefly Relating to the History, Religion, Learning, and Manners of the Hindoos.* London: T. Cadell, 1790.

Dalrymple, William, and Anita Anand. *Koh-i-Noor: The History of the World's Most Infamous Diamond.* London: Bloomsbury, 2017.

Darby, Phillip. *Three Faces of Imperialism: British and American Approaches to Asia and Africa, 1870–1970.* New Haven, Conn.: Yale University Press, 1987.

Delany, Paul. "Introduction: The Peculiarities of the English." In *Literature, Money and the Market: From Trollope to Amis.* Basingstoke: Palgrave Macmillan, 2002.

"The Derivation of 'Duleep Singh.'" *Imperial Oriental Quarterly Review and Oriental Colonial Record* 15/16 (July/October 1894): 188–89.

Derricourt, Robin. *Inventing Africa: History, Archaeology and Ideas.* London: Pluto Press, 2011.

The Diamond Discovery in South Africa: A collection of articles and original correspondence extracted from various colonial journals and original remarks in refutation of the erroneous statements of messrs Harry Emanuel and J. R. Gregory. Colesberg, Cape of Good Hope: Wheatley, 1869.

Dickens, Charles. *Bleak House.* Edited by Steven Gill. London: Oxford University Press, 2008.

———. *Dombey and Son.* Edited by Alan Horsman and with an introduction by Dennis Walder. 2nd ed. London: Oxford University Press, 2008.

———. *Little Dorrit.* Edited by Harvey Peter Sucksmith. London: Oxford University Press, 1982.

Dignam, Dorothy. "Diamonds in Advertisements for Other Products." J. Walter Thompson Diamond Information Center Collection. John W. Hartman Center for Sales, Advertising, and Marketing History, David M. Rubenstein Rare Book and Manuscript Library, Duke University.

———. "Diamond Jubilees—Why and How," n.d., 1–4. J. Walter Thompson Diamond Information Center Collection. John W. Hartman Center for Sales, Advertising, and Marketing History, David M. Rubenstein Rare Book and Manuscript Library, Duke University.

———. "Kaufmann's Famous 12 Points Expanded to 15 for the Promotion of a Diamond Jubilee in Pittsburgh." (1946?). J. Walter Thompson Diamond Information

Center Collection. John W. Hartman Center for Sales, Advertising, and Marketing History, David M. Rubenstein Rare Book and Manuscript Library, Duke University.

———. "Lines and Logic of the Solitaire." J. Walter Thompson Diamond Information Center Collection. John W. Hartman Center for Sales, Advertising, and Marketing History, David M. Rubenstein Rare Book and Manuscript Library, Duke University.

———. "Make the Most of Your Diamond Jubilee." J. Walter Thompson Diamond Information Center Collection. John W. Hartman Center for Sales, Advertising, and Marketing History, David M. Rubenstein Rare Book and Manuscript Library, Duke University.

Dobson, R. B. *The Jewish Communities of Medieval England: The Collected Essays of R. B. Dobson*. Edited by Helen Birkett. York: Borthwick Institute, University of York, 2010.

Doniger, Wendy. *The Ring of Truth and Other Myths of Sex and Jewelry*. New York: Oxford University Press, 2017.

Doyle, Sir Arthur Conan. "The Adventure of the Blue Carbuncle." In *The Complete Sherlock Holmes*. 1:244–57. With preface by Christopher Morley. Garden City, N.Y.: Doubleday, n.d.

———. *The Sign of Four*. Edited by Shafquat Towheed. Peterborough, Ontario: Broadview, 2010.

Drury, Annemarie. *Translation as Transformation in Victorian Poetry*. Cambridge: Cambridge University Press, 2015.

Duby, George. *The Knight, the Lady, and the Priest*. Chicago: University of Chicago Press, 1982.

Duncan, Ian. "*The Moonstone*, the Victorian Novel, and Imperialist Panic." *Modern Language Quarterly* 55 (September 1994): 297–300.

Eliot, George. *Daniel Deronda*. Edited by Graham Handley. Oxford: Clarendon Press, 1984.

Endelman, Todd. *Leaving the Jewish Fold*. Princeton, N.J.: Princeton University Press, 2015.

Entwistle, Joanne. *The Fashioned Body: Fashion, Dress and Modern Social Theory*. Cambridge, UK: Polity, 2010.

Epstein, Edward Jay. *The Rise and Fall of Diamonds: The Shattering of a Brilliant Illusion*. New York: Simon and Schuster, 1982.

Euripides. *Helen*. In vol. 2 of *The Complete Greek Drama*, translated by E. P. Coleridge, edited by Whitney J. Oates and Eugene O'Neill Jr. New York: Random House, 1938.

———. *Helen*. Translated by James Michie and Colin Leach. New York: Oxford University Press, 1982.

Fowler, Marion. *Hope: Adventures of a Diamond*. New York: Ballantine, 2002.

Franklin, J. Jeffrey. *The Lotus and the Lion: Buddhism and the British Empire*. Ithaca, N.Y.: Cornell University Press, 2008.

Freedman, Jonathan. *The Temple of Culture: Assimilation and Anti-Semitism in Literature*. Oxford: Oxford University Press, 2000.

Freud, Sigmund. "Fetishism" (1927). In *The Standard Edition of the Complete Psychological Works,* edited by James Strachey, 21:152–57. London: Hogarth Press, 1961.

———. "On Narcissism: An Introduction." In *The Standard Edition of the Complete Psychological Works,* edited by James Strachey, 14:67–102. London: Hogarth Press, 1961.

Gallagher, Catherine. "George Eliot and *Daniel Deronda:* The Prostitute and the Jewish Question." In *Sex, Politics, and Science in the Nineteenth-Century Novel,* edited by Ruth Yeazell, 39–62. Baltimore: Johns Hopkins University Press, 1986.

Gamman, Lorraine, and Merja Makinen. *Female Fetishism: A New Look.* New York: New York University Press, 1994.

Geertz, Clifford. *The Interpretation of Culture.* New York: Basic Books, 1973.

Gell, Simeran Man Singh. "The Origins of the Sikh 'Look': From Guru Gobind to Dalip Singh." *History and Anthropology* 10 (1996): 37–83.

Glendinning, Victoria. *Anthony Trollope.* New York: Alfred A. Knopf, 1992.

Glowka, Arthur Wayne. "Tennyson's Tailoring of Source in the Geraint Tales." *Victorian Poetry* 19 (Autumn 1981): 302–7.

Goodlad, Lauren M. E. "Anthony Trollope's *The Eustace Diamonds* and the Great Parliamentary Bore." In *The Politics of Gender in Anthony Trollope's Novels: New Readings for the Twenty-First Century,* edited by Margaret Markwick, Deborah Denenholz Morse, and Regenia Gagnier, 99–116. Surrey: Ashgate, 2009.

———. *Victorian Geopolitical Aesthetic: Realism, Sovereignty, and Transnational Experience.* New York: Oxford University Press, 2015.

Goux, Jean-Joseph. *Symbolic Economies: After Marx and Freud.* Ithaca, N.Y.: Cornell University Press, 1990.

Gray, J. M. *Thro' the Vision of the Night: A Study of Source, Evolution and Structure in Tennyson's "Idylls of the King."* Edinburgh: Edinburgh University Press, 1980.

Greenblatt, Stephen J. "Marlowe, Marx, and Anti-Semitism." *Critical Inquiry* 5 (Winter 1978): 291–307.

———. *Renaissance Self-Fashioning from More to Shakespeare.* Chicago: University of Chicago Press, 1980.

Gregory, Alice. "Body of Work." *New Yorker,* 1 August 2016, 26–33.

Griffiths, Andrew. *The New Journalism, the New Imperialism and the Fiction of Empire, 1870–1900.* New York: Palgrave, 2015.

Guitaut, Caroline de. *Diamonds: A Jubilee Celebration.* Royal Collection Trust, 2012.

Haggard. H. Rider. *King Solomon's Mines.* Edited by Dennis Butts. Oxford: Oxford University Press, 1998.

———. *She: A History of Adventure.* Edited by Norman Etherington. Bloomington: Indiana University Press, 1991.

Haidar, Navina Najat. "Diamonds of the Deccan." In *Sultans of Deccan India, 1500–1700: Opulence and Fantasy,* edited by Navina Najat Haidar and Marika Sardar, 325–26. New Haven, Conn.: Yale University Press, 2015.

Hall, Martin. "Great Zimbabwe and the Lost City: The Cultural Colonization of the South African Past." In *Theory in Archaeology: A World Perspective,* edited by Peter J. Ucko, 9–46. New York: Routledge, 2005.

Halpern, Jake. "The Secret of the Temple." *New Yorker,* 30 April 2012, 48–57.

Harlow, George. "What Is Diamond?" In *The Nature of Diamond,* edited by George Harlow, 5–22. Cambridge: Cambridge University Press, 1998.

Harris, G. F. "South African Diamonds." *Belgravia* 13 (1873): 227–28.

Hart, Matthew. *Diamond: A Journey to the History of an Obsession*. New York: Walker, 2001.

Hazan, Robert. *The Diamond Makers: A Compelling Drama of Scientific Discovery*. Cambridge: Cambridge University Press, 1999.

Heller, Tamar. *Dead Secrets: Wilkie Collins and the Female Gothic*. New Haven, Conn.: Yale University Press, 1992.

Hendrie, James H. "Letters from the South African Diamond Fields, 1879–1886." Transcribed by Margaret R. Meyer. Folder 17. Special Collections. Sterling Memorial Library. Yale University.

Herbert, Christopher. "Filthy Lucre: Victorian Ideas of Money." *Victorian Studies* 44 (Winter 2002): 196–204.

———. *War of No Pity: The Indian Mutiny and Victorian Trauma*. Princeton, N.J.: Princeton University Press, 2009.

Herbert, Ivor. *The Diamond Diggers: South Africa to 1866 to the 1970s*. London: Tom Stacey, 1971.

Hirst, Damien. *For the Love of God: The Making of the Diamond Skull*. London: Other Criteria/White Cube, 2007.

"History of the Diamond." *North British Review* 18, no. 35 (1853). Reprinted in *Eclectic Magazine of Foreign Literature* 28 (January 1853).

Hitchens, Christopher. "A Man of Permanent Contradictions." Review of *The Long Recessional: The Imperial Life of Rudyard Kipling* by David Gilmour. *Atlantic Monthly*, June 2002, 289–93.

Homans, Margaret. *Royal Representations: Queen Victoria and British Culture, 1837–1876*. Chicago: University of Chicago Press, 1998.

Homer. *The Iliad*. Translated by Robert Fitzgerald. New York: Anchor Press/Doubleday, 1974.

Hopkins, Gerard Manley. *The Poems of Gerard Manley Hopkins*. Edited by W. H. Gardner and N. H. Mackenzie. 4th ed. London: Oxford University Press, 1967.

Hopkirk, Peter. *Quest for Kim: In Search of Kipling's Great Game*. London: John Murray, 1996.

Houston, Gail Turley. *Royalties: The Queen and Victorian Writers*. Charlottesville: University Press of Virginia, 1999.

Hughes, Diane Owen. "Distinguishing Signs: Ear-Rings, Jews and Franciscan Rhetoric in the Italian Renaissance City." *Past and Present* 112 (1986): 3–59.

Hultgren, Neil. *Melodramatic Imperial Writing: From the Sepoy Rebellion to Cecil Rhodes*. Athens: Ohio University Press, 2014.

Hunt, Linda. "Amy Levy and the 'Jewish Novel': Representing Jewish Life in the Victorian Period." *Studies in the Novel* 26 (1994): 237–38.

Hyde, Ralph, ed. *London Maps: The A to Z of Victorian London*. Reprint of an 1888 Ordnance Atlas, edited and published by George W. Bacon. With notes by Ralph Hyde. Castel, Kent: Harry Margary Lympne in association with Guildhall Library, London, 1987.

Illustrated Exhibitor, no. 6, 12 July 1851, 93.

JanMohamed, Abdul R. "The Economy of Manichean Allegory: The Function of Racial Difference in Colonialist Literature." *Critical Inquiry* 12 (1985): 59–87.

Jeffries, Francis. Review of *Ivanhoe*. *Edinburgh Review, or Critical Journal* 33, no. 65 (January 1820): 3.

Johnson, Barbara. *Persons and Things*. Cambridge, Mass.: Harvard University Press, 2008.

Jones, William. *Crowns and Coronations: A History of Regalia*. London: Chatto and Windus, 1883.

———. *Finger-Ring Lore: Historical, Legendary, Anecdotal*. 2nd ed., revised and enlarged. London: Chatto and Windus, 1890. Reissued, Detroit: Singing Tree Press, 1968.

Kanfer, Stefan. *The Last Empire: De Beers, Diamonds and the World*. London: Hodder and Stoughton, 1993.

Kaufman, Heidi. "'King Solomon's Mines?': African Jewry, British Imperialism, and H. Rider Haggard's Diamonds." *Victorian Literature and Culture* 33 (2005): 517–39.

Keep, Christopher, and Don Randall. "Addiction, Empire, and Narrative in Arthur Conan Doyle's *Sign of Four*." *Novel: A Forum on Fiction* 32 (Spring 1999): 207–21.

Kincaid, James R. *Tennyson's Major Poems: The Comic and Ironic Patterns*. New Haven, Conn.: Yale University Press, 1975.

King, C. W. *The Natural History, Ancient and Modern of Precious Stones and Gems and of Precious Metals*. London: Bell and Daldy, 1865.

Kinsey, Danielle C. "Koh-i-Noor: Empire, Diamonds, and the Performance of British Material Culture." *Journal of British Studies* 48 (April 2009): 391–419.

Kipling, Rudyard. *Kim*. Edited by Zohreh Sullivan. New York: Norton, 2002.

———. "Typhoid at Home." *Civil and Military Gazette,* 14 February 1885. In *Kipling's India: Uncollected Sketches, 1884–88,* edited by Thomas Pinney, 69–73. London: Macmillan, 1986.

Kirkley, Melissa B. "The Origin of Diamonds: Earth Processes." In *The Nature of Diamonds,* edited by George Harlow, 48–65. Cambridge: Cambridge University Press, 1998.

Knox, Robert, M.D. *Races of Men: A Philosophical Enquiry*. London: Henry Renshaw, 1862.

"Koh-i-noor." *Chambers' Edinburgh Journal,* n.s., 291 (28 July 1849): 49.

"Koh-i-noor." http://famousdiamonds.tripod.com/koh-i-noordiamond.html.

Kornbluh, Anna. *Realizing Capital: Financial and Psychic Economies in Victorian Form*. New York: Fordham University Press, 2014.

Koskoff, David. *The Diamond World*. New York: Harper and Row, 1981.

Kower. J. P., Jr. Diary, November 1873: "From Cleveland to South Africa," 1872. Folder 11. Cape Town Library, Cape Town, South Africa.

Krafft-Ebing, Richard von. *Psychopathia Sexualis: A System of Psychology in Sexual Life*. 1886. New York: Pioneer, 1947.

Krebs, Paula. *Gender, Race, and the Writing of Empire: Public Discourse and the Boer War*. Cambridge: Cambridge University Press, 1999.

Kristeva, Julia. *Revolution in Poetic Language*. Translated by Margaret Walter. New York: Columbia University Press, 1984.

Kucich, John. *Imperial Masochism: British Fiction, Fantasy, and Social Class*. Princeton, N.J.: Princeton University Press, 2007.

Kurin, Richard. *Hope Diamond: The Legendary History of a Cursed Gem.* New York: Harper Collins, 2007.
Lagden, Godfrey, Sir. *The Native Races of the Empire.* London: W. Collins, 1924.
Lampert-Weissig, Lisa. *Medieval Literature and Postcolonial Studies.* Edinburgh: Edinburgh University Press, 2010.
Latour, Bruno. *We Have Never Been Modern.* Translated by Helen Porter. Cambridge, Mass.: Harvard University Press, 1991.
Law, Jules. "Transparency and Epistemology in George Eliot's *Daniel Deronda.*" *Nineteenth-Century Literature* 62 (2007): 250–77.
Leasor, James. *Rhodes and Barnato: The Premier and the Prancer.* London: Leo Cooper, 1997.
Lehmann, Ulrich. *Tigersprung: Fashion in Modernity.* Cambridge, Mass.: MIT Press, 2000.
Lenzen, Godehard. *The History of Diamond Production and the Diamond Trade.* London: Barrie and Jenkins, 1970.
Lesjak, Carolyn. "Labours of a Modern Storyteller: George Eliot and the Cultural Project of 'Nationhood.'" In *Victorian Identities: Social and Cultural Formations in Nineteenth-Century Literature,* edited by Ruth Robbins and Julian Wolfreys, 25–42. New York: St. Martin's, 1996.
Levine, Caroline. *Forms: Whole, Rhythm, Hierarchy, Network.* Princeton, N.J.: Princeton University Press, 2015.
Levy, Amy. "The Jew in English Fiction." *Jewish Chronicle,* 4 June 1886, 13. In *Reuben Sachs,* edited by Susan David Bernstein, 175–78. Peterborough, Ontario: Broadview, 2006.
———. *Reuben Sachs.* Edited by Susan David Bernstein. Peterborough, Ontario: Broadview, 2006.
Lewin, Judith. "The 'Distinction of the Beautiful Jewess': Rebecca of Ivanhoe and Walter Scott's Marking of the Jewish Woman." *Jewish Culture and History* 8, no. 1 (2006): 29–48.
Lichtenstein, Rachel. *Diamond Street: The Hidden World of Hatton Garden.* London: Hamish Hamilton, 2012.
Lindley, Augustus. *Adamantia: The Truth About the South African Diamond Fields.* London: W. H. Collingridge, 1873.
Lipovetsky, Gilles. *The Empire of Fashion: Dressing Modern Democracy.* Translated by Catherine Porter with a foreword by Richard Sennett. Princeton, N.J.: Princeton University Press, 1987.
Loewald, Hans W. *Sublimation: Inquiries into Theoretical Psychoanalysis.* New Haven, Conn.: Yale University Press, 1988.
Logan, Peter Melville. *Victorian Fetishism: Intellectuals and Primitives.* New York: SUNY Press, 2009.
Login, Lena. *Sir John Login and Duleep Singh.* With an introduction by Colonel G. B. Malleson. London: W. H. Allen, 1890.
London, M. E. *Life on the Diamond Fields: Extracts from the Private Journal of M. E. London.* Privately printed, 1875.

Lonoff, Sue. *Wilkie Collins and His Victorian Readers: A Study in the Rhetoric of Authorship.* New York: AMS Press, 1982.

MacCarthy, J. R. *Fire in the Earth: The Story of Diamond.* New York: Harper, 1942.

MacDonald, Robert H. *The Language of Empire: Myths and Metaphors of Popular Imperialism, 1880–1918.* Manchester: Manchester University Press, 1994.

Magubane, Zine. *Bringing the Empire Home: Race, Class, and Gender in Britain and Colonial South Africa.* Chicago: University of Chicago Press, 2003.

Makdisi, Saree. *Making England Western: Occidentalism, Race, and Imperial Culture.* Chicago: University of Chicago Press, 2014.

Mallen, Richard D. "The 'Crowned Republic' of Tennyson's 'Idylls of the King.'" *Victorian Poetry* 37 (Fall 1999): 275–90.

Markovits, Stefanie. "Form Things: Looking at Genre through Victorian Diamonds." *Victorian Studies* 52 (Summer 2010): 591–619.

Marlowe, Christopher. *The Jew of Malta.* Edited by N. W. Bawcutt. Baltimore: Johns Hopkins University Press, 1978.

Marx, Karl. "The British Rule in India." *New York Daily Tribune,* 25 June 1853. In *Marx-Engels Reader,* edited by Robert Tucker. New York: W. W. Norton, 1978.

———. "The Fetishism of the Commodity and Its Secret." In *Capital: A Critique of Political Economy,* vol. 1, section 4: 163–81. London: Penguin Books.

McBratney, John. *Imperial Subjects, Imperial Space: Rudyard Kipling's Fiction of the Native Born.* Columbus: Ohio State University Press, 2002.

McCallum, E. L. *Object Lessons: How to Do Things with Fetishism.* Albany: SUNY Press, 1999.

McClintock, Anne. *Imperial Leather: Race, Gender, and Sexuality in the Colonial Contest.* New York: Routledge, 1995.

McDowell, Colin. *Dressed to Kill: Sex, Power, and Clothes.* London: Hutchinson, 1992.

McHugh, James. "Gemstones." In *Handbook of Oriental Studies,* section 2: *South Asia,* vol. 5 of *Brill's Encyclopedia of Hinduism* (vol.: 22/5). Leiden, Netherlands: Brill, 2013.

McLaughlan, Robbie. *Re-imagining the 'Dark Continent' in "Fin de Siècle" Literature.* Edinburgh: University of Edinburgh Press, 2012.

Mehta, Jaya. "English Romance/Indian Violence." *Centennial Review* 39 (1995): 611–57.

Menikoff, Barry. "*New Arabian Nights:* Stevenson's Experiment in Fiction." *Nineteenth-Century Literature* 45 (December 1990): 339–62.

Meredith, Martin. *Diamonds, Gold, and War: The British, the Boers, and the Making of South Africa.* New York: Public Affairs, 2008.

Mersmann, Arndt. "Diamonds Are Forever:—Appropriations of the Koh-i-Noor: An Object Biography." *Journal for the Study of British Cultures* 8 (2001): 175–91.

Meyer, Henry O. A., and Michael Seal. "Natural Diamond." In *Handbook of Industrial Diamonds and Diamond Films,* edited by Mark A. Prelas, Galina Popovici, and Louis K. Bigelow. Boca Raton, Fla.: CRC Press, 1997.

Meyer, Susan. "Safely to Their Own Borders": Proto-Zionism, Feminism, and Nationalism in *Daniel Deronda.*" *ELH* 60 (1993): 733–58.

Mill, James. *History of British India.* Vol. 6. 1858. Reprint of the fifth edition. New York: Chelsea House, 1968.

Mill, J. S. *Principles of Political Economy.* London: John W. Parker, 1848.

Mitchell, Juliet. "Introduction I." In *Feminine Sexuality: Jacques Lacan and the Ecole Freudienne*, 1–26. New York: Norton, 1982.

Mitford, Bertrand. *Renshaw Fanning's Quest*. With introduction by Gerald Monsman. Richmond, Va.: Valancourt Books, 2007.

———. *Through the Zulu Country: Its Battlefields and People*. 1883. Reprint, London: Greenhill Books, 1992.

Mizoguchi, Akiko. "The Colonizer, the Colonized, and the Colonist: A Study of Olive Schreiner's 'My First Adventure at the Cape' and *Undine*." *Eibei bungaku hyoron* 22 (2000): 1–22.

Moffat, Robert. *Missionary Labour and Scenes in Southern Africa*. London: John Snow, 1842.

Monsman, Gerald. "Olive Schreiner: Literature and the Politics of Power." *Texas Studies in Literature and Language* 30 (Winter 1988): 583–610.

Mudimbe, V. Y. *The Invention of Africa*. Bloomington: Indiana University Press, 1988.

Munich, Adrienne. *Queen Victoria's Secrets*. New York: Columbia University Press, 1997.

Munich, Adrienne, and Maura Spiegel. "Heart of the Ocean: Diamonds and Democratic Desire in *Titanic*." In *Titanic: Anatomy of a Blockbuster*, edited by Kevin S. Sandler and Gaylyn Studlar, 155–67. New Brunswick, N.J.: Rutgers University Press, 1999.

Murphy, Margueritte. "The Ethic of the Gift in George Eliot's *Daniel Deronda*." *Victorian Literature and Culture* 34 (2006): 189–207.

Murray, Richard William. *The Diamond Field Keepsake*. Facsimile edition, edited by Brian Roberts. Kimberley, South Africa: Kimberley Historical Society, 1979.

Murthy, S. R. N. *Gemmological Studies in Sanskrit Texts*. 2 vols. Bangalore: Sri. N. Subbaiah Setty, 1990–93.

Newbury, Colin. *The Diamond Ring: Business, Politics, and Precious Stones in South Africa, 1867–1947*. Oxford: Clarendon Press, 1989.

Novak, Daniel. "A Model Jew: 'Literary Photography' and the Jewish Body in *Daniel Deronda*." *Representations* 85 (2004): 58–97.

Pakenham, Thomas. *The Scramble for Africa: White Man's Conquest of the Dark Continent, 1876 to 1912*. New York: Random House, 1990.

Palmer, Edward Henry. *A History of the Jewish Nation: From the Earliest Times to the Present Day*. Boston: D. Lothrop, 1875.

Parker, Ben. "Recognition or Reification?: Capitalist Crisis and Subjectivity in *Little Dorrit*." *New Literary History* 45 (2014): 131–51.

Parry, Benita. *Delusions and Discoveries: Studies on India in the British Imagination, 1880–1930*. Berkeley: University of California Press, 1972.

Patch, Susanne Steinem. *Blue Mystery: The Story of the Hope Diamond*. Washington, D.C.: National Museum of Natural History in association with Harry N. Abrams, 1999.

Patteson, Richard F. "*King Solomon's Mines*: Imperialism and Narrative Structure." *Journal of Narrative Technique* 8 (1978): 112–23.

Payton, Charles A., Sir. *The Diamond Diggings of South Africa: A Personal and Practical Account, with a brief notice of the New Gold Fields*. London: Horace Cox, 1872.

Perfitt, P. W. "The Life and Career of King Solomon." *Pathfinder* 5 (1861).

Pietz, William. "The Problem of the Fetish, I." *res: Journal of Anthropology and Aesthetics* 9 (Spring 1985): 5–17.

———. "The Problem of the Fetish, II: The Origin of the Fetish." *res: Journal of Anthropology and Aesthetics* 13 (Spring 1987): 23–45.

———. "The Problem of the Fetish, IIIa: Bosman's Guinea and the Enlightenment Theory of Fetishism." *res: Journal of Anthropology and Aesthetics* 16 (Autumn 1988): 105–34.

Plotz, John. *Portable Property: Victorian Culture on the Move.* Princeton, N.J.: Princeton University Press, 2008.

Preyer, Robert. "Beyond the Liberal Imagination: Vision and Unreality in *Daniel Deronda*." *Victorian Studies* 6 (1960): 33–54.

Pridmore, Julie. *The Journal of William Clayton Humphereys: Being a Personal Narrative of the Adventures and Experiences of a Trader and Hunter in the Zulu Country During the Months July–October 1851.* Reprint, Durban: Killie Campbell Africana Library, University of Natal Press, Pietermaritzburg, 1993.

Proctor, Robert. "Anti-Agate: "The Great Diamond Hoax and the Semiprecious Stone Scam." *Configurations* 9 (2001): 381–412.

Ragussis, Michael. *Figures of Conversion: The Jewish Question and English National Identity.* Durham, N.C.: Duke University Press, 1995.

Rajan, Balachandra. *Under Western Eyes: India from Milton to Macaulay.* Durham, N.C.: Duke University Press, 1999.

Ranum, Ingrid. "An Adventure in Modern Marriage: Domestic Development in Tennyson's *Geraint and Enid* and *The Marriage of Geraint*." *Victorian Poetry* 47 (2009): 241–57.

Reed, John R. "English Imperialism and the Unacknowledged Crime of *The Moonstone*." *Clio* 2 (1973): 281–90.

Renton, P. *The Lost Synagogues of London.* London: Tymsder Publications, 2000.

Rickets, Harry. *Rudyard Kipling: A Life.* New York: Carroll and Graf, 2000.

Roberts, Brian. *The Diamond Magnates.* London: Hamish Hamilton, 1972.

Roberts, Janine. *Glitter and Greed: The Secret World of the Diamond Cartel.* New York: Disinformation, 2003.

Rosenberg, John D. *The Fall of Camelot.* Cambridge, Mass.: Harvard University Press, 1970.

Roth, Philip. *Everyman.* Boston: Houghton Mifflin, 2006.

Roy, Ashish. "The Fabulous Imperialist Semiotic of Wilkie Collins's *The Moonstone*." *New Literary History* 24 (Summer 1993): 657–81.

Rushby, Kevin. *Chasing the Mountain of Light: Across India on the Trail of the Koh-i-noor Diamond.* New York: St. Martin's, 1999.

Ruskin, John. *Unto This Last.* In vol. 17 of *The Works of John Ruskin.* Edited by E. T. Cook and Alexander Wedderburn. London: George Allen, 1905.

Said, Edward. *Culture and Imperialism.* New York: Vintage, 1987.

Scarisbrick, Diana. *Portrait Jewels: Opulence and Intimacy from the Medici to the Romanovs.* London: Thames and Hudson, 2011.

Scheinberg, Cynthia. "'The beloved ideas made flesh': *Daniel Deronda* and Jewish Poetics." *ELH* 77 (Fall 2010): 813–39.

Schreiner, Olive. "The Boer Woman and the Nineteenth Century Woman Questions." *Cosmopolis* 10 (April 1898): 12–29.

———. *From Man to Man*. Cassandra Editions. Chicago: Academy Press, 1977.

———. "A Letter on the Jew." In *Words in Season: The Public Writings with Her Own Remembrances Collected for the First Time*, 144–53. Johannesburg: Penguin, 2005.

———. "The Problem of Slavery." In *Thoughts on South Africa*, 106–8. Johannesburg: Africana Book Society, 1976.

———. "South Africa: Its Natural Features, Its Diverse Peoples, Its Political Status: The Problem." In *Thoughts on South Africa*, 10:27–64. Africana Reprint Library. Johannesburg: Africana Book Society, 1976.

———. *Undine*. With introduction by S. C. Cronwright-Schreiner. London: Ernest Benn, 1929.

Schreuder, D. M. *The Scramble for Africa, 1877–1895: The Politics of Partition Reappraised*. Cambridge: Cambridge University Press, 1980.

Scott, A., and L. Atkinson. *A Short History of Diamond Cutting*. N.p., n.d.

Scott, Sir Walter. *Ivanhoe*. New York: Dodd, Mead, 1930.

Sedgwick, Eve. *Between Men: English Literature and Male Homosocial Desire*. New York: Columbia University Press, 1985.

Semmel, Bernard. *George Eliot and the Politics of National Inheritance*. Oxford: Oxford University Press, 1994.

Sergeev, Evgeny. *The Great Game, 1856–1907: Russo-British Relations in Central and East Asia*. Baltimore: Johns Hopkins University Press, 2013.

Shakespeare, William. *The Merchant of Venice*. *The Complete Works of William Shakespeare*. The Cambridge Edition Text. Edited by William Aldis Wright. New York: Garden City Books, 1936.

Shell, Mark. "The Wether and the Ewe: Verbal Usury in *The Merchant of Venice*." *Kenyon Review* 1 (1979): 65–92.

Sherman, Lauren. "Will Lab-Grown Stones Save or Sink the Troubled Diamond Market?" *Business of Fashion*, 6 March 2017. https://businessoffashion.com/articles/intelligence/will-lab-grown-stones-save-or-sink-the-troubled-diamond-market.

Simmel, Georg. "Fashion, Adornment and Style." In *Simmel on Culture: Selected Writings*, edited by David Frisby and Mike Featherstone, 187–217. London: Sage, 1997.

———. "Money and Commodity Culture." In *Simmel on Culture: Selected Writings*, edited by David Frisby and Mike Featherstone, 233–58. London: Sage, 1997.

———. *The Philosophy of Money*. London: Routledge and Kegan Paul, 1978.

Simmons, Clare A. *Reversing the Conquest: History and Myth in Nineteenth-Century British Literature*. New Brunswick, N.J.: Rutgers University Press, 1990.

Sinha, Mrinalini. *Colonial Masculinity: The "Manly Englishman" and the "Effeminate Bengali" in the Late Nineteenth Century*. Manchester: Manchester University Press, 1995.

Slaugh-Sanford, Kathleen R. "The Other Woman: Lydia Glasher and the Disruption of English Racial Identity in George Eliot's *Daniel Deronda.*" *Studies in the Novel* 41 (Winter 2009): 401–17.

Snaith, Anna. *Modernist Voyages: Colonial Women Writers in London.* Cambridge: Cambridge University Press, 2014.

"The South African Diamond Fields." *Chambers' Edinburgh Journal* 374 (25 February 1871): 117–20.

Spector, Sheila A. "Introduction." In *British Romanticism and the Jews: History, Culture, Literature,* ed. Spector, 1–16. New York: Palgrave/Macmillan, 2008.

Staines, David. *Tennyson's Camelot: The Idylls of the King and Its Medieval Sources.* Waterloo, Ontario: Wilfrid Laurier University Press, 1982.

Stevenson, Robert Louis. *New Arabian Nights.* Vol. 2 of *The Works of Robert Louis Stevenson.* Classic Library. Cleveland: World Syndicate Publishing., n.d,

———. *Treasure Island.* New York: Grosset and Dunlap, 1975.

Stockley, Cynthia. *Pink Gods and Blue Demons.* London: Cassell, 1920.

Stout, Daniel M. *Corporate Romanticism: Liberalism, Justice, and the Novel.* New York: Fordham University Press, 2016.

Strathern, Marilyn. *The Gender of the Gift: Problems with Women and Problems with Society in Melanesia.* Berkeley: University of California Press, 1988.

Stratton, Jon. *The Desirable Body: Cultural Fetishism and the Erotics of Consumption.* Manchester: University of Manchester Press, 1996.

Sucher, Scott D., and Dale P. Carriere. "The Use of Laser and X-Ray Scanning to Create a Model of the Historic Koh-i-Noor Diamond." *Gems and Gemology* 42 (Summer 2008): 124–41.

Suleri, Sara. *The Rhetoric of English India.* Chicago: University of Chicago Press, 1992.

Sullivan, Courtney. "How Diamonds Became Forever." *New York Times,* 5 May 2013, D23.

Sutherland, John. Introduction and "A Note on Composition, Reception, and Text." In *The Moonstone* by Wilkie Collins, vii–xxxix. Oxford: Oxford World Classics, 1999.

Swiecki, Rafal. "Diamond in Brazil." *Minelinks.* http://www.minelinks.com/alluvial/diamondGeology9.html.

Swinburne, Algernon Charles. "Under the Microscope." 1872. Reprint, Portland, Maine: Thomas B. Mosher, 1899.

Tagore, Sourindro Mohun. *Mani-mālā, or A Treatise on Gems.* 2 vols. Calcutta: Stanhope Press, 1879.

Tavernier, Jean-Baptiste. *Travels in India.* 1676. 2 vols. Translated and edited by V. Ball. London: Macmillan, 1889.

Taylor, Isaac. *The Origin of the Aryans: The Pre-historic Ethnology and the Civilization of Europe.* New York: Humboldt, 1890.

Tennyson, Alfred, Lord. *The Complete Poems of Tennyson.* Edited by Christopher Ricks. London: Longmans, Green, 1970.

Tennyson, Charles. *Alfred Tennyson.* London: Macmillan, 1950.

Tennyson, Hallam. *Tennyson: A Memoir by His Son.* 2 vols. London: Macmillan, 1897.

Thackeray, William Makepeace. *Rebecca and Rowena.* London: Chapman and Hall, 1850.

Thakur, Gautam Basu. "Vernacular Objects/Indian Mutiny/Imperial Panic." *Victorian Literature and Culture* 44 (2016): 557–76.

Thomas, Anthony. *Rhodes: The Race for Africa*. New York: St. Martins, 1996.
Tidrick, Kathryn. *Empire and the English Character: The Illusion of Authority*. London: I. B. Tauris, 1990.
Titanic. Directed by James Cameron. Paramount Pictures, Twentieth Century Fox, and Lightstorm Entertainment, 1997.
Trollope, Anthony. *The Eustace Diamonds*. Edited and with an introduction by W. J. McCormack. Oxford: Oxford University Press, 1982.
———. *South Africa*. 1878. 2 vols. Reprint, London: Dawsons of Pall Mall, 1968.
Tucker, Herbert F. *Epic: Britain's Heroic Muse, 1790–1910*. New York: Oxford University Press, 2013.
———. "Trials of Fiction: Novel and Epic in the Enid and Geraint Episodes from *Idylls of The King*." *Victorian Poetry* 30 (1992): 441–61.
Turrell, Robert Vicat. *Capital and Labour on the Kimberley Diamond Fields, 1871–1890*. Cambridge: Cambridge University Press, 1987.
Valman, Nadia. *The Jewess in Nineteenth-Century British Culture*. Cambridge: Cambridge University Press, 2007.
Veblen, Thorstein. *The Theory of the Leisure Class*. Harmondsworth, UK: Penguin, 1994.
Vescelius-Sheldon. *An I.D.B. in South Africa*. New York: John W. Lovell, 1888.
The Village London Atlas: The Growth of Victorian London, 1822–1903. London: Alterman, 1986.
Viswanathan, Gauri. *Outside the Fold: Conversion, Modernity, and Belief*. Princeton, N.J.: Princeton University Press, 1998.
Walters, Alisha. "A 'white boy . . . who is not a white boy': Rudyard Kipling's *Kim*, Whiteness, and British Identity." *Victorian Literature and Culture* 46 (2018): 331–46.
Weber, Caroline. *Queen of Fashion: What Marie Antoinette Wore to the Revolution*. New York: Henry Holt, 2006.
Weber, Max. *The Protestant Ethic and the Spirit of Capitalism*. Translated by Talcott Parsons. New York: Scribner, 1958.
Wegner, Phillip. "'Life as He Would Have It': The Invention of India in Kipling's *Kim*." *Cultural Critique* 26 (Winter 1993–94): 129–59.
Wheatcroft, Geoffrey. *The Randlords*. London: Weidenfeld and Nicolson, 1985.
Wheeler, Michael. *Ruskin's God*. Cambridge: Cambridge University Press, 1999.
Williams, Gardner F. *The Diamond Mines of South Africa*. 2 vols. New York: B. F. Buck, 1905.
Wilson, Elizabeth. *Adorned in Dreams: Fashion and Modernity*. Revised and updated edition. London: I. B. Tauris, 2003.
Wilson, Kathleen. *A New Imperial History: Culture, Identity, and Modernity in Britain and the Empire, 1660–1840*. Cambridge: Cambridge University Press, 2004.
Wyllie, J. W. S. *Essays on the External Policy of India*. Edited, with a Brief Life, by W. W. Hunter. London: Smith, Elder, 1875.
Xu, Wenying. "The Opium Trade and *Little Dorrit*: A Case of Reading Silences." *Victorian Literature and Culture* 25 (1997): 53–66.
Yogev, Gedalia. *Diamonds and Coral: Anglo-Dutch Jews and Eighteenth-Century Trade*. Leicester, UK: Leicester University Press, 1978.

Young, Robert J. C. *Colonial Desire: Hybridity in Theory, Culture and Race.* London: Routledge, 1995.

Zapata, Janet. "Diamond Jewelry for Everyone." In *The Nature of Diamonds,* edited by George Harlow, 186–98. Cambridge: Cambridge University Press, 1998.

Zimmerman, Bonnie. "'Radiant as a Diamond': George Eliot, Jewelry and the Female Role." *Criticism* 19 (1977): 212–22.

Zoellner, Tom. *The Heartless Stone: A Journey through the World of Diamonds, Deceit and Desire.* London: Picador, 2006.

Index

Italicized page numbers denote illustrations, and an italicized P followed by a number indicates a plate in the gallery following page 130.

Adamantia (Lindley), 146
"Adventure of Prince Florizel and the Detective" (Stevenson), 59. See also *New Arabian Nights* (Stevenson)
"Adventure of the Blue Carbuncle, The" (Conan Doyle), 17, 69–70, 207, 208
Aeneid, The (Virgil), 106
Afghanistan, 45, 68
Africa, 11, 16, 87; Bushmen of, 153, 189–92, 204, 243n20, 244n17; fictional history of Haggard in, 184; gemstones of, 179, 181, 200; races of, 145, 149, 160, 161, 179–81. *See also* South Africa
Albert, Prince, 40, 43, 92
Alexandra, Queen, 44, *P6*
Althusser, Louis, 9
America: diamond exodus to, 181; diamond market in, 8, 18–19, 207–18
Amsterdam, 7, 87
Ancient British Drama, The (Scott), 116
Anglo-Boer War, 194, 203. *See also* Boers
Anglo-Sikh wars, 32, 46
anti-Semitism: in American diamond fiction, 217, 218; in Boer diamond fiction, 202–5; in Diamond Fields of South Africa fiction, 18, 159–92; in English diamond novels, 18, 88, 114–41. *See also* Judaism
Antwerp, 7, 87
Arabian Nights, The, 57, 59, 66, 71, 127, 129, 228n3

Arnot, David, *The Land Question of Griqualand West,* map in, *147*
Arthasatstra (Kautilya), 25
Atwal, Rajpreet (Priya), 36
Austen, Jane, 230n21
Australia, 6–7
Ayers Agency, 213–15

Babe, J. L., 187
Bacon, George, 85–86
Barnato, Barney, 160, 244n5, 246n4
Beecham, Margaret, 100
Beechey, George Duncan, 33–35, 41, 43–44; *Portrait of Duleep Singh, P3*
Beet, George, 151, 204, 205
Beit, Alfred, 160
Belgium, 3
Belgravia (Harris), 159
Benjamin, Walter, 205
Bent, Theodore, 184
Bernhardt, Sarah, 174
Bhatta, Buddha, 27
Bildungsroman, 74, 81, 173
Blackwood's Magazine, 102
Blake, William, 80
Bleak House (Dickens), 110
blood diamonds, 162, 212. *See also* diamonds
Blunt, Sir Wilfred Scawen, 159–60
Boabdil, King Mohammed, 115
"Boer, The" (Schreiner), 193

Boers, 193–206; racism of the, 204. *See also* South Africa

Borneo, 23

Botswana, 212. *See also* Africa

Boyle, Thomas, 145, 153, 164, 194

Brazil, 7

Breitmeyer, Ludwig, 160, 243n40

Brhatsamhita (Varahamihira), 27

Britain. *See* British Empire

British Empire: diamonds of the, 1, 3, 5–11, 18–19, 25, 31–45, 104, *P8;* India in the, 23–70, 86; missionaries of the, 9; trade of the, 11, 85–89. *See also* Victorian era

Brown, Caroline, 42

Brown, Margaret, 209

Browning, Robert, 64

Buddhism, 78; lotus symbol in, 81. *See also* religion

Cameron, James, 207, 218

Cameron, Julia Margaret, 100; *Enid, P7*

Cape Monthly Magazine, 154–55

capitalism: imperatives of, 14; mercantile, 99; spirit of, 96, 97; system of, 108–10, 193–96; Victorian, 95–97. *See also* consumer culture; mining

carats, 219n1

Carlyle, Thomas, 176

Chambers' Edinburgh Journal, 31, 42

Cheyette, Bryan, 180

"Childe Roland to the Dark Tower Came" (Browning), 64

Christianity, 15, 70; conversion to, 121; diamonds in, 17; Kim's version of, 74; Maltese Cross of, 44. *See also* religion

Civitarese, Giuseppe, 119

Cohen, Louis, 161–62

Cohn, Bernard S., 35, 46–47

Coleridge, Samuel Taylor, 24

Collins, Wilkie, 7, 17, 46–55, 62, 69, 81, 217, 227n15, 227nn20–23. *See also* specific works by title

Coming of Arthur, The (Tennyson), 95. See also *Idylls of the King* (Tennyson)

Conan Doyle, Sir Arthur, 17, 61–68

consumer culture, 14, 96–97, 109. *See also* capitalism

Couper, J. R., 156, 161–63, 173–76, 244n4

Dalhousie, Lord, 33–34, 36–37, 39–40, 43

Daniel Deronda (Eliot), 18, 131–40, 211, 239n50, 239n61, 240n64; diamond engagement ring in, 136, 211; diamonds in, 131–41

De Beers, 152, 160, 167, 170, 176, 184, 212–15, 218. *See also* diamonds; mining

democratic desire, 208–11, 218, *P10*

Derricourt, Robin, 184

Diamond Field Keepsake, The (Murray), 159, 167

Diamond Jubilees, 6, 214–18; in advertising, 211, 213, 214; banner of the (Passaic, N.J.), *215;* display of the (Passaic, N.J.), *216;* in the memos of Dorothy Dignam, 214. *See also* consumer culture

Diamond Mines of South Africa, The (Williams), illustrations from, *155, 157, 163, 168, 185*

diamonds: advertisement, *2;* alluvial, 220n17; Asian, 69; bloody, 182–89; blue, 207–10; class system of, 28, 111–13, 207; danger of, 191, 192; divinity of, 27; economics of, 11; English, 85–89, 114–15; feminine, 27; as fetish, 12–15, 60, 61, 67, 103–8, 205; as gifts, 32–39, 50, 51, 58, 60, 66, 118–23; glass as imitation, 4; of Hatton Garden, 87, 122; heart-shaped, 1, *2;* hermaphrodite, 27; identity of, 45; immortal, 16; Indian, 14, 23–70, 81, 82, 88, 89, 208; interpretation in the culture of, 5, 12; jousts for, 108; large, 1, *2,* 13, 17, 59, 191, 205, 212; lore of, 23, 24, 28, 37, 58, 59, 68, 213; and marriage, 108,

119–22, 198, 200, 211–18; masculine, 26–27; myth of, 93; named, 13, 28, 31, 56, 66, 69, 113, 207; neuter, 27; origins of, 4–5; phosphorescence of, 3, 59; planet of, 4, 5; prices of, 1, 4, 60; of public use, 103–8; royal, 91, 103–8; and sexuality, 118–23; structural properties of, 3–5, 61, 85; as talismans, 27, 113; theft of, 170, 173, 197; trophy, 106, 107, 210. *See also* gemology; mining; *and specific gems by name*
Diana, Princess of Wales, 212
Dickens, Charles, 17, 51, 91–92, 109–13, 173, 175, 230n21, 231n1 (ch.5), 235n64; satire of, 112. *See also specific works by title*
Dignam, Dorothy, 213, 214
Dombey and Son (Dickens), 110
Doyle, Arthur Conan, 56–70, 78, 81
Duncan, Ian, 115, 226n10
Durbar of Maharaja Dalip Singh (Hasan-al-din), 33, P2
Dutch East India Company, 193

East India Company, 37, 41, 46, 86. *See also* British Empire
Edward VII, King, 44
Edward VIII, King, 212
Eliot, George, 18, 131–41, 230n21, 239n51, 239n54
Eliot, T. S., 227n14
Elizabeth II, Queen, 44–45, 212, 234n45
England: in the British Empire, 9, 14; diamonds in, 85–89, 118–23, 192, 208, 209; Jewish traders in, 12, 85–89, 118–23; social life of, 88–89. *See also* British Empire; London
Enid (Cameron), P7
Enlightenment, the, 88
Entwhistle, Joanne, 99, 233n39
"Essays in Indian Antiquities" (Prinsep and Thomas), 52
Eureka diamond, 152, 182, 183, P9. *See also* diamonds

Euripides, 94–95
Eustace Diamonds, The (Trollope), 18, 123–32, 134, 137, 207, 210, 240n68
Everyman (Roth), 217
Evil Genius, The: A Domestic Story (Collins), 7

Faith diamond, 204. *See also* diamonds
fashion: and empire, 98–103; imagery of, 98–103; power of, 103; and society, 91, 92, 98–103, 110; and tailoring, 102; visuality of, 91; writing about, 100–102
fetishism: anthropological, 27, 105, 221n34; corporate, 113; cultural, 14, 97, 100, 102, 111, 112, 221nn33–34, 232n15; in Marx, 234n48; and sexuality, 221n33. *See also* diamonds
Fitzgerald, Percy, 86
For the Love of God (Hirst), 16–17, 217, P1
France, crown jewels of, 207–9
Franklin, Jeffrey, 78, 230n13, 230n18
Freud, Sigmund, 12–14, 106, 119; the fetish in, 13, 14, 106, 119
From Man to Man (Schreiner), 199, 202–4

Gaboriau, Émile, 59, 62, 228n7
Geertz, Clifford, 1, 5, 10–11
gemology: compendium of, 7; Indian, 12, 29, 56; lore of, 5, 12, 23–25, 37; skills of, 76; wisdom of, 35. *See also* diamonds
gender: of diamonds, 49–50, 52–53, 121, 202; feminine, 202; masculine, 53, 93; misogyny and, 93; revolution of, 85; Victorian conventions of, 88, 93. *See also* masculinity; women
Gentlemen Prefer Blondes (film; 1953), 19
George IV, King, 208
George VI, King, 45
Gerety, Margaret, 213, 218
Germany, 86
Gloria (Mansfield), 193, 195–98, 246n3

Goa, 86. *See also* India
Goodlad, Lauren, 47, 130, 226n13, 238n34, 238n43
Grandcourt diamonds, 137–39, 210, 239n53. *See also* diamonds
Gray, J. M., 100
Great Exhibition (1851), 8
Great Mogul diamond, 66–67, 229n16. *See also* diamonds
Gregory, Alice, 4
Griqualand West, 145, 146, 153, 163, 246n6; map of, *147*. *See also* South Africa
Guybon, Dr. William, 152

Haggard, H. Rider, 18, 172–75, 182–90, 245n35, 245nn37–38
Harold II, King, 104
Harris, G. F., 159
Hart, Matthew, 4
Heart of the Ocean diamond, 207–10, *P10*. *See also* diamonds
Hendrie, James, 169–70
Heraclitus, 15–16
Hinduism, 17, 47–54, 70; diamonds in, 17, 23–25, 29, 47–49, 51–54, 58; hymns of, 23–24, 52; medieval, 35; sacred writings of, 23, 51. *See also* India; religion; Rig Veda
Hirst, Damien, 16–17, 19, 177, 217; *For the Love of God, P1*
History of British India, The (Mill), 47
History of England during the Middle Ages (Turner), 117
History of the Jewish Nation, A (Palmer), 184
Hockley, Cal, 207, 211, 216
Holland, 86
Holy Grail, The (Tennyson), 95–96, 101. *See also Idylls of the King* (Tennyson)
Homer, 94–95
Hope, Henry Thomas, 208
Hope Diamond, 69, 207, 208, 247nn2–3. *See also* diamonds

Hopkins, Gerard Manley, 15–17, 19, 119, 213, 217
Huguenots, 193, 195. *See also* Boers
Hyde, Ralph, 86

I.D.B. in South Africa, An (Vescelius-Sheldon), 171, 172, 178, 181, 191
Idylls of the King (Tennyson), 17, 91–108, 113, 232n5; diamonds in the, 91–108; fashion in the, 98–103
Iliad, The (Homer), 94–95
India: allusions to, 61–63, 178; ancient, 23; British rule in, 86; diamond production of, 6, 77, 88; gems in, 5–6, 23–82; imitation, 56–70; Occidental views of, 25; parable of, 77; uprising in, 62–65, 71, 81; wealth of, 63. *See also* Hinduism
Industrial Revolution, 92
Interpretation of Cultures, The (Geertz), 1
Iran, 45
Italy, 86
Ivanhoe: A Romance (Scott), 18, 114–41, 177

JanMohamed, Abdul, 78
Jeffrey, Francis, 114
Jew of Malta, The (Marlowe), 116, 120–21, 175
Johannesburg, 195, 196. *See also* South Africa
Johnson, Barbara, 106
Judaism: and diamonds, 85–89, 114–41, 170–84, 202, 217, 218; in European culture, 235n3, 236n10, 237nn19–20, 237n24, 237n31; and identity, 162, 197, 221n42; and trade, 12, 121, 161, 184. *See also* anti-Semitism; religion

karoo. *See under* South Africa
Kaufman, Heidi, 187
Keep, Christopher, 68
Kim (Kipling), 17, 58, 71–82, 199, 230nn16–18
Kimberley Mine, 151–58, *157*, 166,

170–72, 175–79, 186, 187, 204–6, 217, 241n22; map of Diamond Fields, *P9*. *See also* mining; South Africa
kimberlite, 18, 154, *155*, 186, 187, 205, 206
King, Charles William, 3, 45, 51–52, 227nn14–15
King Solomon's Mines (Haggard), 172, 174, 182–89
Kipling, Rudyard, 17, 58, 71–82, 199
Koh-i-noor Diamond, 6, 8, 31–50, 52, 58, 61, 66, 72, 208, 214, 217, 224n28, 224n32, 225n52, 225n55, 226n13, 227n14, 227n16, *P4*, *P6*. *See also* diamonds
Koskoff, David, 206
Kower, J. P., Jr., 169–70

Lacan, Jacques, 104, 106, 234n46
Lahore, 41, 72, 73, 78, 80. *See also* India
Lampert-Weissig, Lisa, 115, 117, 119
Lancelot and Elaine (Tennyson), 91, 93, 106–8. *See also* *Idylls of the King* (Tennyson)
Land Question of Griqualand West, The (Orpen and Arnot), map in, *147*
Last Tournament, The (Tennyson), 106–7, 112. *See also* *Idylls of the King* (Tennyson)
Latour, Bruno, 10–11
Lavoisier, Antoine, 5
Levy, Amy, 18
Life on the Diamonds Fields (London), 151
Lindley, Captain Augustus, 146, 205
Lipovetsky, Gilles, 99–100, 231n2 (ch.5), 233n26, 233n30, 233n38
Little Dorrit (Dickens), 17, 91 109–13
Login, John Spencer, 34, 36, 39, 223n13
London, M. E., 151
London, 7, 12, 40, 62, 109, 182, 183, 199; the diamond trade of, 85–89, 122, 184, 200, 212; Hatton Garden in a map of, 87, *87*. *See also* England
Loos, Anita, 19

Louis XIV, King, 208, 209
Lyonnesse diamond crown, 104, 106–8. *See also* diamonds

Mabinogion, 98–102; Tennyson's adaptation of, 102
MacDonald, Robert, 9
Magid, Jill, 4
Magubane, Zine, 161, 200
Makdisi, Saree, 86, 88
Mani-mālā, or A Treatise on Gems (Tagore), 3, 25, 46
Mansfield, Charlotte, 193–98, 246n3, 246n5
Marlowe, Christopher, 116, 120, 174
Marriage of Geraint and Enid, The (Tennyson), 98–103, 232–33n23. *See also* *Idylls of the King* (Tennyson)
Married Women's Property Act, 127
Marx, Karl, 12, 81
masculinity: abusive, 211; aggressive, 53, 103, 106; black, 185; British, 44, 93, 94; divinely sent, 101; and fetish, 13, 14; insecurity of, 94; Oriental, 40; and power, 97, 103, 106; sacred, 46–55; upper-class, 133; and vulnerability, 97; white, 185. *See also* gender
Mayhew, Henry, 88
McClintock, Anne, 179, 203, 245n33, 245n38
McDowell, Colin, 99–100
McLean, Evalyn Walsh, 209
Mehta, Jaya, 62
Merchant of Venice, The (Shakespeare), 116, 120, 175
Middle Ages: crowns of the, 104; King Arthur of the, 91–108
Mill, James, 47
mining: a book about, 145, 196, 197; cables in, *157*; corporate, 195–97, 205; in India, 23; and manufacturing, 4; oppression in, 204; prospecting for, 18; in South Africa, 151–70, 193–206. *See also* capitalism; diamonds

Mitford, Bertrand, 171, 173, 189–92, 246n43, 246n46
Mixed Humanity (Couper), 156–57, 160–62, 172, 173, 202
Moby Dick (Melville), 197
Moffat, Robert, 189, 190
Moonstone, The (Collins), 8, 17, 46–55, 58, 67–69, 81, 217, 227n14, 228n24
Morte D'Arthur (Tennyson), 100–101, 105
Murray, William, 159
Murthy, S. R. N., 23
Muslims/Mohammedans, 47, 49, 52, 75; associations of, 53; beliefs of, 52; martial power of, 228n26; in Spain, 115; Tipu Sultan among the, 47, 51. *See also* religion

nationalism, 18, 98, 102
New Arabian Nights (Stevenson), 56–59, 81
New York, 214. *See also* America
novel(s): diamond, 8, 18, 29, 71, 114–41, 171–206; domestic, 171–92; imperial, 192; realist, 89; Scottish, 116; sensation, 239n62; socially committed, 91; Victorian, 5–8, 114, 203. *See also* romance

"Of Queen's Gardens" (Ruskin), 49
Orange River, 147, 151, 153. *See also* South Africa
Orloff Diamond, 49, *49,* 66, 226n12, 229n16. *See also* diamonds
Orpen, Francis H. S., *The Land Question of Griqualand West,* map in, *147*

Pakistan, 45
Palmer, Edward, 184
Payton, Sir Charles, 155, 164
Perfitt, P. W., 183, 184
Pietz, William, 12–13
Pink Gods and Blue Demons (Stockley), 172, 175, 177

poetry: allegorical epic, 91–108; nation-making epic, 102
political economy, 96
politics: imperial, 33, 92–93, 98; Reform Acts of English, 100; sexual, 107; structures of, 91–92
Portrait of Duleep Singh (Beechey), 33, *P3*
Portrait of Maharaja Duleep Singh (Winterhalter), 33, 40, *P5*
Portugal, 86
Precious Stones and Gems (Streeter), 85
Prinsep, James, 52
Protestantism, 9, 29; ethic of, 96–97; virtue of, 122. *See also* Christianity
Punjab, 6, 31–35, 40, 45, 72, 74; annexation of the, 6, 31, 35. *See also* India

race: and Africans, 145, 149, 160, 161, 179–81; and Boers, 194; and empire, 9, 65, 73, 74, 160, 187; and Englishness, 18, 114–25, 131–36, 187; and identity, 134, 135; and Judaism, 118–23, 132–40, 162, 180, 189, 203; purity of, 18, 189; and Sikhism, 6, 35, 36, 44, 53, 65, 228n26. *See also* religion
Rachel, 174
Radnadīpikā (*Examination of Precious Stones*; Bhatta), 27, 56
Ragussis, Michael, 115–16, 120
"Rajah's Diamond, The" (Stevenson), 17, 56–58, 61, 68, 71. *See also New Arabian Nights* (Stevenson)
Rajputs, 52–54; martial power of the, 53, 228n26. *See also* Hinduism; India; religion
Randall, Don, 68
Rebecca and Rowena (Thackeray), 121
Reed, John, 51
religion: abandonment of, 120; aura of, 17, 48; of the Boers, 193; conversion in, 41, 44, 46, 73, 80; diamonds and, 47; discarded, 41; evangelical, 9; and fetish, 12; patriarchal, 202; and racism, 193. *See also* race *and specific religions by name*

Renshaw Fanning's Quest (Mitford), 171, 173, 189–92
Reuben Sachs (Levy), 18, 139–41, 240n67. *See also* Judaism
Rhodes, Cecil, 160, 169, 184, 242n1
Richard I, King, 116, 119
Rig Veda, 23–29. *See also* Hinduism
romance, 8, 17, 29, 46–55, 62, 64, 67, 72, 74, 76, 80, 81, 89, 114–41, 171–92, 226n8, 227n14, 230n21. *See also* novel(s)
Roman Empire, 8
Roth, Philip, 217, 218
Ruskin, John, 49, 182

Said, Edward, 80, 230n6, 230n21
Scarisbrick, Diana, 36
Schreiner, Olive, 18, 162, 193–205, 217, 243n20, 244n14, 246n6, 246n11
Scotland, 181. *See also* British Empire
Scott, Sir Walter, 18, 114–41, 184, 212, 230n21
Shah, Nadir, 31
Shakespeare, William, 116, 120, 174, 236n11
Sign of Four, The (Conan Doyle), 17, 61–68, 71
Sikhism, 6, 35, 44, 53, 65; dining rituals of, 41; garments of, 40, 63; martial power of the, 53, 228n26; swords in, 41; turbans in, 33, 35, 40, 41, 63. *See also* religion
Simmel, Georg, 99
Singh, Maharajah Duleep, 6, 32–36, 39–41, 43, 45–46, 49, 65, 72–76, 224n33, 224n41, *P2, P3, P5*
Singh, Maharajah Ranjit, 36–37, 42, 47, 72, 223n18
Singh, Maharajah Yadavindra, *26*
slavery: in Africa, 7, 193, 246n44; in Brazil, 7, 129; in imperial history, 221n42
Smith, Adam, 109
Smithsonian Institution, 208
social change: in the Middle Ages, 99, 231n2 (ch.5); in South Africa, 146–47; in the Victorian period, 91–93, 100, 123–27
Solomon, King, 182–84, 186–89
South Africa: African diggers of, 163–67, *163, 168,* 170, 195, 200; in the British Empire, 9, 104, 194, 203; diamond production of, 6, 8, 14, 18, 86–87, 151–206; discovery of diamonds in, 146–48; karoo in, 146, 155, 158–61, 171, 172, 190–99, 202–5, 246n6; as native territory, 145, 146, 153, 156, 160–67, 172–74, 179–86, 190–93, 196, 197, 200, 204, 244n6. *See also* Africa; Boers; Griqualand West; Orange River; Vaal River; Zulus
South Africa (Trollope), 158; map of Kimberley Mine in, *157*
Southey, Richard, 145, 240n1 (p.III)
Spain: colony of, 68; Jews of, 115, 217; racial type of, 133
Star of Africa diamond, 205. *See also* diamonds
Star of South Africa diamond, 152, 153, 182, 183, 240n1 (p.III). *See also* diamonds
Stevenson, Robert Louis, 17, 56–71, 81, 188. *See also specific works by title*
Stockley, Cynthia, 172, 175, 178, 181
Stoker, Bram, 173
Story of an African Farm, The (Schreiner), 194, 198, 199, 202, 203
"Story of the Bandbox" (Stevenson), 57–58. *See also New Arabian Nights* (Stevenson)
"Story of the House with the Green Blinds, The" (Stevenson), 59–60. *See also New Arabian Nights* (Stevenson)
"Story of the Young Man in Holy Orders" (Stevenson), 59. *See also New Arabian Nights* (Stevenson)
Stout, Daniel, 88, 231n1 (ch.5), 235n58
Strathern, Marilyn, 121, 237n29
Stratton, Jon, 14, 232n15
Streeter, Edwin, 85, 189

"Suicide Club, The" (Stevenson), 60. See also *New Arabian Nights* (Stevenson)
Suleri, Sara, 79, 230n18
Survey of the Cities of London and Westminster (Roque), detail of Hatton Garden in map from, *87*
Swinburne, Algernon Charles, 98

Tagore, Raja Sir Sourindro Mohun, 3, 7, 25, 28
Tavernier, Jean-Baptiste, 24, 28, 42, 66, 77, 208
Tennyson, Lord Alfred, 17, 91–108, 112, 113, 217, 231n1 (ch.5), 234n44, 234n46, 234n51; apocalyptic revelation in, 93; fashion consciousness of, 100–102. See also specific works by title
Thackeray, William, 121; under the pseudonym of Mr. M. A. Titmarsh, 121
Thakur, Gautam Basu, 29
"That Nature is a Heraclitean Fire and of the Comfort of the Resurrection" (Hopkins), 15
Thomas, Edward, 52
Thoughts on South Africa (Schreiner), 204
Thousand and One Nights, The, 24, 56; Sinbad in the, 24, 66, 228n6
Tidrick, Kathryn, 9
Tiffany Jewelers, 207, 247n1. See also diamonds
Times (London), 159
Tipu Sultan, 46–47, 49, 51, 52, 225n1, 226nn3–4
Titanic (film; 1997), 207–11
To the Cape for Diamonds (Boyle), 145, 46
Travels in India (Tavernier), 24
Treasure Island (Stevenson), 188
Trollope, Anthony, 18, 123–31, 133, 158, 166, 173, 174, 207, 238n46; Ivanhoe and Rebecca in, 123–27

Turner, Sharon, 117
Turrell, Robert, 163

Undine (Schreiner), 199–204

Vaal River, 147, 153, 163. See also South Africa
Veblen, Thorstein, 88, 97
Vescelius-Sheldon, Louise, 171, 172, 178–81
Victoria, Queen, 3, 5–6, 31–36, 40–45, 49–50, 52, 92, 105, 176, 180, 214, 233n40; small diamond crown, *P8*
Victorian era: biblical exegesis of the, 182; cultural revolutions of the, 92–97; ethnology in the, 9; fashion in the, 98–103; fiction in the, 28, 69; imperialism of the, 187; melodrama of the, 113; novels of the, 5–8, 114; political economies of the, 15, 95; society of the, 88–89, 92–93, 96–97; women's magazines of the, 100. See also British Empire
violence: of diamonds, 49, 55; of imperialism, 160, 226n7; and malice, 25; reciprocal, 107; and romance, 226n8; sexual, 101; in theft, 47, 156
Virgil, 106

Weber, Max, 1, 9, 96, 244n10
Wegner, Philip, 77
We Have Never Been Modern (Latour), 10
Welles, Frederick, 205
William I, King (William the Conqueror), 104
Williams, Gardner F., 164–65, 176, 240–41n2
Wilson, Elizabeth, 99
Winston, Harry, 208
Winterhalter, Franz Xavier, 33, 40; *Portrait of Maharaja Duleep Singh*, *P5*
women: adultery of, 98; bondage of, 199, 200, 202; chastity of, 103; death of, 108, 199, 201–4; desires of, 97, 98, 102; English diamonds for, 88, 111,

200; idealization of Jewish, 119–20; inaccessible, 106; insecurity of, 98; loneliness of, 204; misogyny and, 93; and prostitution, 199, 200, 202; sensuality of, 120–21; as trophies, 88, 94, 97, 98, 101, 102, 108, 110, 111. *See also* gender

Wyllie, J. W. S., 52–55, 227n20, 227n22

Zimbabwe, Great Ruins of, 184, 186, 187. *See also* Africa

Zulus, 179, 180, 184–86, 191; King Cetewayo of the, 180; warrior (probably Jim Caneel) of the, *185*. *See also* South Africa

"Zulu War Dance, A" (Haggard), 186